Ghosts of Mississippi

Ghosts of Mississippi

The Murder
of Medgar Evers,
the Trials of
Byron De La Beckwith,
and the Haunting
of the New South

Maryanne Vollers

LITTLE, BROWN AND COMPANY

BOSTON   NEW YORK   TORONTO   LONDON

First Edition

Library of Congress Cataloging-in-Publication Data

Vollers, Maryanne.
    Ghosts of Mississippi : the murder of Medgar Evers, the trials of
Byron De La Beckwith, and the haunting of the new South /
Maryanne Vollers. — 1st ed.
        p.   cm.
    ISBN 0-316-91485-1
    1. Evers, Medgar Wiley, 1925–1963 — Assassination.
2. Beckwith, Byron De La.   I. Title.
F349.J13V65   1995
364.1'524'092 — dc20   94-31108

10 9 8 7 6 5 4 3 2 1

MV-NY

Published simultaneously in Canada
by Little, Brown & Company (Canada) Limited

Printed in the United States of America

For Bill Campbell
All the roads lead home to you.

The arc of the moral universe is long,
but it bends toward justice.

— Theodore Parker,
abolitionist

Contents

Ghosts of Mississippi

1

Ghosts of the Old South

BYRON DE LA BECKWITH was not an ordinary prisoner, and he was not treated like one.

When he arrived at the Hinds County Detention Center in the fall of 1991, he was seventy years old and suffering from blocked arteries and bad hearing. Beckwith was confined to an eight-by-ten-foot private cell, with its own shower, in the medical block of the jail. His meals were brought to him in his cell. He had a cot, a little black-and-white TV, a bookcase, a reading light, a public-school-issue desk-chair, and boxes and boxes of paper, pens, special foods, vitamins, letters, note-pads, envelopes, and assorted ultra-right-wing political literature.

Beckwith had to be kept away from the other prisoners, who were mostly black. He was such a garrulous, uninhibited racist that he was as likely to call someone a "nigger" to his face now as he was back in 1964, the last time he was in jail in Jackson, Mississippi. It was clear to those who remembered him, and many did, that the man hadn't changed much in three decades. Neither had his predicament. Beckwith was charged with killing a civil rights leader named Medgar Evers, of shooting him in the back in his driveway one hot June night in 1963 and leaving him to bleed to death in front of his wife and young children.

Beckwith's rifle was found at the scene, but nobody had seen him pull the trigger. He was tried twice for the crime, and both times juries of twelve white men couldn't decide on a verdict. After the second mistrial, Beckwith was set loose. The murder charge, however, hung over him for three decades.

Then new evidence surfaced in the dormant case, and Byron De La Beckwith was arrested again. By now the story of Beckwith and Evers was so old and famous that songs had been written about it and passed down through a generation. A legend was about to be tried for killing a legend.

As the new case against Beckwith slowly worked its way through the courts, there was a feeling that a cycle was being completed in the state's history: a time of revelation, of epiphany, perhaps even of judgment was about to visit Mississippi.

In the years that had gone by between the first and most recent incarcerations of Byron De La Beckwith, the Deep South started calling itself the New South, and its optimistic leaders tried to shake off the past like a lingering nightmare. But history will not be ignored, not in Mississippi, where people live long with their memories and their grandfather's memories, where outraged and querulous ghosts still haunt the future.

An eerie déjà vu settled over the state. For those who were paying attention, the tenor of the times seemed more like the early sixties than the nineties.

Slender, rolled-up broadsides began appearing on people's lawns, just like they did in the days when the Ku Klux Klan had paralyzed whole counties with fear. The little papers advised potential jurors that Byron De La Beckwith was a hero and an innocent man.

One steamy August morning, ten months after Beckwith's arrival in the Jackson jail, a cousin named Kim McGeoy and a guest showed up to visit him. The smiling guard buzzed McGeoy into the corridor as two of Beckwith's earlier visitors exited. A middle-aged man and woman nodded cheerfully. They both carried clear plastic garbage sacks loaded with hundreds of folded white papers and tiny booklets titled *Citizens' Rule Book*. The couple were not searched going out, and Kim and his guest were not searched or even run through a metal detector after they signed in.

Another electric door opened, and they walked, unescorted, into a narrow hallway. There were a dozen or so solid doors, each with a small, rectangular glass window. The door to cell 121 was open.

Byron De La Beckwith lounged on his prison cot, chatting with John Branton, an old Klan friend, and another cousin whose family owned miles of cotton land around Greenwood, Mississippi, where Beckwith was raised.

Beckwith wore a dark blue prison jumpsuit and jail slippers. His face and arms were white as pipe clay after so many months in lockup. He glanced up at Kim and smiled broadly.

"Greetings, cousin!" he chirped.

"Hello, Delay," said Kim, calling him by the name his friends used.

The cell walls were cinder block painted a sickly yellow. There was a narrow horizontal window near the top of the back wall that admitted a thin wash of sunlight. From time to time Beckwith would leap onto his cot and strain to look out the window, maybe just for a glimpse of natural color in the world outside.

The cot took up most of the length of his cell. Next to it his small bookcase was stuffed with Bibles and other books on subjects that interested him. There was a large paperback titled *Gun Parts*.

The wall by his desk was taped over with clippings, cartoons, snapshots, and fan mail. One cartoon, clipped from a newspaper editorial page, depicted the nine U.S. Supreme Court justices seated for a group photo. It showed a beaming Clarence Thomas with his hand on the thigh of a startled Sandra Day O'Connor. Beneath the image of the new African-American justice, Beckwith had penned, "Who dat?"

One of the snapshots taped to the wall showed a group of smiling white folks on a sunny day. There were maybe a dozen lined up in two rows, not unlike the Supreme Court justices, each holding a round red battle shield emblazoned with the white cross and red blood-drop emblem of the Ku Klux Klan.

The banty little prisoner was in high spirits. He was looking forward to his court appearance on Monday, at a hearing set to decide whether his right to a speedy trial had been violated. He expected to be set free any day now, either because the murder charge would be dropped or because the judge would finally allow him out on bond.

"I think they'll let me go. It's costing them too much money to keep me in this hospital," Beckwith told his guests. He was holding court now, a princeling among his subjects. Every gesture was exaggerated: a hearty backslap, a doubled-over guffaw. The heart patient seemed as spry as a teenager as he bounded around the small cell, talking.

"You know we got AIDS here, right next door?" Beckwith said. "A white boy."

Someone in the room suggested that the AIDS victim should go plant a kiss on the district attorney, and they all laughed.

"Then there's this nigger down the hall!" Beckwith said in his loud deaf-man's voice. As he said it, a black male nurse walked past his cell, not even glancing at the open door.

"Now Delay, you know the sheriff warned you about that kind of language around here," said Kim, shutting the door.

Beckwith was unrepentant. He asked his visitors if they'd heard the new joke going around town. It was about the petrified forest, a small tourist attraction north of Jackson, and the recently unveiled bronze statue of Medgar Evers on Medgar Evers Boulevard, formerly Delta Drive.

"Do you know how to get to the petrified forest?" Beckwith asked archly.

Pause.

"Just head out Delta Drive and turn left at the petrified nigger!"

The laughter from his friends further energized Beckwith. He pounded his chest and bragged, "I don't have a heart problem!"

But something was bothering Beckwith. It was the stranger who came in with Kim. She was one of the book writers who had been trading letters with him. He hadn't invited her, but for some reason he told her she could stay and write down whatever she wanted. Now a weird current was singing in Beckwith, working at him, and he was changing in front of everyone's eyes.

"You look like a white woman, but are you a Jew?" he asked.

Kim broke in and told him his visitor was a Catholic. But Beckwith was suspicious. If he hated any group more than blacks, it was Jews.

"A Catholic would know the Hail Mary," he said. "You say it after me: Hail Mary . . ."

She looked at him, then realized what he wanted.

"Full of grace. The Lord is with thee . . . ," she said.

"Blessed art thou amongst women . . . ," he continued, staring hard, gesturing with his hand for her to finish.

"And blessed is the fruit of thy womb, Jesus."

"Holy Mary, Mother of God . . ."

"Pray for us sinners, now and at the hour of our death . . ."

Beckwith was satisfied only for a few moments. He couldn't relax. He started to pace, and he began to sermonize, raising his finger to the sky, and before long he was ranting about "filthy Jews." Every time he said the word "Jew" he hooked one bony finger next to his nose and made a sniveling, sneering face. Jews were imposters, he said, and the white men of True Israel, like himself, had a mission.

"It is in Luke!" he shouted. "As I wrote to you, thus it is today: 'But those mine enemies, who would not that I should reign over them, bring hither, and slay them before me!' "

He was panting now, and his three friends looked worried. He sat down on the cot to catch his breath, while his visitors changed the subject. They talked about mutual friends, and guns, and that got the old man's attention.

Beckwith was calm now, and he launched into a long, elaborate story about going squirrel hunting with his visiting cousin from Greenwood.

"I wanted to show him you could hunt squirrel with a pistol," said Beckwith, nodding at the dapper businessman in the nice khakis seated on his cot. "This was in the days before there were scopes for pistols. I knew my pistol could shoot because my wife was always shooting at me with it!"

He was laughing now, loose. His friends exchanged nervous looks. "This was my first wife. She was a terrible shot, always missed me!

"Anyway, we were out in the woods and I took a green walnut and put it on a stick, and shot it." He assumed the stance of a man firing a gun, his pale blue eyes peering over the sight at the imaginary target.

"BAM!"

Beckwith stood up.

"He thought it was a lucky shot, so I did it again."

He crouched again in the shooting posture, aiming at the back wall, his eyes narrowed in pure concentration on the imagined target, somewhere beyond the window, out in the world.

"BAM!"

2

Decatur

We were all close, but different. Medgar was more quietish. I used to see him go way down in himself, like he's in a deep, deep studying. He'd just walk down the yard and out in the pasture where we'd keep the cow and the horse, and he'd be looking way over there somewhere.

He used to always carve his name on the trees and things: M. W. Evers. Everywhere you'd go: M. W. Evers. Mama had a wash place down by the spring where she built a shed to keep out of the rain. You'd see M. W. Evers all over it.

Now when I drive along the expressway in Chicago I see his name again: Medgar Evers School. All over the country. Medgar Evers Boulevard. Or whatever.

See, he had a dream, it was something in him, that he wanted. He'd carve his name and he'd stand back and he'd look. Even he didn't know. It all come back to me, after it happened. Now I see his name everywhere.

— *Elizabeth Evers Jordan*

Decatur didn't have much going for it as a town, but it did have a court-house. It was an impressive building, a Greek Revival marvel with brick walls, jaunty striped awnings over the windows, and massive Doric columns at the north and south ends. A wide expanse of stone steps led up to the formal north door, and that was where, in the summer of 1934, Theodore Bilbo delivered a speech to the white citizens of Newton County, Mississippi.

It was a Saturday night, hot as it could be, and the town was packed with men who rode in from the county to listen to the ex-governor from Poplarville. This time around, Bilbo was running for the U.S. Senate. The topic of the night was the same as always: niggers and what to do with them. Bilbo knew his audience and what they wanted to hear. It had worked for him for thirty years, and it would carry him through the rest of his career as the most racist politician in Washington.

"Nigger women!" shouted Bilbo, warming to his subject. "All they do is wash clothes and have babies. So don't pay them money! Give them old clothes!"

Medgar and Charles Evers had slipped into town that night to hear the man speak. They were small then, eight and eleven, so they wormed their way between the legs of the men in the crowd. The brothers ended up sitting on the courthouse steps, directly beneath the fat little white man.

Charles remembers Bilbo was so short he had to stand on a pedestal just to be seen. He wore his trademark white suit and red suspenders and red tie. The boys raised their faces, and the gaslight from the courthouse must have caught them in the shadows, because Bilbo looked down and saw them.

"See those two little nigger boys sitting here," Bilbo shrilled through his bullhorn. "If we don't watch out, we will live to see the day when these two nigger boys will be asking to represent us in Washington!"

A murmur passed through the crowd. The boys could feel all those sets of eyes staring down at them in the hot night. They didn't move, and Bilbo resumed talking.

Later Charles would say that the speech was downright inspirational.

For two boys growing up in rural Mississippi during the Depression, Charles Evers and his little brother, Medgar, had some powerful dreams. Late at night, with the house dark and quiet and their sisters and parents asleep, the brothers would lie in their bed on the sleeping porch and talk about their future together.

They had a plan. They would buy some land down in South Amer-

ica — Brazil! — and build two houses on two hills separated by a valley.
The houses would look out on each other, and the brothers could walk
across the valley to visit. They were going to put a big, tall fence around
the property with a guard at the gate and big dogs running patrol around
the grounds.

"We won't let any white folks in," said Medgar.

"And very few niggers," said Charles. And the boys would laugh until
Daddy Jim shouted for quiet.

The dream kept growing, expanding as the years went by. In Brazil
they would have their own plantation, have their own women, their own
children, and keep out the world. They would be free and live close
together.

Another thing they agreed: they would never get married.

Medgar and Charles Evers grew up in a painted white house with a tin
roof on an acre of farmland near the railroad tracks in Decatur.

Their father, James Evers, was a public worker. That meant he never
sharecropped on a plantation; he was his own man. When there were
jobs, he worked on the railroad. Mostly he stacked planks in the lum-
beryard at the sawmill. He was a lanky, powerful man, more than six feet
tall. His father had owned his own land, and so did Jim Evers, and he
built by hand the house where he raised his family.

Jessie, his wife, worked as a domestic for some white folks in town.
She took in laundry. The Everses kept milk cows and chickens and
planted crops, and while they were often short of cash, the family always
had food on the table.

Jessie Evers had been divorced before she met Jim Evers. Her first
husband's name was Grimm. For all their life together that's what Jim
Evers called her, Grimm. She brought three children with her to the
second marriage: Eddie, Eva, and Gene. She had four more children with
Jim: James Charles, Elizabeth, Medgar, and Mary Ruth.

Jessie was a tiny woman, not five foot two, with tiny feet and hands.
She was born Jessie Wright in Scott County, just west of Decatur. Her
grandfather was a half-Indian slave, and according to the family legend,
he was the most troublesome, uncooperative slave in east Mississippi.
His name was Medgar Wright, and Jessie named her fourth son for him.

Her father was so light-skinned he could pass for white. He was, in fact, the son of a white man, which was common enough in the piney hills of Scott County.

Jessie Wright's daddy, the story goes, once shot a white man, or maybe two, or maybe just shot at them. The reason, it's said, is that someone called him a "half-assed mulatto," and he pulled his gun and started shooting. That was the last he was seen, at least officially, around Scott County. He hit the road to save his life. Over the years he'd show up from time to time.

Liz Evers tells a story of how she and Eva were staying with her Aunt Dora, Jessie's sister, down in Forest. One summer's day a white stranger came to the door.

"Aunt Dora!" Eva shouted. "There's a white feller calling!"

Dora took a look and laughed. "That's no white man!" she said. "That's your granddaddy."

Jessie Evers was a religious woman. She helped build the Church of God in Christ, the Pentecostal Holiness church just up the street in Decatur. She read from the Bible, and she reared her children with a firm, loving hand. The children went to church all day every Sunday. Jim was a Baptist, so sometimes they went to two churches. They weren't allowed to carry on and go to dances. Ball games and church. That was all the entertainment that was allowed.

As religious as she was, Jessie Evers had a spitfire in her too. She was a plump woman in her later years, but she moved herself like a queen. People would tease her, saying, "Mama Jessie, the way you walk, you carry your hips like each side is worth a million dollars!"

"Baby, more than that!" she would laugh.

She was an excellent cook, and her macaroni and cheese, fried corn, biscuits, and banana pudding were a minor legend in Decatur. Naturally she was very popular with visiting ministers around supper time.

Liz remembers how it irked Medgar that the preachers would eat all the best food and leave scraps for the children. One Sunday he sat at the table and watched one buttery biscuit after the next disappear into the preacher's mouth. When there was just one left, Medgar couldn't contain himself.

"Pass 'em!" he said, and reached across the preacher for the last biscuit. He got whipped for that.

Medgar didn't get whipped all that much. He had a mischievous streak — he would torment his sisters and sneak food, like all boys will — but he was basically a studious, serious child.

Not like Charles. All their lives Charles and Medgar were held up against each other. Medgar was always the good boy, and Charles was the bad one. They were so close but so different, like flip sides of the same copper coin.

Charles was sneaky and tough, prickly and defensive. He wouldn't let anybody get the better of him, and in that he was like his father. Medgar was more like his mother. Good-natured. Tender.

Charles would tease Medgar without mercy. He nicknamed him "Lope" after Brother Loper, a deacon in Mama's church whom Medgar disliked. He pushed Medgar into the fishing hole to teach him how to swim.

Still it broke Charles's heart to see Medgar get cold or hurt. He would do things for him, like every frosty winter night when Daddy ordered the boys to bed, Charles would climb in first to warm up the spot where Medgar would sleep. Medgar was the only one who could reach him that way. Charles protected his younger brother like he would protect the soft part of himself.

The neighborhood boys called Charles "Dermp." That was the white man who would come into the Negro section to sell housewares and Bibles. Charles got that name because he would do anything to make a nickel: he would sell the tinfoil from cigarette packs, dig up scrap metal from old fields, sell pop bottles. Charles knew instinctively that money was freedom, money was power.

Charles and Medgar hated the white salesmen who came to the Quarter. They would walk into a Negro's house uninvited, without a knock, and sell their goods. Colored folks couldn't sell to the whites.

So Charles and Medgar took their small revenge, organizing little rebellions to help even the score. Things would go wrong. The furniture man's tire would spring a leak, or the gate to the watermelon truck would swing open, spilling the melons all over the road. Medgar and Charles put bags on their heads to jump the white paperboys and scatter their newspapers. If Medgar and Charles weren't allowed to be paperboys in their own neighborhood, neither would they. Mama had always taught them they were no better or worse than anyone else, and they believed her.

Still, the world of black and white is hazy to a young child. Black or white, all a child knows at first is his family, and only as years go on do the outlines of the outside world take shape and sharpen. The rules of race, the stilted etiquette that goes along with it, is as incomprehensible as all the other rules a child must learn: wash your hands before supper, go to bed before dark, don't go out of the yard, stay out of puddles, always call a white man mister, always say yessir or no ma'am, never look them in the eye. Never show them what you feel.

In the rural south in the days of Jim Crow, the story was the same everywhere. It is a story told by blacks and by whites, by boys and girls who grew up together until they reached a certain age, when suddenly the shadow of race fell between them. In one summer, over a few weeks, sometimes in an afternoon, they would lose their friend and, in a way, their innocence.

It happened to the Evers boys like it happened to all the others. Medgar and Charles used to play with the Gaines children, Margaret and Bobby, the children of the family that hired Mama Jessie to clean and cook. All through childhood the Evers and Gaines children would run and tumble and nap together. And then one day Mama wouldn't let the boys come with her to the Gaines house anymore. Margaret was getting too old for them to come around.

One of Medgar's best friends was a white boy who lived nearby. One summer he stopped coming over. Before long he was standing in the street with his white friends, and when Medgar walked by, he called him a nigger.

Nobody had to remind the Evers brothers of how it was.

Every weekday Medgar and Charles walked to school a mile or more, along the tracks and across the muddy roads of Decatur. Sometimes a bus full of white kids going to their own school passed by, and the children screamed names at them, and the bus driver ran hard into the puddles just to watch the colored boys jump. They often got to school covered with mud.

The town of Decatur lay on the edge of the hill country, midway between Philadelphia, Mississippi, and the main road that would later become Interstate 20. It was a part of the state where most of the white folks were dirt farmers, and they outnumbered their black neighbors. The whites were a different breed here than they were in the Delta or on the Gulf Coast. Their ancestors came from Appalachia, and they spoke their words with a hard mountain twang. They were clannish and insular, fundamentalist Protestant, and, as a group, they had little tolerance for anyone different.

Decatur in the thirties was as segregated as it gets. The colored folks couldn't even drive their cars into town on Saturday. They had to park them at the edge of the Quarter and go in on foot.

Town was the domain of whites, enemy territory. A black man knew he'd better keep his eyes down, and God help him if a white woman should brush against him on the sidewalk. That alone could get him beaten, even lynched. The best policy was to just walk in the road, get right off the sidewalk if a white was on it. Do your trading in the shops where you could, and head back to the safe part of town.

There were ways around most rules, even the biggest ones. The white men who prowled the Quarter for Negro girlfriends called the practice "backdoor integration." It was something the white men might brag about in certain company.

But if a black man got caught with a white girl, he was as good as dead, or bound for Chicago forever, if he was lucky enough to get out of town.

Everybody knew what happened to Willie Tingle.

The full story is passing out of living memory around Decatur, and the old folks remember only what they were told as children. Everyone agrees on this: Willie Tingle was somehow involved with a white girl — whether he wrote her a letter, insulted her, or actually slept with her depends on who's talking. He was grabbed by a mob of white men right off the streets of Decatur, dragged past the Quarter, tied to a tree outside of town, and shot.

Jim Evers knew Tingle. Medgar was in his early teens when he was lynched. The killers stripped Tingle's body and left the clothes to rot under the tree where he died. Years later Medgar would talk about that lynching, how it disgusted him that a few men could grab Tingle and not one Negro in the town would try to stop it. For months after the killing, Medgar would visit the pasture where it happened and stare at the scraps of clothes, the bloodstains rusted brown, and remember. Charles recalls asking his father why Mister Tingle had to die.

"Because he was colored, son" was all his father would say.

Medgar and Charles didn't have to be told.

When they walked into town alone, they were vulnerable, two little barefoot colored boys open to the sport of whites. With Daddy it was different.

For some reason, Jim Evers wasn't afraid of the white folks. He wouldn't step off the sidewalk for anyone, and he got away with it.

Every Christmas Eve the white boys made a game of throwing firecrackers at the black shoppers to make them dance in the street. Jim Evers led his boys to the store and nobody threw anything at them. "They don't bother us," Jim Evers told his sons. "Don't let anyone bother you."

Medgar and Charles saw how wild the old man could be one morning at the sawmill commissary. The story of what happened that day is part of the Evers legend now, often repeated and embellished with each retelling.

On this particular Saturday morning a small crowd of whites was gathered in the store, shooting the breeze around the flour sacks, when Jim Evers came in to settle his bill. Evers bought everything on credit, then paid up at the end of the week. He couldn't read or write, but he had a talent for numbers, and he could figure sums in his head. And he wouldn't be cheated.

The clerk named the figure, and Jim knew it was wrong, maybe five or six dollars more than he owed. He told him so.

"Nigger, you callin' me a liar?" the white man asked. The others stopped talking and watched. Charles and Medgar stood by the door, too scared to move.

"I don't owe that much," Evers said quietly. "And I'm not goin' pay it."

The clerk reached behind the counter to get his gun, but Jim Evers moved quick. He grabbed an empty Coke bottle from a crate on the floor and smashed it on the edge of the counter.

"If you make another move, I'll bust your brains out," he said. He aimed the broken glass at the man's throat.

The story has been told many times, in different ways. In one version the boys ran out the door and straight on home. The way Charles remembers it, he and Medgar each grabbed a bottle to help, but Jim Evers ordered them out the door. The old man slowly backed out of the store, the white men standing slack jawed, the little clerk shaking and sputtering with outrage.

"I'll kill you, nigger," he shouted.

"You better not move," said Evers as he made the door.

The boys expected the white farmers to pour out after them, whip them or worse, so they started to run.

"Don't run, don't run," said Evers. "They're nothing but a bunch of cowards."

They walked home together. Charles remembers his daddy putting his big rough hands on the boys' heads. "Don't let anybody beat you," he told them.

Charles took his father's words to heart. He was always willing to get the first lick in. That was how he and Medgar were different. Medgar was a peacemaker.

Charles tested his strong head against other boys, even against his father.

"You be quiet," Jim Evers might tell him when he mouthed off at the table.

"No, *you* be quiet!"

Bam! James would knock him in the temple, lay him out. Charles took what Daddy said and lived by it.

Medgar listened to Mama. Mama would pray for you. Charles would come home after a fight with another boy, and she'd say, "Don't do that; do unto others as you would have them do unto you."

"But *Mom*, he's kicking my behind!"

"No, don't fight, that's not the best way."

But James Evers would say, "Knock his head off!"

One morning the family was gathered around the table for Sunday breakfast. It was the bottom of the Depression, breadlines everywhere, hardly any work to go around. The Everses' table always had something, eggs from the chickens, biscuits, maybe some bacon left over from hog-killing time. Charles sat on one side of his father and Medgar on the other, and the family got to discussing the commodity lines downtown for the out-of-work.

"Boys, let me tell you something," said Jim Evers. "I don't ever want to think of one of you in that soup line, heah? If I thought we were gonna be in that shape, have to go in that soup line, I'd kill every one of you and kill myself too! Don't you *ever* get on no soup line, get no commodity."

In the quiet that followed, Charles looked at his father, the old man's face hard with anger, and imagined him actually killing them all.

Medgar and Charles had a half-brother, Eddie, who was a wanderer. Eddie was a good fifteen years older than Charles. When the boys were half grown, ten and thirteen, they would listen to Eddie's stories of his travels. He used to ride the rails, he could never sit still, and the young brothers thought he was hopelessly glamorous. They would ride the rails from Decatur to Newton and back, just to be like Eddie.

One day Eddie came home complaining of a headache. He took to bed and died without ever seeing a doctor. The family thought later it must have been a brain tumor.

Charles was crushed. It was the first time anybody that close to him had died. He couldn't eat and he couldn't cry. He would just sit on the porch, listening to the trains roll through town.

Mama Jessie took in boarders to make extra money, and one of these men taught Charles to drive a car. He also taught him the bootlegging business.

When Prohibition ended, Mississippi stayed dry. There were enough Baptists to vote against liquor in every county and enough sheriffs and tax collectors getting rich from payoffs that nobody wanted to ruin the system. This didn't mean liquor wasn't available, or even sold openly in some places. The illegal sale of liquor was even taxed by the state — it was called the bootleg tax. Bootlegging was big business, and Charles wanted in. So he found out where the boarder bought his whiskey wholesale, and he started buying it too. Jim and Jessie Evers hated bootlegging, and they never knew what he was doing.

Charles would never touch a drop — he never has in his life, he says. And he never smoked or gambled. It was a waste of money, for one thing. And he wouldn't have anything control him, nothing habit-forming. He always had to be in control.

Charles later went to live in the town of Forest with Mark Thomas, an uncle who owned a funeral business. Since Charles could drive, he helped out with the ambulance-hearse. And when Uncle Mark was out of town, Charles would sometimes take Medgar to Vicksburg, where he could buy bottled whiskey from Louisiana. Charles would load it up in the back of the hearse and run back to Forest with the siren wailing. Nobody would think to stop a Negro ambulance.

Charles would stack the liquor behind the bottles of embalming fluid in his uncle's storeroom and sell pints to the honky-tonks in Scott County. It was the beginning of his serious business career.

When Medgar Evers outgrew the one-room schoolhouse in Decatur, he had to walk the twelve miles to the nearest Negro high school in Newton. Eventually he boarded there during the week. There was never any question that he would go to school or that he would finish. Even the girls in the Evers family got some higher education, and that was rare in those days. But then World War II came, and Medgar dropped out in the eleventh grade to join the army. Charles had already signed up.

The war separated the brothers at last. Charles was sent to the Pacific, and Medgar went to Europe.

Medgar sent his salary home to his mother. A person could keep an account at the post office, up to twenty-five hundred dollars. Medgar filled his limit. Charles sent money home as well. By the time the brothers came back from the service, there were four new rooms on the house and indoor plumbing, and the old woodstove was gone at last.

3

The Veteran

THE PHOTOGRAPH of Byron De La Beckwith in his high school annual reveals a somewhat homely boy with slick black hair brushed from a wide forehead, prominent ears, intensely friendly eyes, and a broad grin. His is a salesman's face, the face of a future Rotarian, Kiwanian, or Shriner. It is the face of someone who has to compensate for the fact that the list of activities printed under his picture shows only one entry: Study Club, 3. It is the face of someone who won second place in two senior categories. He was voted the second friendliest boy and second wittiest boy in the Greenwood High School Class of 1940. If there had been a category for most eccentric, Beckwith might have, for once in his life, come in first.

His Greenwood neighbors remember Byron De La Beckwith as a sweet, lonely child. He was raised by men, very strange gentlemen bachelors who lived in a big, spooky old house near the center of town. His father died when he was five, and he was twelve when his mother succumbed to cancer. It was a somewhat unmentionable disease in those days. Her death made Beckwith even more conspicuous in a small town where he had the social disadvantage of being born in California. He was an outsider, and he was an orphan in a community that valued conformity and tradition. His strongest suit was his family name and his relation to the Southworths and the Yergers and the Kimbroughs, who were among the oldest and most powerful families in the Delta.

Beckwith's maternal grandfather was Lemuel Purnell Yerger, who ran off to join the Confederate army when he was sixteen. He rode as a courier with the wild Tennessee general Nathan Bedford Forrest until he was wounded and captured by Yankees. After the war the young man returned from a P.O.W. camp, still a private but with a limp and a legend that enhanced his status in town. He soon started calling himself the Colonel.

L. P. Yerger set up a law practice and married well, to Susan Fisher Southworth, a Delta socialite from a family of planters. The Yerger family had cotton land as well, a 10,000-acre plantation called Glen Oak on the Tallahatchie River.

The Colonel and his wife had four children, the youngest of whom was a high-strung, attractive girl named Susie Southworth Yerger, Beckwith's mother. There are more stories than facts available about "Miss Susie," as she was called all her life. Some say she was among the most popular debutantes in the Delta. Others say she had mental problems. Certainly Miss Susie was overshadowed by her flamboyant first cousin Mary Craig Kimbrough, who married the socialist author Upton Sinclair. Mary Craig later wrote a book about her life in Greenwood, appropriately titled *Southern Belle*. It captures perfectly the idealized life of the Southworths and Kimbroughs.

"I was born in the midst of vast cotton plantations," she wrote. The South of her childhood was, she said, "an enchanted land." She described her family as "these proud white people [who] thought they were the lords of creation, and no 'damyankees' could make them change their minds or their ways. Pleasure was their chief concern, and they sought it and had it, just as their parents had done in the old days."

In fact this enchanted land was a child's fantasy; the Delta was nobody's paradise. It was a dull, flat, utilitarian landscape that flooded or parched, sweltered or froze depending on the time of year. It was a place of pestilence and isolation — so bad that few stately homes were actually built in the alluvial flatlands, but instead were set in the hills of Carrollton or Vicksburg, or somewhere high up in the breezes and out of the typhoid.

The Yergers and Kimbroughs were exceptional. Delta folk to their bones, they built their big houses in Greenwood. They saw no reason to look any farther than Memphis, the shopping capital of the Delta. They lived chasing the myth of the Old South, and they passed the fantasy down through generations.

No one knows precisely why Miss Susie ventured to Colusa, California, to visit her great-aunt Sallie Green. She may have simply needed a change of scenery. Certainly she needed a husband, since she was still a spinster at twenty-five.

Aunt Sallie found a match for Susie in Colusa: Byron De La Beckwith, the town's twenty-nine-year-old bachelor postmaster. The couple were married back in Greenwood in 1912. Her father, the Colonel, wore his Confederate uniform, and people remarked at the time at the sea of gray coats at the wedding reception, as the aging veterans paraded their colors.

A picture of Miss Susie taken that year shows a handsome but wan woman with long, thick chestnut hair twisted up in the fashion of the day. Her chin is strong, her nose straight, but there is an air of melancholy about her that could have been the photographer's sad music or something of her own.

A picture of Beckwith shows a compact, square-jawed, black-haired man. His lips are thin and pursed, the eyes not friendly, as he poses in his stiff California National Guard uniform.

The young couple settled in Colusa and soon moved into a brand-new Craftsman-style bungalow.

For a native of Mississippi, Colusa would not have seemed terribly foreign. In fact it was like a little Delta town that had died and gone to heaven. It was a conservative community with broad, tree-lined streets, churches, neatly tended houses, and serious citizens of good pioneer stock. It was laid out in a rich, flat valley along the volatile Sacramento River, which was held back by a familiar barrier of earthen levees.

After eight years of marriage, Susie and Byron De La Beckwith finally produced a child. He was born in the nearest hospital, in Sacramento, on November 9, 1920. The baby was, predictably, named Byron De La Beckwith, Jr., although years later he would refer to himself as Beckwith the Sixth.

By now Beckwith, Sr., had inherited a small fortune from his late father's real estate ventures. He acquired a title and abstract company in Colusa and bought himself a 700-acre farm on the east bank of the

Sacramento River, where he planted prune trees. Outwardly he seemed like a solid businessman. But Beckwith was a heavy drinker, and, apparently, a philanderer and a gambler. Before long all of his properties were heavily mortgaged.

Beckwith, Jr., would later say that his childhood in Colusa was pleasant enough "to a point." Beckwith's mother, increasingly unable to cope with her life, had a startling habit of locking her son in the hall closet. He claims it never scared him. All he had to do was calm down and smile, and the door would open. Others say the hyperactive child was sometimes locked in his nursery for hours.

The father was an avid hunter who collected hundreds of rifles, knives, pistols, and swords of all descriptions. He sometimes took the family to a rustic, shotgun-style cabin high in the mountains at Berry Camp, where he fished and hunted deer. One early photograph of "Little Delay," as he was called, taken when he was a toddler, shows him with curly, golden baby locks down to his shoulders, wearing a little playsuit and holding a small revolver in his pudgy fist. Another picture reveals a slightly older boy, his hair trimmed in what might be his first haircut, looking serious and leaning possessively against a bolt-action rifle that is taller than he. In the foreground is the body of a buck his father had shot.

Beckwith has another enduring memory from his California childhood. He remembers the white robes and tall caps of the Ku Klux Klansmen when they walked through town. The twenties were the heyday of Klandom in America. There were two million known members. In 1925 forty thousand hooded marchers converged on Washington, D.C. The Klan vote elected at least two U.S. senators and a raft of governors, including the governor of California.

The main enemies then were Jews and Catholics, not to mention the "Yellow Plague" in the West, the Chinese, Filipinos, and Japanese and every other sort of enterprising immigrant.

Beckwith recalls seeing the Klansmen and describes the sensual impact that moment had on him. He wrote in one letter, "In the drugstore soda fountains — cafes, etc. in California in the 20's, robed Klansmen with tall dunce caps (seemingly made of a good grade of white poster board), neat and clean — snowwhite — would take turns in walking through the towns just to be seen and were then as prominent as the bell-ringers, volunteers who used to drum up money for the Salvation Army! And now that too is fading."

In August 1926 Beckwith's father died of pneumonia. His death certificate mentioned "contributory alcoholism." He was forty-two years old. His son was not quite six.

Unfortunately for all concerned, Susie Yerger Beckwith was now alone with her young son and practically destitute. The estate, including the prune orchard, was sold for fifty-seven thousand dollars, all of which went to pay debts. Her family dispatched a sober, responsible nephew, Yerger Moorehead — who was also a lawyer — to bring Susie and the boy back to Mississippi.

The Yergers lived in a big, gabled wood-frame house on George Street in Greenwood. It was a fine, tree-lined street with large, stately homes and lots of children running on the sidewalks.

In 1926 both the Colonel and his wife were alive. Miss Susie's forty-two-year-old bachelor brother, Will, still lived at home. There were plenty of people to occupy "Little Delay" and places to explore. Beckwith especially liked the attic, where guns and books were stored. An old muzzleloader interested him more than the books.

Beckwith was a rambunctious boy, and he remembers his childhood as happy and indulged. "I am an only child and a spoiled child," he would later write, explaining why he demanded to have things exactly his way.

There was a lot to learn about southern manners, and Delay learned it the hard way. Once an uncle whipped his behind for responding to a request with "Okay," instead of the required "Yes, sir."

Delay was astonished by how many black faces he saw in Mississippi. He had known only one Negro before in his life, and that was Aunt Sallie's housemaid. The boy was constantly talking and asking questions, and one night at dinner he asked his cousin Yerger Moorehead what they were and where they all came from.

Yerger smirked and told him that *that's* what happens to smart-aleck white boys from out west who ask too many questions: they get rolled in gumbo mud and hung on the fence to dry. When they come down, they've turned into black pickaninnies. The six-year-old sat wide-eyed and believing, as six-year-olds will, and stopped asking questions for a while.

Beckwith had disliked Yerger Moorehead from the outset. He thought he was strict and dull and sarcastic, but he was more or less safe from the man as long as his mother was around or he was out of sight.

His eccentric uncle, Will, took day-to-day responsibility for the boy. Little Delay spent summer days out at the Glen Oak plantation, the large family-owned cotton farm that Will managed.

There Will was known to the servants and farmhands as "Master." They called Delay "Little Cap'n." Beckwith would later recall these plantation days as an ideal arrangement. He felt the races were happy in their separation, kind after kind, as it says in the Bible. The "nigras" expected the white man to care for them and to be courteous and soft-spoken. The white man expected loyalty and subservience. The white man, he came to believe, was put on earth "to rule over the dusky races," and this was how it was done.

Delay joined the Boy Scouts and spent his idle days with his friends in the swamps killing birds and garfish and turtles and frogs with their .22 rifles. A boy in the Delta had to know how to shoot.

The Colonel died in 1928, and his wife followed him four years later. Neighbors on George Street remember the peculiar, old-fashioned mourning Miss Susie put herself through. For months she would wear only black, then only white, and then only lavender.

The Depression cut hard into the Delta way of life. A lot of big farms went broke, and the banks in Greenwood closed one after the next. Fortunes were halved and halved again, and the great tracts of cotton land that the Yergers and the Southworths controlled dwindled.

Still, depending on the price of cotton and the yield of Glen Oak, Beckwith's family would sometimes have enough money to journey en masse to the health spas at Battle Creek, Michigan, or nearby Allison Wells. Going to spas was a fashion of the time, but there must have been more of an attraction for Miss Susie. She was occasionally hospitalized — some say for mental disorders — while a cancer slowly spread through her body.

Delay noticed his mother was spending more and more time in her room, skipping family meals. She assured him she was getting better, just resting. He would often sit with her in the evenings, watching as she brushed her long brown hair, and she would tell him stories about his father and their life in California.

Through those hours with his mother, and through the letters his father had written to Will, which Delay was later given, he learned that his father had some strong ideas on race and culture. The Chinese, he wrote, were diligent people, but unwelcome in America "because their pagan practices and racial characteristics can not fit into Caucasian culture nor civilization."

Beckwith has said that after his father, Uncle Will was the main male influence in his life. He would spend endless hours in the creaking old house, listening to stories about the War Between the States, also known in these parts as the War of Northern Aggression.

The Greenwood relatives, the Yergers and the Southworths and Morgans and Kimbroughs, were all Confederate patriots of the first order. Their exploits were drummed into young Beckwith, as they were drummed into so many white boys of the South, boys born in defeat but still talking about the glory of the lost cause.

The stories gained new luster with each passing year. The women devoted themselves to keeping the faith alive. Beckwith's grandmother, Susie Fisher Southworth Yerger, helped create a monument to the fallen Confederate heroes in front of the Greenwood courthouse. She was the model for one of the stone figures: a brave rebel woman cradling a fallen soldier.

Beckwith's aunt, Mrs. Allan McCaskill Kimbrough (born Mary Hunter Southworth, and Mary Craig's mother), was, along with his maternal grandmother, a friend of Varina Davis, wife of the Confederate president. Mrs. Kimbrough's crowning achievement was to restore Belvoir, the Jefferson Davis house on the Mississippi Gulf Coast, and turn it into a monument and a home for Confederate veterans. To this end she gave a rousing speech before the state legislature in 1917, echoing the sentiments that were heard, would be heard, at the house on George Street in Greenwood for many years. She said to them: "The old South has not forgotten, and the young South will ever remember the great lessons of heroic faithfulness which is its final inheritance. . . . None in the history of the world shows greater courage nor fidelity to a principle than does the conduct of the Confederate men and women who are our ancestors. Theirs was called the defeated cause. It has never been defeated and stands triumphant today before the world."

Considering the ruins of the post-war South, it is hard to imagine a greater self-delusion, but there it was.

*   *   *

Delay Beckwith was at a Boy Scout meeting when his mother died in her
bed upstairs in the big house on George Street. Uncle Will broke the
news, and told Delay to change into some good clothes to greet the
mourners. Within hours of his mother's death, the twelve-year-old was
mingling with a houseful of visitors, in the old southern way.

To Beckwith's horror and dismay, Yerger Moorehead was made his
legal guardian. Not only was he an orphan, but his boring, disciplinarian
cousin now controlled his money. Their mutual animosity grew to the
point where, as Beckwith later wrote, "his face generally revealed gloom
at my approaches and satisfaction at my departures."

Children were wary of the rambling house he lived in with his peculiar bachelor uncle and cousins. One neighbor remembers hearing Beckwith, as a small boy, tell her mother how lonely it was living in that
house with all those men.

One of them, an older cousin named Hunter Holmes Southworth,
apparently did nothing for a living. He would often dress up in full
hunting livery and, with a servant appropriately attired, take his old
Ford out for country jaunts.

Uncle Will grew increasingly odd. It seems he was a capable manager
of the Glen Oak plantation while he was young. As he aged, that streak
of eccentricity that ran through the family surfaced in him. He was always a cheerful man, a little scary to the neighborhood children on
George Street, but he would win them over with little gifts he pulled
from his pockets. As he got older, his behavior grew more bizarre, and
he could be seen walking through town collecting scraps of wood and
metal. Junk piled up in the yard of the house — people remember this as
far back as the early fifties. To neighborhood children, it was always a
spooky, haunted house.

Eventually Will became forgetful. He would buy fish for supper, or
maybe catch some, and then stuff them in a bureau drawer for safekeep-
ing, and forget them for a few days or weeks. He was a generous, addled
soul who contributed to Democratic causes and politicians, neighbors in
need, whatever took his fancy. Years later some family members had him
committed to an institution to stop his squandering of family funds.
Delay, who never thought there was anything terribly wrong with Will,
had to bail him out.

In his freshman year of high school Beckwith was shipped off to the

Webb School in Bell Buckle, Tennessee. Beckwith liked the male comradery of boarding school, but he chafed under the discipline and academic requirements: Latin, physics, four years of English and history. He lasted one year, then transferred to the infinitely more fun and less demanding Columbia Military Academy in southern Mississippi. There he got to wear a red-caped overcoat over his miniature Confederate uniform. In 1938 he dropped out of the military academy and returned to Greenwood to finish his education in public high school.

As a teenager Beckwith wasn't much of a lady's man. He wasn't exactly ugly — "just so-so," one of his friends recalls. But he wasn't a dater, more interested in men's activities, like hunting and fishing. He was always attached to a gun of some kind. He boasted to his friends that his father had been a "military man" and that he had owned a big gun collection in California.

One of his schoolmates remembers he was popular among the girls who couldn't get a date. If a girl's date fell through, she could always call on Delay. He was the extra man, always a gentleman and very funny. A chum more than a boyfriend. There were dances every weekend at the country club, and Delay was often there with a girl who considered him a safe choice — better than going alone.

Another classmate — and few want their names mentioned — remembers Delay as "a screwball," blazingly eccentric even in a town where genteel eccentricity was borne with honor and not discussed in public, like a string of bad paper debts. He would do unusual things, like circulate a petition to demand that all the high school dances be formal balls and to mandate the wearing of tuxedos. This was in the depth of the Depression.

He finally graduated when he was twenty years old. This is his prediction in the "Class Prophecy" pages of his high school annual: "De La Beckwith has turned reformer and missionary in the South Sea Islands."

It is unclear whether this was meant to be ironic. It turned out to be partly right. He ended up in the South Seas, although his mission was not yet religious.

In the fall of 1940 Beckwith enrolled at Mississippi State College in Starkville. His grades were so bad that he dropped out after midterm and returned to Greenwood.

Beckwith went to work in a steam laundry and later at the nearby

Pepsi-Cola bottling plant. He did well enough to be made a salesman. It was not an easy thing, but he managed to break this new beverage into the Delta marketplace, where Coca-Cola and RC were nearly sacred traditions. Apparently Beckwith found his calling as a salesman. By all accounts he was not interested in much except learning the trade, enjoying his Scotch and soda, and generally having a good time.

But before he could decide whether to return to college or make his career in sales, the Japanese bombed Pearl Harbor. There was never a question that Beckwith would sign up, like every able-bodied Mississippi boy was expected to do. In January 1942 Beckwith joined the Marines. He was twenty-one years old, five foot eight, and not quite 140 pounds.

He trained at San Diego and shipped out with the Second Marine Division for the first Battle of Guadalcanal and the Solomon Islands campaign. Beckwith saw some action and then cooled his heels in New Zealand for nine months. He took up reading for the first time and managed to memorize the entire *Rubáiyat of Omar Khayyám*. In November 1943 his division was positioned to join one of the bloodiest campaigns of the Pacific, in the Gilbert Islands.

The Tarawa atoll had been British territory until the Japanese captured the island group in December 1941. They had heavily fortified an air base at Betio, and that was the object of the Marine assault.

In *Line of Departure*, a book later written about the Battle of Tarawa, Corporal Byron De La Beckwith is mentioned as a "happy-go-lucky youngster," who went into battle with copies of the Bible and *The Rubáiyat* in his pack. The stroppy little Marine also carried a straight razor in case an enemy soldier jumped him during the assault. He was a forward machine gunner on an amphibious tractor vehicle in the first wave of Marines to land at Betio.

The night before the landing Beckwith prayed "fervently" to keep from showing fear. The next morning, as Beckwith's amtrac churned across the shallow reef, the invading force came under withering fire. There were nearly 5,000 Japanese troops dug in on Betio. There were 5,600 Marines and 125 amtracs to take the beach.

Four hundred yards from shore, Beckwith's .50-caliber machine gun jammed. Rather than hit the deck with his fellow Marines, who were taking heavy casualties as bullets ripped straight through the armored bow, Beckwith scrambled aft and yanked out the .30-caliber gun. He wrestled it forward and placed it in the forward mount. Beckwith kept firing as the amtrac hit a reef one hundred yards from the beach. Then a spray of machine gun fire splintered the gun mount and jammed his weapon. As the story was told, Beckwith still didn't duck. Rather than discourage the men, a third of whom were wounded by now, he made a show of pretending to fire the big gun. This, of course, drew Japanese fire right at him, and he was flipped back to the deck with a bullet in the thigh. The vehicle made it to shore, dispatched the Marines who could still walk, and withdrew with the wounded, including Beckwith.

As it pulled back, the vessel was hit by a mortar round. Beckwith and the others plunged into the sea. Machine gun fire continued to rake the water.

"Disperse!" someone yelled.

"Disperse, hell!" shouted Beckwith. "Submerge!"

Beckwith dove and grabbed onto coral as bullets dropped around him. He floated in that reef for hours until the battle subsided and he was rescued by a light tanker. From there he was evacuated to the hospital ship *Solace* to begin a long rehabilitation. His war was over.

Tarawa was one of the most savage battles in the history of the Marine Corps. In Beckwith's unit of 500 men there were 343 casualties. In all 1,027 Americans were killed and 2,292 wounded. Of the Japanese troops defending the atoll only 17 survived.

Beckwith returned to Greenwood at the end of the war with a Purple Heart, which he gave to Uncle Will. He also brought home a bride. Mary Louise Williams was a Wave, a big, dark-haired, broad-hipped woman from east Tennessee. They met while he was recuperating from his wounds.

She was not at all the southern ideal of a suitable gentleman's wife. Although her family descended from Roger Williams, she was considered lower-class by Greenwood society. She was not ladylike. Her nickname, in fact, was "Willie." And she spoke with a grating hill twang, not a soft Delta drawl. She talked loud and she swore like a sailor. She drank hard.

Beckwith was deeply in love with her. Their marriage distanced him from his rich planter cousins, but Delay didn't seem to care. He came visiting with her anyway, proud as he could be. But people noticed that he would sometimes correct her in front of them, criticize her grammar or her manners, and she would get mad. Before long there would be a fight. As the years went on, the fights got worse.

Delay and Willie lived in the big old George Street house for a time after the war. Then Beckwith used the GI Bill to buy a small place in town. Before long Willie gave birth to a son, who was named, naturally, Byron De La Beckwith. They called him "Little Delay."

Beckwith's old friends and cousins noticed that he was cockier than before, as if he figured he could take on anything and anybody. Beckwith was drinking quite a bit, going out at night with other couples and men who had been through the war.

Beckwith had always been mischievous and carefee; now he was edgy and more serious than before. He had a strong opinion about most everything. And there was something else: he was bitter. About what, it was hard to say. Nobody can remember him carrying on about blacks and Jews in these days. His bitterness didn't seem to have a focus. There was just a hardness to him that hadn't been there before, a pervading sense of loss and regret and disappointment at the way things were.

To those who knew him casually Beckwith was still as gregarious and courtly as ever. His natural eccentricity percolated to the surface time and again, manifesting in harmless ways. It showed up as exaggerated courtesy, strange jokes, and increasing religious fundamentalism. None of these things set him that far apart in the rural South, where eccentricity was expected and deep religious beliefs were the norm. Beckwith even seemed to be joining Greenwood's postwar middle class. He found his calling as a salesman for the New Deal Tobacco Company. The little firm, owned by a family of Italian immigrants, issued him a car, which he used to hawk cigarettes and snuff to one-room country stores up and down the Mississippi Delta.

It is tempting to imagine him then, tooling along the arrow-straight back roads, through towns named Panther Burn, Money, and Midnight, passing in the dust, unaware, another car bearing a traveling businessman, a veteran, a black man whose path would someday cross with his own.

4

Brave New World

AMERICA NEEDED SOLDIERS, and it didn't care what color they were. For the first time black men were actively recruited for the army. But the services were still segregated in World War II and Medgar Evers was assigned to the 325th Port Company, where only the officers were white. The 325th followed the Normandy invasion into France and moved inland and south with the Allied troops.

The names of the cities were like strange music to a seventeen-year-old from Mississippi: Le Havre, Cherbourg, Antwerp. Europe was exotic and exciting, and the white folks didn't seem to have the same attitudes as those back home. There was no Jim Crow, not once you got away from your unit. Even there it was different. There was a white lieutenant who took an interest in him, encouraged him to work on his vocabulary and take pride in himself. Medgar was befriended by one family of French farmers, and he even started courting their daughter. He felt comfortable with whites for the first time in his life. For the first time, he learned that the whole world wasn't like Mississippi.

Charles was learning his own lessons on the other side of the world. In basic training he ran crap games and sold bootleg to the soldiers, always on the hustle. That was nothing new. Then he was shipped to the Pacific theater — Australia, then New Guinea. He served with a battalion of combat engineers. He hurt his leg jumping into a foxhole and got reassigned to administrative duty. It increased his business opportunities.

After the Philippine invasion, Charles Evers found a new line of work. He opened his first brothel in Quezon City. He had ten girls working for him, turning tricks for five dollars each — twice that for officers. It was an integrated establishment and, Charles insists, a clean one. Money was money, and Evers was going to make it by providing services to those in need.

Meanwhile Charles took some classes in English at the University of Manila business school. That was where he met a good Filipino girl named Felicia. Charles loved Felicia like he never loved anybody before or since. He never even slept with her. He wanted to marry her, but there was no way to do it. He couldn't stay in the Philippines, and he couldn't take Felicia back to Mississippi because she was part French and her skin was white. He knew they wouldn't survive five minutes back home. When he shipped out, it just tore him up. He knew he would never see her again.

Medgar also left his French girlfriend behind. He even had to stop writing to her once he got back to Decatur. If certain people found out that he had a white girl in Europe, then Medgar and his family would be in terrible danger.

The war changed the Evers boys, but it didn't change Mississippi. Medgar and Charles Evers went overseas to fight fascism and now they had to live under it in their own country. It wasn't right, and there wasn't anything to do but change it.

So in the summer of 1946, Medgar, Charles, and a handful of other young veterans from Decatur took the first step toward resistance. They registered to vote.

At first they made a big show of walking into the registrar's office, and they were turned away. Later they quietly slipped onto the rolls. Of the nine hundred or so registered voters in Decatur, they were the only blacks.

As the primary approached, somebody noticed what had happened, and the nightly visits began. At first it was concerned white people who would knock on Jim and Jessie Evers's door, warning them that their sons were making a mistake. Then black proxies would show up with the same message and the same vague threats.

The night before the election, Senator Theodore Bilbo visited Decatur. He told the white people of Newton County that the best way to keep a nigger from voting was to visit him the night before.

Medgar and Charles and Jim Evers stayed up that night. The brothers set up a cross fire on the road to the house, Medgar with a .22, Charles with his army carbine, but nobody came to visit.

The next morning, July 2, 1946, was Medgar Evers's twenty-first birthday. The town of Decatur was so still and empty you could feel the trouble through your skin. Medgar and Charles and the neighbor brothers A. J. and C. B. Needham and two other friends put on their good clothes and walked together to the courthouse. There were rough white men in every doorway, farmers and pulp haulers. The Evers brothers knew every one of them.

Charles had a pistol in his pocket; C.B. had a .22 strapped to his ankle. The group split up and tried to get in different entrances. Medgar and Charles walked in the front.

Charles remembers one of the rednecks calling out, "You niggers gonna wind up getting yourself killed, and everyone around you killed."

Charles wheeled toward the man. He felt half crazy anyway, like it was time to put it all on the line. Then he felt a tugging at his shirt sleeve and a quiet voice."Charley, it ain't worth it," said Medgar, and he slowly backed them out the door.

"You better not follow us!" Charles shouted back, as the six men retreated across the courthouse square. Nobody followed. It only proved to Charles that the white man was a coward, just like his daddy had told him. The people in Decatur might have thought the black veterans were whipped, but Charles and Medgar told themselves they were just waiting for their time to come. Someday they would vote.

Medgar had been working as a construction laborer after the war while he decided what to do with his life. The incident at the Decatur Courthouse seemed to give him some direction. He decided to finish his education and be somebody.

World War II was the great social leveler in Mississippi. Not only did it reveal the modern world to a generation of farm boys, but postwar programs, like the GI Bill, offered them their first ticket to that world. Veterans were eligible for scholarships. In 1946 Charles was already enrolled at Alcorn College in southwestern Mississippi. Medgar was able to attend a special high school on the campus until he got his diploma.

Alcorn Agricultural and Mechanical College was the main state college for black students in Mississippi. Jackson State had opened, but Alcorn was the best and oldest public institution. It had been founded on the grounds of Oakland College, a Presbyterian finishing school for the sons of white cotton barons before the Civil War. After the war the white school closed, and the state bought the campus to create a school for the education of newly freed Negro men. It emphasized vocational training in farming and industry.

When Medgar Evers arrived on campus, all that remained of the original school was Oakland Chapel, a stately Greek Revival edifice that had been built by slave labor, and a rolling lawn of massive live oaks and magnolias.

Alcorn was a liberal arts school with a limited curriculum. What it did best was turn out teachers for the segregated school system. In 1946 a black teacher's average salary in Mississippi was $426 per year. A white made $1,211. The educational system was as outrageously unequal as the salaries. Negro children were expected to attend school only a few months of the year when they weren't needed in the fields. At that time fewer than one-quarter of black children made it to high school, while 62 percent of white children reached the ninth grade.

Medgar Evers wanted no part of that system. He decided to study business administration. He wanted to own his own business, be his own man. Charles majored in social sciences.

Both brothers made the football team, and Medgar became a star halfback. Charles always found a way to make a buck, even in college. He started a taxi service for Alcorn students. He and Medgar even sold ham sandwiches out of their dorm room for a profit.

Meanwhile Medgar was making a name for himself. Not only was he a football star in a sports-obsessed state, but he also was on the track team and debating team, and in the choir and the business club. He edited the campus newspaper. He worked with the YMCA and took part in interracial discussions at Millsaps College in Jackson. He was listed in the national publication *Who's Who Among Students in American Colleges and Universities.* He was the editor of the 1951 Alcorn yearbook.

Like his brother Charles, Medgar dated a lot of women. He never committed to one of them until Myrlie Beasley arrived at Alcorn.

They met during her first afternoon on campus in the fall of 1950. She was a seventeen-year-old freshman, a tall, thin girl with a strong face that could be beautiful or handsome, depending on the set of her jaw. Her hair was shoulder length and carefully straightened.

She was standing in her first pair of high heels with a cluster of other freshmen women in front of the student union. Medgar came by with a group of football players, casually checking out the new talent. He saw Myrlie leaning against a lamppost, chatting with a new girlfriend.

"I think you better get off that light post," said Medgar. "You might get electrocuted."

Myrlie answered with a coltish toss of her head.

Medgar Evers was tall, good-looking, older than the other students, and polite, with a subtle sense of humor. What he liked about Myrlie was that she was sheltered and innocent and naive. What she liked about him was that he wasn't.

Myrlie Beasley was born on March 17, 1933, in the river port city of Vicksburg. Her mother, Mildred Washington Beasley, was only sixteen. Her father, James Van Dyke Beasley, was a twenty-eight-year-old delivery truck driver. The couple separated when Myrlie was an infant, and she was taken in by her paternal grandmother, Annie Beasley. Although her parents drifted in and out of her life in an amiable way for the rest of their days, it was Grandmother Beasley who reared her. Myrlie called her Mama.

Myrlie grew up in a world of women, in the heart of the Negro middle class in Vicksburg. The family had status. Mama was a retired teacher who had been trained at the Hampton Institute in Virginia. Myrlie's namesake, Aunt Myrlie Polk, also was a schoolteacher, and her husband, John, was a county agent for the Department of Agriculture.

There were other strong women in her life. Her mother's mother, Alice Washington, lived across the street and worked as a domestic servant for a rich white family in town. And in one room of Mama's house lived Myrlie's great-great-grandmother, Martha Hoover, an ancient blind woman who had been born in slavery. The Beasley side of the family was so light-skinned because Grandma, as they all knew her, had been "taken in" by a white overseer named McCain. She gave birth to his son, Mama's father, who looked just like a white man.

Myrlie remembers her childhood home as a warm and secure place. Aunt Myrlie taught her piano; Uncle John indulged her with rides in his shiny black Ford and trips to the candy store. She was the only child, and she was treated like a precious diamond, and as carefully guarded.

Grandmother Washington cooked and cleaned for a white family, the Robinsons. They were the only white people Myrlie knew.

She remembers visiting the Robinsons every Christmas to play the piano. Mama would straighten her hair and dress her in white tights and her very best dress. It was always an exciting day, but Myrlie instinctively bristled at having to come in through the kitchen door, not the front door, like the other guests. It was a small but painful nick in her self-esteem, the kind most whites could never, can never understand. Myrlie would play for the family. There would always be a gift for her under the tree. But she was never invited to stay and open it. She left the way she came in.

There was never a moment when Myrlie Beasley didn't know that she was a Negro in a white world. She would later say that she knew what she was the moment she took her first breath, born in a bedroom at home instead of a hospital.

As she got older, she learned the rules of race by instinct, by osmosis. Segregation was just part of the air you breathed back then; it was the way things were. When she went to town, the buses, the water fountains, and rest rooms were separate for whites and blacks, and she knew there were things whites had that she couldn't use, like pools and libraries. But nobody challenged segregation in her world. Nobody even discussed it.

Mama and Aunt Myrlie sheltered her as best they could. But there was no way to disguise the meaning of the shabby, used uniforms the Magnolia High School football team had to wear. If you wanted to escape that world for a while in the flickering unreality of the picture show, there was still the dirty "buzzard's roost" where you had to sit, up away from the white kids, to remind you of what you were. It spoke in a language as loud and clear as the voices that called "nigger" from the shiny yellow school bus as it passed you by.

It was second-class citizenship, and it felt wrong, but there was nothing to be done about it. You just had to do your best in the world you were given. Myrlie wasn't particularly interested in the white world. It was enough to have family and friends in a separate but spiritually rich and nurturing all-black society, a parallel world of educated, professional people, a world of books and parties and music. Myrlie felt special and talented. But she knew she had little control over the direction of her life.

Myrlie was an excellent student and she graduated second in her high school class. She was a gifted pianist by then, and it was Mama's and Aunt Myrlie's dream that she would go to college and earn a fine arts degree in music. Myrlie was an obedient child, and she wanted to please the women who brought her up. Their dreams became her own. A college degree meant prestige and employment as a teacher — the highest status a Negro woman could reasonably hope to achieve.

But there was a problem: Mississippi colleges for Negroes did not offer music majors. Their curricula were designed by the white men on the Board of Higher Learning to offer Mississippi blacks just enough education to keep the federal government off the state's back. If a family had money, and very few did, they could send their children to private colleges to finish their education. The rest of Mississippi's blacks were at the mercy of the state.

The approved majors were in education, business, and agriculture, as these were the professions needed to keep the separate Negro society functioning. If a black student wanted to study medicine, law, dentistry, or other specialties, the state could grant scholarships to out-of-state universities. It was a way to keep costs to a minimum at the black colleges while discouraging the development of a highly educated class of blacks who might threaten or compete with white society.

Myrlie wanted to go to Fisk University in Nashville, Tennessee. The family couldn't afford the tuition, so Myrlie applied for a scholarship to study out of state.

First, the presidents of the Negro colleges in Mississippi had to review her application and write a letter to the Board to Higher Learning to confirm that they did not offer the music degree she wanted. But the president of Jackson State crushed her hopes when he wrote that his college offered all the courses she needed — meaning that she didn't need to major in music. Her scholarship was denied.

There was no way she would apply to Jackson State. So, in the fall of 1950 she entered Alcorn College. Her major was education.

It was the first time Myrlie could remember feeling an open rage at Mississippi's segregated system. But she didn't direct her anger at the white power structure. She blamed the Negro president of a Negro college who wrote the letter that killed her dreams of studying music. It wasn't until she met Medgar Evers that she learned whom and what to blame.

After they started dating, Medgar took Myrlie to Millsaps College, a white Methodist school in Jackson, to take part in an interracial discussion group. It was a terribly daring, even frightening thing to do. Myrlie was learning, but her politics were still unformed. She did what she did to please Medgar. This man was all business. He wanted to discuss current events; she hungrily read the newspaper every morning to have something to talk about.

He wanted her to argue with him, challenge him. She might breezily mention, "The sky was blue; it was a beautiful day," and he would say, "No, Myrlie, the sky was gray, and it was a terrible day." He did it just to get her going, to make her debate him. He was already shaping her, forcing her to take a stand when she had always been taught to back off from fights, smooth the waters, go along.

He was clear about what he wanted in a girlfriend: he liked her long hair, her looks, her manners. When they got more serious, he told her, "I want you to be the mother of my children." He told her he wanted her to be smart but innocent. She would be pliable, like clay for him to mold.

"How romantic," she wanted to say sarcastically, because she had that tart side of her too. But she said nothing.

This serious, mysterious older man was exactly what Myrlie Beasley wanted. She had imagined him when she was fourteen years old, not what he would look like, but the way he would be. The man she would marry would be an athlete, and he would be brilliant and educated and fun to be around. Her father was like that, witty and smart and charming. But most important, she wanted a man who would be responsible, who would meet his obligations to his family. In that way she wanted someone very much unlike her father. She could sense right away that Medgar would keep his word, that he would make a commitment.

Mama and Aunt Myrlie did not see this side of Medgar Evers. All they saw was a sophisticated veteran out to plunder their precious girl. Myrlie's upbringing had been almost Victorian. Aunt Myrlie went along on her eighth-grade prom date. She had a formal "coming out" party when she was sixteen, and Mama carefully screened her suitors. They forbade her to see Medgar Evers. He was too old and too experienced, and he would make her quit school.

Naturally the couple became engaged. It was the summer before her sophomore year.

Myrlie and Medgar headed north to Chicago — separately — to earn money over the summer of 1951. Myrlie was closely chaperoned by the relatives she was staying with. But sometimes she and Medgar would slip away for a ride along Lake Shore Drive. Medgar cruised down the wide, peaceful, tree-lined streets in the rich white neighborhoods, and he talked about his dreams.

He showed her one special place, a neat suburban house with a landscaped lawn.

What he wanted, he told her, was to live in a house like this some day.

Myrlie broke the news of their engagement to her distraught grandmother at the end of the summer. They were married on Christmas Eve.

It was a hapless, almost comical wedding night, where everything seemed to go wrong. Medgar dropped the ring under the stairs and had to break into the house because the key was locked inside; Myrlie erupted in a painful rash; Mama would barely speak to them.

Charles Evers, who should have been Medgar's best man, did not attend the wedding. The Korean War had begun, and Charles had been called back to his Army Reserve unit. But he would have sulked at the ceremony, even if he could have been there. To Charles, this wedding was a betrayal. He just couldn't understand why Medgar would go and do something as foolish as get married. Why did he need to? He could have any girl he wanted. What about Brazil? Charles ripped and tore at Medgar over this "mistake." But Medgar loved Myrlie, and he wouldn't be talked out of the marriage. Charles never forgave Myrlie for marrying his brother and ruining all his plans for them.

The formal portrait of the bride and groom on their wedding night belies the turmoil backstage. The photograph shows a handsome, beaming couple posed before a display of ferns and candles. Medgar wears a dark, wide-lapeled tuxedo and a white boutonniere. Myrlie wears a simple, ankle-length white tulle gown. Her illusion veil is swept back from her face. The newlyweds lean together, smiling, but clutch each other's arms as if to keep from falling.

All Myrlie wanted was an ordinary life, the kind that would fit into Medgar's suburban dream house. She wanted a decent income and kids and her husband working nine to five and coming home to her in the evenings. She wanted to get out of Mississippi, maybe move to Chicago, where she could finish school.

But the more Medgar was away from Mississippi, the more he wanted to come home. There was no other place for him. And the safe middle-class life would never satisfy him.

Myrlie and Medgar finished the school year at Alcorn. Medgar graduated that July. He was recruited to work for the Magnolia Mutual Life Insurance Company, an enterprise owned and operated by a black man, Dr. Theodore Roosevelt Mason "T. R. M." Howard of Mound Bayou, Mississippi.

To most travelers, Mound Bayou was just an eye-blink traffic stop on Highway 61, just north of Cleveland in the heart of the Delta. But Mound Bayou had a unique distinction in Mississippi. It was the only place where blacks founded, settled, and still governed their own town. It was where Medgar and Myrlie Evers made their first home together in the sweltering summer of 1952.

Mound Bayou was founded in 1887 in a lowland wilderness swamp as an experimental all-black community.

In 1940, when a newspaperman named Hodding Carter, Sr., visited Mound Bayou while researching a book about the lower Mississippi, there were about one thousand residents. The town was a shabby collection of buildings with twenty-four stores, three groceries, five churches, a high school and grammar school, and precisely enough professionals to keep the town self-sufficient: a doctor, a lawyer, a dentist, and a pharmacist. At the north end of town a forty-bed hospital was being built with funds donated by a black philanthropical organization called The Knights and Daughters of Tabor.

By 1952, there were about thirteen hundred people within the town limits. Mound Bayou was a safe haven for Mississippi blacks. Crime was low, and there was little white harassment at the time. But it was a dull town, self-conscious and staid.

Myrlie Evers hated it. During the day she worked as a secretary in the Magnolia Mutual office. Medgar usually came home late from work, and there was little entertainment in town. The picture show was a joke, there was nothing new to read. There was no television.

Medgar Evers didn't notice it was boring in Mound Bayou. He was completely absorbed in this new world.

Dr. Howard became Medgar's mentor. Howard was rich by anyone's standards. He owned hundreds of acres of rich Delta land. He lived in a nice brick house outside of town. Howard was portly, light-skinned, bespectacled and outspoken. He had flashy, almost effete tastes. He rode around in a red Buick convertible and had a fondness for skeet shooting and gentlemanly blood sports such as quail hunting. Medgar, who was an avid hunter, fit right into Howard's social arena.

Howard was ahead of his time in many ways. He founded the Delta-based Regional Council of Negro Leadership with a handful of other prominent businessmen. It was a homegrown lobby group, a sort of grassroots NAACP. Howard recognized the native xenophobia of white Mississippians, and he decided that they would be more likely to bargain with their "own Negroes," than with a foreign, New York outfit. The group spearheaded the first known black economic boycott in the Delta, aimed at service stations with toilets for whites only. The campaign was simple and specific, summarized in the bumper sticker the group distributed: "Don't Buy Gas Where You Can't Use the Restroom."

There was also a Mound Bayou chapter of the NAACP, and Medgar joined it. Through the NAACP and the Regional Council, Medgar met a group of veterans and hard-core activists who would be his allies for the rest of his life, including Aaron Henry, a pharmacist in Clarksdale and local NAACP chapter president, and Amzie Moore, a fearless businessman from Cleveland, Mississippi.

Medgar started out selling insurance policies in the town of Clarksdale. Later his beat included the rural areas, the plantations where few sharecroppers even knew what insurance was.

One of his closest colleagues was Thomas Moore, a tall, handsome young veteran and Mound Bayou native. Evers and Moore would often ride together to the big plantations to try to crack the insurance market out there. They also had another mission. They were recruiting for the NAACP, urging people to register to vote, and setting up new chapters across the Delta. Every working day in the summer of 1953 Moore and Evers dressed up in blue jeans and casual shirts and climbed into Medgar's Mercury to head out into the cotton fields.

The roads in the Delta don't seem to bend. They slice through the swamp flats like a child's exercise drawing in perspective, where the shimmering pinpoint of infinity is the Mississippi River, unseen but felt in the distance. In the summer months the river spreads its hot, fetid air over the breezeless floodplain, engulfing everything with its smell and its presence. The sun pounds down on the fat black topsoil, the best in the world for growing cotton, built up with layers of silt from millennia of wild spring floods.

It was here, in the Delta, that Mississippi found its wealth while it perfected a system of slavery in a nominally free country. The system was called sharecropping.

Medgar Evers thought he knew what poverty was until he started working the plantations. But every time he went out into the Delta, he was astonished by the squalid, leaky shacks, barely big enough for chicken coops, where families of twelve might live.

Thomas Moore remembers the children wore handmade clothes and no shoes. They were dirty, and you could tell they were hungry. They didn't talk much, just sat in the corner picking at their daily ration of hoecakes and greens, while the college-educated salesmen tried to sell their daddies insurance.

Evers and Moore had to be careful out there. They had to get permission to be out on the plantation, or they might get beaten up by some foreman. They talked their way onto the big spreads, like the huge King and Anderson plantation up near Clarksdale, by convincing the farm manager that it would be in his best interest for the sharecroppers to buy their own insurance. Then the planter wouldn't have to bury them or pay their medical bills. It would be taken care of. This tactic usually worked. You had to outfox the man, use psychology against him. Evers taught Moore that you can't sell anybody anything unless you convince him he needs it, that there's something in it for him.

Evers also taught Moore some tricks for selling insurance. The sharecroppers were terribly superstitious; many of them believed in spirits. The young salesmen would use that knowledge. For instance, they would pick their mark and ask the neighbors all about him. That way when they came to his shack, they knew him by name, knew his children's names, and knew other things about him. It got his attention. It was a way to make the sale, maybe $1.50 or $2.00 a week for the minimal health, life, and burial insurance. Burial insurance was the most important. While a person may have nothing in life, he would have himself a funeral, and it would be paid for. Evers and Moore figured they were selling dignity. And if they didn't do it, some white insurance agent would be out there selling policies. Besides, they gave something back.

If the white man wasn't watching, Evers and Moore would call together meetings in those dark little shacks and start teaching the sharecroppers something about their history. It was a program they devised on their own, with the local NAACP chapter. Most of the sharecroppers couldn't read, didn't pay attention to the radio, and were almost cut off from the rest of the world. So Medgar Evers would pull a George Washington Carver commemorative silver half-dollar from his pocket and show the folks: "This is a colored man." They could relate to that. He would tell them about Marcus Garvey, Harriet Tubman, Frederick Douglass, Marian Anderson. People, heroes, whose names they never learned in school, if they ever went to school at all.

On the long rides down those Delta back roads, Evers and Moore would talk about their lives. Medgar was always offering good advice to his younger friend, trying to make peace between Moore and his wife, who were having problems. The two men would talk about their dreams and their frustrations.

Once Medgar swept his hand across the flat horizon beyond the windshield and said, "This is like a virgin country, man. If everything got straight here, this would be the best place in the world to live."

Sometimes he would be angry, pumped up, frustrated over the beaten-down, hopeless sharecroppers out on the plantations. "We've got to get these people to *do* something," he would say, bouncing his fist on the dashboard.

For the past year, Medgar Evers had been toying with a wild plan to strike back at the white man in Mississippi. He was thinking about fighting fire with fire. Guerrilla warfare in the Delta. Black night riders, the Negro answer to the Klan, give the man a taste of his own fear, slip in and take out the bad guys in their sleep. The Mississippi Mau Mau.

Evers, Moore, and every other informed black person in America were aware that something was happening on the other side of the world. Africans were starting to shake off their colonial masters.

In Kenya a Kikuyu leader named Jomo Kenyatta was leading his people to fight British rule. He was in jail, but his followers were waging a campaign of terror in the African highlands. They called themselves Mau Mau. Dozens of white farmers were killed (the newspaper reports overlooked the thousands of Africans who died in the conflict).

Kenyatta was Medgar Evers's hero. His name, in Kikuyu, meant "Burning Spear." He was an intellectual who had written books outlining the plight of his nation and the need for an end to colonialism. Apparently by any means necessary.

Charles Evers had by then settled in Philadelphia, Mississippi. He and Medgar got to talking about it, and actually started making plans for a Mississippi Mau Mau. It was more than just a fantasy. They had guns and knew how to get more. They could have started the war anytime. But Medgar had a change of heart.

Myrlie remembers that it was a close reading of the Bible and his mother's influence that turned Medgar away from violence.

Medgar was always a cautious, deliberate person. He thought it over and read and talked about it, and finally he came to the conclusion that a vigilante campaign would never work. It would only bring more violence, more misery. Instead, Medgar devoted himself to the work of the largest, and, at the time, most radical nonviolent organization available to him, the NAACP.

In June of 1953 Myrlie gave birth to a boy, the Everses' first child. Medgar was so happy and nervous he backed his car into a ditch on the way to the hospital. He already had a name picked out for his son. He would call him Kenyatta.

Myrlie was mortified. When it came time to fill out the birth certificate, she quietly altered the child's name to Darrell Kenyatta Evers. Medgar didn't complain, but he still sometimes called his son Kenyatta.

Over the years Myrlie would have to endure the smirks and casual little jokes their friends would make. "How's the little Mau Mau?" they would ask. Unphased, Medgar would reply, "Burning Spear is just fine."

By now, Myrlie Evers realized that her life with Medgar was not going to be at all ordinary.

5

Black Monday

SOMETHING was bothering E. J. Stringer. It was weighing on his mind as he rose to speak to a group of black professionals at the American Legion Hall in Mound Bayou. This was Stringer's first speech in his new role as president of the Mississippi State Conference of the NAACP. A lot of members in the audience were, like himself, veterans of World War II.

Stringer was thinking about education. He was a graduate of Alcorn College, but he had been compelled to leave the state to get his degree in dentistry. Yet in Mississippi's white universities, where no black man had ever studied, there were German, Japanese, and Italian students. The white schools of Mississippi were good enough for our former enemies, but not for the black veterans who fought them to keep America free. The thought, Stringer recalls, irritated him. So he asked a question of his audience that night: "Is there anyone here who will help us to integrate the university system of Mississippi?"

When the speech was over, Medgar Evers stepped up to E. J. Stringer and told him that he was willing.

On Monday, January 11, 1954, Evers took his first step into the arena. On that day he filed an application to the University of Mississippi Law

School. Thurgood Marshall, who was then director-counsel of the NAACP Legal Defense and Educational Fund, agreed to act as Evers's attorney.

The Jackson *Daily News* picked up the story after E. J. Stringer made the formal announcement. The headline read, "Mound Bayou Man Files Application at 'U' Law School."

It shouldn't have been such big news. After all, eight southern states had already quietly accepted a few Negroes at the university level, and legal trends were running in the direction of desegregation. The NAACP had, since the late 1940s, been winning a series of lower court decisions on the issue.

Mississippi, of course, was different from other states. There were signs that the state would not yield an inch.

Myrlie Evers was furious. She knew what this meant, that there would be years of harassment, danger, not to mention poverty. How would they afford law school? Besides, she was pregnant again.

Medgar said he was doing it for her, for the children. She didn't see it that way. They were still arguing about it when the family visited Medgar's parents in Decatur.

Myrlie adored Mama Jessie. She was such a decent, loving, light-hearted woman. Myrlie loved Daddy Jim too, but he was harder to get close to. She thought he was like a diamond in the rough. He could be stern, somber, thoughtful, but he just lit up when he saw his only grandson, Darrell. Daddy Jim would rub his rough old face against that baby's skin, chuckling and clucking while Darrell ran his little legs all over the old man's chest.

Jim Evers was completely bald then, and very thin. His heavy-lidded eyes were tired in a deep way. But he was still the law in that household. When he spoke, everyone heard him.

As always the Evers family did their talking at the dinner table. Medgar told his parents he was applying to Ole Miss law school. Myrlie told them she was pregnant again. And suddenly the delightful reunion turned into a pandemonium of tears and angry words and people stomping away from the table.

Jessie was terrified for her son and worried about his children. Medgar laid out his reasons for his decision. His father listened without a word and then spoke to him as if he were a child.

"Your first duty is to your family," Jim Evers said in a voice like a slow roll of thunder.

Medgar jumped up and left the table. He was twenty-eight years old, and he still couldn't dispute his father. But he would not be treated as anything other than a man. Not by anyone.

Myrlie Evers remembers that nobody could understand what was driving Medgar. She thinks even he didn't realize how far he would have to go, or why.

Only a few months later Jessie phoned her sons to tell them Jim Evers was dying. Charles, who was teaching school and coaching football and running a funeral business in Philadelphia, carried him to the closest hospital, in Union. Medgar jumped in his car to meet them. What he found was appalling. The nurses had put the old man on a cot in the damp hospital basement. There was nothing Charles or Medgar could say, no kind of hell they could raise, that would get that man upstairs where the whites were treated.

The brothers took shifts staying with their father. Medgar was with him the night he died. Jim Evers was suffering a hemorrhage, and Medgar was standing over him, waiting for the end, when he heard a terrible commotion outside the hospital. A nurse came down and asked for Medgar's help. She led him to a frightened black patient with a bleeding leg. There had been a shooting, and a white lynch mob was roiling outside, hoping to string up the wounded man. There was nothing Medgar could do. Eventually the mob gave up. But Medgar's father died in that hospital basement listening to the sound of white men muttering "nigger."

Charles drove down from Philadelphia with his own hearse and took Jim Evers's body away from the hospital. Then he dressed his father for the funeral.

The state Board of Higher Learning went through the motions of considering Medgar Evers's application to the University of Mississippi Law School. Evers was even called in for a personal interview with the state attorney general and soon-to-be-governor, James P. Coleman.

Coleman grilled Evers about his motives for applying, why he wanted to be a lawyer, and why he wouldn't apply for a grant to attend an out-of-state school. Medgar answered the questions calmly, including the last one: Where would he live and dine if he were accepted at Ole Miss?

Medgar said he planned to live where everybody else lived: in a campus dormitory. "I'm very hygienic. I bathe every day. And I assure you that this brown won't rub off."

Three days after Myrlie gave birth to a daughter, Reena, Medgar was notified that his application was rejected. There was a problem with his letters of reference. The board had ruled that his recommendations had to come from the county where he resided, not the county where he was born. It was too late to reapply for the fall term. He could try again next year.

But by the time that decision was made, the stakes had changed in the segregation game.

On Monday, May 17, 1954, the chief justice of the U.S. Supreme Court, Earl Warren, read the court's decision in the case of *Brown v. Board of Education of Topeka, Kansas:* "We conclude, unanimously, that in the field of public education the doctrine of 'separate but equal' has no place. Separate educational facilities are inherently unequal." He gave the southern states until October to come up with a plan to integrate.

The race-obsessed government of Mississippi had been monitoring the Supreme Court for years, watching for early warning signs that the unthinkable integration of schools would become the law. Anticipating that the battle would probably be lost, the legislature had tried to find ways around the inevitable decision. As early as 1952 the state was officially studying the disparity between black and white education, and by 1953 the legislature appropriated thirty million dollars to "equalize" Negro schools. The idea was to approach the *Plessy v. Ferguson* standard of "separate but equal" facilities that had been established in 1896. In this dirt-poor state segregation had a high price tag. It would get higher.

In Mound Bayou that night Medgar and Myrlie Evers twisted the dial on the radio, tuning in every crackling news report on the decision. Medgar was hopeful but guarded. It was obvious that the whites of Mississippi wouldn't give up without a fight.

By the end of the day the South was already sending up howls of protest. Georgia governor Herman Talmadge dismissed the decision as "a mere scrap of paper." Integration of schools, he said, would lead to "mongrelization." Governor James Byrnes of South Carolina raved that the decision would end "civilization in the South as we have known it."

On May 27, Mississippi senator James O. Eastland, the blustering cornpone plutocrat who had replaced the late Theodore Bilbo, delivered his assessment on the floor of the Senate. It was the essence of white supremacist delusion: "Segregation is not discrimination," he purred. "Segregation promotes racial harmony. . . . There is no racial hatred in the South. The Negro race is not an oppressed race."

The Supreme Court decision blindsided most southern states, but not Mississippi. While the governors and senators sputtered and strained, Mississippi's segregationists were getting organized.

Within a few weeks the ideologues of legal racism had prepared their arguments. Among their heroes was a dapper, bespectacled judge from Brookhaven named Thomas P. Brady. The judge was no backwoods demagogue. He had attended the toney Lawrenceville prep school in New Jersey; he graduated from Yale and studied law at Ole Miss. The classical education had not made much of a humanist of him; Brady used his broad knowledge to lash together a pseudoscientific justification for white supremacy.

One night in June 1954 Judge Brady became the prophet and voice of Mississippi's white resistance when he spoke at the Sons of the American Revolution Hall in Greenwood, Mississippi.

A rapt Byron De La Beckwith sat in the audience, soaking in every word. Some say he was never the same again.

Brady's speech was such a hit that he felt compelled to expand on it and publish it few weeks later. The booklet's title was *Black Monday,* which is what segregationists call May 17, 1954, the day, Brady wrote, when "the declaration of socialist doctrine was officially proclaimed throughout this nation."

These were the times of Senator Joe McCarthy's communist witch-hunts and the great Red Scare. These were the years of the Rosenbergs and the Russian bomb and the cold war. Superpatriotic, elaborately Christian white men and women were banding together to stave off the frightening postwar social upheaval. They were convinced that godless communists lurked behind every social movement, from unionism to ecumenicism. Every group that made them uncomfortable was conveniently identified as a "communist front," and the NAACP was near the top of that list. To the radical right in the fifties integration was just another form of communism forced on the American people. Any concessions would signal a victory to the forces of atheism and collectivism and would lead not only to the destruction of the white race but also to the imminent invasion of the American homeland. As Judge Brady put it, "The great threat to this nation is that of creeping Socialism and Communism. The interracial angle is but a tool, a means to an end, in the overall effort to socialize and communize our government."

In most states the radical rightists stood on the sidelines and heckled the government for not doing enough to combat the communist threat. In Mississippi they *were* the government.

This was the climate in which the Supreme Court offered its mandate to end segregation in schools "with all due speed," and in this atmosphere Judge Brady delivered his humdinger of a speech.

He began with a treatise on the origins of man: At the dawn of history there were three "species of man": "Homo Caucasius" — the "Great White Race"; "Homo Mongoloideus" — the "yellow man"; and "Homo Africanus" — the Negro. While the first two races made strides in developing civilizations, he said, "the negroid man, like the modern lizard, evolved not."

He hammered away at the greatest fear of a self-respecting white supremacist: race mixing, mongrelization, and the defilement of white women. Mongrelization, he pointed out, had caused the destruction of past civilizations: "Whenever and wherever the white man has drunk the cup of black hemlock . . . his blood has been infused with the blood of the negro, the white man, his intellect and culture have died."

He said Africans should have been grateful for the opportunity to be slaves. He compared them to well-broken horses, beasts of burden.

Among his more memorable observations was this: "The loveliest and the purest of God's creatures, the nearest thing to an angelic being that treads this terrestrial ball is a well-bred, cultured Southern white woman and her blue-eyed, golden-haired little girl."

Naturally Judge Brady called to memory the outrages of the War Between the States and the humiliation of Radical Reconstruction. He warned Washington against pursuing its plans to force integration on the South: "Pour a little coal oil of political expediency and hope of racial amalgamation upon the flickering blaze which you have created and you will start a conflagration in the South which all of Neptune's mighty ocean cannot quench."

As soon as Brady published his speech in booklet form, Beckwith took to the streets of Greenwood to sell copies. His missionary zeal was ignited. The enemy had been identified. The troika of communism, atheism, and integration were now linked in Beckwith's mind as the root of evil. As he once put it, his "race, color and creed innards got out of sorts."

Robert Patterson was another Deltan inspired by *Black Monday*. Patterson was a beefy red-haired cotton planter from Sunflower County and a local celebrity of sorts. Before he joined the army, he had been a college football star and captain of his Mississippi State team in 1942. He had always held some radical conservative views, and he had quietly contributed anti-Semitic articles to fringe publications. But after he read *Black Monday*, he decided to devote himself to the cause of fighting integration.

One night in July Patterson and thirteen other prominent white men got together in an Indianola living room and set up a new organization called the Citizens' Council. A week later a hundred men attended an open meeting at city hall. Within four years there would be 80,000 paid members in Mississippi and 300,000 in councils across the South.

It was the end, for a while, of the white southern liberal. Any opposition to segregation was labeled traitorous. The Citizens' Councils controlled the local, and in some cases state, elections. Their common enemy was the NAACP, the "communist front group" that had brought the lawsuit that threatened the southern way of life.

As soon as Beckwith heard about the Citizens' Councils he signed right up. He was a big joiner. On a business résumé he compiled thirty years later, Beckwith listed all of his affiliations, starting with the Boy Scouts. Along with his church groups, there was the 4-H Club, Knights of Pythias, American Legion, Veterans of Foreign Wars, Masons, Knights Templar, Shriners, LeFlore County Hunting and Fishing Association, Greenwood Historical Society, Sons of Confederate Veterans, Sons of the American Revolution (he held state offices in that one), the NRA, the National Muzzle Loading Rifle Association, and the Moose Lodge of Greenwood.

Yet Byron De La Beckwith would never admit that he had joined the

Ku Klux Klan. In later years, after his name was linked with various hate crimes around the South, Beckwith would issue a standard non-denial when asked outright if he was a member: "I've been accused of it." He often added that he found the group to be a wholesome outfit.

Back in the fifties there was not much of a Klan in Mississippi. There wasn't any reason to have one. The state government was so radically segregationist, and the Citizens' Councils, often called the white-collar Klan, were so firmly in control of business, that a Ku Klux Klan would have seemed redundant.

There was a group across the border in Louisiana called the Original Knights of the KKK, and some scattered members of old, traditional outfits like the Knights of the White Camellia in southern Mississippi. People joined out of family tradition more than anything else. It was a racist's low-rent fraternity, with costumes and funny titles. All that would change after John F. Kennedy sent federal troops to Oxford in 1962 to integrate Ole Miss. But back in the halcyon fifties, a racist could be fairly secure without organized vigilante groups. The violence was ad hoc and applied as necessary.

By 1956 the State of Mississippi had organized itself to battle integration by creating the Sovereignty Commission. It had a broad mandate and a long leash. Nowhere in its charter were the words *integration* or *segregation* mentioned. The code words were *encroachment* and *sovereignty*.

The law that the state legislature passed in establishing the commission read, in part, "It shall be the duty of the Commission to do and perform any and all acts and things deemed necessary and proper to protect the sovereignty of the state of Mississippi . . . from encroachment thereon by the Federal Government or any branch, department or agency thereof; and to resist the usurpation of the rights and powers reserved to this state."

The original purpose of the Sovereignty Commission was to serve as a big PR agency, to educate the nation about the benefits of the southern system, and to lobby against outside interference. It quickly became much more than that. An investigative department was established, headed by L. C. Hicks, the former head of the Mississippi Highway Patrol (which had its own intelligence unit). A former FBI agent named Zack Van Landingham was hired to do the "investigations." A two-year appropriation of $250,000 was set aside for the commission, some of which was quietly diverted to the Citizens' Councils. People quickly caught on to the true nature of the Sovereignty Commission. It was Mississippi's state spy agency.

Now here was an organization Byron De La Beckwith could get behind. He wrote to Governor Coleman on May 16, 1956, asking for a job as an investigator to help in "uncovering plots by the NAACP to intergrate [sic] our beloved State."

The letter was written in a distinctive style that would be recognized by prosecutors and FBI agents in the years to come. Beckwith outlined his current obsession: "To me [the fight for segregation] is a life or death struggle and NOTHING ELSE IS MORE IMPORTANT AT THIS TIME! I . . . will tear the mask from the face of the NAACP and forever rid this fair land of the DISEASE OF INTEGRATion with which it is plagued with."

He wrote that it would be a sin to squander his talents selling tobacco when his "useful energy may be expended in acquiring the information needed to thwart efforts of the power mad integration mongers."

He mentioned in his résumé his favorable war record, his happy home life, and that he was on the Membership Committee of the Greenwood Citizens' Council (it later booted him out for his overly zestful recruitment techniques). Other skills that he felt qualified him for the job were "expert with a pistol, good with a rifle and fair with a shotgun — and — RABID ON THE SUBJECT OF SEGREGATION!"

The letter was found many years later in Coleman's papers after the governor's death. The Sovereignty Commission sent Beckwith a form letter saying that it would consider his application. It is not generally known whether he was ever called upon to help out.

6

The Association

GLOSTER CURRENT knew he had his man. E. J. Stringer and Aaron Henry had told him that Medgar Evers had what it took for the job. Right away he could see it too. Medgar Evers was not afraid. Besides, he had the most important qualification to be the first field secretary of the NAACP for Mississippi: he was available.

They met for the first time on October 29, 1954. Medgar drove to Stringer's hometown of Columbus for an airport interview with Current, who was NAACP director of branches. After the *Brown* decision in May, Thurgood Marshall had suggested the NAACP increase its field staff to monitor compliance and gather affidavits for further school desegregation suits. Mississippi was a hard position to fill. It was essentially a suicide mission.

Gloster Current was a tall, dark-skinned man with a prominent nose and a dour countenance. He was an abstemious Methodist preacher, which somehow contradicted his previous claim to fame as the leader of a Detroit swing band called Gloster Current's Nightingales. Current had joined the NAACP youth council back in the thirties and later assumed the leadership of the Detroit branch. In 1946 he had been hired as the director of branches by the legendary NAACP leader, Walter White.

Although almost all its foot soldiers were black, the NAACP was an integrated organization. In fact it had been founded by whites in 1909. By the beginning of World War II the association had some eighty-five thousand paid members. About 10 percent were whites, most of them occupying executive roles. There were nearly five hundred branches.

Policy was directed from the NAACP's national office in New York, where a dozen or so salaried executives worked. They were all Negroes, including the secretary, who ran the operation. The president of the NAACP was traditionally a white man.

The NAACP's weakness was its inability to attract working-class Negroes. It had a reputation as an elitist, bourgeois organization. All policy came from the New York office, which dictated goals and strategies to the branches. The branches were semiautonomous units that elected state leaders and met in state conferences.

The NAACP strategy was simple and focused: change the laws and then change society. In a world with so many injustices the organization narrowed its mission to attacking legalized racism in the forms of Jim Crow laws and school discrimination and promoting voting rights and new laws, such as antilynching legislation, to protect the lives of black people. The organization lobbied state legislatures and the U.S. Congress. The independent legal section fought in the courts. Every case was carefully selected to build a precedent. The association was opportunistic, and it was capable of sacrificing short-term gains for long-term goals. The NAACP never advocated violence — or even civil disobedience. It was, above all, a "respectable" organization. But this did not prevent NAACP branches, particularly in the South, from being labeled radical and subversive.

During the early years, when the NAACP had a near monopoly on black activism, it was directed by Walter White, an amazing, tireless crusader. White set the standard for NAACP endurance by working eighteen-hour days, often risking his own life to investigate hate crimes. What made White all the more remarkable was the way he looked.

With his blue eyes and fair skin and silky straight hair he could easily have slipped into the white world — "passed" — and abandoned his Negro identity. Instead Walter White, the son of an Atlanta postman, used his white skin to infiltrate southern towns to investigate lynch-ings.

Under White the NAACP grew strong and influential. He demanded and got complete loyalty from his New York lieutenants, and they in turn required the same from the field staff. Working for the association was more than a job; it was expected to be a way of life.

Gloster Current recognized that Evers was NAACP material. In his recommendation to Roy Wilkins, who had succeeded White as execu-tive director, Current described him as "qualified, courageous, and im-pressive." The association offered Evers the job for forty-five hundred dollars a year, as well as a secretarial job for Myrlie. They would have to move to the capital, Jackson.

Myrlie was not thrilled. Not only was this a dangerous job, but it meant the end of Medgar's career at Magnolia Mutual. But there was no way to dissuade Medgar, and at least the job got them out of Mound Bayou.

Medgar accepted the offer on November 27. He was expected to be-gin work on December 15. On November 29, Medgar's new immediate boss, Ruby Hurley, the regional director who was then based in Birming-ham, wrote him a curt letter. She realized he was not being paid yet, but she needed a detailed report on the state of affairs in Mississippi, includ-ing documentation of intimidation by the Citizens' Councils. She had to have it in two weeks, in time for a regional meeting in Columbus.

The pattern of demanding the impossible, yesterday, had begun. So had Myrlie Evers's simmering resentment. She knew already she had met her most powerful rival.

Within two weeks Evers's first official report was ready. It sizzled with the enthusiasm of a fresh recruit. He wrote about Mississippi's "progress" in 1954, due to the "phenomenal . . . unequaled leadership" of the NAACP, as well as Dr. Howard's Regional Council of Negro Lead-ership.

It was encouraging to Evers that black leaders had defied Governor Hugh White at a state-sponsored meeting called to demonstrate Negro support for voluntary segregation. "On that momentous day, July 30, 1954, 99 out of 100 Negro leaders before the Governor of Mississippi and his Legal Educational Advisory Committee . . . told him in no un-certain terms that they would have no part in any scheme to circumvent the U.S. Supreme Court's decision on segregation in the Public Schools," Evers wrote. The bad news was that the governor then decided to back a plan to abolish public education instead of desegregating schools.

The report outlined the ominous rise of the Citizens' Councils, which Evers called "the up-town Ku Klux Klan." By the end of 1954, according to T. R. M. Howard's estimates, councils had been organized in thirty-five of eighty-two counties. The objective of the councils, Evers wrote, was to "keep the Negro in his place" by keeping him out of white schools, keeping the ballot out of his reach, and keeping him dependent on the white man's dollar.

Since the time of Evers's application to Ole Miss, public universities had begun requiring recommendations from five alumni. In addition, an amendment had been passed in the November state elections allowing circuit clerks the authority to reject anyone who registered to vote if he or she could not interpret the U.S. Constitution.

Meanwhile the Citizens' Councils plotted to keep Negroes in low-paying jobs and to organize economic reprisals against troublemakers.

In his report Evers told the story of one black farmer who had owed five thousand dollars on his house and 120 acres to a bank in Hollandale. The president of the bank called him in and told him his note was due and that it would not be renewed. "We are not going to renew notes for any of you niggers in the Negro Council or the NAACP. We are going to use peaceful means but if that won't work, we shall use other means," the bank president said.

White employers who extended credit, called "scrip," to their workers or sharecroppers to get medical or dental attention refused to give credit for Dr. Howard or Stringer or any other practitioner associated with the NAACP or the Regional Council. The intimidation extended to the local draft board. Dr. Howard, who was forty-seven years old, received a notice telling him that he might be reclassified as 1-A.

Evers concluded his presentation with a number of recommendations. The most important one was that the national NAACP set up a cash fund to loan money to Negroes who were under pressure from the banks. To a limited degree the association accepted his recommendations and made some funds available.

Evers's first job for the national office would be to collect signed affidavits attesting to intimidation by the Citizens' Councils. But first he

was flown to New York City on New Year's Day, 1955, and put through
an intensive training course in NAACP history and procedures, everything from how to take a deposition to how to dress.

Medgar and Myrlie moved into a two-bedroom apartment in Jackson.
Myrlie's grandmother came to live with them to watch the babies while
Myrlie worked as Medgar's secretary at the NAACP office.

The organized backlash against integration in Mississippi grew stronger with each passing month. In April 1955 Ruby Hurley and Medgar
Evers traveled together through the Delta on a fact-finding mission. Hurley was a tall, elegant single woman with a taste for good clothes and fine
Scotch. She smoked long cigarettes. She was utterly fearless and totally
devoted to the NAACP. Whenever there was a crisis in Mississippi or
anywhere in the Deep South, Hurley would wade right into it. She and
Medgar Evers would drive this route again and again during the long,
bloody months that followed.

Like foreign correspondents in hostile territory, Evers and Hurley
discreetly met with Negroes in the Delta and recorded their statements:
Fit Simmons once hauled wood for a sawmill owned by a member of the
local Citizens' Council. The sawmill owner had threatened to repossess
Simmons's truck if he didn't quit the NAACP and remove his name from
the voter rolls. The truck driver still owed $800 on a $2,200 note. Simmons did what he was told, but the white man took his truck anyway.
There were other incidents: Just before Hurley and Evers arrived, the
windshields of ten cars had been smashed outside an NAACP branch
meeting. About that time, a white woman had told some Negroes that
"the Yazoo river was muddy now, but it would be muddier than that
when some of their bodies were thrown in." Tensions had been building
in the small town of Belzoni since 1953, when a group of local black
businessmen filed a complaint with the Justice Department that Sheriff
Ike Shelton was preventing Negroes from voting in Humphreys County.

A voter had to pay two dollars a year for the right to register; blacks
were forced to pay for two years to qualify. But when they showed up to
vote, their receipts were torn up in front of them. The money was never
refunded. No black had managed to vote in Humphreys County since
Reconstruction, but there were still about four hundred Negroes on the
register.

Evers and Hurley dropped in on Gus Courts, who ran a small grocery store and owned a bus that transported laborers to the cotton fields. He told them some frightening stories.

Courts had been the first president of the new Belzoni branch of the NAACP, chartered on February 8, 1954, with a membership of sixty-four. That summer a branch of the Citizens' Councils was founded in a town just a few miles west of Belzoni. Courts found himself at ground zero of the white backlash. The newly organized planters and local businessmen lined their sights on the nearest NAACP fledgling branch.

Belzoni, with about four thousand residents, a third of them white, was virtually run by the newly formed Citizens' Council. Its first target was Courts. He was a big man who talked slow and thought fast, though, like most Delta blacks of his generation, he could barely read and write. Soon after the NAACP chapter was formed, Courts was called into the local bank for a meeting. The bank president wanted to see the NAACP books. When Courts refused, he was told that if he wanted to keep his credit, he'd better resign from the NAACP.

"We will tie up your bus and tie up your store," the man said. "We will run you out of town." Before long the wholesaler who sold him groceries cut off his supplies. His landlord evicted him from his store. And he started getting death threats.

In August 1954 Gloster Current had received a sad, painfully typed letter, special delivery, from Gus Courts: "This is to nofie you. that thay have fosted me under preasher to resine as preaident of Belzoni branch NAACP.

"And thay are so putting preasher on other members of the branch Thay say we cant oprate hear.

"Any mail sent to me pleas send in A plain Envelope and leave NAACP of. I have a reason for this.

"Yours truely Gus Courts."

The grocer managed to find another location for his store, across the street in a building owned by another NAACP member. But the harassment didn't end. And Courts didn't give up. When the man who took over Courts's position at the local NAACP branch left town, Gus Courts resumed his job as president.

Courts told Evers and Hurley that the planters were pressuring share-croppers to boycott NAACP-connected businesses and, more serious, were forcing the ones who were registered to vote to tear up their poll tax receipts or face eviction. By then the number of qualified black voters in Humphreys County had dropped from four hundred to about ninety-one. All Ruby Hurley and Medgar Evers could do was write down the details and report back to New York, hoping to secure some financial relief for the people of Belzoni.

Reverend George Lee also ran a grocery store, just like his friend Gus Courts. The fifty-one-year-old Baptist minister was active in the NAACP, and he was having the same financial problems as Courts. He also had been told to take his name off the voting rolls.

On Saturday afternoon, May 7, 1955, Courts stopped by Lee's store. Lee told him a white man at the courthouse warned him to take his name off the list.

"I've got a funny feeling," George told Gus.

"You're not afraid, are you?" Court asked.

"No, I'm not afraid."

Around midnight that same night Alex Hudson was sitting on the porch of a house on Church Street, in the black section of Belzoni. He was talking to his girlfriend, Angie Wellsby, when he noticed a black Buick pass slowly by the house, followed by a two-tone Ford or Mercury convertible. The second car, with the top up on a clear, warm night, was gaining speed, trying to catch up with the Buick. Then Hudson heard what he thought was a loud backfire. He looked up and saw the convertible pull next to the Buick. He saw the muzzle flash as a second shot rang out. The Buick veered off the road and crashed into the house of a neighbor, Catherine Blair.

Blair heard the first shot and got out of bed to look out the window at whoever was fighting. It was Saturday night, after all, so she figured the neighbors were at it again. From the window she saw the convertible and some white men in it. Then there was a flash and an explosion. Moments later Reverend George Lee's Buick crashed through her bedroom wall, knocking her house off its foundation and crushing the bed where she had slept.

George Lee crawled out of the wreckage and collapsed, blood gushing from a ragged hole where his lower jaw used to be. The neighbors who crowded around loaded him into a passing cab, but he died before he reached Humphreys County Memorial Hospital.

Dr. A. H. McCoy, the new NAACP state president, arrived in Belzoni the next day, in time to be present for the coroner's inquest into Lee's death. Every member of the coroner's jury belonged to the local Citizens' Council. Although McCoy and two black physicians brought in by Lee's widow examined the body and found powder burns on the minister's face and lead pellets in his head, the jury ruled the death accidental.

McCoy sat in astonishment as the white men discussed their theories of how it could have happened.

"A scantling could have punched him in the jaw and killed him where he crashed into the house," said one.

"He could have died from shock."

"The noise which sounded like a gun could have been tire blowouts."

The lead pellets in Lee's mangled jaw, they decided, must be fragments from his dental fillings.

When McCoy, who was a dentist, pointed out that lead is not used in fillings, one of the jurors remarked, "We will have to find the dentist who filled his teeth to see if he used lead, if it is proved that this is lead."

The newspapers were already calling the death an "odd incident," but police found a bullet in the tire of Lee's wrecked car, and they were toying with a new theory. Reverend Lee, said Sheriff Ike Shelton, might well have been shot "by a jealous nigger." Police hinted at rumors, which no black in Belzoni had ever heard or believed, that there was "another woman" involved.

Back in New York Roy Wilkins and Gloster Current were reading about Lee's death in the newspapers and placing increasingly angry calls to Jackson and Birmingham.

On the night Lee was murdered, Medgar Evers was traveling in southern Mississippi, trying to drum up NAACP members in rural communities where there were no phones and no electricity. It would be days before Evers checked in at a prearranged contact point and found himself in the middle of the first crisis of his career in the NAACP.

When he finally heard the news, Evers raced back to Jackson, where he met Ruby Hurley. She hadn't heard about the killing until Monday morning, when she arrived back in Birmingham from a conference in Florida. Their job now was to get the facts, report to New York, and alert the press.

By the time Evers and Hurley arrived in Belzoni to investigate the shooting, a number of the terrified witnesses had scattered or gone into hiding. Alex Hudson had fled to a relative's house in East St. Louis. Neither official questioned anyone until Lee's funeral on Thursday, May 12.

As a bureaucracy the national NAACP organization could rival the most ossified federal agency. Wilkins and Current applied an almost religious devotion to decorum, chain of command, and centralized decision making. Blood and teeth could be splattered from Belzoni to Birmingham, but no steps would be taken until a neatly typed report appeared on Wilkins's desk in Manhattan.

On Friday the 13th, the day after the funeral, Ruby Hurley phoned in her first report to Gloster Current. Because she was afraid an operator might be listening, Hurley vaguely described the witnesses she and Evers had located and threats that had been made against Lee. Because she was the ranking NAACP staffer on the scene, Hurley was taking heat from the national office for the clumsy investigation. She used the opportunity to divert the blame to the new recruit, Medgar Evers.

For the first and only time, someone accused Medgar Evers of being afraid. Hurley complained that Evers seemed relieved that a mass meeting had been canceled the night before the funeral. She also questioned Evers's continuing loyalty to the cautious, moderate T. R. M. Howard, who was increasingly at odds with the association. Evers seemed to be promoting a merger between Howard's Regional Council and the NAACP. The NAACP, like all bureaucracies, was jealous of its territory. It was not about to share the limelight, or the membership fees, with a homegrown organization.

Wilkins was furious. On May 16, he fired off a curt memo to Current: "I still have no report on my desk on the Belzoni, Miss., incident. It is now more that a week since it occurred. As you know, we were not able to take any steps or to send out any kind of story in our press release last Thursday because we had still not heard from our people in Mississippi."

He added a sarcastic snipe at his new field secretary: "Is Mr. Evers, by chance, working for some other organization?"

So it went. Hurley offered to quit; Current persuaded her to stay. Evers was given another chance to prove himself.

Many things were mentioned in the memos that flew back and forth between Mississippi and New York during those hysterical days in May of 1955. Only one mention was made of something almost every black person in Mississippi was aware of by now: there was a death list. It was a list of enemies of Mississippi's old way of life, and it had been published in newspapers in the Delta. Reverend Lee's name was on it. And so was Medgar Evers's.

Medgar Evers took the lessons of the Lee murder to heart. From now on he would be ready. And nobody would ever again say he was afraid.

Lee's case showed the NAACP that the federal government was not going to help its cause. The FBI sent agents to investigate the murder. The FBI lab in Washington analyzed the pellets in Lee's jaw and found they were indeed number 3 buckshot. But nothing was done. No arrests were ever made in the case.

Evers was learning how futile it was to expect help from the FBI. Its leader, J. Edgar Hoover, dismissed the NAACP as a communist front organization. The few resident agents who lived in Mississippi were white and mostly southern born, and they enjoyed a cozy relationship with the local police. They were not eager to protect NAACP workers or to investigate race crimes. The southern agents were even suspected of complicity. In one report, Ruby Hurley noted that when the FBI sent investigators to Belzoni, members of the Citizens' Council boasted that they planned to recruit the agents.

A month after Lee was gunned down, the U.S. Supreme Court declared that the desegregation of schools would proceed "with all deliberate speed."

This was the NAACP's cue to start a fresh campaign in the most segregated state in the country. The parents of schoolchildren, a handful of NAACP leaders, and Medgar Evers took on the monolithic white power structure to enforce the Supreme Court's decision. The Justice Department did nothing.

Medgar Evers stepped out in front, getting people across Mississippi to sign petitions to reorganize the schools. In Vicksburg 140 parents put their names on a petition. In Natchez 75 signed. The Citizens' Councils retaliated quickly. Petition signers were fired from jobs, threatened, harassed, and driven out of business. Many community leaders fled north to Chicago. Evers spent his days and nights cajoling people, begging them to keep their names on the list, spiriting them out of town, lending them money, listening to their stories.

On August 17, in Judge Tom Brady's hometown of Brookhaven, Lamar Smith was shot dead at ten o'clock on a Saturday morning on the

Lincoln County Courthouse lawn. Smith was a sixty-year-old farmer who had managed, along with a few of his relatives, to stay on the voter rolls and actually vote in the recent primary elections. He had been organizing a campaign to get blacks to vote by absentee ballot when he was killed in front of half the town on a busy shopping day. Oddly enough, there were no witnesses.

By the end of the year, the NAACP would put out a concise pamphlet chronicling the state-sanctioned campaign of terror. And once that little booklet was published, Mississippi became a place name linked with an atrocity, like Waterloo, Pearl Harbor, Dachau. For decades to come, "M" would stand for Mississippi and murder.

7

The Stirring

EMMETT TILL was born and raised in Chicago. His mother warned him to stay away from the white folks in Mississippi, but he was sure of himself and his charm. He was only fourteen, big for his age. His friends called him "Bobo."

On August 21, 1955, Emmett Till arrived in Money, Mississippi, population fifty-five, a flyblown speck on the map a dozen miles north of Greenwood. He expected to spend the rest of a lazy summer with his mother's uncle, Mose Wright, a sixty-four-year-old preacher, and his large extended family.

Three days later Till and six of his teenage cousins piled into the preacher's old '46 Ford to go for a drive. They ended up at the tiny grocery store in Money. The store was operated by a young couple, Roy and Carolyn Bryant, who lived with their two small sons behind the shop. Roy was away that afternoon.

Outside on the porch Till and his cousins were joking around. Till pulled out his wallet and showed them a picture of a white girl he knew in Chicago, started boasting he'd "had" her.

If he was so good with white girls, one cousin told him, why didn't he go on in and talk to the woman in the store? Or was he chicken? The cousins giggled, wide-eyed, as Emmett Till walked into the store alone.

Carolyn Bryant later testified that Till grabbed her and asked her for a date. All the kids outside heard was Emmett Till saying, "Bye, baby," as he came back out on the porch. Some say he whistled, a wolf whistle. Some say that since the boy stuttered, his words sometimes came out in a whistle. He didn't mean anything by it.

The cousins hustled Till into the old Ford and drove back to the preacher's house. Nobody told Mose what had happened.

That Saturday night Mose Wright woke up to a pounding at his cabin door. Roy Bryant and his brother, J. H. "Big" Milam, had come for Emmett Till.

Three days later some fishermen found Till floating in the Tallahatchie River. The body was bloated and eaten by fish. One eye was missing; part of the head was crushed. A seventy-four-pound cotton gin fan had been fastened to the neck with barbed wire. There was a bullet in the skull.

For all the black men who wound up dead in the Mississippi swamps, this lynching was different. He was a stranger from Chicago, and his grieving mother wanted an open casket for his funeral. *Jet* magazine printed a photograph of the corpse. A red spotlight was focused on Mississippi. The lynching of a fourteen-year-old Negro boy made headlines in every state. Before long the Delta was crawling with reporters. They sent back stories about the conditions in Mississippi that a hundred NAACP press releases never could have inspired. Emmett Till's murder gave a name and a face to the unspeakable.

For Negroes in Mississippi the lynching telegraphed an unmistakable message: the white man could kill you for any reason. It didn't matter whether you tried to vote or joined the NAACP or did nothing at all. They would kill you just for being black.

Milam and Bryant were arrested and charged with murder within days of the abduction, and tried two weeks later.

The NAACP scrambled to investigate the case. Medgar Evers, Ruby Hurley, and Sam Baily put on dungarees and field hats and drove north to Money to look for witnesses to the abduction.

Mose Wright was the prosecution's star witness. The old man sat in the witness box in his Sunday best and slowly told the story of the night

Milam and Bryant had come for the boy. Milam had said he was going to take the boy.

Do you see this man in the courtroom?

Mose Wright stretched out a long bony finger, and in a courtroom so quiet you could hear sweat drop, said, "Dar he," as his finger fell to Milam. The judge was already pounding his gavel, shouting, "Order, order!"

The white men never denied kidnapping the boy to teach him a lesson. They just said he was alive the last time they saw him.

A jury of twelve white men took one hour and seven minutes to acquit the killers. Two months later Milam and Bryant sold their story to *Look* magazine and described in great detail how they had killed Emmett Till. Since they couldn't be tried again for the same crime, they felt that they could say whatever they wanted. They insisted they never meant to kill the boy, just teach him a lesson he wouldn't forget. It was the boy's smart mouth that killed him. He just wouldn't back down, they said, wouldn't see the error of his ways. He told them that he'd had white women. They said he told them he was as good as they were. So they stripped him naked, beat him, and made him carry the heavy metal fan to the river. Then Big Milam shot him in the head.

This is what J. W. Milam told the *Look* writer: "Well, what else could we do? He was hopeless."

This is more of what Milam told that writer:

"I'm no bully. I never hurt a nigger in my life. I like niggers in their place — I know how to work 'em. But I just decided it was time a few people got put on notice."

Back in Belzoni Gus Courts refused to be intimidated. The murders of George Lee and Emmett Till only hardened his determination to fight back. All through 1955 he recruited new members for the local NAACP, doubling its charter. That summer he started talking about filing a lawsuit against the Citizens' Councils.

Courts owned a bus that he used to transport field hands to cotton plantations around the Delta. One local planter and Citizens' Council leader made it his business to follow the bus every morning. When it stopped at a plantation, the white man would get out of his car and have a talk with the owner. Before long there wasn't a plantation in the Delta that would hire field hands hauled by Courts.

Courts consulted a local white lawyer about filing a suit over his loss of business. Apparently word got around. In late November another white citizen stopped by Courts's grocery store.

"They're planning to get rid of you," the man told Courts. "I don't know how, and I don't want to know." It was a threat as much as a caution. And Courts had no doubt who "they" were.

Three nights later, at 8:30 on November 28, 1955, Courts had just rung up a sale and was standing behind the counter of his store when a shotgun blast shattered the front window and hit him in the left arm and abdomen. Savannah Luton, who had just bought a can of kerosene, ran outside and saw a two-tone green sedan pull away in the darkness. She clearly saw a white man in the rear window.

Someone called Sheriff Ike Shelton, but nobody could find him. Courts was bleeding and in pain when another police officer arrived at the scene and the witnesses described what had happened. Friends gently lifted Courts into a car and drove sixty miles to the hospital in Mound Bayou.

Medgar Evers got the call in Jackson that night. This time he followed procedure: he called Ruby Hurley, the national office, and the press. And then he got in his car and drove to Mound Bayou.

Roy Wilkins would often show people a picture of Gus Courts lying in his hospital bed. In the photograph was a grim young man standing next to Courts, one hand gripping the bed, the other plunged deep in his coat pocket, like a vengeful guardian angel, ready for anything. The man in the picture was Medgar Evers.

Gus Courts lived. He gave a number of bedside interviews to northern reporters who flocked south to cover the latest outrage.

Courts was philosophical. He said he'd known his time was coming, that he had "tried to prepare my mind for it." The hard part, he said, was knowing that his enemies could slip up on him any time, and that the shot would come out of the darkness.

A reporter from the New York *Post* drove to Belzoni to ask Sheriff Shelton whether he had located any suspects.

"I honestly think some damn nigger just drove there and shot him," Shelton told him. He still hadn't interviewed Courts.

Two FBI agents from Greenville were assigned to the case, but they got sidetracked by a bank robbery before they could interview Courts or any witnesses.

Incredibly the Belzoni Citizens' Council posted a $250 reward for information leading to the conviction of the gunman. It was never claimed. No arrests were made.

The brave old man finally packed it in and moved to Chicago. It was, for many, the only way to stay alive.

The Citizens' Council of Philadelphia, Mississippi, worked long hours to drive Charles Evers out of town. He held out as long as he could.

By the end of 1954 Charles had so many things going it was hard to keep track of them all. He was married with children now. His wife, Nan, was a smart, patient woman. She had to be to stick with Charles, who never believed a man should be anything but free. But he had responsibilities for his family. He wanted a good life for his daughters.

Like his brother, Medgar, Charles had returned from World War II with an active hatred of racism. The NAACP was the most practical outlet for change, and so Charles got involved. He was chairman of voter registration for the NAACP state conference, and he was as passionate a recruiter as Medgar. When the position of NAACP field secretary came up, Charles thought about taking it himself. But he had his businesses to consider, and he knew himself well enough to realize that he wasn't suited to the NAACP management style. He decided to leave the civil rights work to Medgar, reasoning that he'd make enough money for both of them.

Charles Evers had by then built a small business empire in Neshoba County. He was acquiring a new funeral home, he was selling burial insurance, he ran a café, and was starting up a motel in the black section of Philadelphia. He had started the town's first black taxi service. Charles was so legitimate and prosperous, he had even opened a bank account.

The Citizens' Councils didn't like to see a black businessman succeed. But what really brought Charles down was his radio show.

Charles Evers was Mississippi's first and only Negro disc jockey. A white man owned WOKJ in Philadelphia, but he gave Charles a chance to go on the air. Charles didn't have the slightest idea how to be a disc jockey, but he learned fast, and the sponsors of his blues and gospel show were happy with the response in the black community. Charles made the most of his radio hour. He opened and closed every show by saying, "Pay your poll tax. Register and vote!" He had added two hundred new names to the rolls with his one-man campaign.

The pressure started right away. He couldn't renew the lease on his café or taxi stand. His coffin suppliers were demanding cash up front. Somebody loosened the lug nuts on his car wheels. A white man called warning him about an assassination plot.

The Citizens' Councils boycotted his radio sponsors. The station owner was a good man, but he was eventually pressured into firing Charles Evers. Charles said he understood. No hard feelings.

But as he was driving away from the station, a woman ran her car into his. She sued him and won. Finally Charles Evers was wiped out. The last straw was when his creditors repossessed his furniture, set it out in the street for everyone to see.

Charles sent Nan and the girls to stay with her mother in Mt. Olive, Mississippi. All he had was twenty-six dollars in change. He loaded up his beat-up car and headed north.

The killings and beatings and financial ruinations of 1955 had the desired chilling effect on the black people of Mississippi. Membership in the NAACP in Mississippi had dropped from 4,639 to 1,716. Soon it was practically an underground organization.

People were paralyzed with fear, terrified of the Citizens' Councils. There was little for Medgar Evers to do but try to stay alive and hold on to as much of the NAACP membership as he could.

In December 1955 Medgar Evers watched with growing excitement as the civil rights movement took a new direction in Montgomery, Alabama. One cold evening a former NAACP secretary and seamstress named Rosa Parks was arrested for refusing to give up her bus seat to a white man. In the wake of indignation that followed the incident, a young minister named Dr. Martin Luther King, Jr., led fifty thousand Negroes in a mass boycott of public buses to end Jim Crow practices in the city.

In New York Roy Wilkins and Thurgood Marshall watched the same movement with growing alarm. King and his legions in Montgomery were grabbing public attention — and donations — away from the NAACP. For the first time the old association had a serious rival in the Deep South.

The dilemma of what to do about Martin Luther King threatened to become a crisis in January 1956, a few weeks after the boycott had begun, when the NAACP held its annual national convention in San Francisco. King showed up to give a speech and was heartily welcomed by Mississippi's fledgling field secretary, Medgar Evers. Evers publicly invited King to visit Mississippi to inspire a movement there. On the first night of the convention a group of renegade delegates met in Evers's hotel room and hammered out a three-page resolution calling for total NAACP support of King and his boycott.

Both Wilkins and Marshall were stunned and angered, but Wilkins averted a floor fight with Evers and his group by offering to give "careful consideration" to adopting the boycott as a civil rights tactic and, further, by offering the resources of the NAACP Legal Defense and Educational Fund to cover legal fees incurred by the Montgomery movement. This mollified Evers and the other Young Turks, but the tug-of-war between the NAACP old guard and Martin Luther King had only begun.

Later that year King founded a new national group called the Southern Christian Leadership Conference (SCLC) and invited Medgar Evers to attend its first convention in New Orleans. Evers was duly elected secretary of the SCLC.

Roy Wilkins was outraged. Evers was ordered to resign. He could serve only one cause, and it had to be the NAACP. Evers agreed to abandon the SCLC.

Evers privately fretted about Wilkins's refusal to cooperate with other civil rights groups, but he had made his choice. He followed instructions from New York and used his influence to keep the SCLC from setting up an office in Jackson.

The NAACP strategy remained unchanged: avoid violent confrontations while slowly challenging segregation in the courts. But the NAACP needed test cases to bring to court. In early March 1958 Medgar Evers decided, on his own, to test the law forbidding segregation on interstate transport. On his way home from an NAACP conference in Greensboro, North Carolina, he switched buses in Meridian, Mississippi.

C. B. Needham, one of Evers's friends in Decatur, knew that Medgar was planning to ride in the front of the bus. He offered to come along, at least follow in a car, but Evers insisted on going alone.

When it came time to board, he took a seat in the front row. The white bus driver told him to move to the back of the bus. He politely declined. The driver called in the cops, who took Evers to the police station for

questioning. They told him he was going to destroy the good race relations in Meridian. They let him go with a warning a few minutes later.

Evers got back on the bus and took the same seat. This time the bus
driver pulled out of the station without a word. A few miles down the
road to Jackson a white cabdriver in a black '55 Ford flagged down the
bus. The driver opened the door for the cabbie who stormed on board
and slugged Medgar Evers with a roundhouse right that made half of
Evers's face go numb. Medgar didn't strike back. He just sat there and
took it. The bus driver broke it up, and the bus went on to Jackson.
Medgar never gave up his seat.

Evers's plan was to file a lawsuit against the bus company to challenge the state's bus segregation laws. But the NAACP preferred not to
involve staffers in test cases, and for a number of reasons the complaint
was never pursued.

In early 1958 *Ebony* magazine ran an "as told to" feature article on
Medgar Evers titled "Why I Live in Mississippi." There were pictures of
Medgar at work, fishing, and playing with his children. The article recounted the landmarks of Medgar's life: the speech by Bilbo that Medgar
and Charles had witnessed as boys in Decatur, the lynching of Mr. Tingle,
the showdown at the Decatur Courthouse on primary day. It told the
story of Medgar's impossible love for his state, "the land that produced
Bilbo and exterminated Emmett Till," that could still, in his mind, be the
best place in America. What the article revealed about Medgar Evers was
his utterly middle-class optimism and his belief in the American system.

But what readers, particularly his white enemies, remember about
the article was his admission that he was an admirer of Jomo Kenyatta
and had once considered starting a Mississippi Mau Mau. No matter that
Evers explained why he had turned against violence. "It didn't take much
reading of the Bible," Evers said, "to convince me that two wrongs would
not make the situation any different, and that I couldn't hate the white
man and at the same time hope to convert him."

That fall the Citizens' Councils newsletter reprinted parts of the *Ebony* article, accompanied by a cartoon with the caption "The Mau-Mau's
are Coming." A brief article described Medgar Evers's supposed dream of
a Mississippi Mau Mau "roaming the Delta in search of blood." They
managed to quote him correctly in one instance. Medgar Evers did say,
"I'll be damned if I'm going to let a white man lick me."

The longer Evers survived, the bolder he became. In early 1958 the Mississippi legislature passed a bill to authorize an investigation of the NAACP. Evers said that he welcomed the probe. "In fact, we'd gloat at the opportunity. . . . We condemn other countries that deny freedom of the ballot, [but] we here in Mississippi, in the so called American way of life, are denied the right to vote."

Gloating in front of white men was not a posture Mississippi Negroes lived to tell about, but Evers defied them over and over again. It was as if by his own brazen example he could give some courage to his people.

Still things hadn't improved for the NAACP in Mississippi. Evers put seventy-eight thousand miles on his Oldsmobile in 1958 trying to drum up new members and new voters. The numbers were slipping in both areas.

Myrlie wished that just once she and her husband could go out and have a good time and not end up in a debate over "the race issue." Medgar was a Mason and an Elk and a member of the American Legion, and these organizations threw a lot of formal dinner parties and banquets. Like any salesman, Medgar would use these occasions to push his product. Only Medgar Evers's product was freedom.

Evers never missed an opportunity to take an open mike and make a pitch for the NAACP or ask people to vote and get involved. Sometimes Myrlie would sit in her good dress in front of her half-eaten plate of party food and cringe when Medgar stood up to speak. Immediately the heckling would start: "C'mon, man! We came here to *party*." He would finish what he had to say as if there was no problem at all. Sometimes, on the ride home, Myrlie couldn't hold her tongue anymore.

"Why?" she would moan. "Why can't you ever relax? Why does it always have to be you who makes the speeches and does the work?"

Medgar would get mad. "You don't understand," he would snap. "If I don't do it, who will?"

8

The Spy Agency

THE SOVEREIGNTY COMMISSION kept track of Mississippi's NAACP field secretary in a file labeled "Medgar Evers — Race Agitator." At first all the novice spy outfit did was clip newspaper articles about the NAACP. But in late November 1958 Governor Coleman suggested having a closer look at Evers. He ordered the commission to conduct "spot checks" day and night on Evers, "to determine whether he is violating any law." The Sovereignty Commission was particularly irritated by Evers's verbal attacks on the new Negro schoolhouses popping up throughout the state in a slick response to the Supreme Court order to integrate.

L. C. Hicks, the commission's chief investigator, asked state and local police to check out Evers. On December 2, 1958, Hicks submitted his first intelligence report. He got the Evers's home address right, but he described Evers as five foot five, 160 pounds, and thirty-eight years old. Medgar was nearly six feet tall and thirty-four years old.

The brief memo mentioned that Evers had at one time lived around Philadelphia, Mississippi, "and his actions were such that he left on somebody's request." It seems the cops had confused Medgar with Charles, who had moved to Chicago.

Over the months and years that followed, Medgar Evers's file grew thicker. Percy Greene, publisher of the black newspaper, the *Jackson Advocate,* eagerly supplied what information he could: where Evers had gone to school, how he had gotten his ideas about integration during his army days.

Greene, who was once a leading black Democrat and voting rights activist, had turned against the NAACP after the *Brown* decision in 1954. He did not believe that integration would benefit the black community. He and Medgar Evers had become bitter enemies, and he was an easy mark for the Sovereignty Commission, which recruited him to inform on Evers and other NAACP leaders. He was paid in subscriptions to the *Advocate* for school libraries, seed money for anti-NAACP organizations, all-expenses-paid trips for speaking engagements, and just outright pay-offs of cash. There were other, less prominent spies on the commission's payroll.

By January 1959 Zack Van Landingham, the former FBI agent who had been hired to conduct Sovereignty Commission investigations, was starting to get better information on Evers, including his military record, post office information, and employment records. For the first time a confidential source was mentioned, known only as T-1.

That March the Hinds County district attorney helpfully supplied the transcript of supposedly secret grand jury testimony by Medgar Evers involving a school desegregation case. The memo from Van Landingham to the commission director notes that D.A. Louis Nichols furnished the transcripts to both William Simmons, head of the Citizens' Councils, and Governor Coleman.

The Sovereignty Commission was, in fact, the link between the state government and the supposedly private segregation groups. For years it funneled money — as much as fifty thousand dollars a year — to support the Citizens' Councils. The files from April and May 1959 reveal how the Sovereignty Commission and the Citizens' Councils sometimes cooperated and shared information and other times battled each other for control of the state's segregation policy.

On April 13, 1959, Van Landingham notified Governor Coleman that an informant had tipped him off to an impending visit by Roy Wilkins to

Jackson on May 17, the fifth anniversary of the *Brown* decision. At that time Evers and Wilkins planned to map out a desegregation suit targeting Hinds County schools.

The next entry in the file was written on May 18. It reads like a Keystone Kops script, with the Mississippi attorney general grappling with the Jackson police after stumbling across a right-wing plot by the Capitol Street crowd to have Wilkins and Medgar Evers arrested.

On the afternoon of May 17, Van Landingham and Joe Patterson, the state's attorney general, decided to drive over to the Masonic Temple on Lynch Street to have a firsthand look at the crowd that had gathered to hear the NAACP leaders speak. They found the street jammed with out-of-county cars and a few Jackson patrolmen jotting down all the tag numbers. Before long Meady Pierce, chief of detectives, who apparently worked closely with the Sovereignty Commission, pulled the state men aside and said, "You know what some damn fools have done? They have gone and gotten out warrants for Roy Wilkins and Medgar Evers."

Van Landingham, Patterson, and Pierce drove down to police headquarters to talk it over with the chief of police. It seems that an active Citizens' Council member named Elmore Greaves had, the day before, sworn out a complaint against Evers and Wilkins for defying a state "breach of the peace" law that forbade advocating integration. Everyone in the room agreed that a move like that would be a disaster from a PR point of view. They knew that the law was unconstitutional, the arrests would never stick, and the incident would gain the NAACP a million dollars' worth of publicity, while making the authorities in Mississippi look like morons.

The chief thought that the warrant would be ignored, until he got a call that morning from the D.A. saying that he was under so much pressure he had ordered the warrant to be served. The pressure was coming from top-ranking officials in the Citizens' Councils.

Patterson got on the phone and tried to reach anyone he could, including a relative of Elmore Greaves, to get the warrant withdrawn. Greaves, through this intermediary, informed the state official that there was no way he would withdraw it. He said the Citizens' Councils had decided that the governor was afraid of Medgar Evers and Roy Wilkins, "and they were going on their own to secure their arrest." Greaves said that the arrests had been planned for weeks and a lot of people had been in on the decision, including a judge named Russel Moore.

Eventually the attorney general contacted the governor, and he managed to call off the warrants. Wilkins and Evers were able to speak without being arrested.

A rift was growing between the Sovereignty Commission, the governor, and Citizens' Councils extremists. The split would only be mended, temporarily, when Governor Coleman's "moderate" handpicked successor was defeated that summer in the Democratic primary by the Citizens' Councils' choice for governor, Ross Barnett. At that point the councils effectively ran the state government.

The files show that the Citizens' Councils thought that the state was too soft on the NAACP and that it was afraid to challenge Medgar Evers. Council leaders, with the cooperation of law enforcement and the judiciary, executed a plan to show Medgar Evers the inside of a jail, despite the wishes of the governor.

The Citizens' Councils used a fanatic front man, Greaves, to carry out its actions. Elmore Greaves was soon to become, if he wasn't already, a close colleague of Byron De La Beckwith.

Beckwith had grown more radical and more outspoken over the years. After hearing the famous Black Monday speech in Greenwood, he had started sending colorful letters to the editors of local newspapers, to his congressman and senators, and to anyone else who might listen to his pro-segregation screeds.

A classic example appeared in the Jackson *Daily News* in March 1956. Beckwith was outraged at the liberal attitudes shown by clergy in his beloved Episcopal Church. "Let's get the race mixers out of the Episcopal Church, for it is rapidly becoming the 'Devil's Workshop.'" In his mind the NAACP was Satan's agency: "These men, disguised in the robes of the clergy, deliberately and maliciously defy the laws of God and drag the sacred name of Jesus Christ through the mud in the attempt to crucify the white race on the black cross of the NAACP."

Beckwith was pleased with his letter-writing campaign and the attention it brought him. He even tried to lobby President Eisenhower in the cause of segregation. One day he walked into the local office of his congressman, Frank Smith, and gave him a letter to deliver to Eisenhower. The letter was so vicious, so sloppy, and so ignorant that Smith refused to forward it to anyone. It was eventually printed verbatim in the Greenwood *Morning Star*. Part of it reads, "We have had an overdose of the NAACP and all its affiliates and their fiendish associates. Arise with us to unite and destroy the madmen who sow the seeds of mongreliza-tion."

In town Beckwith, who was once a considered a harmless, friendly eccentric, was becoming increasingly tedious and disruptive. He would dress in his white linen planter's suits and, clutching a black Bible to his breast, preach the gospel of segregation to anyone he could collar. He sold copies of *Black Monday* on Howard Street during lunch hour. He cornered strollers and pressed them with anti-integration literature.

Some people avoided attending meetings of the Sons of the American Revolution because of Beckwith's endless hectoring on the race issue. His Sunday school classes became forums for his radical views. Every conversation would eventually turn to the subject of race, and soon the little man's countenance would change: his face would turn red and blustery; veins would stand out on his forehead. Once he started on the subject, there was no turning him off.

The rector of the Episcopal Church in Greenwood reproached Beck-with for standing at the door on Sundays with a clearly visible pistol in his belt "in case any niggers tried to integrate the church." Beckwith later switched to a local Methodist congregation, which he felt was more suitably pro-segregation.

Although this kind of obsessive behavior might have won Delay some admirers at the communal table at the Crystal Grill, where the "nigger problem" was the main topic of gossip, it isolated him from the saner members of his family and most of Greenwood. And as his political fanaticism increased, his life with his wife, Willie, deteriorated. From all accounts husband and wife drank a good deal, and when they got drunk, they got violent.

In 1957 Beckwith began to complain of terrible headaches and numb-ness in his face and limbs. He quit smoking and tried to stop drinking, but his symptoms remained.

About that time Willie checked into Greenwood LeFlore Hospital for the first of many visits to treat what had become acute alcoholism. She was a binge drinker, and she later said that it was the only way she felt she could escape her husband. She said that he had started hitting her shortly after Little Delay was born.

Willie divorced Beckwith in October 1960. She cited as the reason the cruel and unusual treatment by her husband of fifteen years. In her complaint she claimed that their problems had intensified around 1955. She said that Beckwith cursed her, beat her with his fists, kicked her and knocked her down and threatened to kill her if she told anyone about it.

In the past year, she said, the violence had grown worse. He would slap her in public. She alleged that on June 21, 1960, Beckwith tied her hands and feet together and left her hog-tied on the floor all night. That was when she filed for divorce.

The judge awarded her custody of Little Delay, now fifteen, and twenty-five dollars a week in support. As soon as they were divorced, Beckwith set out to win her back, and sure enough, Willie and Delay were remarried on Valentine's Day, 1961. The beatings and brawls began almost immediately, according to her second divorce petition, filed in 1962. In it she complained that Beckwith had driven her near to a complete nervous breakdown. In one fight he broke her finger while trying to pull off her wedding ring. She'd had to take out a restraining order to keep him from attacking her.

Beckwith answered this complaint with his own brief. In it he denied cursing his wife and said that he hit her only in self-defense. He accused her of being a violent drunk, "addicted to use of intoxicating liquor . . . of a mean and quarrelsome disposition." He said that she had shot at him with a pistol and he had had to disarm her. He said that her repeated hospitalizations were caused by alcoholism.

At the time Beckwith was making $255.88 per month from his sales job and his government disability pension. He said that he had inherited a "considerable" sum of money from an uncle's estate (Will had died in 1961) and that he had shared it with Willie. In fact they had used the inheritance to buy a new house on Montgomery Street in Greenwood, which Beckwith had put in her name.

On October 9, 1962, the judge granted Mary Louise Williams Beckwith her second divorce. Beckwith was ordered to pay costs. Once again he showered her with promises and apologies and flowers. They married for the third time three weeks later.

Beckwith agreed to see a psychiatrist as part of the reconciliation. Willie and Delay drove together down to Jackson for the visit. Later, in the car outside the doctor's office, Delay repeated what the psychiatrist had told him. The diagnosis, he said, was schizophrenia with paranoid tendencies.

9

The Freedom Riders

On A BREEZY MARCH DAY in 1961 nine students from Tougaloo College filed into a whites-only public library and sat down to read.

Naturally the cops showed up and told the students to leave. The chief of detectives suggested that they use the "colored" library. The students kept their eyes on their open books and didn't move.

They were duly arrested, charged with failing to disperse when ordered, and taken to jail. They were released on bond the next day. That morning about sixty students from Jackson State marched down Lynch Street, heading toward the city jail to protest the arrests. The first civil rights march in Jackson was broken up by cops with billy clubs and police dogs and tear gas.

Two days later on March 29 the nine students were set to be tried in municipal court. The seats reserved for Negroes in the courtroom filled up early, and about one hundred black spectators were directed to stand in a parking lot across Pascagoula Street. Newspaper accounts say that about one hundred whites were gathered on the other side of the courthouse. The trial was set for 4 P.M.

Medgar Evers arrived at about 3:35. He dropped off some colleagues and parked his car in the commercial lot. As he was walking toward the courthouse, he passed the Jackson Police Department headquarters. He saw three policemen in the window, and he didn't recognize any of them; at least one of them recognized Medgar Evers.

"There he is," said the cop, loud, as Evers walked by. "We ought to kill him." Medgar Evers later told the FBI that he "just smiled" at the policemen and walked over to meet his friends.

When the students arrived for their trial, a few in the Negro crowd started to applaud. Without warning, a police captain yelled "Move 'em out!" and some twenty-five cops waded in, swinging clubs.

Although the police had tried to chase off the white spectators, seventy or so stayed behind. One of them was a big-time bootlegger and locally famous racist named G. W. "Red" Hydrick. The stout little man broke through the lines to practice some freelance crowd control. He chased down a black photographer and beat him with his pistol butt. Then he spotted Medgar Evers walking by.

All Evers saw was a white man in a dark suit and hat who snuck up behind him and pistol-whipped him in the back of the head with a blue-steel .38. The blow staggered Evers, but he didn't fall. As he walked away, two uniformed cops ran up to him, and one shouted, "Get going, boy."

Medgar assured them that he was going. But as he passed by, both officers clubbed him from behind, aiming for the kidneys. Evers was whisked off the street by two friends who recognized him.

After a doctor examined him and found that he wasn't seriously injured, Medgar Evers started gathering up witnesses to sign affidavits of police brutality. He made his own statement to the FBI that night.

In the subsequent FBI reports the group of Negroes standing outside the courthouse is consistently referred to as a "mob." Apparently no action was taken against the police. But a few weeks later, the new U.S. assistant attorney general for civil rights, Burke Marshall, made a specific request for an immediate FBI investigation of the incident.

Marshall told reporters, "I have Evers's story. I'm trying to find out if it's true. If it is, it's a disgrace."

Marshall added diplomatically, "I may say, though, that I've been told by local authorities that the instructions to the police were not to use force."

It was not much, but at least it was something. The investigation never led to any charges, but the fact that the Justice Department waded into the fray signaled a real change in policy. The difference now, of course, was that John F. Kennedy had been inaugurated president that January.

Kennedy's brother Robert was the new attorney general. Although Robert Kennedy later admitted, "I won't say I stayed awake nights worrying about civil rights," he and his brother soon came to take the Negro cause very seriously.

The Civil Rights Division of the Justice Department that the Kennedys inherited didn't have much bite, but it did have some good attorneys. One of them was named John Doar.

Doar was a slow-talking, long-legged trial lawyer from Wisconsin. His father was a trial lawyer too, and the two of them used to ride the circuit from small town to small town. It taught Doar how to do his own investigating, and it taught him something about how small-town courthouses work.

In 1960 a classmate from Princeton recruited Doar to join him at the Justice Department, as first assistant secretary in the Civil Rights Division. The division was trying to enforce the 1957 and 1960 Civil Rights Acts, two weak laws that made it possible for the Justice Department to bring suit against counties where registrars discriminated against Negro voters. Doar stayed with the Justice Department when Robert Kennedy came into office.

The new attorney general walked into Doar's office one day early in 1961 and told him that the president wanted to do something about civil rights — now. Doar persuaded Robert Kennedy to pursue a voting rights case in Macon County, Alabama, before Judge Frank Johnson. They tried the case in the spring of 1961 and quickly produced a groundbreaking victory for black voters.

One thing Doar had learned by then was that the FBI had to be poked and prodded into doing the legwork to prepare voter discrimination cases. Doar would compose long lists of specific questions for the agents to ask. One questionnaire was two hundred pages long. It was clear that J. Edgar Hoover and his men were not on the civil rights bandwagon. Because of that Doar ended up doing a lot of his own investigating, which is how he met Medgar Evers.

The next voting rights target, Doar decided, would be the southern counties of Mississippi. As it turned out, a number of affidavits from that region were already in the department's files. They had been generated over the years by the NAACP field secretary in Mississippi.

When John Doar and his associate George Owen showed up at Medgar Evers's door in Jackson, Medgar invited them in for coffee. Doar liked Evers instantly. Here was a levelheaded man, not a whiner or a screamer, someone with great conviction and dignity.

Medgar Evers took out a map of Mississippi and showed the two white men from Washington where they needed to go. He gave them contacts. He called ahead when he could. With Evers's help Doar began preparing the first federal voting rights cases in Mississippi.

It would turn out to be a long, painful process, nothing like Alabama. Part of the problem was a deal that was already being made in Washington. By then Jim Eastland had achieved a lumbering seniority in the Senate, and with it the chairmanship of the key Judiciary Committee. He was in a prime position to block any of the appointments President Kennedy wanted to make. He had the power to deal, and he used it.

Kennedy was keen on making Thurgood Marshall a federal judge. Eastland knew that, and he had his price. One day early in the administration, the story goes, Eastland bumped into Robert Kennedy in the Senate hallway and said to him, "Tell your brother if he'll give me Harold Cox, I'll give him the nigger."

In the end Kennedy got Thurgood Marshall on the bench, along with nine other black judges. Cox was the cup of hemlock he had to swallow.

On paper William Harold Cox seemed harmless enough. He had been Jim Eastland's college roommate. He had no judicial record to speak of and no blatant alliances with white supremacist groups. Despite Roy Wilkins's warning that Cox was a disastrous choice, Kennedy appointed him to the Fifth Circuit, which included the southern half of Mississippi.

It was there that Cox ran head-on into John Doar. The two men sparred from the outset. Over the years Cox would refuse to schedule Doar's cases, and Doar would try to have Cox censured for his outrageous behavior on the bench. In open court the judge called a group of black plaintiffs "a bunch of niggers . . . acting like a bunch of chimpanzees." He called Doar "stupid." Predictably, many of the Justice Department's cases were beached on the Fifth Circuit.

As the Justice Department began its slow, painstaking, churning advance into civil rights litigation, a mass movement sprang up around the department's young lawyers and pushed them in directions they hadn't planned to go. In the spring of 1961 the energy of Doar's division was diverted when a group of protesters from the Congress of Racial Equality (CORE) decided to test court orders desegregating interstate transportation facilities (two years after Medgar Evers's solo attempt). They called themselves the Freedom Riders.

The plan, conceived by the CORE director, James Farmer, was for two groups of experienced black and white nonviolent protesters to ride interstate buses across the South. The route would take them from Washington, D.C., through the Carolinas, Georgia, Alabama and Mississippi, and end up in New Orleans on May 17, the anniversary of *Brown v. Board of Education*.

The SCLC gave the Freedom Riders full support, and even the NAACP's Wilkins gave his quiet blessing to the enterprise. But one man who did not seem happy to see the Freedom Riders come through Mississippi was Medgar Evers.

Mississippi was sacred ground for the NAACP. The association would not tolerate the sort of membership raiding that might take place if the CORE people established a beachhead in the state.

Evers took five weeks to answer a letter from Farmer requesting support in the form of housing and food for the Freedom Riders when they reached Jackson. When he did respond, Evers's tone was icy: "As much as we would like to help, we feel that CORE's coming into Jackson at this time . . . will not have the effect intended and possibly hamper some of the efforts already in progress. . . . It would perhaps be better for you to bypass Mississippi and proceed to your destination."

As soon as the Freedom Ride began, it turned into a bloody fiasco. The worst incidents occurred in Alabama, where buses were attacked by mobs of Klansmen and burned. As each group of Freedom Riders were hospitalized or arrested, CORE sent another group to take their place. The next stop was Mississippi.

Robert Kennedy was desperate to stop the bloodshed, and he was forced into the awkward position of challenging Democrats in the South. He made another deal with Eastland to avoid more violence: Eastland would "allow" the Freedom Riders safe passage into Mississippi as long as they could be arrested in Jackson for "inflaming public opinion."

The first group of riders were arrested by Jackson police as soon as they walked through the bus terminal. So were the next group. Wave after wave of Freedom Riders kept coming. By the end of the summer two hundred or more had been arrested. The jails were full, so the riders were sent to the notorious Parchman State Penitentiary up in the Delta. Some of the convicted activists remained there for months.

Court costs and bail money depleted the CORE reserves. Roy Wilkins grudgingly gave CORE a thousand dollars — just enough to charter more buses.

There were so many cases that the city of Jackson hired a special prosecutor to deal with them. His name was Alvin Binder, an ambitious lawyer and, coincidentally, a member of Mississippi's small Jewish community.

Being a Jew did not automatically translate into being a political liberal, or even a moderate, in Mississippi. Binder was a staunch segregationist from Clarksdale. He allowed himself, for a while, to be used by the Sovereignty Commission as an out-of-state speaker promoting Mississippi-style race relations. He quit after he was inadvertently sent to a Ku Klux Klan meeting. He became more disillusioned soon after he began prosecuting the Freedom Riders. After one swift conviction Binder noticed a group of jurors emerge, smiling, from the mayor's office. Binder quietly resigned.

Meanwhile Medgar Evers was becoming a civil rights celebrity. By now the mere mention of Mississippi would send a shiver of dread down the spine of an outsider, and Medgar Evers's name had become attached to the danger and the glamour the state represented. He was the man the reporters called when Mack Charles Parker was lynched, when Roman Duckworth was dragged from a bus and shot, when Herbert Lee was gunned down. The newspaper reports, the *Ebony* article, and Evers's increasing visibility on the television news added to his legend. The NAACP often sent Medgar to branches in other states to lecture on the situation in Mississippi. People would listen, awestruck, to news from the front line.

In the spring of 1961 Medgar attended the annual NAACP conference, held that year in Philadelphia, Pennsylvania. It was his seventh national meeting.

The meeting was the first for a newly hired field secretary from Atlanta named Vernon Jordan. He was just one year out of Howard University Law School and dazzled by Medgar Evers, the star among the field secretaries. Medgar took to the new recruit. Jordan remembers him as a mentor, a big brother who guided him through the tangled internal politics of the NAACP.

Jordan says that he and Evers "bonded" that summer at a retreat for the southeastern regional NAACP at Beaufort, South Carolina. It was like a summer camp for activists, held in a big wooden house and dormitory run by a Quaker group. Jordan, whose mother was a famous caterer in Atlanta, mainly remembers how bad the food was and how little of it they got to eat.

There would be meetings and workshops all day, then dinner at about four o'clock. Nothing else was scheduled for the rest of the evening. Jordan persuaded Evers and Ruby Hurley, their boss, to drive into Beaufort to look for something to eat.

Every Negro restaurant in the area was closed. This presented a problem: NAACP staffers were forbidden to trade at segregated establishments. They cruised downtown Beaufort looking for a place to eat, and all they could find was a white truck stop. Jordan remembers the big neon sign flashing STEAKS, CHOPS, FISH!

He pulled into the back.

"Where are you going?" Ruby Hurley asked.

"Right in here, Miss Hurley," Jordan said.

"You cannot go in this place! It violates NAACP policy!"

Jordan snatched the car keys and headed for the kitchen door. He explained the situation to the cook, who was of course black, and placed his order. While he was waiting, Medgar Evers came to the door.

"You better come on out of here, man," said Evers. "You're going to get into a world of trouble with Ruby. She's raising hell with you!"

Jordan just smiled. As strong as Medgar was, he had an astonishing respect for authority, for following the rules and obeying the leaders. He was the kind of NAACP man Jordan would soon find out he could never be.

The cook handed Jordan a big box of steaks and laughed as he said, "This white man is going to buy the NAACP these dinners."

Ruby Hurley was blowing the horn when they got back to the car. Jordan put the steaks in the trunk and, without a word, drove back to the retreat. Medgar said nothing. Ruby was tearing into Jordan, lecturing him on his responsibilities. Meanwhile the aroma from the steaks and the fried onions was drifting into the car.

"Miss Hurley, those steaks sure do smell good," said Medgar.

Ruby Hurley caved in. "Well, I guess they do . . . "

When they got back to the old house, the three of them sat in the kitchen and just devoured those steaks and drank and talked into the night. It was a magic moment for Vernon Jordan, so full of contradictions and friendships forged in the strangest of times.

Jordan and Evers became close friends, and Vernon would take every opportunity to visit Jackson. His favorite place to eat was a restaurant on Farish Street called Steven's, where everybody who was anybody in civil rights could be found at lunchtime. The walk there with Evers from the Masonic Temple offices seemed to take forever because Medgar stopped in every store along the way to chat with the owner. He seemed to know everybody on the sidewalk, asked about their health and their family, and knew their kids by name. Medgar Evers left no hand unshaken.

The sad thing, Jordan remembers, was that the NAACP didn't seem to realize what a star Evers was until he was gone. He remembers with anger a scene the following spring, when the national conference was being held in Jackson. It was a big success, Jordan recalls. Jackie Robinson and the boxing champion Archie Moore were there. There was a big turnout.

Jordan has never forgotten going with Medgar to drop Gloster Current off at the old Jackson airport after the conference was over. Current was criticizing Medgar mercilessly, hammering away at him for the low membership figures and giving him hell for not recruiting hard enough. Vernon Jordan watched in agony as Medgar Evers broke down in tears.

That was 1962. Ross Barnett was governor and the Citizens' Councils were at the height of their power. Everyone could see Medgar Evers was risking his life every day, and here was Gloster Current, who could get on an airplane and go back to the safety of his nice home in Queens, New York, badgering him to tears. Jordan couldn't hold his tongue another minute.

"You leave Medgar alone!" he shouted at his boss. "You have no right to pressure him."

"No, Vernon," said Medgar mildly. "Now you leave us alone."

That was the way it was at the NAACP. Medgar would take it in the neck from his bosses, then go out and work even harder for them.

The conference marked the end of a difficult year. While Medgar Evers carried on the timeworn NAACP strategy — fight segregation in the courts and avoid civil disobedience — he watched a small stream of activists set up shop in his state.

In an October 1961 report to Roy Wilkins, Evers listed the newcomer organizations wading into the dangerous waters of Mississippi. He reported on the Freedom Riders and the growth of other nonviolent groups in the state. In a part of the report that must have alarmed Wilkins, who loathed Martin Luther King, Evers noted that King had drawn a crowd of twenty-five hundred to three thousand people to a mass meeting in Jackson sponsored by the Student Nonviolent Coordinating Committee (SNCC). "Less than eight hundred dollars was collected," Evers pointed out.

The tone of the report reveals a simmering rivalry, a condescending, world-weary attitude that the NAACP would sustain throughout the decade. When Evers described the upstart civil rights groups, his tone was that of a disapproving father whose teenager had flipped the Buick. Listen to his description of SNCC, whose team, led by Bob Moses, had tried a frontal attack on the most Klan-ridden, terror-stricken counties in southern Mississippi:

> It was not until they began to run into difficulties securing bonds for young people they had caused to be arrested and until they themselves [Moses and other leaders] became involved with some hoodlums, law enforcement officers and voter registrars which landed them either in jail or gave them severe beatings; did they ask for NAACP assistance publicly and cooperatively.

NAACP lawyer Jack Young represented them, "frequently at the expense of the association."

Evers sounded like a true Mississippian; he didn't much care for outside interference. By mid-October, Evers reported, SNCC was a "skeleton operation" in Jackson. Most of the leaders who had been arrested were now out on heavy bonds.

Even Roy Wilkins recognized the problem. In 1960 he had told

Farmer, who had left the NAACP to join CORE, "You're going to be riding a mustang pony, while I'm riding a dinosaur."

The SCLC, SNCC, and CORE were scooping up a whole generation of students by offering them something the NAACP would not: action. The movement train was pulling out of the station, and once again Medgar Evers had to decide whether to try to stop it or jump on board.

10

Ole Miss

IF THERE WAS ONE SYMBOL of Mississippi's white heritage and a concentration of its oligarchic impulses, it was the University of Mississippi at Oxford, affectionately known as Ole Miss. The rolling green lawns, the stately columned mansions, and Greek Revival buildings were artifacts from the mythical antebellum South. The school mascot was a character called "Colonel Reb." The Confederate battle flag was the school symbol.

The sorority and fraternity systems at Ole Miss were actually redundant. The social status of students was established at birth through the complex blood ties and relationships of families: girls were born Tri Delts or not, and boys Sigma Chis, or not, and one hardly needed rush week to draw the distinction. This was white Mississippi society distilled. It was this ossified, tight-knit, lily-white world that became the object of James Meredith's obsession in the spring of 1961.

Meredith was a junior at Jackson State. He was an air force veteran, a short, wiry man with a smooth moon face that made him seem years younger than he was. At college in Jackson, Meredith studied history and political science. He surrounded himself with a loyal coterie of friends, an "underground" made up of fellow veterans, intellectuals, and others with a militant interest in civil rights. They sought the perfect gesture, the first opening in which to place the wedge between the white man and his power.

On January 21, 1961, the day after John F. Kennedy was inaugurated, Meredith wrote to the registrar at Ole Miss asking for application forms. Then he contacted Medgar Evers.

Although Meredith admired Evers, he had never had much use for the cautious, moderate NAACP. He knew, however, that he would need the legal and financial clout of the old association if he ever expected to see the inside of Ole Miss.

Quietly, behind the scenes, Medgar Evers shepherded James Meredith through the maze of the NAACP bureaucracy. Evers steered Meredith to Thurgood Marshall and the Legal Defense and Educational Fund. When Marshall (who would soon be appointed to the federal bench) wanted more information from Meredith about his qualifications, Evers put the call through from his own home.

Marshall, already famous for his bluntness, wanted proof that Meredith's record was as good as he claimed it was. Meredith, who would prove to be as stubborn as the lawyer, hung up on him. Nobody questioned his integrity. He refused to speak to Marshall again.

Meredith credits Medgar Evers for saving the whole enterprise. Medgar soothed both men. He convinced Meredith that producing documentation was good legal strategy, and, more important, he convinced Marshall that Meredith was not as flaky as he seemed. It was Evers's sheer force of will and persuasiveness that enabled Meredith to proceed with the lawsuit. Evers knew that Meredith was hotheaded, stubborn, arrogant, and maybe a little crazy. But Evers also instinctively knew that Meredith could take the pressure and the abuse and the threats that were ahead of him. That counted more than anything else.

It took eighteen months of court battles, but finally a federal judge ordered Ole Miss to admit James Meredith. Mississippi's governor, Ross Barnett, chose to ignore the court order, saying it usurped the rights reserved for the states.

On September 20, 1962, James Meredith made his first attempt to register on the Ole Miss campus. Ross Barnett and a screaming mob of four thousand segregationists turned him away.

Five days later, after another round in the courts, Meredith tried again, this time at a registry office in Jackson. He was accompanied by the head of the U.S. Marshals and by John Doar of the Justice Department. The NAACP had by now taken a backseat to the government lawyers who were handling the case.

Again there was an ugly crowd of hecklers shouting, "Nigger, go home!" Meredith was hustled through the mob and up to the registry door, where the governor stood to block him. Barnett scrutinized the men and then deadpanned, for the benefit of Doar and the other bystanders, "Which one of you is James Meredith?"

Meredith grinned, but Doar was less amused, particularly as Barnett read a statement concluding, "I do hereby finally deny you admission to the University of Mississippi." Then the governor paused and smiled at Meredith. "But I do so politely," he added.

"Thank you," Doar said dryly. "We leave politely."

For the next week the governor haggled with the attorney general and even President Kennedy over Meredith's admission. At one point Barnett agreed to let him in if the U.S. marshals would pull guns on the governor to make it look like he was putting up a fight.

By Saturday, September 29, the Kennedys thought they had a deal: the marshals would sneak Meredith onto the campus without making a show of it. There would be no incident.

The big Ole Miss–Kentucky football game was scheduled for that afternoon. The university wisely decided to move the game to the stadium in Jackson rather than draw huge crowds to the already volatile Oxford campus. When Ross Barnett made his appearance in the stands, the band struck up "Dixie," and the crowd cheered wildly. Rebel flags were waving alongside banners declaring "Go Get 'em Ross." A huge rebel yell issued from the crowd as Barnett took his seat. They all sang the college fight song with new vigor: "Never, never, never! We will not yield an inch."

Ross Barnett changed his mind again.

President Kennedy federalized the Mississippi National Guard and signed an executive order authorizing the armed forces to enforce the law in the state. On Sunday morning Barnett again told the Kennedys he would quietly allow Meredith onto the campus. He then called on four of his closest allies to fly to Oxford and act as his personal representatives, with a mission to "protect the citizens of Mississippi." They included the speaker of the Mississippi House, a state senator, a state representative from the lower Delta named C. B. "Buddie" Newman, and Judge Russel Moore. Barnett failed to mention that he had already cut a deal with the government.

Meanwhile it was becoming clear that the situation was not in the hands of the governor or his envoys. Another figure had come to town, and he was organizing his own brand of resistance.

General Edwin Walker was already a familiar figure in Mississippi. He was one of the most rabid anticommunist radicals in the country. Ironically Walker had been in command of the 101st Airborne when Eisenhower had sent in troops to carry out the Supreme Court desegregation order at Little Rock's Central High School in 1957. After that Walker had been posted to Germany, where he was forced to resign after he was discovered indoctrinating U.S. troops with right-wing John Birch Society literature.

When it was announced that James Meredith would be enrolled at Ole Miss by court order, Walker sprang to action from his Dallas, Texas, home. He went on the radio calling for ten thousand volunteers to go to Oxford to rally behind Governor Barnett. He told his followers to bring knapsacks and skillets to Ole Miss. It could be a long siege.

Byron De La Beckwith was a big fan of General Walker, and by Sunday afternoon, September 30, he was on his way to Oxford with a pickup truck full of weapons. Just outside Greenwood, Beckwith was stopped by some "friendly police." They said they expected he would be coming, and, with some difficulty, they convinced him to turn back.

Hundreds of like-minded citizens from all over Dixie did not turn back. By nightfall the Ole Miss campus was swarming with hard, armed men with a mind to fight the last battle of the Civil War. General Edwin Walker was among them, leading the charge.

James Meredith arrived from Memphis by small plane just before dark. With an escort of armed marshals and John Doar by his side, he slipped onto the Ole Miss campus without incident and was taken to his dorm room at Baxter Hall. A contingent of armed guards was posted there, with orders to shoot to protect him.

They were never necessary. The action was taking place on the other side of campus in front of the elegant, Greek-columned Lyceum building, where the registrar was located. By 7 P.M., two thousand angry drunks were taunting some 170 marshals who had taken positions around the building. More outsiders were joining the angry white students, and finally the marshals fired tear gas. At that point the Mississippi Highway Patrol withdrew, and so did the hapless envoys whom Ross Barnett had sent to keep the peace.

Both sides blamed the other for starting the bloodshed. A trooper was hit in the chest with a tear gas canister and nearly killed. A marshal was shot in the throat and lay bleeding for hours because the crowd wouldn't let an ambulance through. The only reinforcements to arrive all night were a group of local guardsmen led by the writer William Faulkner's cousin. He was injured in the fight.

Although they begged to use their side arms, the marshals were not authorized to use deadly force. All they could do was fire tear gas and swing billy clubs against a mob with shotguns, pistols, sniper rifles, and, in one case, a rampaging bulldozer used as a tank. Dozens of rioters were arrested and hurled into a makeshift jail in the Lyceum basement. During the night one bystander and a French reporter were killed by .38 bullets.

In the early morning hours the first contingent of army MPs swept the campus. By dawn it was over.

At 8 A.M. Meredith, under heavy guard, walked across the once-lovely campus, now strewn with burned-out vehicles and stinking of tear gas, to register at the university. With his bodyguards he made it in time for his first class, a lesson in colonial American history. Walker was arrested at a roadblock as he was heading out of town.

Although it is said that an organized, violent Klan was not present in Mississippi until early 1964, the retaliation that followed Meredith's admission to Ole Miss showed a pattern indicating that someone was directing a terror campaign in the state. Whoever it was knew the targets, what they owned, and where they lived.

According to Medgar Evers's field report from that period, on the night of October 2, a Molotov cocktail was pitched at Dr. Gilbert Mason's medical clinic in Biloxi. That same night, in a nearby coastal city, another firebomb was thrown into the office of a gas station owned by Dr. Felix Dunn, president of the Gulfport NAACP branch. Evers surmised that the same people were responsible for both bombings. Whoever it was knew quite a bit about both men and their real estate. On October 3, the home of a prominent NAACP leader in Columbus, Mississippi, 250 miles north of Gulfport, was similarly bombed. The next night, in central Leake County, someone fired shots into the houses of Negroes who had signed petitions to integrate the public schools.

At Ole Miss Meredith was accompanied by U.S. marshals wherever he went. There were no other serious incidents, just some bottle throwing at the dorm and kids calling him names. Some white students started talking to Meredith. A few even joined him at the lunch table. He was getting a lot of mail. Much of it was supportive, but some of it wasn't. One letter contained a simple piece of verse:

> Roses are red, violets are blue;
> I've killed one nigger and might as well make it two.

11

The Jackson Movement

THE FRIENDLY OLD WHITE MAN at the gas station on the Louisiana line wanted to share the latest Kennedy joke with his customer. "How can Kennedy expect to get a man on the moon," he asked, chuckling, "when he can't even get a busload of niggers across Mississippi?"

John Salter just shook his head. Around him a thick mist rose from the swamps. He wondered what he was getting himself into.

Just after midnight, on the first day of September 1961, Salter and his wife, Eldri, crossed the Mississippi River bridge into Vicksburg and headed for Jackson. With his light eyes, blond crew cut, and square jaw, Salter looked more like an Anglo football coach than a half-Indian social activist and union organizer who was soon to become one of Mississippi's most famous "outside agitators."

The Salters, who were in their twenties, were on their way from Arizona to Tougaloo College, just north of Jackson, where John had been hired to teach sociology. He was attracted to Tougaloo because it was a sanctuary of reason and racial tolerance in the roughest part of the South. Tougaloo was a black, private Christian school, now with a handful of white students from the North and an integrated, somewhat international teaching staff. When the Freedom Riders had come through that summer, they'd bunked at Tougaloo.

Among the first peculiar things Salter noticed about his new job was that his otherwise friendly students avoided him on the streets of Jackson because he looked white. The races had no contact at all. He was astonished at the total segregation of the city and the fear of the people, who could seem as despondent as whipped dogs.

Almost immediately John Salter was sucked into Mississippi's racial politics. It was as natural as breathing air.

One of his students in his American government class was Colia Liddell, president of the NAACP's North Jackson Youth Council. She asked him to speak to the group, and before long he had signed up as its adult adviser.

The first time Salter met Medgar Evers was at the annual NAACP Freedom Fund dinner in Jackson that fall. John and Eldri felt the stares as they walked up to the Masonic Temple that night. Besides the cops taking down tag numbers, they were the only non-black people there. Medgar Evers greeted them at the door like old friends. He knew them by name; Colia had told him they were coming. Salter was taken by Medgar's ease and warmth and passion. They agreed to meet again.

The Salters listened as each NAACP chapter reported in with a litany of beatings, and harassment, and economic disaster. But no story haunted them as much as the one Medgar Evers told about his friend Clyde Kennard, a black Mississippian who was dying in prison for the crime of wanting to go to college.

The case was probably the most frustrating and tragic fight of Medgar Evers's career. It was particularly painful because Kennard was so much like Evers. They were the same age, they came from the same kind of hardworking rural family, and neither of them was intimidated by the sound of a white man saying no. Evers knew that but for the grace of God, he could have been in Kennard's place.

Like Evers, Kennard was an army veteran who had served in World War II.

After Kennard left the service, he continued his college education at the University of Chicago. Then his stepfather got sick, and Kennard dropped out of school to return to Mississippi to take over the family farm for his mother.

The closest college was the all-white state school, Mississippi Southern College in Hattiesburg. That was where Kennard wanted to finish his degree. Three times he tried to enroll. On the morning of his last rejection in September 1959, Kennard was arrested on campus by local constables for reckless driving and illegal possession of whiskey. Kennard was a Baptist who didn't drink. Even Zack Van Landingham, the Sovereignty Commission investigator assigned to the case, thought Kennard had been framed. He also discovered an aborted plot to plant dynamite in Kennard's car.

None of this mattered to the judge. Kennard was convicted and fined six hundred dollars. The local Citizens' Council was out to ruin him. The bank foreclosed on his farm (a Jackson businessman and later the NAACP bought the mortgage for his mother). Then he was arrested on another outlandish charge: a well-known local thief accused Kennard of hiring him to steal chicken feed. Although the burglar was released, Kennard was sentenced to seven years' hard labor at Parchman.

Soon after Kennard reported to the prison farm, he complained of stomach pains. The condition was left undiagnosed and untreated for months before a doctor found the massive cancer in his colon. Even then he was sent back to work in the fields. He was thirty-three years old.

When Medgar Evers tried to tell the nicely dressed crowd at the Freedom Fund dinner about the efforts to get Kennard of out of prison, the words would not come to him, and his eyes filled with tears. It was the only time anyone could remember seeing Medgar Evers break down in public. Twice he started the speech, and twice his voice failed him. Aaron Henry offered to take over, but Evers forced his way through to the end of his talk, and by then everyone in the hall was weeping for Clyde Kennard, and perhaps for Medgar Evers, and perhaps, too, for themselves.

That December Medgar Evers and the Jackson NAACP led a modest, mainly symbolic consumer boycott of Capitol Street, the white shopping district where black clerks were never hired and black shoppers could not try on the clothes they bought.

The merchants refused to negotiate. The boycott was ineffective, and it received no local publicity. News coverage in Mississippi was outrageously biased because the media were almost totally controlled by members of the Citizens' Councils. The two TV stations in Jackson were cheerleaders for white supremacy. They sometimes blacked out national broadcasts that offered an alternative viewpoint. They even censored network news segments that dealt with civil rights demonstrations and boycotts. Fred Beard, the general manager of WLBT, the NBC affiliate, was a prominent member of the Jackson Citizens' Council. Members of the Hederman family, who owned the state's two biggest newspapers, the Jackson *Clarion-Ledger* and the Jackson *Daily News,* were notorious segregationists. Only a handful of regional newspapers, most notably Hodding Carter's Greenville *Democrat-Times*, offered reasonably balanced coverage of the biggest story of the day.

Lawsuits were simmering in the courts, including one to desegregate the county bus line and another to desegregate the public schools. The plaintiffs in the latter case included Reena and Darrell Kenyatta Evers, Medgar and Myrlie's two older children.

In February of 1962 Medgar Evers made his separate peace with the idealistic outsiders from CORE and SNCC who were treading on NAACP territory. Evers saw the need to coordinate all local, state, and national civil rights organizations operating in Mississippi. He joined in talks to set up an alliance called The Council of Federated Organizations (COFO). Despite Evers's support, the national NAACP refused to join COFO. Aaron Henry took the titular post of president, but the project was driven by its director, Bob Moses, and assistant director, Dave Dennis.

By then Medgar Evers and Dave Dennis had become close friends. They would slip off together to a little steak restaurant on the outskirts of Jackson to have a drink — Medgar was careful about who saw him relaxing — and talk. Mostly they talked about sports and women while they tried to slough off the tension of their work. But inevitably the conversation would come around to the movement. At this time Medgar was still struggling with his impulse to confront the system the way the SCLC, SNCC, and CORE took it on, while keeping his loyalty to the NAACP. The support he gave Dennis and Moses was still mainly under the table.

When James Meredith cracked Ole Miss, the confrontation gained new momentum. After troops were sent to Oxford, a thousand new members joined the Citizens' Council in Jackson alone. About the same time, the Negroes of Jackson staged their first successful boycott of the segregated Mississippi State Fair.

The atmosphere of tension and hope spilled over into the Seventeenth Annual State Conference of Mississippi Branches of the NAACP in November 1962. It was a big event in Jackson, full of national staffers and celebrities. Roy Wilkins gave a speech, and Dick Gregory entertained the crowd.

Dick Gregory had grown up broke and hungry in a St. Louis slum. By 1962 he was a famous nightclub comedian who rode into the big time on a wave of race jokes. He was the Negro's answer to Lenny Bruce, but without the bitter edge. Gregory could disarm the whites in his audience and make them laugh with him.

"Last time I was down South I walked into this restaurant, and this white waitress came up to me and said, 'We don't serve colored people.' "

"I said, 'That's all right, I don't eat colored people.' "

By the end of 1962 Gregory had been on *The Jack Paar Show* and on *The David Susskind Show,* he had cut a comedy album, and he was a Playboy Club regular. Because of the nature of his material and his high profile, he was increasingly drawn into the civil rights movement. He met Roy Wilkins and Martin Luther King, Jr., and he performed at fundraisers and rallies. But he never really got emotionally involved in the movement until Medgar Evers asked him to come to Jackson, Mississippi.

It was a one-night gig, and he was eager to get it over with. Gregory didn't like being in Mississippi; there was such an outrageous atmosphere of hostility and fear. He had to admit he held the same prejudice so many northern blacks did against their hayseed brethren down in Mississippi, the ones who'd been left behind in the great move north, the ones Gregory called "verb-busters" for the way they mangled the language. He came down to Mississippi out of a sense of duty, but he was already thinking about the flight home when an old man took the stage.

Gregory later recalled in his autobiography, *Nigger,* how the seventy-eight-year-old man was telling the crowd about his years in jail, where he had done time for killing a Negro who had been sent to burn his house down. The old man had been trying to register voters. "I didn't mind going to jail for freedom," the man said, but he had never spent a night apart from his wife. When he finally got out of jail, his wife had died. It tore Dick Gregory up. He gave Medgar Evers a train ticket and some money for the old man to visit his son in California. Something had turned over in his heart. He was involved now.

That night Gregory heard the story of Clyde Kennard for the first time, and Medgar introduced him to Kennard's mother, Leona Smith. Evers sent him more information about the case when Gregory got back to Chicago, and Gregory began to push to get Kennard out of jail. He got the story into the national press, including the news that Kennard was dying of cancer. (The bad publicity finally convinced Governor Ross Barnett to pardon Kennard in the spring of 1963. Kennard died in a Chicago hospital on July 14, 1963, three weeks after his thirty-sixth birthday.)

By the fall of 1962 black folks across the Delta were organizing to resist white supremacy in ways that were unthinkable half a decade earlier. Aaron Henry, the state NAACP president, was leading a boycott of white-owned shops in Clarksdale. A full-blown movement had sprouted in Greenwood, where a hundred blacks at a time were lining up at the courthouse to attempt to register to vote.

In Jackson, home of fifty thousand Negro citizens, there was scant activity. Conservative ministers and business leaders were reluctant to challenge the system. Medgar Evers spent most of his time in other parts of Mississippi, where black communities were more receptive to the civil rights message.

But as the 1962 Christmas season approached, student activists started talking about another boycott. A strategy meeting was held in John Salter's home where it was decided that blacks would boycott all 150 Capitol Street businesses, not just a few big stores or specific products. They printed five thousand leaflets outlining their demands: equality in hiring and promoting employees; the end of segregated drinking fountains, rest rooms, and seating; the use of courtesy titles — Mrs., Miss, and Mr. — for all races; and service on a first-come, first-served basis.

The organizations that signed the leaflet were the North Jackson Youth Council; the Tougaloo chapter of the NAACP; SNCC, represented on campus by Joan Trumpauer; and CORE, represented by Dave Dennis. In the future they would call themselves the Jackson Movement.

Salter spoke to Medgar Evers about setting up some pickets on Capitol Street. It would mean getting bail money together, and Medgar agreed to try to raise some from the national NAACP.

At the last minute the NAACP turned them down. Desperate, Salter turned to a New York civil rights lawyer named William Kunstler, whose daughter attended Tougaloo. Kunstler agreed to help and found donors, including an arm of the SCLC, to pledge a total of three thousand dollars for bail.

On December 12, 1962, Salter and the others drove to Capitol Street and managed to walk up and down in front of Woolworth's one time before they were hauled off by the Jackson police. Salter counted at least fifty cops and a hundred white spectators. It took two days to bail everyone out, but the publicity payoff was worth it to Salter. The TV crews played into the demonstrators' hands. They clearly showed the picket signs calling for a boycott on the news.

Mayor Allen Thompson was outraged. The former college Greek professor was a hard-core segregationist, and he was in no mood to bargain. He threatened to sue the pickets for a million dollars. He offered to line Capitol Street with a thousand police to prevent more picketing. And he further vowed to remain calm.

The boycott attracted an avalanche of hate mail and hate calls to the Salter home on the Tougaloo campus. Just before Christmas someone fired a shot into the house, barely missing their sleeping infant daughter.

Medgar continued to give the movement his quiet support. He helped raise property bonds outside the auspices of the NAACP, and he and John Salter became friends.

Evers fascinated John Salter, who was drawn to his calm and his kindness and something else. There was a quality in Evers's eyes, a wild calculation that reminded Salter of a lone wolf or a coyote. He was regal and untamable.

John and Eldri Salter spent Christmas Day with the Everses, and Myrlie cooked them all dinner. It was a grim, rainy afternoon and the mood was no better. Medgar showed Salter the collection of guns he kept in the house and the German shepherd named Heidi who patrolled the backyard. They agreed that the beast was stirring in the state. A change was coming, and everyone knew the price.

"The white man won't change easily," Salter remembers Medgar saying. "Some of these people are going to fight hard. And more of our people could get killed."

Salter watched Myrlie listening quietly. He knew that she knew whose life was on the line.

*   *   *

COFO divided Mississippi into regions for each civil rights group to conquer. SNCC intensified its voter registration campaign in the Delta. In retaliation, the white fathers of LeFlore County decided to cut off surplus federal food aid, which was used to help the desperately poor part-time field hands and their families through the winter. People were literally starving in Greenwood.

SNCC organized a drive to distribute food and supplies and medicine to the Negroes of LeFlore County. Dick Gregory chartered a plane to fly fourteen thousand pounds of food from Chicago to Memphis, Tennessee, and then truck it down to Greenwood. The more food that was handed out, the more status SNCC gained among the people.

On Wednesday, February 20, 1963, six hundred people lined up in Greenwood for their rations. Two days later fifty Negroes silently lined up at the courthouse to register. That week several houses in the black part of Greenwood were torched.

On the night of February 28 Bob Moses and two other SNCC workers named Randolph Blackwell and James Travis drove out of town for a meeting in Greenville. A white Buick without license plates and carrying three white men followed them. About seven miles out of Greenwood the Buick pulled up beside them on the dark highway and sprayed the SNCC car with bullets.

Travis, who was driving, was hit in the neck and shoulder. Moses grabbed the wheel and stomped on the brakes as the car swerved off the road. Jimmy Travis survived, but only after a copper-jacketed slug was removed millimeters from his spinal cord.

Rather than run, Moses and the SNCC leadership called for an intensified campaign in Greenwood — more canvassers, more marches. The whites struck back. The SNCC office was destroyed by a firebomb. Sam Block and three others were showered with glass when someone fired a shotgun into their car.

That March John Salter and a group from Jackson drove to Greenwood with Medgar Evers. A mass rally was being held in the church now used as SNCC headquarters. Fifteen hundred people packed the church; three hundred more stood outside while police cruisers circled.

Medgar Evers was called to the stage to say a few words. The Greenwood campaign had moved him deeply. He saw what was possible when people overcame their fear and marched. If the movement could draw this kind of crowd in a redneck Delta backwater like Greenwood, think of what could be accomplished in the capital city.

Salter thinks it was a turning point for Evers. He could feel it in the words he spoke that night: "It's very good to see the number of persons out here tonight, and certainly this indicates that we're ready for freedom and ready to march for it. . . . We're going to go back to Jackson and fight for freedom as you're fighting for it here in Greenwood. . . . When we get this unity, ladies and gentlemen, nothing can stop us."

Dick Gregory was spending more and more time in Mississippi. He had an affinity for SNCC, and since the group was organizing in Greenwood, that is where Dick Gregory went. He waged a personal war with the police, defying them to arrest him, taunting them back when they taunted him.

"Nigger," he would hear a cop mutter.

"Yo' mother's a nigger!" Gregory would reply.

The cop would just gape at the pudgy black man in the big, audacious cowboy hat. The police took it from him, because word must have gotten out not to arrest Dick Gregory and make a martyr out of him. He couldn't get himself arrested. So he marched, and he watched while the cops beat on old ladies and young kids. The whites in Greenwood had no idea what to do with a black man who didn't fear them.

That wasn't the case in Alabama.

Gregory went from Greenwood to Birmingham that spring to join Martin Luther King's massive civil rights demonstrations. King had been arrested, and Dick Gregory was promptly thrown in jail as soon as he marched. It was in the Birmingham jail, he later said, that he received the first truly professional beating of his life.

By then Birmingham had cornered America's attention. The media ate it up. It was an allegorical pageant, a classic conflict of good versus evil, the easiest kind of symbolism for the nation to absorb. The saintly, nonviolent Dr. King battling the forces of evil represented by Eugene "Bull" Connor and his dogs. The TV cameras were rolling when the dogs were set loose on the peaceful marchers and the fire department opened up its power hoses on women and children, hurtling them into brick walls and down slick sidewalks. Charles Moore of *Life* magazine was there to capture every contortion and grimace on film.

The images from Birmingham probably turned the tide of public opinion against the segregationist South. King was anointed leader of the civil rights movement.

This was very disturbing to Roy Wilkins, particularly when UPI reported that Martin Luther King was considering a similar campaign in Mississippi. Not only was Wilkins jealous of King, but he and Gloster Current worried about the aftermath of massive demonstrations. What would happen to the people of Birmingham and Jackson and Greenwood once the outsiders got their headlines and packed up and moved on?

By now Medgar Evers had more or less committed himself to the idea of direct action. He quietly encouraged Martin Luther King to come to Jackson. Meanwhile the national leadership of the NAACP scrambled to keep King out of Mississippi.

The boycott of Capitol Street in Jackson had continued into the spring of 1963. The whites would not negotiate. When they could raise the bail money, the Youth Council kept up its pickets. In April Roy Wilkins ponied up five hundred dollars for the group and in a letter assured Salter that "we stand ready to assist in any way until success has been achieved." Salter was encouraged but baffled. He suspected that Wilkins's sudden interest had something to do with Birmingham.

By mid-May the Jackson Movement had gained momentum, and it was ready to throw down the gauntlet. A letter was sent to the governor and the mayor demanding an end to all racial discrimination in Jackson's stores, parks, public facilities, and schools. It put the Capitol Street gang on notice that they were about to have another Birmingham on their hands. Unless negotiations brought results, the letter promised to "step up and broaden our selective buying campaign." To accomplish the end of segregation, the letter said, "we shall use all lawful means of protest — picketing, marches, mass meetings, litigation, and whatever other means we deem necessary."

The letter was signed by John Salter, Doris Allison, and Medgar Evers.

On May 13 Mayor Thompson went on television to respond that he would never negotiate. Salter, Allison, and a number of other leaders and students piled into Medgar's office in the Masonic Temple and listened, slack jawed with disbelief, to the mayor's unctuous speech.

Thompson looked straight into the camera and said that Jackson was a place where the races lived "side by side in peace and harmony." Where the Negroes had "twenty-four-hour police protection." Where there were "no slums."

Speaking directly to his Negro citizens, he said, "You live in a city where you can work, where you can make a comfortable living. You are treated, no matter what anybody else tells you, with dignity, courtesy and respect. Ah, what a wonderful thing it is to live in this city. . . ! Refuse to pay any attention to any of these outside agitators who are interested only in getting money out of you, using you for their own selfish purposes."

Evers decided to demand equal time. For one thing he wanted the people to know that he was no outside agitator. He was a Mississippian.

Medgar Evers appealed to the station WLBT and the Federal Communications Commission to get equal time to reply to Allen Thompson's televised speech. The TV station, which was about to lose its broadcasting license because of biased coverage, gave in without a fight.

Medgar raced back from an out-of-town trip and arrived at the studio just in time to prerecord his speech on May 20.

Dave Dennis remembers feeling uneasy. Before this moment, Medgar Evers had just been a name in the newspapers. Very few white people could recognize him. The televised reply put Medgar too far out in front. It focused the attention, and the danger, on one man instead of spreading it around to many.

But someone from Mississippi had to reply to the mayor's charge that the demonstrations and boycotts were being led by "outside agitators." And so Medgar Evers began his speech with the words, "I speak as a native Mississippian."

Although many hands went into writing and revising the speech, it was pure Medgar: reasonable, forceful, and relentlessly logical. It must have rattled white Mississippians. Most of them knew Negroes only as farmhands and domestic workers. Here was a well-spoken, smart black man, a college graduate with a Yankee accent. And in a state where it was still the custom for a black to step off the sidewalk to let a white pass, here was a Negro talking back to the mayor of the capital city. Disputing him.

"Now, the mayor says that if the so-called outside agitators would leave us alone everything would be all right," Evers said. "This has always been the position of those who would deny Negro citizens their constitutional rights. . . . Never in history has the South, as a region, without outside pressure, granted the Negro his citizenship rights."

Evers moved lightly into the new world order: the winds of change that were sweeping Africa stirred hardly a breeze in his own home state.

"Tonight the Negro knows from his radio and television . . . about the new free nations in Africa, and knows that a Congo native can be a locomotive engineer, but in Jackson he cannot even drive a garbage truck.

". . . Then he looks about his home community and what does he see. . . ? He sees a city where Negro citizens are refused admittance to the City Auditorium and the Coliseum; his children refused a ticket to a good movie in a downtown theatre. . . . He sees a city of over 150,000, of which forty percent is Negro, in which there is not a single Negro policeman or policewoman, school crossing guard, fireman, clerk, stenographer, or supervisor employed in a city department. . . .

"What does the Negro want? He wants to get rid of racial segregation in Mississippi life because he knows it has not been good for him nor for the State. . . .

"Jackson can change if it wills to do so. . . . We believe there are white Mississippians who want to go forward on the race question. Their religion tells them there is something wrong with the old system. Their sense of justice and fair play send them the same message.

"But whether Jackson and the state choose change or not, the years of change are upon us. . . . History has reached a turning point, here and over the world."

Medgar Evers may have lacked the fire and poetry of Martin Luther King, but rarely has a better case been made for desegregation. King appealed to the heart; Evers went for the mind and the soul. He knew how to appeal to the sympathy of whites, and he knew he needed to win at least some of them to his cause. By his own example he could show whites that a black man could be reasonable, and educated, and well spoken. To a white supremacist, Medgar Evers, at that moment, must have seemed like the most dangerous man in Mississippi.

Even the Hederman newspapers couldn't completely ignore the speech, but the Jackson *Daily News* brushed it aside with a couple of columns and a glib headline: "Mix Drive Talked Up."

On Tuesday morning, May 28, the heat was building on the asphalt of Capitol Street. Three black Tougaloo students, all members of the Youth Council, walked into Woolworth's and sat down at the whites-only lunch counter.

Nervous waitresses turned off the lights and stopped serving. Ann Moody, Pearlena Lewis, and Memphis Norman sat impassively on the stools as word spread through town and a crowd of white men assembled around them.

It started with a few insults and grew into something unspeakable. Raucous teenagers dumped ketchup and mustard on the heads of the demonstrators. Then an ex-policeman named Benny Oliver grabbed Memphis Norman and threw him to the floor. He was stomped and kicked in the head while white cops stood by and watched.

When word of the sit-in reached NAACP headquarters, Medgar Evers wanted to ride over to Woolworth's, but John Salter talked him out of it. Salter went, along with some others, and waded into an ugly, surreal scene. Reporters and photographers and TV crews hovered around the counter while the mob threw food and screamed and slapped at the demonstrators. Norman had been hauled away unconscious, under arrest for disorderly conduct. Joan Trumpauer, the white student activist at Tougaloo, took his place and others came to join her. Salter sat down with them. A radio reporter was calling out the blows like a sports announcer at a ball game. BAM! Someone hit Salter on the side of the head, nearly knocking him off the stool. CRACK! Another blow from behind. Someone threw a mixture of water and pepper into Salter's eyes.

Medgar Evers later told Salter that FBI agents were in the store that day. They took notes but made no move to stop the violence. Police broke up the mob only when they started to smash the merchandise.

Many pictures were taken of this scene. One in particular captured the moment and went out over the wires to newspapers around the country. It shows John Salter hunched over the stainless steel counter covered with blood and ketchup and globs of mustard, his blond crew cut dusted with salt and sugar. Behind him a teenager in a checked shirt reaches to pour a canister of sugar over Trumpauer's neatly coiled hair and down the back of her summer dress. Ann Moody, covered with slop, stares down at her hands, holding back tears. The mob is literally on top of them, leering boys laughing and dragging on cigarettes. There are no police visible in the frame. There is one older man clearly seen at the edge of the mob, Red Hydrick, seems to be pushing his way to the front with a hungry, excited grin on his face.

By the end of the day, the mayor was ready to talk. Every network was carrying the sit-in footage, and Thompson seemed anxious to end the bad publicity. He offered to hire a Negro patrolman and a school crossing guard and a fireman, and he would support the gradual desegregation of public facilities — even schools — in Jackson.

The mayor's concessions were announced at a jubilant rally that evening. Later that night, however, Mayor Thompson went on the radio to deny that he had ever made such statements. All he had offered, he claimed, was to hire a few policemen and crossing guards, and not right away.

Medgar Evers got a message that night, too. The children were asleep in their beds, and Myrlie was waiting up for Medgar, reading a book. Just after midnight someone threw a Molotov cocktail at the house. A sheet of flames engulfed the carport.

Myrlie ran outside and turned a garden hose on the fire that was still burning near the gas tank of her car. When the police arrived, they sniffed around the carport for a while and picked up a broken brown bottle. One of the cops told Myrlie that the fire was probably just a prank.

A neighbor had called Medgar at NAACP headquarters, and he raced up in his car while police were questioning his wife. The reason he was late, he told Myrlie with a guilty smile, was that he had called a reporter with the story before leaving the office.

Heidi, the German shepherd, had been out in the carport waiting for Medgar when the firebomb hit. She disappeared for hours, then finally wandered home, wild-eyed and jumpy. She was never right again after that night.

12

The Last Warning

On THURSDAY, May 30, 1963, a group of students at Lanier High School started singing freedom songs on the school lawn. It was a spontaneous protest; nothing had been planned. Before long dozens of children poured out of their classrooms and started singing with them. The Jackson police surrounded the school and eventually drove the students back into the building with dogs and clubs. Some parents who came to take their children home also were beaten.

Charles Diggs, the black congressman from Detroit who was a longtime advocate for civil rights in Mississippi, sent an urgent telegram to President Kennedy. Diggs protested the police violence at Lanier High School and implored the president to send federal troops to Jackson to avoid a disaster.

"As bad as Burmingham was," the congressman wired, "will it take the death or maiming of someone before you realize that Mississippi is even worse?"

Lee C. White, a White House counsel, responded for the President. All he would say was that the Justice Department was following the situation closely.

*　　　*　　　*

That afternoon John Salter noticed an odd sight downtown. There was a Shriners convention in Jackson that day, and white men wearing red fezzes were wandering around the city streets.

He didn't think much of it. Salter and a group of teachers and clergy were on their way to demonstrate at the federal building in Jackson, thinking that they might be safe on U.S. property. They were wrong. Police arrested them all.

Salter had a new friend and ally with him that day. Ed King was a rare bird: a young white Methodist minister and a native-born Mississippian who had joined the Tougaloo staff as chaplain a few months earlier. King had studied at Millsaps College and later at Boston University and was already a veteran of the civil rights struggle. He had been arrested for demonstrating in Montgomery. Now he was fully committed to the Jackson Movement.

On Friday afternoon six hundred high school students gathered at the Farish Street Baptist Church, emptied their pockets of anything sharp that might be considered a dangerous weapon, and grabbed hold of little American flags. Medgar Evers and John Salter gave them encouraging speeches, and then they marched, two by two, out of the church, singing freedom songs.

The slow march turned right, heading toward Capitol Street, into the late spring heat, and ran straight into a phalanx of blue-helmeted riot cops. Behind the riot police were rows and rows of county sheriffs and state cops. When the children reached them, the cops shouted "Run!" and when some of them did, the police fired shots over their heads. The cops pounced on the others, ripping the flags from their hands and throwing them in the dust.

Medgar and Salter stood on the sidewalk watching. Salter saw Medgar's face darken, the deep lines grow deeper.

The police arrested everyone on the street. They manhandled the children back through the ranks of officers and threw them into hot, stinking trucks that were used to haul garbage. The children were then carted off, still singing, to the state fairgrounds animal stockades that had been specially prepared for demonstrators.

That night Roy Wilkins came down from New York and spoke to fifteen hundred people jammed into the Masonic Temple auditorium. This was not the usual middle-class NAACP crowd. There were black folks from every part of town. Their children were getting arrested, and now they were involved. Wilkins, who was usually a wooden, boring speaker, caught fire that night. He compared Mississippi to Hitler's Germany, and he had the people rocking. But Wilkins never mentioned more demonstrations. The students, who had planned to remain in the stockades — like the demonstrators in Birmingham — were being quietly bailed out by NAACP lawyers.

The phone threats were increasing at the Evers house.

Medgar had become more concerned about an ambush after the firebombing. He would stand out in front of the carport and stare at the vacant lot across the street. He told Myrlie he was going to see if he could get that brush cleared.

On a hot Saturday morning, the first day of June, John Salter drove Medgar, Roy Wilkins, and a Jackson woman named Helen Wilcher down to Capitol Street. They carried hand-printed placards in paper bags and took them out when they arrived in front of Woolworth's. Wilkins's sign said, "Don't buy on Capitol Street." Medgar Evers's said, "End brutality in Jackson — NAACP."

As soon as they arrived, they were arrested. The news crews were on hand, and a picture of the arrest shows Medgar in a puckered summer suit, white shirt, and thin dark tie. He glares at a policeman who is about to take the sign from him. He seems to be containing himself from fighting back. In the foreground, a white hand holds a cattle prod.

They were out on bond before they saw the inside of a cell. John Salter was preparing to march with two hundred more demonstrators when Evers and Wilkins arrived back at the Masonic Temple.

Wilkins, Salter remembers, looked at them silently, then said, "No more marches. Not today, anyway, and probably not for a while."

Medgar said nothing. Ed King and Salter pleaded with Wilkins to relent, and he did. "Well, go ahead and have it," he said.

Once again the marchers were run down and thrown into garbage trucks. Some were clubbed. In all some seven hundred demonstrators, mostly children, were jailed in the stockades.

That night Martin Luther King, Jr., was on the phone to his adviser, Stanley Levison, in New York. We know this because the FBI was taping the call. King gleefully reported that the NAACP chairman had finally gotten himself arrested. "We've finally baptized brother Wilkins!" he said.

Dick Gregory had just been released after five days in the Birmingham jail. He was in San Francisco to do his show at the hungry i when he heard about the demonstrations in Jackson. He called Medgar Evers to see if he could help. He felt he owed Medgar, since it was Evers who had first brought him to Mississippi, introduced him to Clyde Kennard, and changed his life.

As Gregory was getting ready to fly south, he had a premonition that someone was about to die. He thought it would be him, that he would be gunned down in Mississippi. So he checked to make sure his will was valid. And then he headed for Jackson.

Dick Gregory flew all night and got to Jackson late. He was asleep at a minister's house when Medgar Evers called him. "Greg, you better call home," Evers said.

"What happened?"

"I don't know. Your son's sick."

"Medgar?"

"I'm sorry, Greg. Your son's dead."

Richard Gregory, Jr., had died sleeping in his crib. The baby wasn't three months old. Gregory canceled his appearance and flew home to Chicago. He told Medgar he'd be back as soon as he could.

In Chicago he was getting calls from Greenwood. Mean white voices told him they were glad his son was dead, that it served him right.

Martin Luther King and other civil rights leaders were waiting in the wings, hesitant to join the fight in Mississippi and risk the wrath of the NAACP. In Jackson the political lines had been drawn: the direct-action group, comprised of Salter, Ed King, Dave Dennis, and the youth leaders, versus the NAACP leadership and a timid group of ministers who had yet to join in any demonstration. The old guard was winning.

Gloster Current recalls that the decision to stop the direct-action campaign in Jackson was a simple one. The bail money had run out. Demonstrations and arrests were just too expensive. Besides they were not really the NAACP's style. And the last thing the NAACP wanted was some outsider like Martin Luther King, Jr., coming in, stirring things up, and getting people killed, and then picking up and leaving the NAACP to clean up the mess.

Medgar Evers was caught in the middle. He was even thinking about quitting. He had been offered a job in Los Angeles. Maybe he could take it and get out. Or he could join forces with King and start a real movement in Jackson.

Evers's friend Vernon Jordan had quit the NAACP in April. He had called Medgar in Jackson with the news, telling him that he had taken a big job with better pay at the Southern Regional Council. Ruby Hurley, he said, was furious and refused to talk to him.

Medgar told Vernon that he was happy for him. Evers said that he knew it was the right decision and that he should do the same. "But I can't leave," he told his friend. "This is my place, and this is what I've got to do and where I've got to be." They promised to keep in touch.

What Medgar Evers eventually wanted to do was go to law school, get his degree, and then run for Congress. But right now he couldn't leave Mississippi; he couldn't leave the NAACP. He might as well try to quit his own family, abandon his own heart.

On Monday, June 3, students showed up for demonstrations and were told by NAACP national staff to go home. It was a cooling-off period, they said. Small groups of pickets were still being brought down to Woolworth's, but the big street marches were over.

That afternoon Mayor Allen Thompson told the press that the crisis was over. He said he would begin taking applications for Negro policemen and school crossing guards.

Medgar Evers implored the national press to stick around, telling them that the Jackson Movement was still rolling. But they left for bigger stories. A showdown was building between the Kennedys and the governor of Alabama. The local newspapers were crowing the demise of the movement.

On Wednesday, June 5, nine demonstrators were arrested on Capitol Street. Their crime was walking on the sidewalk while wearing NAACP T-shirts and holding American flags.

About this time a young reporter from the New York *Amsterdam News* named Sara Slack got an interview with Medgar Evers. She had been trailing him for days, but there had never been time to talk. One afternoon he invited her to drive down to Capitol Street with him. Three teenage demonstrators huddled in the back of his Oldsmobile, below the window line, so they wouldn't be arrested before they got there. He watched them take the gold points off their American flags so they wouldn't be charged with carrying dangerous weapons.

On the drive downtown Medgar pointed out the sights to Slack, like a tour guide in purgatory: There's City Hall and the Governor's Mansion. See those white men walking over there? That's the secretary and treasurer of the Citizens' Councils.

Medgar dropped off the boys, who were promptly arrested. As he drove away to report the arrests to the children's parents, a police car pulled up beside the Olds. The passenger rolled down his window. Evers did the same.

"Hello, Medgar. How ya' doin?" said police chief James L. Ray.

Evers said hello. The two men exchanged pleasant words and drove off to different parts of the city.

Medgar asked Sara Slack if she had noticed the red eyes and weary faces of the cops on Capitol Street. "It's a wonderful thing," he said, chuckling. "We're keeping these cops as busy as hell."

Slack asked Medgar about his heroes, and he told her that the two men who had most influenced him were Jomo Kenyatta and Dr. T. R. M. Howard. But it was World War II that shaped him. When he came back from France at the end of the war, he saw his own country with new eyes. "I knew if I didn't fight for what we are entitled to," he told her, "I'd be less than a man."

W. C. "Dub" Shoemaker was a young reporter for the Jackson *Daily News,* and the Negro movement was part of his beat. During the days of demonstrations, Shoemaker attended every NAACP mass meeting that was open to the press. Sometimes he went alone. Sometimes he went with a new undercover detective named Jim Black, who was gathering information for an injunction against the leaders of the movement.

Shoemaker happened to be by himself at a meeting at the African Methodist Episcopal (AME) Church on West Street where one firebrand preacher was, in Dub's opinion, stirring up the crowd. Some unfavorable news broadcast had aired that night, and the preacher was shouting about the unfair press coverage. Before long the crowd was on its feet, yelling, "Get 'em, get 'em!" Dub suddenly felt conspicuously white and definitely in the wrong line of work, and he started glancing at the door. Suddenly Medgar Evers stood up, grabbed the preacher by the shoulders, and tossed the man away from the microphone.

"Sit down!" Evers said.

To Shoemaker's amazement the hard, angry crowd instantly melted. People sank down in their chairs, and Medgar Evers quietly continued the meeting.

On Thursday, June 6, Salter was served with an injunction — *City of Jackson v. John Salter Jr. et al.* — naming Medgar Evers, Dick Gregory, Dave Dennis, and a slew of others and preventing them from sponsoring, encouraging, or engaging in any picketing, demonstrations, or anything else that annoyed the city fathers. Jack Young and the other NAACP lawyers drew up a proper legal response, but no mass defiance was planned, just a few pickets every day.

John Salter reluctantly decided to send his wife and infant daughter back to her parents in Minnesota. It was too dangerous for them to stay in Jackson. Carloads of white boys prowled the roads between the city and Tougaloo. Someone loosened the lug nuts on Salter's car. It felt to John like it was only a matter of time.

More than three thousand people crammed into the Masonic Temple auditorium on the night of Friday, June 7. Riot police lined Lynch Street. It was a big night for the faltering movement. Lena Horne was there to give a speech and a performance; Dick Gregory had left his son's graveside to be there for Medgar Evers.

Ruby Hurley introduced Lena Horne to the crowd. While Ruby was speaking, Medgar handed her a note to ask some white men in the audience to quit smoking, since the fire codes prohibited it. When she made the announcement, people turned and looked at the white strangers. Instead of putting out the cigarettes, they got up and left.

Gloster Current, NAACP director of branches, saw the white men in the audience, sitting over by the right side of the auditorium. Current thought he had seen one of the men earlier that day. That afternoon he had been typing in the upstairs NAACP office where background material was made available to the press. He noticed two white men looking around. When Lillian Louie, the secretary, asked them what they wanted, they left.

Henry Kirksey, who worked for the Mississippi Teachers' Association in another office in the building, had seen the men in the stairwell. One, a short, dark-haired man, was acting out something to his friend. He was crouching down, pretending to fire a pistol. Kirksey would later say the man looked a lot like Byron De La Beckwith. John Salter thought that Beckwith was one of the white men in the audience that night, and so did Ruby Hurley.

Dick Gregory remembers that the auditorium was hot and crowded. There was a bad feeling in the air, and a fear. He thought someone might try to bomb the place. Anything could happen.

"You people here in the state of Mississippi carry the key," Gregory said. "When you finish freeing yourselves, you'll free the North. When you shake the vicious beast — the white man — off your backs, even the Indians will run off the reservations."

Gregory got a dozen standing ovations that night. As he picked up momentum, he tried to lighten the atmosphere a little. That was his job — to name what people feared and make them laugh about it.

Gregory joked about his attraction to white women. It was the white man's fault, he declared. "You can't advertise Bufferins without a blonde. So, I need a blonde to help me get rid of my headaches."

Roars of laughter.

"The white man thinks he knows us! He doesn't. He can't! . . . What this foolish white man doesn't know is that for all that time, we've been sitting there in the back of the bus studying him, watching him and knowing him better than he knows himself."

Gregory saw some white faces in the crowd. "I know you policemen are down there at the press tables taking notes and pretending to be reporters," he said. "Well write this. Go downtown and tell your white daddy to get the barbed wire ready, 'cause we're coming tomorrow!" The crowd reacted with great waves of applause and shouts and stomping ovations.

There were many speakers that night. Gene Young, a nine-year-old boy who was small for his age, stood on a packing crate to reach the microphone. He told the crowd how he had been a prisoner in the stockades and a policeman had twisted his arm in its socket because the boy wouldn't call him "sir." He was willing to do it all again, he said.

"Let's march!" Gene shouted, poking his little fist to the sky. One of the NAACP staffers gently ushered him off the stage.

No marches were announced that night. The people of Jackson didn't know it yet, but a decision had been made in New York. No more bail money. No more demonstrations.

Medgar Evers gave the final, wrap-up speech. Myrlie sat in the audience in her cauldron of emotions — pride, excitement, love, and fear. Mainly she felt fear when the list of events and fund-raisers was finished and he began to speak from his heart.

"Freedom has never been free," he told the crowd. ". . . I love my children and I love my wife with all my heart. And I would die, die gladly, if that would make a better life for them."

After the meeting, Dick Gregory talked to Medgar Evers. He was scared for him. He could feel it in the air, he could see it in the faces of the police — they *knew* something was going to happen. Now that his son was dead, Gregory no longer thought it was his turn to die. He just hugged Medgar and said, "I probably won't be seeing you no more."

Dick Gregory left Jackson the next day.

There was a rare party after the mass meeting at the Masonic Temple. Myrlie thought it was wonderful just to have a drink and talk; it seemed almost normal. Medgar seemed unusually attentive. The children were being minded by a friend, so Myrlie and Medgar didn't leave until two in the morning. They left in separate cars, dropping off friends along the way.

Medgar and his group discussed the white strangers they had seen in the audience that night. And then someone mentioned that he had seen the white men follow them when they left the temple.

Medgar stepped on the gas and got home just as Myrlie and the kids drove up. She wondered why he had driven so fast.

Dave Dennis was living in the Maple Street apartments in Jackson, where Medgar and Myrlie had first lived. He was organizing the mean little town of Canton in the spring of 1963. It was rough up there, just twenty miles north of Jackson. The whole town was run by the Citizen's Council, and there were some bad cops and worse deputies. It was getting so that Dennis's white station wagon was recognized and stopped every night.

On Saturday, June 8, Dennis asked Medgar Evers if they could switch cars for the day. Maybe he wouldn't be recognized in Canton for a change.

That night Dennis went to a meeting up in Madison County, and on the way back to Jackson two or three carloads of white men pulled alongside and stopped him. They forced him out of the car. They said they knew who he was, and they asked him where he was going, called him nigger this and nigger that. Dennis thought, *This is it,* and he got ready for the worst. But it was cotton-chopping time in Madison County, and two big truckloads of fieldhands out working late came churning down the road. The rednecks had to move their cars and Dennis took the opportunity to jump back into his and fly back to Jackson as fast as Medgar's car would go. Medgar had a fast car.

When Dennis met Evers at the mass meeting in Jackson that night, he joked about it. "A man could get killed driving your car!" he said. Medgar laughed. He told Dennis a cop had tried to run him down that afternoon when he stepped out of Dennis's car. He said, "Why don't you come back to the house and have a drink?" But Dave Dennis was tired, and he wanted to get some sleep.

Everyone could see that Medgar Evers was exhausted. He was making himself sick. So that Sunday Myrlie made him stay home most of the day. Later she remembered some of the things he had said to her that day. She wanted him to buy a new suit. They argued about it in a playful way. Where would he get the money? When she pressed him, he got serious. "Myrlie, I won't be needing a suit," he said.

Medgar worried that night that his life insurance wasn't up to date. He needed to borrow some money to pay the premium. Myrlie persuaded him to wait for his next paycheck.

Medgar spent most of the day at home, and ate Sunday dinner with the family. He played with the children. He took a nap and was starting to feel better.

Later that night Medgar phoned his brother, Charles, in Chicago. They called each other often, at least twice a month. Medgar was worried about Charlie. He knew that he was having trouble with the Chicago mob.

Charles Evers was a rich man now, the owner of three taverns, including the Club Mississippi on the South Side and a twenty-four-unit apartment house at Sixty-second and Normal, where he lived with his family. He had arrived broke, but Charles Evers knew how to make money every way there is to make it.

He started using some of his old business skills. He worked as a washroom attendant. He took a day job as a science teacher in a public school. But his energy went into building up the nightclubs, a prostitution ring, a jukebox business, and a numbers racket. That's where he was running into some trouble with the Mafia, who felt that all jukeboxes and numbers games should be in their control.

Medgar usually didn't want to hear about his brother's businesses, and Charles kept him in the dark as much as he could. He knew Medgar didn't approve. But Medgar knew there was a turf battle brewing in Chicago. Charles tried to reassure him.

"These damn dagos are trying to take over, but I'm goin' to lay with 'em."

Medgar said, "Charles, you be careful now. They'll kill you."

"No, *you* be careful about those damn Klukkers down there. They are much more detrimental than these dagos up here. I got my hoods, too."

Charles knew about the threats against Medgar and how some fool had thrown a Molotov cocktail at the house. He was planning to carry his brother out of there for a long vacation. Neither man had taken time off in years. Charles had bought a brand-new shiny black Cadillac, and they were going to drive as far south as they could, then somehow get to Brazil, where they had bought some land. Forty acres. Just like in their dreams, when they were kids.

Charles had it all planned out. They would leave in early July, for Medgar's birthday, spend a month relaxing, and be back in Chicago in time for the NAACP convention.

There was a little pause in the conversation.

"Charles, I worry about y'all," Medgar said.

"Don't worry about me. I won't be here!" said Charles, trying to lighten it up. "You just be careful. Don't go in the woods, some ol' redneck down there may lay around there and shoot your brains out."

"Don't you worry, I'll take care of that."

"Lope, I'll see ya in July."

"I hope so."

"Wha'dya mean, you *hope* so?"

"If I'm not too busy."

It was the way he said it that bothered Charles.

"You want me to come down there?"

"Nope, I'm all right. I'll be all right."

"Okay, I'll check you later."

Both men were crying when they hung up. Charles almost called back to tell him to come up to Chicago for a few days, but he knew Medgar would never leave.

On Monday it got even hotter.

There was another angry meeting at the Masonic Temple that evening, and John Salter suggested inviting the SCLC into Jackson to pick up the pieces of the direct-action movement. He recalls that the NAACP staffers shouted him down. Medgar Evers sat tight and silent.

As it turns out, Medgar had received a phone call from Dr. Felix Dunn, the Gulfport NAACP president. Dunn had learned through a white lawyer he knew that the Ku Klux Klan had Medgar on a hit list. There would be an assassination attempt, soon. He should put some guards around his house.

On Tuesday, June 11, the police presence around the Masonic Temple had vaporized. Only a handful of riot cops guarded Capitol Street. But surveillance seemed to be at an all-time peak.

That afternoon John Salter and Steve Rutledge, another white NAACP worker from Tougaloo, drove a group of students wearing NAACP T-shirts downtown to walk around Capitol Street. Police cars trailed behind wherever they went. Finally Salter parked on Farish Street and walked back to the unmarked car that pulled in, as expected, right behind him. He wanted to know why he was being followed so closely. Suddenly the detective's door swung open, hitting Salter and nearly knocking him off his feet.

When Salter went to the Masonic Temple to report the incident, he found Medgar Evers in the almost-empty auditorium. Medgar said the same thing had happened to him the Saturday before: a police car had nearly hit him as he crossed the street. He said he was being followed too.

At 3:45 P.M. Medgar called the FBI to report the incident with the Jackson police car. He told the FBI that between 4 and 5 P.M. the previous Saturday, he had been walking down Lynch Street, crossing Franklin, when a police car had shot out at him, causing him to jump back on the curb. The cops inside had laughed. He gave the FBI man the police car license number.

He told them something else. Today he was being followed everywhere he went by a police car. The FBI man said he would pass the information on to the Justice Department.

Medgar called home three times that day, just to tell Myrlie he loved her and to chat with the children. Once he called to talk about the scene on television that afternoon. Governor George Wallace had stepped aside to allow the registration of two black students at the University of Alabama.

It was a tense time across the South, but the red spotlight was now on Alabama. The Kennedys feared another performance like the one at Oxford the previous fall. To their relief George Wallace kept his word. He postured and huffed and strutted and declared the federal government unconstitutional.Then he backed down and allowed the students to enter the university without bloodshed.

President Kennedy seized the moment and lashed together a speech for broadcast that night. It was one of the best of his career.

The speech aired in Mississippi at 7 P.M. Myrlie gathered the children around the TV set. Kennedy described the "moral crisis" of race relations. He called for changes in the law and in "all of our daily lives." And he outlined a new civil rights bill he had in mind to break down the legal barriers between the races.

Myrlie was elated. She couldn't wait to talk about it with Medgar when he got home.

A lot of people say they saw Medgar Evers that night. Henry Lamb, one of Medgar's childhood friends from Forest, Mississippi, was in Jackson to attend a convention of Negro Elks. He says he had dinner with Medgar at a restaurant in Jackson. Others remember Medgar stopping by the Elks Lodge later for a drink and a talk with his old friends. There was a poker game going on, but Medgar didn't stay long. Gloster Current, a Methodist minister, was in town, and Medgar couldn't very well bring him there. And there was the mass meeting, usually at a different place but at the same time every night.

People remember that Medgar Evers came late to the mass meeting at the New Jerusalem Baptist Church. The enthusiasm for the movement had waned, and the church wasn't full. Some NAACP staffers from New York and Memphis talked about voter registration in Jackson. There was a discussion of T-shirt sales. John Salter saw Medgar on his way out. Medgar seemed so tired.

Salter drove home to Tougaloo after the meeting ended at about eleven o'clock. When he got back to his empty house, he took out the .44/40 rifle that Medgar Evers had loaned him and set it by the bed before he fell into an uneasy sleep.

Clarie Harvey's family owned the biggest Negro funeral home in Jackson. She was a prominent person, and her income did not depend on the white man's business, so it was possible for her to keep a high profile in the civil rights movement. She and some other women had formed a support group for the Freedom Riders, and now she was backing the Jackson Movement as best she could. She met Medgar in the church vestibule and was shocked by the look on his face. It was just awful, taut like a death mask. He smiled when he saw her and offered her a ride home. She said thanks, but she didn't need one. She had her bodyguards with her.

Medgar Evers didn't have any bodyguards. But he did have James Wells, who had come by to check on him.

Wells had been fishing that day, but he stopped at the meeting on his way home. He had a bad feeling. Evers was gathering up a group of students to drive them home. Wells told him to get on back to his family; Wells would take care of the students. Medgar said no, he had to go see his lawyer later anyway. So James Wells drove home.

At about 11:30 P.M. Medgar pulled up to Jack and Aurelia Young's house, hoping to find something to eat. He knew Aurelia Young had a crowd staying with her, and she always kept a pot of something on the stove. He didn't want Myrlie to have to get up and cook for him when he got home.

Jack was the only black lawyer in Jackson, and he spent most of his time working for the NAACP. He had put himself through law school while working as a postman. Aurelia was a gifted composer who taught music at Jackson State. They were close friends of the Everses.

Aurelia was on the phone when Medgar came to the door. She was talking to Jack. He was telling her they needed some more mimeograph paper at the law office. They were preparing a brief to respond to the injunction against demonstrations in Jackson. Was that Medgar? Great. He could bring it.

Medgar didn't stop to eat. He went back to the Masonic Temple to get the paper. Gloster Current, who was visiting the Youngs, offered to go with him. When they got to the temple, Gloster looked up at the clock. It was ten minutes to midnight.

Evers got the paper, then drove his boss back to the Youngs' house. Current picked up his rental car to drive the supplies to the law office.

Medgar dropped him at the door and shook his hand, holding it for a long time. Gloster was leaving town the next morning for an NAACP conference.

"Mississippi will never be the same," he told Gloster. "It will never be the same." He let go at last and said, "I'm tired. I want to get home to my family."

Then he drove off.

13

The Hour of Lead

THE HEAT SETTLED in that night of June 11, 1963. Myrlie Evers propped open the bedroom window, and the air filled with the heavy scent of honeysuckle carried in on a sluggish breeze.

That evening Myrlie had allowed the children to wait up for their father. She had moved the television into the bedroom. She let the dog, Heidi, out to wait at the front door. Then she lay down on the bed. By midnight the baby was sleeping (a third child, James Van Dyke Evers, had arrived in 1960) and Myrlie was half-dozing, while the two older children watched a late movie.

Just before 12:30 A.M., the children heard the sound of their father's car and the crackle of tires on the drive.

"There's Daddy!"

Evers parked his pale blue Oldsmobile behind his wife's station wagon. The assassin was waiting in the overgrown lot across the street. He had cleared out a nest in a honeysuckle thicket two hundred feet from the Everses' front door.

Medgar Evers wore a white shirt that night, and it must have glowed like a beacon in the crosshairs of the sniper's scope as Evers climbed out of the car and into the moonlight. He picked up an arm-load of paperwork and NAACP T-shirts, then slammed the car door shut.

Betty Coley wanted to get out of the house for a while. She had been arguing with her mother all night, and she thought she might as well go for a walk to cool off. Kenneth Adcock, the seventeen-year-old boarder, went along with her.

It was late when they left, about 11:15. The streets were lit by moon-light. The two talked as they walked in the lambent night air, down Merrydale Street, where they lived, down Missouri, past the Negro neighborhood on Guynes, and across Delta Drive to Hawkins Field, the airport, just a short stroll to the west. They watched the planes landing and taking off. It was after midnight when they began to retrace their steps back home.

Kenneth Adcock remembers passing the intersection of Guynes and Missouri and his shoulder brushing against the overgrown honeysuckle in front of a vacant lot. He remembers seeing the headlights of a car on Guynes Street. Then something exploded in the bushes, right behind him.

There is something about a close shot that leaves a vacuum behind, as if the blast sucks all the air out of the atmosphere around it. Things slow down while your senses rearrange themselves. As Betty Coley and Ken-neth Adcock stood in the road, in that frozen moment, they both heard the same thing: the crunching of undergrowth as someone ran back into the woods.

The bullet smashed into Evers's back, just below the right shoulder blade. The slug tore through him, then through a window and a kitchen wall, before it glanced off the refrigerator and landed on a counter. When Myrlie Evers ran to the front door, she found her husband sprawled facedown, one arm stretched out, his fingers still gripping the house keys. Medgar had somehow dragged himself around her car, leaving a jagged trail of blood.

When Darrell and Reena heard the shot, they pulled Van down to the floor, just like their daddy had taught them. Then they followed their mother to the door.

Myrlie was hysterical. The children ran over to their father's body, screaming, "Daddy! Get up!"

Houston and Jean Wells were asleep when they heard the shot next door. Houston looked out the window and saw Medgar lying facedown on the ground. Wells grabbed his pistol and crept outside. Whoever was doing the shooting was about to find out that there weren't going to be any more soft targets on Guynes Street. Wells fired a shot in the air. Jean called his brother James to come help.

It was 12:45 A.M., June 12, 1963, when Detective Captain B. D. Harrell picked up the ringing telephone at Jackson police headquarters. The caller said there had been a shooting at 2332 Guynes Street. Harrell told Fred Sanders and John Chamblee, the two detectives on duty, to drive right over there. He told the dispatcher to radio for the nearest patrol car to respond to the scene.

Aurelia Young picked up the phone again, thinking it was Jack wanting something else. She heard Myrlie Evers on the line, wailing and weeping.

"Medgar's been shot!"

That couldn't be, Aurelia thought. Medgar was just here.

"Well get off the phone!" she said. "I'll get a doctor!"

Aurelia tried to call Jack at his office, but the line was busy.

When Gloster Current reached Jack Young's office, the phone was ringing. Myrlie was on the line, shouting that someone had killed her husband.

Gloster and Jack Young jumped into Jack's car. They stopped to pick up Aurelia and headed toward Guynes Street. Young kept a gun in the glove compartment, and he checked to be sure it was there.

James Wells lived on Crawford Street, only a few minutes south of Guynes. When his sister-in-law called, he jumped in his truck, where he knew there was a loaded shotgun, and raced up Delta Drive toward Medgar's house. He turned onto Missouri Street where it hit Delta and was almost at the intersection of Missouri and Guynes when he saw a man running between two houses, heading toward the highway. He couldn't see whether the man was white or black. It seemed he was tall, but then Wells was sitting in a pickup, and it was hard to tell. The man's clothes were dark, but he wore white shoes that glowed in the moonlight as he ran.

At this point James Wells figured the gunman was still out there; maybe there was a whole group of them. So Wells got out of his car and fired the shotgun at the ground, hoping to scare them off.

Wells reached the Everses' driveway just as his brother Houston was carrying out a mattress to lift Medgar into his station wagon. It looked bad. A cop car was at the house, with two uniformed patrolmen just sitting there watching. People from all over the neighborhood were gathering in the driveway.

Myrlie, who was thirty years old and strong, clawed through the crowd to climb into the station wagon with her husband, but her neighbors held her back. The squad car pulled out in front of the station wagon to escort it to University Hospital.

Medgar Evers came awake during that ride to the hospital. He tried to sit up. He mumbled and thrashed and fought while his chest filled with blood. Houston Wells, who was driving, remembers the last thing he said before he died was, "Turn me loose."

Myrlie Evers was left behind in the bloody carport with her weeping children and the stunned, murmuring neighbors. The street filled with squad cars, then reporters and photographers arrived, popping flashbulbs and trampling the lawn. Myrlie felt a searing, molten hatred rising through her. If she had a machine gun, she thought, she would mow down every white man in the crowd. She had no doubt who murdered her husband. His name didn't matter; it was all of them. She could have killed them all.

As soon as he got the call, Dr. Albert Britton, the Everses' family doctor, drove straight to the University of Mississippi Hospital, where Medgar was taken. When Britton got there he found the emergency room doctors trying to revive Evers. Britton didn't think they were moving fast enough. He could not treat his old friend because he was a Negro and this was a white man's hospital. But Britton made sure the doctors knew who they were working on.

"This man is Medgar Evers, field secretary of the NAACP!" Britton told them.

One of the white doctors whispered, "Oh, my God."

Dr. Britton sat by Medgar's side. He realized there was nothing anyone could do for the man. Evers's chest was torn to pieces. It was amazing he could still breathe. Britton called his name, and Medgar turned his head, gulped for air, and was gone.

By the time Jack and Aurelia Young and Gloster Current arrived at the Evers house, Medgar had already been moved. Aurelia stayed with Myrlie while the men went to the hospital.

Aurelia Young had never seen so much human blood before, and it was not as she had imagined. It was thick, like blobs of jelly; it didn't run. Myrlie couldn't keep still. She kept walking out onto the carport, stepping over those blobs of blood, and Aurelia kept coaxing her back inside, trying to keep her occupied. She started to pack some of Medgar's things to take to the hospital, although they knew it was probably hopeless.

Another friend, Hattie Tate, walked into the bedroom. She couldn't speak. There had been a phone call. Hattie's face was like a crumpled paper bag. Medgar's death was all over it. Myrlie took one look at Hattie Tate and fell down weeping.

Dr. Britton drove over to see what he could do for Myrlie. He held her as he told her he was there with Medgar at the end. She was already starting to ask herself whether she could have saved him if she hadn't panicked. Britton assured her there was nothing anyone could have done to keep Medgar alive. On the level of reason she believed him. On another level she never would.

The children were across the street at a neighbor's house, still crying and hysterical. Myrlie had to gather up everything she had left in her to go over there to calm them down. Then she had to tell them that their father was dead.

John Salter was asleep in his house on the Tougaloo campus when he heard a knock at the door. He reached for the .44/40 Medgar had loaned him and shouted through the door. The voice of his friend George Owen, a Tougaloo official, called back. George Owen had bad news. Medgar Evers had been shot. Salter called Houston Wells, who told him that Medgar was dead.

*   *   *

Dave Dennis had just come back from Canton after an exhausting night of organizing. He was drifting to sleep when the phone rang in his Maple Street apartment. The news that Medgar was dead sat like a stone inside him. He couldn't make himself go to the house, or the hospital, or the funeral home. Instead for the next few days he hung on the fringes, like a shadow, where he could be comfortable and invisible to all but his own people.

The police were crawling all over the place for the rest of the night. One detective asked her if Medgar had any enemies, and she laughed. He asked if Medgar had been having an affair, and she tried to throw him out.

Myrlie wondered what had happened to the family dog during all this commotion. She'd never heard her bark, and there was no sign of her now. Much later, when the shepherd finally came home, the light seemed to be gone from her eyes.

Television news crews had arrived before dawn, and they set up their lights in the driveway. The footage that survives from that time shows the essential elements of the crime scene: the thick blood on the concrete, the cars, the crowd of distraught people huddled at the front door around Myrlie Evers. She wears a light-colored dress, and there is a look of shock and distraction on her face as she waves her hand dismissively at the crowd or the lights or the scene itself, as if she could wash it all away with a gesture. Her eyes are the eyes of a blind woman.

The camera follows the detectives as they measure the crime scene. It lingers on a neat hole in the front window. Then the camera moves inside the house, and you can imagine these white strangers tramping through the hallways, gaping at another hole in the living room wall beneath the bronze plaque — some sort of award — and into the kitchen. There is a spotless ceramic sink, a wire rack of draining dishes, a watermelon set out on the counter for the next day's lunch, and a pencil stub on the counter marking the spot where the bullet that killed Medgar Evers came to rest.

It was Detective Fred Sanders who found the bullet, wrapped it up, put it in his pocket and marked the spot. Sanders and his partner, John Chamblee, then traced the path of the bullet back to the window. They completed the trajectory by standing next to the hole in the window and shining a flashlight beam over the car and the spot where blood marked the place where Evers had been hit. The beam traveled across Guynes Street, over a triangular corner of lawn and a four-foot chain-link fence. From there the beam crossed Missouri Street and illuminated a clump of honeysuckle under a sweet gum tree in an overgrown vacant lot.

Outside the detectives got down on hands and knees, and shining the flashlight over the grass in the corner lot, they looked for signs that the dew had been disturbed by footsteps. They checked the fence to see whether any dust had been brushed away, perhaps by a gunman leaning against it with a rifle. They found nothing.

The detectives turned their attention to the vacant lot. That was where they found a sniper's nest carefully hollowed in the honeysuckle and a path leading back toward Delta Drive, to the dark end of a parking lot attached to a burger joint known as Joe's Drive In.

Chamblee examined the spot in the bushes where the grass was flattened. There were no spent cartridges, no cigarette butts, no gum wrappers, nothing left behind. All he found were freshly mashed leaves and a broken branch forming a hole in the thicket four and a half feet above ground level.

It was a spot perfectly concealed from passersby, or customers at the stores out on Delta Drive, two hundred feet west. A man standing in the hollow would have had a clear view of Medgar Evers's house and driveway.

Detective Sergeant O. M. Luke arrived around eight in the morning. All kinds of gawkers and newspaper people were hanging around. Cars were everywhere, and maybe fifteen cops were stationed around to make sure things didn't get trampled worse than they were. It was already getting hot.

Luke and his partner, R. O. Turner, drove over to University Hospital, where an autopsy was being performed on the body of Medgar Evers. An orderly handed them an envelope containing all the personal effects removed from the body.

When the detectives examined the contents, they learned that Medgar Evers died with $1.12 in change in his pocket. They were curious about an address book with, according to their written report, phone numbers and addresses of "people out of state and no doubt cohorts in his work." A number of papers were tucked into the address book, but they were glued together by dried blood. They pried open one folded yellow note paper to find a five-dollar bill and the receipt for a donation from Mr. Clennon F. Jones of Jackson.

The detectives methodically recorded the contents of Medgar Evers's pockets, creating a catalog of the physical concerns of his finished life. His checkbook showed a balance of $109.33. An Elks Club membership card was dated June 11, 1963, the last day of his life. His wallet contained two poll tax receipts, a hunting and fishing license, a driver' license, a Western Union credit card, a Bell System card, and an Air Travel Card. Other cards showed his membership in the Farish Street YMCA, the AFL-CIO, the M. W. Stringer Masonic Lodge, the American Veterans Committee, and the NAACP.

When they were done, the detectives went to Evers's office and asked to look around. Gloster Current was there, and he showed them Evers's private files. The officers were looking for threatening letters, but they found nothing, they said, that would "shed any light on this case." Current told the detectives that Medgar had felt like he was being followed yesterday, not just by the police, but someone else. He had a premonition, Current told them, that something was about to happen.

Luke went back to the crime scene at 10 A.M. and joined the search for evidence along the paths and fields between Missouri Street and the businesses on Delta Drive. He was hoping to find a cartridge hull from the rifle — something, anything, the sniper might have dropped.

It was hot work. Luke was a stocky man and nearly bald except for a thin strip of black hair running down the crest of his skull. The detective crept along the trail leading to an overgrown field behind Joe's Drive In. He found a concrete slab where someone had recently kept a trailer, a little ditch, and a pile of asphalt. By eleven o'clock the sun was almost directly overhead. Because of the sharp sunlight and because he was low to the ground, looking hard, Luke saw something he might not have noticed: Something looked wrong with the hedge next to the ditch. It wasn't much of a hedge, more like a tangle of honeysuckle vines with an apron of knee-high weeds. He peered closer and he saw it: the dark end of a rifle stock.

It was obvious to Luke that the rifle had been placed carefully in the tangle, shoved way back and about a foot off the ground. Luke thought somebody had to do some work with the long barrel to make a hole in that thick hedge big enough to slide the rifle in without the scope catching on the branches. A leafy vine had been pulled down to conceal it.

Ralph Hargrove, the superintendent of police investigations, came over and took pictures while Luke took a long stick and slid the gun out of its nest. The detectives hustled their find back to police headquarters. Hargrove dusted the rifle and scope for latent fingerprints. There were smears and smudges all over the gun and one nearly complete print on the black metal scope. It popped right up. Hargrove was certain it was fresh. He lifted it and photographed it.

That done, Luke pulled back the bolt and a spent hull ejected from the chamber. A live round popped into place. Whoever had fired the rifle hadn't bothered to get ready for another shot. He must have figured one was all he needed. The gun had been fully loaded. Luke fished out six more rounds in the magazine. All were lead-tipped .30-caliber bullets.

Dutifully the detectives packaged it all up and sent the evidence to the FBI crime lab in Washington, D.C.

One of the many things Medgar Evers had managed to make time to do on the last night of his life was drive Aaron Henry to the airport. Henry was due to address a convention of the Texas Pharmaceutical Association in Houston on Tuesday, then fly from there to Washington, D.C. He and Medgar had been given twenty minutes to testify before the House Judiciary Committee to support a new civil rights bill. Medgar gave Aaron a copy of the speech he planned to give, so that the two witnesses wouldn't duplicate their testimony. They would meet again in Washington.

Aaron Henry woke up the next morning in his Houston hotel room and snapped on the TV to watch the *Today Show*. Henry smiled when he saw Roy Wilkins and Lena Horne on the screen — he hadn't known that his friends would be on that morning. But his rejoicing turned to horror when he heard the announcer explain that because of the tragic assassination of Medgar Evers in Jackson, Roy Wilkins had been asked to . . .

Henry sat back on the bed and wondered what to do. He felt like the life had been punched out of him. His old friend, his buddy, Medgar.

Henry made that speech in Houston, then flew to Washington. Since he had a copy of Medgar's testimony with him, he testified before Congress for his friend. He let them know he was speaking for Medgar Evers, who could not be there. Then he flew back to Jackson to prepare to bury him.

It was about three o'clock Wednesday morning when Charles Evers rode in from collecting cash from his tavern operations. He saw all the cars around his property, and he knew it was something bad. First he thought something had happened to his daughter, Pat. As always he had his gun in his hand as he got out of his car. You never want to let them get you first. That's how he had lived so long.

He stepped up on his porch and peered in the window. His living room was packed with people. They all stared as he walked in the door. Nobody could look him in the eye.

"C'mon in Charles," someone said.

"What's goin' on?"

"Your wife's back there; go back there."

He saw Nan in the bedroom, and she said, "Come in, Charlie. Sit down."

"Is there something wrong with Pat?"

"No. Medgar."

"What?"

"They shot him."

Charles tried to make a picture of it in his mind, but he couldn't.

"Oh, well," he said. "They can't kill 'im. They just winged him."

"No, Charlie. He's dead."

That was all he could remember. Somebody must have made reservations for him, must have gotten him out to the airport, because he came to his senses as his plane was landing in Jackson the next day. He looked out at the haze, and he knew where he was. A plan was forming in his head.

Somebody picked him up and drove him to Guynes Street. He saw Myrlie walking around like a zombie. There were reporters and so many other people milling around the house.

His anger was burning through now, like a hot sun. Charles Evers was preparing to kill every peckerwood in Mississippi. Just like the Mau Mau he and Medgar had talked about years ago. He could do it; he had money now. He'd hire people to help him, pay cooks to poison the food in white folks' homes, grind up glass in their hamburgers. He was half crazy, plotting his revenge. They were going to pay for this.

There was one thing he had to do first. He had to get over to the funeral home and take care of his brother's body. He had been in the funeral business, after all. He knew what they did to bodies. So he went down to the basement at Collins Funeral Home on Farish Street, and he fixed Medgar up in his suit, got his hair looking good in that low English style they both always favored.

Then Charles Evers walked across the street to Medgar's office in the Masonic Temple and started throwing things into the hall. The secretaries and NAACP brass from New York watched him trash the place, just crazy with grief. One of them said, "Who's going to take Medgar's place?"

Charles said, "Don't look no further. I'm here. I'm taking his place."

They looked scared. He figured they knew he was thinking about killing white folks, and they knew what his business was in Chicago, but there was nothing they could do to stop him. How would it look in the press if Roy Wilkins was feuding with Medgar's only living brother?

Medgar and Charles had made a pact. If something happened to one, the other would take over. It was that simple. The best part of Charles had been torn away and lost. He would have to live for both of them now and search for Medgar inside himself.

Roy Wilkins quickly agreed to appoint Charles Evers Mississippi's new field secretary. Charles left the jukeboxes and the numbers and the businesses in Chicago behind him. He never went back.

The death of Medgar Evers revived the Jackson Movement, if only temporarily. The morning after the murder thirteen ministers marched downtown. They were immediately arrested and released later that afternoon. Medgar, in his death, had accomplished what he couldn't do in his life: he got those ministers on their feet.

That morning the NAACP staffers, Salter, Dave Dennis, and hundreds of Tougaloo students drifted into the Masonic Temple, pulled in like filings to a magnet, looking for a purpose in their grief, looking for something to do with their anger. When they heard that the ministers had marched, they also took to the streets. Two hundred student demonstrators marched from the Masonic Temple. One hundred police met them head-on. With some skull cracking and shoving, 145 marchers, half of them under age seventeen, were arrested and hauled off to the fairgrounds stockade.

The doctor gave Myrlie Evers a sedative, but she couldn't sleep. When the sun came up, the police and the gawkers were still at her house. Then Charles flew in from Chicago, there were NAACP people around, somehow newsmen were in the house taking pictures, and she couldn't figure out how to make them all leave.

Myrlie tried to go out with a bucket to clean the blood off the carport. Someone hustled her back inside. She tried to be alone in her room, but friends would come in and sit with her to keep her from brooding.

When Myrlie heard there was a meeting at the Pearl Street Baptist Church that night, an idea formed in her mind: she had to speak. It was the most important thing right then, and nobody could stop her.

Myrlie Evers was wearing a green summer dress and white gloves when she walked into the church where the Reverend R. L. T. Smith was speaking, and he introduced her from the podium.

It was the first speech she had made since her school days. She was surprised to hear her own voice so calm, like it was coming from somewhere else, disembodied — and she felt Medgar was there with her. She spoke softly at first.

"I come to you tonight with a broken heart," she said to the immensely quiet crowd. "I am left without my husband, and my children without a father, but I am left with the strong determination to try to take up where he left off. And I come to make a plea that all of you here and those who are not here will, by his death, be able to draw some of his strength, some of his courage, and some of his determination to finish this fight.

"Nothing can bring Medgar back, but the cause can live on. . . . We cannot let his death be in vain."

Then Myrlie Evers walked past the hushed, weeping people in the church and into the waiting car and back to her lonely, empty room to begin the grieving that would never truly end. She had made the first step in a journey that would take her thirty years to finish.

14

Funeral

NEWS OF MEDGAR EVERS's assassination was covered on television, in weekly magazines, on every wire service, and in every major newspaper. Evers became, in death, more famous than he had been in life.

On its editorial page the day after the murder, the *New York Times* noted the grim irony of Evers's assassination following Kennedy's compelling nationwide address on America's moral awakening, noting that "Mr. Evers's martyrdom [has] advanced the prospect for strong Civil Rights legislation."

The Thursday morning *Clarion-Ledger* reported that "the most intensive manhunt in recent Jackson history" was under way to find the killer or killers of Medgar Evers.

President John F. Kennedy issued a statement from the White House saying that he was "appalled by the barbarity of the act." He and Mrs. Kennedy sent a personal note of condolence to the widow.

The white leaders of Mississippi expressed suitably shocked sentiments: Governor Ross Barnett called the murder "a dastardly act." Mayor Allen Thompson, who for some reason was taking time off from the municipal crisis at his vacation home in Destin, Florida, immediately returned to the city. "I am dreadfully shocked, humiliated and sick at heart that such a terrible tragedy should happen in our city," he said.

A total of $22,350 was by now being offered for information leading to the conviction of Evers's killer, including a $10,000 reward from the NAACP and smaller ones such as $50 from District Attorney Bill Waller, $100 from Sheriff J. R. Gilfoy, and, most ironically, $1,000 from the Hederman newspapers — the *Clarion-Ledger* and Jackson *Daily News,* which had done so much to deride Evers while he was alive. The reward offer in the *Clarion-Ledger* was accompanied by its own tepid, back-handed editorial. "The death of Medgar Evers is most regrettable," it began, going on to denounce the "outside agitators" who had supposedly started all the trouble. "Continued demonstrations can lead only to more bloodshed," the paper warned.

As soon as he learned that Medgar Evers had been shot, Roy Wilkins summoned his NAACP troops to Jackson. Gloster Current canceled his plans and stayed in Mississippi. Ruby Hurley flew in from Atlanta. The Washington and New York staffs piled in to manage the crisis.

One of the men Wilkins called to Jackson to help with the funeral was Vernon Jordan, who had quit the association only two months earlier. Jordan was heartsick, but he was not surprised that his friend was dead. When he got the call that Medgar had been shot down he couldn't cry. He was just angry deep down inside himself, and it was not the emotion that brings tears. Medgar knew he was going to die, the way a soldier knows.

Jordan's eyes were still dry when he and Roy Wilkins walked into the room at Collins Funeral Home on North Farish Street where Medgar's body was laid out for viewing. Both men noticed that the funeral home had put a phony handkerchief in Evers's blue suit pocket. It was a cardboard square with a cloth triangle glued to the top. Without a word they exchanged looks and agreed that this was not good enough for Medgar. Vernon Jordan watched as Roy Wilkins removed the cardboard square and placed his own handkerchief carefully in Medgar's pocket.

The NAACP staff took over the funeral arrangements. Medgar had told Myrlie that he wanted his funeral to be short, "no long eulogies," and, typically, he didn't want anything expensive. "When I'm gone, I'm gone, and I won't know anything about it."

The NAACP had other plans. Myrlie fretted about the expense of a big funeral, but Ruby Hurley told her not to worry about it. Ruby was taking charge, managing the event. Clarie Harvey noticed with some resentment the way Ruby was pushing people out of the way, making it an NAACP show.

Hurley even chose the clothes Myrlie and Reena were to wear to the funeral.

When she walked into the Masonic Temple on Saturday morning, Myrlie Evers was wearing a simple black dress, a double strand of pearls, elbow-length gloves, and a beaded black toque, a style popular in New York that season. Four thousand people crammed into and around the simple, sand-colored temple. For three days temperatures had gone past one hundred degrees, and the hot, damp-flannel air settled around the mourners. It was an effort to breathe.

The only sound was the stirring of a thousand paper fans and the murmuring of voices. There were flowers on the stage around the glossy casket draped with an American flag. Medgar Evers was dressed in the suit Myrlie had chosen for him. He wore a blue NAACP tie imprinted with the scales of justice, a white Masonic apron trimmed in blue, and an Elks emblem around his neck.

Photographers flashed pictures. Reporters scribbled on notepads. Myrlie knew this was not what Medgar had wanted. But by now the funeral was a runaway train; she could not apply the brakes if she wanted to. Her life, her future, and her children's future were attached, maybe forever, to these people, this organization that had stolen her husband while he had lived and claimed him now, more than ever, in death. She took her seat in the front row of folding chairs, with Charles on one side and Darrell on the other, and stared at the open coffin.

The temple was packed with prominent blacks and a few white officials: Bayard Rustin, Ralph Bunche, Dick Gregory, James Meredith, and John Doar.

Doar and the usual crew from the Justice Department had been standing by in Tuscaloosa when Governor George Wallace had stood in front of the Alabama campus gate to protest the entry of two black students. Doar had rushed back to Jackson when he heard that Evers had been shot. Then he had been immediately diverted to another crisis just north of Greenwood, in the town of Winona. Fannie Lou Hamer, Lawrence Guyot, and two other SNCC workers had been unlawfully arrested and brutally beaten in the Winona jail in the days before Evers was killed. Doar had spent much of that week preparing lawsuits against the Winona police.

Now he was here to pay his respects to his friend. John Doar did not "fraternize" with the government's clients, and he would not let his lawyers get too close to people in the movement. It wasn't proper. But Doar had worked so hard and so long with Medgar Evers that he couldn't call him anything but his friend. Doar sat quietly and pondered what might have been done.

Martin Luther King, Jr., sat up front in the sweltering room. He had not been invited to speak, and he made no statements to the press.

An organist played Fox's "Requiem." A black-robed choir sang gospel songs. And the speeches began.

Dr. T. R. M. Howard, who had come down from Chicago, spoke about Medgar's days in Mound Bayou, how he had organized the state's "first non-violent protest," the 1952 bumper sticker campaign to boycott gas stations that had no rest rooms for Negroes. Medgar's old mentor was always ahead of his time, and even as the movement's leading Gandhian pacifist sat in the audience, Howard's words foreshadowed the era of militancy this first of many assassinations would bring down on the nation: "For over a hundred years, now, we have been turning first one cheek, then the other cheek," Howard bellowed in anger. "Our neck has gotten tired of turning now!" The crowd roared its approval.

The speeches, the gospel music, and the eulogies went on for an hour and a half. Roy Wilkins delivered the final words: If Medgar Evers "could live in Mississippi and not hate, so shall we," he said. "Medgar Evers was a symbol of our victory and of their defeat. The bullet that tore away his life four days ago, tore away at the system and helped to signal its end."

Darrell, who was ten years old, sat quietly through the long ordeal, his face a mask of grief. By the end of the ceremony, the little boy who hid his tears at home tucked his chin and sobbed.

As the crowd filed out and the pallbearers lifted Medgar's casket, Myrlie slumped against Charles. "Don't break down now," he murmured, and held her up until she took her place, alone, behind the white hearse as it slowly rolled down Lynch Street.

The rest of the mourners followed behind, three and four abreast, walking in silence. Martin Luther King, Jr., and Roy Wilkins, in a tense public display of unity, walked side by side as the line stretched along the mile-and-a-half route to Farish Street.

Earlier that week the Jackson City Council had issued a permit allowing a silent march from the Masonic Temple to the Collins Funeral Home on North Farish Street after the funeral services. It was a classic Thompson push-and-pull gesture. Yes, you can walk, but you cannot run. Or talk or sing or carry placards.

When the procession crossed the railroad tracks and skirted the white part of town, the police lining the route thickened. Row after row of blue-helmeted riot police stood at the corner of Farish and Capitol Streets, their backs to the granite dome of the statehouse, their batons at the ready across their chests.

Myrlie was alone in her grief, her mind gone somewhere else, when Aaron Henry came up next to her and said, "Look behind you, Myrlie." She saw them then, thousands of people, young people walking through Jackson, and she realized that Medgar had taken them past their fear. She wished Medgar could see them now.

Aurelia Young opened her house on Pearl Street, a few blocks west of Farish, to the NAACP representatives and their guests. They were sitting on the floors, on the beds, on every available space in the great living room, eating a buffet lunch, when the phone rang. It was for John Doar, someone saying there was a riot breaking out on Farish Street. Jack Young and Doar jumped in a car and headed back to the funeral home.

It had started with a song. The crowd stood outside the Collins Funeral Home, some finding shelter under sidewalk awnings, most just standing in the searing sunlight, grief-stricken and helpless and angry.

Suddenly the thin soprano voice of a young girl broke the quiet vigil. "Ohhhh, freedom . . ."

A hole opened in the crowd, and the girl stepped into it, her voice gaining strength. "Ohhhh, freedom . . ."

A few voices joined hers.

"Before I'll be a slave, I'll be buried in my grave. . . ."
Then they were all singing:

> *No more killing,*
> *No more killing, over me, over me . . .*

The cops were starting to notice, and the dogs grew restless at the edge of Farish Street. After a pause someone picked up another song, more up-tempo, and everyone was singing and clapping.

> *This little light of mine,*
> *I'm gonna let it shine . . .*

Someone started pointing at the tall buildings and the domed state-house, and the lyrics changed. "All over Capitol Street, I'm gonna let it shine . . ."

The crowd turned south and started moving. Hundreds more were pouring in from the side streets and porches along Farish, shouting "We want the killer," moving fast now, running. Running in front of them were the Jackson police, retreating to Capitol Street and the riot squads. It was as far as the crowd would get. Hundreds of police, some with weapons drawn and dogs straining at the leash, advanced on them slowly, deliberately driving them back from the white business district.

The news footage from that day shows the riot squad in a human chain from sidewalk to sidewalk. At the edge of the crowd cops rough people up, using their batons. The crowd pulls back, leaving a wide gap between them and the riot police, backed up by a fire department pumper truck with a hose at the ready and some itchy-fingered county deputies who are starting to look real nervous.

John Salter and Ed King watched the rush to Capitol Street and thought one thing: we've got to get Martin Luther King back here to lead this. They ran into a building and up a flight of stairs, desperately searching for a telephone to call the airport and stop King from leaving. They found an open office but no phone. As they paused to look out the window at the crowd, some cops spotted them, and within minutes police had charged into the building, grabbed the two, and thrown them into a paddy wagon. A black man with a bleeding head wound and a black woman with a torn dress were thrown in after them. They were taken to the stockade.

Reporters who were there that day described a pandemonium of singing, chants of "Shoot! Shoot!" from the street kids taunting the cops,
cops cursing, dogs barking and growling, policemen grabbing people
and clubbing them with batons and rifle butts, officers pounding on cars
with their nightsticks and shouting, "Get on out of here!" and a rain of
bottles and chunks of brick flying through the air and skidding along the
pavement at the advancing police.

Then a tall, thin man in a white shirt rolled up at the sleeves stepped
between the demonstrators and the police and began to shout his name
in a clipped Yankee accent: "I'm John Doar! That's D-O-A-R! I'm from
the Justice Department in Washington, and anybody around here knows
that I stand for what's right! This is not the way! You are not going to
win anything with bricks and bottles."

The crowd stopped for a moment, as if they were looking at a crazy
man, or a ghost.

Doar spotted Dave Dennis along the side of the street and shouted,
"C'mon Dave. Let's get this stopped!"

Doar never saw the man with the tire iron taking aim at his head who
appeared in the picture on the front page of the *New York Times* the next
day. "Medgar Evers wouldn't want it this way," Doar shouted.

The man with the tire iron ran off.

"Hold hands with me and help us move these people along," Doar
said. A few people linked hands, and they slowly walked the crowd away
from the police line.

Dave Dennis was ducking in the alleys, trying to talk sense to a bunch
of pumped-up street kids with rifles. He stopped one teenager who was
taking aim at John Doar. Just one shot would be all it would take, and
there would be a massacre. Dennis knew that.

He had stayed on the outskirts of the crowd all day. He couldn't face
the funeral, never went inside or viewed the body. He had lost his heart
for it. So he hovered on the edges, trying to keep things cool. Somehow
it worked.

The crowd slowly dispersed. There would be no one else to bury that
day.

Inside the funeral home Clarie Collins Harvey prepared the body of
Medgar Evers for its last journey on a slow train through the South, to

the nation's capital. Harvey and Mary Cox, an insurance agent, took the casket to the train station in Meridian and rode with it to Washington. Clarie remembers the crowds that gathered at every station along the way, silent black folks lining the tracks, some of them weeping. There was no sign or funeral bunting on the train, no announcement beforehand. Somehow they knew it was Medgar Evers, and so they came.

The next day, Tuesday, Salter and King learned that they were being indicted for "inciting to riot." It was on their minds as they drove back to Tougaloo along North West Street, as usual.

It was about 11:30 A.M. and the lunchtime traffic was just starting. John Salter caught a glimpse of the white boy driving a car that ran the stop sign just ahead of them. That car plowed into the southbound lane, causing another driver to swerve and hit Salter and King head-on.

Salter woke up in a blood-drenched haze. There was a jagged hole in the passenger side windshield. Ed King was slumped by the door, blood gushing from his face.

In the emergency room Salter saw a contingent of Jackson plainclothesmen taking a good look at him as he lay helpless and drugged on the gurney. One was the man who had slammed him with the car door a week earlier.

Salter and King drifted in and out of consciousness all week. On Wednesday Jeanette King brought a copy of the Jackson *Daily News* to the hospital, and Salter learned that his dreams for another Birmingham were over.

The paper was full of news of "easing tensions." Five Negro leaders from Jackson had met with Mayor Thompson, who had offered a compromise to end the demonstrations. He would hire Negro policemen for Negro areas, have Negro school crossing guards, upgrade salaries for municipal workers, and continue meetings with Negro leaders. It was essentially the same package Medgar Evers and the local NAACP had already rejected. It did not include public accommodations integration or school integration or a biracial committee. But it was being sold to the folks as a great victory. The deal was voted on in a mass meeting and accepted. Charles Evers backed the compromise. The next big push would be a voter registration drive.

John Salter sighed. His head was pounding, and rain was falling on the streets outside his hospital room, cooling the city at last. The Jackson Movement ended for him that day. Within weeks he would leave the state to take a job as a field representative for the Southern Conference Educational Fund, based in New Orleans.

That afternoon Medgar Evers was buried in Arlington Cemetery, a long way from home.

Myrlie and Charles and Reena and Darrell flew to Washington for the burial ceremony. Medgar had wanted to be buried in Jackson, and Myrlie wanted that too, but the NAACP had other ideas. There would be a big ceremony and speeches at the national cemetery. Medgar would be working for the NAACP even in his grave.

Five hundred people met the funeral train at Union Station and accompanied the body to the funeral home. Twenty-five thousand more came to view the body.

Myrlie and Charles followed the hearse to Arlington.

Charles Evers could hardly stand it. He could barely drag himself out of the limousine when it reached the grave. This was the brother he had kept warm all those years, whose side of the bed he would heat up with his own body each night before they went to sleep. And now they were going to lower that brother into a cold, dark grave, and it just about tore Charles's heart out. He could never stand for Medgar to be cold.

Hundreds of people gathered on the green slopes of Arlington National Cemetery as Medgar Evers was lowered into his grave. The crowd was filled with senators and congressmen, grim-faced officials from the Justice Department and the president's cabinet. While Kennedy did not attend, he had invited Charles and Myrlie and the children to visit him at the White House after the funeral.

Charles remembers looking out over the gravesite and the rolling lawns with the great monuments of Washington in the distance, and feeling a memory surface from deep in the past.

"Well, Bilbo," he thought to himself. "We finally made it to Washington."

Medgar Evers was given a full military burial, with a six-man honor guard and a three-gun salute. After a bugler sounded taps, a soldier handed Myrlie the American flag that had draped Medgar's casket.

Two days later, she and her family flew home alone.

15

A Pawn in the Game

EVEN BEFORE he saw the rifle in the newspaper, Thorn McIntyre wondered whether Byron De La Beckwith might be the killer. There was a rumor going around Greenwood that Delay had been involved somehow. Then McIntyre saw the Enfield rifle on the front page of the Jackson *Daily News*, and his stomach seized up. He was almost sure that was Beckwith's gun. But he had to be certain. So he called the number they gave in the paper and asked some questions about the markings on the Enfield. The sergeant who answered the phone told him the rifle had the inscription "Eddystone" and the numbers 9-18 on top of the barrel. Now Thorn was in a genuine fix.

Innes Thornton McIntyre III was a solid citizen. Around Greenwood they said he came from a good family, and that meant a lot. In the spring of 1963 he was twenty-five years old, a handsome veteran with a lovely wife and two small children. He'd had two years of college at Mississippi State and now managed Greenbriar, the family's cotton plantation, a few miles outside Greenwood.

McIntyre was a typical man of his time and place: he loved sports, he collected guns, he went to church, he was a patriot and a segregationist.

A bumper sticker seen in the South summed up how he felt about his heritage: "Born in the USA by Chance; Born a Southerner by the Grace of God." Being a southerner meant being genteel, showing respect and good manners. It meant feeling a separateness from the rest of the country, a distinction to be proud of. But Thorn considered himself a regular person. Growing up he had been more concerned with dates and football than politics. In 1963 the integration problem was on most people's minds, but it wasn't the most pressing issue in their lives. For white people like Thorn it was more important to put food on the table and pay the bills than to stay up nights worrying about the "Negro question."

Thorn McIntyre had grown up around black folks, and he felt, like many white men of his generation, that he had a "special bond" with the servants and laborers on his place, many of whom had worked for his family for years. There was a personal connection, even though blacks and whites occupied separate worlds. There were rules: you didn't cross over into their world, and they didn't cross over into yours. As long as you respected that, everyone got along just fine. Thorn, like everyone else in his white world, was worried that this cherished "relationship," this hallmark of the "southern way of life," was threatened by the outside agitators coming in to stir things up. He was opposed to it. But there was a point beyond which he would not go.

Delay Beckwith was different. In Thorn's estimation he was more than willing to cross that line, and he was capable of anything.

In Greenwood in those days everybody knew everybody. So naturally McIntyre and Beckwith were acquaintances. Like every other white man in Beckwith's line of sight, McIntyre had been pestered with anti-integrationist literature, and Beckwith would use every conversation as an excuse to talk politics.

The only thing Beckwith cared about as much as segregation was guns, and in that he and McIntyre had something in common. Both men loved guns and loved to trade them.

In 1959 McIntyre ordered an old Enfield rifle from a catalog. When Beckwith laid eyes on it, according to McIntyre, he simply had to have it. He kept pestering McIntrye, suggesting all kinds of trades, until one day in January 1960 Thorn finally caved in and traded with him, just to get rid of him. That was the kind of salesman Beckwith was: persistent. He would just wear you down until he got his way.

Beckwith got the barrel and action of the old Enfield, and Thorn kept the original wooden stock. Beckwith gave him a new .244 Remington rifle barrel and another old Enfield action with a rusty barrel.

Three and a half years later there Thorn was: a decent man caught between the proverbial rock and hard place. The reward money didn't interest him, even though there was now $22,000 up for grabs. If he turned Beckwith in, some people would think he was a rat and a traitor. On the other hand, that rifle could be traced to McIntyre, and he didn't want to be accused of murder. And as much as he hated the idea of integration, shooting a man in the back in his driveway was not the way to go. McIntyre suspected that his life was never going to be the same as he picked up the phone and made another call to the Jackson Police Department.

McIntyre's call was one of dozens that came in during the days following the murder. There were more leads than the police could check out in a month, but they ran down dozens of them.

Some seemed promising, such as the White Top cab that Medgar Evers's neighbors had seen cruising around on the night of the murder. It turned out to have been delivering a telegram.

Detectives came up with more helpful information when they canvassed the neighborhood. The weekend before the murder Mr. and Mrs. Leroy Pittman, owners of the local grocery store, had seen a well-dressed white man nosing around the vacant lot they had for sale. He was of average height and drove a white, late-model Valiant or Dodge with a long aerial in the back. They wouldn't have thought much of it except that he had been wearing sunglasses after dark.

Two cabdrivers at the Trailways bus station in Jackson said that a white man had been asking for directions to Medgar Evers's house, but they couldn't help him. They said he had a local accent and told them he needed to find out where Evers lived in the next couple of days. They described him as tall, in his early forties, and wearing dark pants and shirt and a brown hat.

This seemed very promising, although there was also a report of a man fitting the same description arriving about that time on a bus from Shreveport, Louisiana. The man, according to witnesses, seemed like a "nut" because he had accused a ticket agent and the bus driver of being communists.

*   *   *

While the police combed the city for leads, the local FBI office was running down its list of the usual suspects. Informants called in tips. One said that Red Hydrick, the bootlegger, had something to do with the murder. Another said a former policeman had been involved. Someone spotted a blue pickup truck with a rifle in the gun rack in Joe's Drive In parking lot before the murder. The same truck also had been seen at a civil rights demonstration in Jackson on May 28. The FBI shared much of this information with the Jackson police. What the FBI did not tell the police was that they were closing in on the real suspect.

The FBI hadn't done much for Medgar Evers when he was alive. Now that he was dead, J. Edgar Hoover mobilized hundreds of agents in forty-eight field divisions to help find his killer.

They started with the obvious: who owned the rifle and scope? Unfortunately the .30/06 rifle was more than forty years old, and nearly two million Enfields had been made at the end of World War I. They had been sold as surplus, and they were a popular collector's item throughout the country, a big mover at gun fairs. Records were hard to trace.

The Japanese-made Golden Hawk scope was more promising. There were only fifteen-thousand in the country, and they were sold through one importer in Chicago. He kept good records. Only five scopes had been shipped to Mississippi, one of them to Duck's Tackle Shop in Grenada, about twenty miles north of Greenwood. The FBI traced each of the scopes, sometimes through several owners. They found all but the one that had been shipped to Grenada. FBI agents questioned the shop owner, John "Duck" Goza, three times before he finally said, "Wait a minute, I'll tell you what I think you want to know." He was almost sure that he had traded the scope to a Byron De La Beckwith from Greenwood, but he didn't want to "get him in trouble."

The two agents drove down to Greenwood to check Beckwith out. At dusk, while they were parked outside his house waiting for him to show, Beckwith drove up in his white Valiant.

Beckwith instantly recognized the FBI agents, who were dressed in coats and ties. He walked over and told them to get off his street. When they asked to talk to him, he said, "No comment." When they asked him if he knew anything about the Golden Hawk scope, he said nothing and walked into his house.

Once they had a name, workers at the FBI lab in Washington were able to come up with a set of prints from Beckwith's Marine Corps records. In the early morning hours of Saturday, June 22, they had a match with the latent print on the scope.

On Saturday afternoon Beckwith's neighbors on George Street noticed a nondescript American car and some conspicuously overdressed white men hanging out in front of the old Yerger place. They were asking passersby where Beckwith might be found. One of the neighbors called Yerger Moorehead to tell him that the FBI was snooping around, and he in turn called Beckwith, who was working at the fertilizer company in Greenville that day.

Beckwith called Hardy Lott, the family lawyer, who was also city attorney for Greenwood, to ask for advice. They decided that Beckwith would turn himself in at Hardy's office. Yerger negotiated with the FBI agents, saying that Beckwith wanted time to shave and change out of his field clothes before he met them.

At eleven o'clock Saturday night Beckwith was arrested in Lott's office. He was charged under the 1957 Civil Rights Act for conspiring to injure, oppress, and intimidate Medgar Evers in the free exercise of his constitutional rights. The federal warrant charged Beckwith and "persons unknown" with this conspiracy, but no one else was arrested.

When Beckwith was taken into custody, he was wearing what would become his trademark outfit: a neat dark suit, a monogrammed shirt with French cuffs, a good tie, and a pocket square. He was, of course, going to behave like a gentleman. There was no need for handcuffs.

Fred Blackwell, the young photographer for the Jackson *Daily News*, had gotten a tip that there would be an arrest in the Evers case. He was waiting at the police station. Fred was surprised that Beckwith was all dressed up, like a real dandy, and that he did not seem at all upset about being charged with murder.

The FBI agents turned Beckwith over to the Jackson police, who planned to file state murder charges. He spent what was left of the night at the city jail.

On Sunday the police put together a lineup. Both cabdrivers were brought in to identify the man who had been asking for directions to Evers's house. Only one, Herbert Speight, was positive the man was Beckwith.

The Pittmans also were shown the six-man lineup. Mr. Pittman picked out Beckwith as the man he had seen prowling around the vacant lot, but he said he couldn't be absolutely positive.

Detectives Luke and Turner tried to get Beckwith to talk to them about the case. Beckwith would gab about the weather and the baseball scores and gun collecting, but he had nothing to say about the murder. When they asked him to take a lie detector test, he said he had "no statement to make at this time." When they tried to bait him into talking about segregation, he told them that Mississippi could use a Ku Klux Klan, that it could do a lot of good. But that was all he would say.

Monday's *Clarion-Ledger* carried a banner headline that read: "Californian Charged with Murder of Evers." The paper pointed out that Beckwith had not been born in Mississippi.

On Monday the federal charges against Beckwith were "deferred" while state murder charges were filed. After a preliminary hearing on Tuesday the judge ordered Beckwith held without bail, pending an indictment from the grand jury. Hinds County district attorney Bill Waller said that he would ask for the death penalty.

After Beckwith's picture appeared in the newspapers, the Jackson police got several calls from people who thought they had seen him snooping around the Masonic Temple on June 7, the night Lena Horne and Dick Gregory had spoken.

Lillian Louie, the NAACP office secretary, said that she had seen Beckwith at the meeting and a few days later, on June 11, had seen him in the office. But Louie could not pick him out from a photo lineup.

The police identified two other white men who resembled Beckwith and had been seen at the Masonic Temple on June 7 and June 11. One was a strange man from Michigan who had been hanging around asking questions. The other was an undercover cop.

They still couldn't definitely place Beckwith in Evers's vicinity.

Bill Waller was thirty-seven years old and ambitious. He was a sixth-generation Mississippian from a big landowning family near Oxford, William Faulkner's hometown.

Bill Waller was not a tall man, but he was powerfully built, with a large head and a peculiar hairline. His straight dark hair came down low at his forehead and jutted sharply back at the temple. It emphasized his heavy, low-slung face, which was often set in an expression that explained, somehow, why the Waller family inevitably chose bulldogs as pets.

Waller had followed a conventional career path that could lead to the Governor's Mansion and beyond: Ole Miss law school, military service (he had been in army intelligence during the Korean War), a law practice in the capital city. In 1960 Waller was elected Hinds County D.A. It was a part-time job, but he brought in his law partner, John Fox, to help him out. They kept their private practice going, which was perfectly legal at the time, while they prosecuted all the felonies in four counties.

In the summer of 1963 Bill Waller was not exactly a household name in Mississippi. Before long, everyone who read the paper or watched the TV news knew him. But name recognition can sometimes backfire. Bill Waller and John Fox claim that it never entered their minds, but vigorously prosecuting a controversial race murder case, even against a man like Beckwith, was not going to win them friends among the Citizens' Councils clique, which still had a powerful influence in Mississippi.

To be honest, people were shocked that there had been an arrest in the Evers case. And so many white men had walked away from killing a Negro that nobody really thought that Beckwith would ever be tried, much less convicted. Charles Evers and Myrlie Evers made hopeful, cautious statements to the press. Aaron Henry was typically blunt: "I don't think they will indict him." He speculated that Beckwith would get off on "the lunacy angle" and might get a suspended sentence. Henry predicted large demonstrations in Jackson and across the country if that happened.

Detectives John Chamblee and Fred Sanders rode out to Greenville with a court seizure order to take possession of Beckwith's company car at Delta Liquid Plant Food. Sanders was furious that the FBI had arrested Beckwith without including, or even notifying, the Jackson police. He felt that the police would have solved the case eventually. Now all he could do was to strengthen what evidence he had.

There was nothing inside the white 1962 Valiant that interested the detectives. They took photographs of the exterior, which had a long whip-type antenna attached to the bumper and a large, boxy trailer hitch.

The detectives also searched Beckwith's crumbling old house on George Street in Greenwood. Yerger Moorehead met them at the door and showed them around.

Most of the rooms in the house were empty. Beckwith seemed to occupy one upstairs bedroom and a bare sitting room downstairs. In the bedroom the detectives found a box of newspaper clippings about integration, along with a folder of letters Beckwith had written on the subject and part of the manuscript for an anti-integration book that Beckwith was writing. They also found three guns in the bedroom: a Remington rifle and a double-barreled shotgun, both fully loaded, and a .25-caliber automatic pistol. There were several hundred rounds of ammunition, but nothing usable in a .30/06 rifle. There was, however, a booklet advertising Peters ammunition, and someone had circled the .30/30 and .30/06 specifications. They also found a letter from a Jackson psychiatrist named Dr. Roland E. Toms and a canceled check for the purchase of field glasses.

Detectives Luke and Turner brought in two young women who had been working at Joe's Drive In on the night of the murder to look at another lineup. Neither could pick out Beckwith, although both identified his Valiant as the car they had seen in the lot that night. Martha Jean O'Brien, a seventeen-year-old carhop, repeated her observation that the man she had seen get out of the Valiant had been six foot two or taller and 160 to 165 pounds with a dark complexion, black curly hair, a black mustache covering his lip, and an erect posture. He had been wearing black pants and a black long-sleeved shirt. When the police later took a signed statement from O'Brien, this detailed description was not in it.

On Tuesday, July 2, two weeks after his arrest, Beckwith was formally indicted for murder by the grand jury. Medgar Evers would have turned thirty-eight that day.

It wasn't long after John Chamblee and Fred Sanders had arrived in Greenwood and started asking questions about Delay Beckwith that they realized that the townspeople were closing ranks around one of their own. In one frustrated report Sanders referred to Greenwood archly as a "clannish" kind of town.

People were generally cordial, even friendly, but they said nothing useful. One deputy sheriff told Sanders that no outsider would get the whole story from anyone.

The detectives heard about Beckwith's well-known segregationist ardor, the "funny" straw hat he wore, and the pistol he toted to church. He was almost universally regarded as a "blowhard" and a "nut."

During this initial visit Chamblee and Sanders met and interviewed Thorn McIntyre, who had already been visited by the FBI. In what must have been the best news they got all week, McIntyre told the Jackson detectives that he was willing to testify that he had traded the rifle to Delay. He also told them he wanted to keep things quiet, and he didn't want any reward. That was a good thing because the reward was not going to be given to him or anyone else, since Beckwith technically had been located through routine police work in tracing the scope and fingerprint.

The rest of the investigation was standard fare. The detectives checked Beckwith's company credit card record to see whether he had bought gas in Jackson. Meanwhile Luke and Turner checked motel records to see whether Beckwith had stayed in the city. They continued to interview potential witnesses, and they tracked down rumors that Beckwith had been seen hanging around Lynch Street before Evers had been shot.

The long, exhausting process of trying Beckwith began with a flurry of motions from both sides. Most interesting was one by the prosecution: Waller wanted Beckwith sent to the state mental hospital at Whitfield for a competency evaluation. Waller stated, magnanimously, that "it was something that should be done," even though the defense never asked for an exam.

It was an unusual move in those days. Waller wanted to go fishing in Beckwith's head. If Beckwith was found competent to stand trial, that diagnosis could be used against him should he later decide to plead insanity. If he was found to be mentally incompetent, he could be committed to a mental hospital, which would spare everyone the trouble of trying him. At least it got the issue of sanity out of the way.

Beckwith was indignant. The defense cried foul, and a three-hour hearing was held on the subject on July 18.

Yerger Moorehead testified for the prosecution. "I will say he is able to consult with attorneys and to prepare a defense," Beckwith's cousin and former guardian told the court. "But I don't believe he is mentally capable of being guilty of a crime of violence. I'm not making that statement without a great deal of background to make it on." Moorehead said that he had noticed a change in Delay's mental state after he had come home from World War II.

Waller also called Dr. Roland Toms, the Jackson psychiatrist to whom Beckwith had been referred by his family doctor in 1962. Toms had reached a diagnosis, but a defense objection stopped him from repeating what that diagnosis was. Toms also was prevented from answering whether Beckwith had been packing a pistol when he had come in for his appointment.

Waller managed to squeeze Beckwith's alarming divorce papers into the record, as well as the judgment from a peace bond hearing in July 1962, in which Beckwith had been found guilty of "threatening to kill his wife . . . and likely to carry out the threat."

Judge Leon Hendrick ordered Beckwith to Whitfield for a month-long psychiatric exam. A week later another judge overturned the ruling. While Waller appealed, Beckwith was sent to the Rankin County Jail, near the Whitfield hospital.

Rankin County lies just across the Pearl River, east of Jackson. But crossing the bridge means entering a somewhat different, more primitive world. To this day some older black cabdrivers get a little nervous leaving the city limits to take a fare to the big airport in Rankin County late at night. It's a reflex. In the past Negroes knew they had better not be caught out on Lakeland Drive or Highway 80 after dark without a note from a white man saying they had business there. The county was the realm of bootleggers and tough redneck deputies. It was where, before 1968, in the days when the whole state was dry, the teenagers of South Jackson and the blue-haired ladies of Belhaven would drive out to pick up a bottle. It was the place where the White Knights of the Ku Klux Klan had established a foothold in the early sixties and where towns like Florence and Brandon and Star are still shorthand for "Klanland" to some people who remember.

By all accounts Byron De La Beckwith was treated like visiting royalty at the Rankin County Jail, where he spent most of the rest of the year.

Local housewives brought him special meals. He kept a TV set and part of his personal gun collection in his cell. He later bragged that the sheriff let him out from time to time to get his hair cut or go shopping. The sheriff just reminded him to be back by dark.

Beckwith had as many visitors as he wanted. Red Hydrick dropped by and gave him two hundred dollars walking-around money. According to Bill Minor, a respected local reporter, Hydrick told Beckwith, "I've killed a hundred niggers and they haven't never done anything to me yet. You don't tell them anything."

Another visitor was former General Edwin Walker, himself having escaped punishment for his role in the Ole Miss riots after a lunacy exam. Walker briskly answered a few reporters' questions after his visit. He said that Byron De La Beckwith was a "fine Southern gentleman." All he would say about the murder charge was that Medgar Evers had been "working against the good of the country."

Bill Waller had to get a state supreme court order to pry Beckwith out of his open cell in Rankin County. Beckwith seemed peeved when the Hinds County sheriff took away his guns.

A television news crew recorded Beckwith's transfer to Jackson on a cold December day. He wore a natty brown wool suit. His personal effects were at his feet on the pavement: an elegant umbrella, a portable typewriter, and a box labeled "Health Guardian Isometric Exerciser." Beckwith sucked on a huge, lit cigar as he strode into his new confinement. "Mighty glad to be here, sir," he said to the jailer.

It was immediately clear to all those who knew them that Charles Evers was not at all like his brother. Where Medgar was smooth, Charles was rough. Where Medgar would choose to persuade, Charles would twist an arm.

The people in the movement who had worked so long with Medgar were wary at first, but hopeful. Nobody really knew Charles or what he would do. It didn't take long for the SNCC kids and the CORE people to stay out of his way.

Dave Dennis liked Charles Evers's roguish charm, his slick charisma. It was hard not to like him on a personal level, as long as you didn't cross him. On the job he was unpredictable, mercurial, moody. But Charles's main crime was not being Medgar.

One day that summer Dennis walked up the steps to the old NAACP office in the Masonic Temple to visit Charles and found the floors covered with red wall-to-wall carpeting. He thought, *This is a desecration.* That was his last visit to the office.

Everywhere Myrlie Evers turned in her house on Guynes Street, there was something to remind her of the night of the killing. There was the blood that would never quite wash off the carport; the dent in the refrigerator where a fingertip would fit; the stack of crisp white shirts still carefully folded in the closet, that she didn't have the heart to give away.

The children were shattered. Van, the three-year-old, talked endlessly about the blood on the steps and about his father. He would answer the phone and the door with the same words: "Have you seen my Daddy?" He must have said it a hundred times a day.

Reena kept her grief hidden, and Darrell retreated into deep silences. Sometimes he would just sit under the plum tree and stare out at nothing. He had trouble at school. He slept with a toy gun by his bed. And when his mother went away, as she often did, he was terrified that she would never come back.

The NAACP stepped in to take care of the family. Gloster Current and Roy Wilkins made sure that Myrlie and the children had enough money to live on. They knew Medgar had died without insurance, so the NAACP board voted to keep her on the payroll as a consultant, earning Medgar's salary of seventy-five hundred dollars a year. They voted to give her a twenty-thousand-dollar tax-free gift over four years. They set up a trust fund for the children to shelter donations. The NAACP took care of everything. All the association asked for in return was her cooperation and loyalty.

Myrlie signed a document authorizing only the NAACP to use Medgar Evers's name to raise funds. Every few days a packet of checks would arrive from New York for her to endorse, along with a list of thank-you notes for her to copy and sign. The NAACP staff wrote the text for her.

Almost immediately Myrlie Evers was in demand on the speaking circuit. Shortly after Byron De La Beckwith was arrested for the murder, she made her first out-of-state appearance. She accepted for Medgar the NAACP's highest honor, the Spingarn Medal, which was awarded posthumously at the annual convention in Chicago. After that she was on the road most weekends, giving speeches to NAACP branches.

She remembers the time as one remembers an unpleasant dream — the kind in which you never catch the plane you are late for, never find your way to the train. She was disconnected and depressed, just walking through her life, which no longer had any meaning. Coming home to the house on Guynes Street was agony.

Alarmed, Gloster Current and Roy Wilkins arranged for Myrlie and the children to see a psychiatrist in New York. They urged her to move away from Jackson.

16

Trial by Ambush

THE TRIAL of Byron De La Beckwith began in Jackson on a raw, windy morning January 27, 1964. A small, curious crowd gathered on the steps of the huge limestone-and-granite courthouse on the corner of Pascagoula and Congress Streets. A vendor selling peanuts was disappointed by the turnout. It could have turned into a circus, but the NAACP deliberately kept a lid on demonstrations that might detract from the "dignity" and "fairness" of the trial.

The Hinds County Courthouse had been built on a grand scale, with heavy, oversize bronzed-wood doors, a cool, vaulted marble foyer, high ceilings, lots of dark polished wood and oil paintings in the public rooms. Despite the grand trappings it was an all-purpose building: three floors of judges' chambers, courtrooms, and witness rooms. The top two floors, accessed from a separate entrance, served as the Hinds County jail, where Beckwith was a prisoner. One wing of the fifth floor held the old gallows chamber, used frequently in the days when executions had been a local event. The state now dispatched its condemned inmates in the gas chamber at Parchman prison, deep in the Delta.

Security was heavy on the second floor, at the entrance to courtroom number three. The bailiffs were expecting big crowds and trouble. Each spectator and journalist had to sign in at the door, submit to being frisked, and receive a badge to enter. There were new rules for this trial: anyone could sit wherever he or she wished. There was no need for demonstrations. For the time being the courthouse was integrated by order of the judge.

The wood-paneled chamber was the biggest the city had to offer, with seating for three hundred and a balcony. The judge's bench towered over the assembly.

Circuit court judge Leon Hendrick was sixty-nine years old, tall and slim, with pure white hair and spectacles. He was generally a soft-spoken man, but he could summon a big courtroom voice when he needed it. This was not the southern cracker of a judge the northern press was expecting to find. Hendrick was, reporters would point out, a "dignified" professional.

At 8:30 A.M. the first batch of veniremen took their seats in the courtroom. There were two hundred names on the roster of potential jurors picked from the voting rolls of Hinds County. All were men. Women wouldn't serve on state juries in Mississippi for another four years.

Of the one hundred veniremen who sat in the courthouse, seven were Negroes. It was a little charade the courts had to go through, since there were no laws barring blacks from juries. They just never were chosen.

Three Negroes were actually interviewed. Each was dismissed because of work conflicts or opposition to the death penalty, which was reason enough to dismiss a potential juror in a capital case. District Attorney Bill Waller simply skipped calling the others.

Bill Waller kicked things off with a question for each man in the jury pool: "Do you think it's a crime to kill a nigger in Mississippi?"

Black spectators, including Aaron Henry, shifted angrily in their seats. So it was going to be like this after all. Another kangaroo court, a whitewash, a quick acquittal. Another Emmett Till.

But Waller had a strategy going. He assumed certain things: that white men of goodwill would have a hard time sympathizing with the victim; that they might find Beckwith sympathetic — particularly if he didn't testify, and Waller had no way of knowing whether he would; that they were segregationists. But just as he did, they could set all those things aside and follow the law. His questions were designed to put himself squarely in their corner, lead them through the facts, and show them that they could do the right thing together.

He asked practical questions: Had they contributed to Beckwith's defense fund? Would rendering an unpopular verdict affect their relationship with their customers?

And he dug deeper, putting himself inside the skin of his potential jurors, seeing how it fit. "The deceased worked in a way obnoxious and emotionally repulsive to you as a businessman and me as a lawyer — can you put this out of your mind and judge this case like any other case?" he asked.

Ed King sat in the balcony and watched with growing disgust. It seemed to him that Medgar was on trial, not Beckwith. He would refer to this proceeding as "Medgar's trial" for the rest of his days.

Meanwhile Waller kept on hammering on his theme: "I'm a little upset myself right now with all these nigras in the courtroom — does that bother you?"

The strategy seemed to pay off. When Waller put the big question — Is it a crime to kill a nigger? — to one venireman, the man sat quiet.

"What did he say?" asked Judge Hendrick.

"Nothing, Judge," said Bill Waller. "He's trying to make up his mind." The man was sent home.

This went on for four days, both sides picking through the minds of the jurors, looking for an advantage. Of the first twelve men to come up, the prosecution dismissed eleven.

The normally stoic judge took to fidgeting with a ring on his finger. The three defense attorneys cradled their chins in their hands as they scrutinized each juror.

Beckwith seemed thoroughly at ease. Wearing a dark blue suit with a red tie-and-sock combination, he lounged in his chair at the defense table. Spectators noted that he looked more like a prince awaiting coronation than an innocent chump on trial for his life. He casually draped one arm across his chair and the other on the defense table, chin raised and black wire-frame glasses balanced on his nose. During breaks he smoked a cigar while he chatted with his guards.

He was elated by the appearance — apparently a surprise — of his long-estranged wife, Willie. She was a big woman with dark hair and an unpleasant expression on her face. She wore a modest little knit suit, two big strands of faux pearls, and pale gloves. In later appearances she sometimes wore a little fur stole over her shoulders.

The first time Beckwith saw her in court, he rushed over and kissed her. She sat behind him throughout the trial.

There were other regulars as well. Reverend R. L. T. Smith sat in the same front-row seat every day. Judge Russel Moore, the Citizens' Councils stalwart who had once conspired to arrest Medgar Evers and Roy Wilkins, was a constant fixture in the spectator pews.

Jury selection wore on into night sessions. Finally both sides agreed on twelve jurors and one alternate who represented a cross section of white Jackson. Among them were two electricians, two business executives, an engineer, a plumber, a bakery manager, and assorted salesmen.

Opening statements were heard on Friday, January 31. This time the courtroom was packed with spectators, and a line curled around the hallway with the overflow crowd.

John Fox sat with Bill Waller at the prosecution table. Like Waller he was an old-family Mississippian. He could trace his roots through seven generations, back to a Revolutionary War veteran who had migrated from South Carolina. The family still owned a farm outside Jackson that had belonged to the Indians before the first Fox ancestor bought the land and planted crops. But while Fox could out-Mississippi any witness he interviewed, he was nobody's redneck. He was raised in Oxford, where his father was a professor and registrar at the University of Mississippi Law School. Fox went straight through Ole Miss, undergraduate and law school. After a stint in the army he went into practice with his friend Bill Waller in 1958. Now in his thirties, Fox still looked like a college boy, or maybe a member of the Kingston Trio, in his white shirt and thin tie and crew cut, which made his perfectly round ears stick out like apricot halves.

Beckwith's troika of lawyers — Hardy Lott, his partner Stanny Sanders, and Hugh Cunningham — were older, more established attorneys. Physically they were almost interchangeable: fleshy-faced white men in advanced middle age with similar cases of male-pattern baldness.

Ross Barnett, who by law could not succeed himself, had turned over the governorship to Paul Johnson earlier that month. He had resumed an active partnership in Cunningham's law firm, and he made frequent appearances at the defense table. Barnett developed a habit of wandering into the courtroom almost every morning of the trial. More than once the former governor shook Beckwith's hand and clapped him on the back in full view of the jurors.

The bailiff called the court to order, and Waller began to lay out his case for the jury. "Our witnesses will show in ten ways that Byron De La Beckwith is guilty of this crime," he said.

The first state witness was B. D. Harrell, the officer who had taken the call about a shooting on Guynes Street.

The next witness was Myrlie Evers.

Myrlie chose a royal blue dress and black gloves for her court appearance. As the bailiff led her to the stand, Myrlie's eyes flicked over the courtroom, looking for Beckwith. She had dreaded this moment and wondered how she would react when she saw him. When she took her seat and her eyes came to rest on him, she felt nothing at all. She was utterly composed.

Byron De La Beckwith sat at the defense table, watching impassively. From time to time he squirmed in his chair to scan the crowd of spectators for familiar faces. Sometimes he scrawled furiously on a yellow legal pad.

Bill Waller began his questioning by asking her name.

"Mrs. Medgar Evers," she said.

"Your first name, please?"

"Myrlie — M-Y-R-L-I-E."

Waller was walking a minefield here. He needed her testimony. She had to describe the crime scene, how she had heard the shot and found her husband in the pool of blood. With luck the jury would sympathize with the well-dressed, well-spoken widow. But the whole thing could backfire if Myrlie balked at being called by her first name, which every white person in the courthouse knew was the way you were supposed to address a Negro.

The prosecutor and the widow had argued over the issue of courtroom decorum for months. Myrlie refused to address anyone as sir, not even the judge. And she assured Waller that she would not answer any questions in which she was addressed as "Myrlie" instead of "Mrs. Evers."

Waller could just see it blowing up in his face. He was going to play along, but what about Hardy Lott? What if he called her Myrlie and she refused to answer? Would the court haul her off for contempt? And even if that didn't happen, what would the jury think of such an uppity attitude? The whole case could be wrecked over a piece of foolishness.

Waller proceeded with caution. He solved his own problem by not using her name at all when prefacing his questions. Evers calmly answered questions about her husband: when they were married, where he went to school. Then Waller led her to the day of the murder.

She testified that she had spoken to her husband on the phone three times that day, the last time around 5:30 P.M. In a clear, strong voice she described how the children had heard the car pull into the driveway, and then the shot.

"After that there was complete silence," she said.

"What did you do?"

"The moment I heard the blast I ran to the door. . . . I turned on the light and opened the door at the same time and I saw my husband where he had fallen." She described the keys in his hand, the blood on the ground.

"I believe that's all," said Waller.

The prosecutor sat down, and Hardy Lott walked to the lectern. "After you heard this loud blast," he asked, "did you hear any more shots?"

"I heard another shot after I had gotten to my husband."

Bill Waller relaxed. Lott was going along; he wouldn't use her name at all. Maybe Lott wanted her testimony in cross-examination more than he needed to alienate the jury against her by provoking a scene. It could be his only chance to bring up Medgar Evers's career as an integrationist and to establish other motives for the killing.

Myrlie didn't remember hearing any shots after the second blast. Then Lott asked her whether she had accused anyone at the scene of killing her husband. She said she had not.

"You didn't say to anyone, 'You shot my husband'?" he asked.

"No, I did not."

Lott was trying to bring out what some witnesses had heard on the night of the murder, when Myrlie was hysterical and shouting at a group of white boys who came to gawk at the crime scene. She yelled some things she could no longer remember.

Lott wanted to show the jury that there could be more than one suspect in Medgar Evers's murder.

The lawyer asked Myrlie whether her husband had received death threats, and she said that he had. She then testified that Medgar Evers was the NAACP field secretary and that he was active in the integration movement.

"Was he — he was the first person as a matter of fact who attempted integration of the University of Mississippi."

Myrlie opened her mouth to answer yes. It was something she was proud of. But Waller wasn't going to allow Hardy Lott to get into this if he could help it.

"Your Honor," he barked. "We don't see that this has any bearing on this!"

"I sustain the objection to that," the judge said.

Lott tried a different approach.

"Now, at the time your husband was shot he had filed and had pending in Jackson a suit to integrate the white public schools of this city . . .?"

Waller jumped up again.

"Your Honor, we can't see that this is material on cross-examination of this woman. She is a housewife. She wasn't in the movement. It has nothing to do with this slaying at the time, in the middle of the night at his home."

This time Judge Hendrick allowed the question.

Lott resumed: "My question was, if it wasn't a fact that at the time your husband was killed he had pending a lawsuit filed by him on behalf of his children to integrate the white schools of Jackson, Mississippi?"

"My husband was not the only plaintiff. There were other plaintiffs in the case."

"But he was a plaintiff in it?"

"He was one of the plaintiffs."

"You were another?"

"That's correct."

"It was brought on behalf of all the colored children in Jackson to integrate the schools here?"

"We were not the only plaintiffs."

"There were others. Is that suit still pending?"

"To my knowledge, it is."

"Now I believe one of your children who you stated was present that night is Thomas Kenyatta Evers?"

"No, that is not correct."

"What is his name?"

"Darrell." She spelled it out. "D-A-R-R-E-L-L K-E-N-Y-A-T-T-A Evers — E-V-E-R-S."

"I see. He was named after Kenyatta . . ."

"Your Honor, we object to this! This is a deliberate attempt to poison the minds of the jury about some child's name!"

"I sustain the objection," the judge said.

Lott gave up.

"No further questions."

As Myrlie stood to leave the witness box, she felt somehow disappointed. She was just getting warmed up, and it was over. She had made it through without losing her temper or breaking down. Medgar would have been proud of her. It was the last she would see of the inside of the courtroom for the rest of the trial. Witnesses could not listen to testimony, and to the relief of the defense the grieving widow could not take a front-row seat for the jury to see. If Waller hadn't called her, Lott might well have, just to keep her out of court.

The next witness was Houston Wells, the Everses' next-door neighbor, who had fired his pistol to scare off the assassin. Wells owned a furniture company, and he was a good friend of Medgar Evers. Bill Waller wasn't going to tiptoe around this witness. He was a good ol' boy again.

"You are Houston Wells?"

"Yes, sir, I am."

"Where do you live, Houston?"

It was established that Wells was a neighbor and that he heard the shot that killed Evers, his daughter screamed, and some two minutes later he fired a .38 pistol in the air before running next door. He told the court that his brother James drove over to help, it took James about five minutes to get there, and that James fired a shotgun in the air just as Medgar was being carried to the hospital.

"Well, I believe just as I was leaving another shot was fired."

"You know who fired that shot?"

"My brother."

"You all are not trigger happy are you, Houston?"

"No, we were aware it had to be somebody . . . in that area . . ."

Waller had one last question. He wanted the jury to hear just what Houston Wells found when he saw his friend lying, gasping in his own blood.

"Did you see the wife of Medgar Evers?"

"Yes, sir. . . . She was coming out the door and was screaming. . . . And the children were screaming. She was screaming and the children were screaming. She was just a wreck."

"That's all."

The next witness was Joe Alford, a Jackson patrolman who arrived at the scene some three minutes after the call came in at 12:45 A.M. that there had been a shooting on Guynes Street. He escorted Wells's car, with Evers inside, to the hospital.

Then came Dr. Forrest Bratley, a pathologist who performed the autopsy on Medgar Evers. He was called in at 2:15 A.M. He said the body was still warm. The cause of death: hemorrhage.

In a matter-of-fact voice Dr. Bratley described Evers's wounds. There were two. The smaller wound, he said, was in the back, some ten inches below the right shoulder blade and about six inches to the right of his spine. It was oval in shape and measured fourteen by nine millimeters, a little smaller than a dime. From that entry point he had tracked the path of the bullet through Evers's body. It was a grisly education in the damage one shot from a military weapon could inflict in the blink of an eye, tearing up lung tissue and arteries and shattering bones before it exited the chest in a jagged gash roughly the shape of a half-dollar coin.

The next witness was John Chamblee, a thirteen-year veteran of the Jackson police who had been a detective for eight of those years. He said he had investigated maybe twenty murders in the past decade. Jackson was a small, slow town back then. Chamblee was well-spoken but a little nervous. Bill Waller kept asking him to speak up and slow down as he described the crime scene in the early morning hours of June 12.

When he and his partner arrived at the scene at 12:54 A.M., they found Myrlie Evers standing in the carport with a neighbor. Then they saw the blood. It was "a tremendous amount of blood," Chamblee said. "In fact it looked liked somebody had butchered a hog at that point."

The detective told the court that Myrlie Evers was nearly incoherent with shock. He described a crowd of about twenty-five people milling around on the lawn, but nobody had seen anything. So Detective Chamblee and his partner, Fred Sanders, started to look for physical evidence to piece together what had happened.

At this point the prosecution entered into evidence a stack of black-and-white photos of the crime scene and the surrounding neighborhood, some of them aerial shots.

After lunch Hardy Lott cross-examined Chamblee.

"Did you take in a boy, a young white man, that night for questioning about having shot Evers?" he asked.

Chamblee told him that he and other officers "took several people in for questioning and collaboration [sic] of what had happened out there. But as far as a suspect, we didn't take anybody in as a suspect, purely as a witness in the material."

Chamblee was asked whether he had heard Myrlie Evers accuse someone at the scene of shooting her husband. He had not.

Fred Sanders also testified that afternoon. Waller handed the thirty-two-year-old detective a glass bottle containing fragments of a .30-caliber lead-tipped bullet. Sanders identified it as the bullet he had found on Medgar Evers's kitchen counter. It was in pieces now because it had been dissected and tested by the FBI laboratory. It was, he said, over the strenuous objection of Hardy Lott, the same bullet that had killed Medgar Evers.

Next up was Betty Coley, the woman who had been walking with Kenneth Adcock along Missouri Street when the shot was fired. She remembered how beautiful the moon had been that night. Bill Waller let her tell her story:

"We were walking, as has been pointed out, toward my home. Just walking slowly, talking and we were very startled when we heard the sound of the bullet because we were positive that the shot had been fired at us. Kenneth grabbed me. We stood there for a second and Kenneth said, 'The best thing we can do is just to walk on slowly like we've been walking and act as if nothing had happened.' And that's what we did. We walked on to the house."

Right after the shot was fired, Coley heard the sound of someone running. From what she could tell, the person had been heading in the direction of Joe's Drive In.

After a short break Hardy Lott took the witness.

"You, of course, couldn't tell, for example, whether that was a man or a woman running," Lott said.

"No, sir."

"Just somebody running in that field. And you naturally stayed there, or didn't you, for a while, you and the young man, after that running over in there and you didn't see anything."

"Not very long. But we were there. We didn't walk away immediately."

"Did you hear any car start up or leave or anything?"

"Not that I recall."

Adcock took the stand next and corroborated Coley's testimony. Like Coley, he heard the sound of someone running, but he never heard a car start up.

Detective O. M. Luke was born and raised in Neshoba County, not far from Medgar Evers's hometown of Decatur. He had been a police officer in Jackson for just over thirteen years when he took the stand that day.

Luke described his search of the crime scene on the morning of June 12. He described the weedy field behind Joe's Drive In where he found the Enfield rifle and scope carefully concealed in a clump of vines. The weapon, he said, had not been dropped, but had been carefully placed upright in the honeysuckle, more than a foot off the ground.

The rifle, he testified, was an Eddystone, serial number 1052682. The scope on it was a United Golden Hawk, six by thirty-two power, serial number 69431. Before the rifle was shipped off to the FBI lab in Washington, Luke had scratched his initials and the date into the barrel action.

Bill Waller held up the rifle, clearly heavy in his hands, and all attention in the courtroom focused on the long, black gunmetal of the barrel and the heavy wooden stock. As a mere prop the gun was an effective prosecution device. Its physical presence was mesmerizing. It looked mean and evil and deadly.

"Is this the gun — the exact gun — that you pulled out of the honeysuckle vine?" Waller asked.

"This is the gun, the same gun," Luke replied.

And so, State's exhibit number 21 was entered into evidence.

Delay Beckwith had a hard time sitting still under the best of circumstances. During the sometimes tedious examination of evidence, the crime scene photographs, and particularly the rifle, Beckwith trailed his lawyers around the room, peering over their shoulders, dogging them, keeping the focus of attention on himself.

During one break that day Beckwith and his attorneys holed up in an empty jury room. The door swung open for a moment, and a reporter caught a glimpse of Beckwith handling the rifle, aiming it across the table.

As Luke left the courtroom, Bill Waller arranged the papers at his table and got ready for the last witness of the day. "The State calls Thorn McIntyre."

There was a tension in the courtroom as the young farmer stepped up to the bench.

In 1964 the rules for state trials in Mississippi were different than they are now. The exchange of evidence we know as discovery didn't exist then. Both parties went to trial more or less blind. Neither side had to reveal anything except alibi witnesses. It was called "trial by ambush."

Innes Thornton McIntyre III was a surprise witness. He wore green sunglasses for the occasion.

McIntyre said that he had known Byron De La Beckwith since he had gotten out of the service in 1958. He told the court that he also knew Hardy Lott and Stanny Sanders. In fact they had been his personal attorneys "for a long time."

Waller then asked him, "Did you in the year 1959 own a British or American Enfield, I'm not sure which it is called, but did you own an Enfield 30.06 rifle?"

"That's correct," McIntyre said. "I ordered the rifle from International Firearms, as I remember, in Connecticut."

He had seen an ad in a magazine, and had ordered it COD for $29.50. He remembered that the invoice was from Quebec, Canada. He recalled picking it up at the Railway Express office in Greenwood. Waller gave him a Railway Express invoice dated February 2, 1959.

McIntyre had never seen this piece of paper before. It was a copy of the shipping company's invoice, which the FBI had dug up in its investigation. McIntyre couldn't find the original invoice he had received from Quebec. McIntyre told the court that the information on the shipping company's invoice was similar to his recollection of when and how he had received the gun, but Waller was not allowed to enter the invoice into evidence.

The D.A. then handed McIntyre exhibit number 21, the rifle found near the crime scene.

"How does that weapon compare to the one you owned?"

"The type of weapon is exactly the same. There is no doubt of that. The weapon was made at the Eddystone arsenal and this one is also as shown by the markings on this weapon here. The weapon I owned was made in the ninth month of the year 1918. Those are the only definite markings that I do remember but I do remember those definitely."

"Does this gun in every way appear to be the gun that you owned?"

"When I traded my rifle, I kept the wooden stock. I couldn't testify to that. I still have my stock in my possession."

"You mean you took the stock off the barrel?"

"Yes, sir."

"You traded a gun without a stock?"

"That's correct."

"Who did you trade guns with?"

Over a volley of objections from Hardy Lott, McIntyre was allowed to answer: "A man from Greenwood named De La Beckwith."

"Do you see that man in the courtroom now?"

"I do."

Thorn told the jury that he had once had a general conversation about guns with Beckwith on the street in Greenwood. Beckwith had driven twelve miles out to McIntyre's house to trade with him. He told the jury that it was his opinion that the gun in evidence was the same gun he had traded to Beckwith. He said he had fired that gun two hundred or three hundred times and had turned over some empty cartridge cases to the FBI. He was sure they had come from this weapon.

Now Hardy Lott took the lectern. This might be the best witness the state was likely to come up with, and Lott knew he had to do his best to demolish him. But he did it gently.

What he had to make clear was that the rifle in evidence looked nothing like the one McIntyre had traded to Delay Beckwith. Lott led McIntyre through the details of the trade: the rusty Enfield barrel and action and the new Springfield for McIntyre's good Eddystone-type Enfield.

"All right," Lott said. "Now he kept the stock on his rifle?"

"He kept his stock and I kept mine."

"Now the thing you traded him didn't have any scope on it, did it?"

"No."

"And it didn't have any stock?"

"No. . . . That's not my stock."

Lott asked him how, without having seen the stock or scope before, he could identify the rifle in the newspaper. He said it was because the barrel had been made at the Eddystone arsenal in September 1918.

"Would it surprise you to learn that there were more than two million manufactured in that month?"

"No, it wouldn't."

The court recessed until 9 A.M., Saturday.

That night there was another murder in Mississippi. Somebody lured Louis Allen to his front gate and blew his head off with a shotgun.

Allen was a thirty-six-year-old logger with a wife and three children who lived in Liberty, Mississippi. To this day some folks around the little community on the Louisiana line say Allen was killed for a bad debt. Others know better. They say it was because Allen had witnessed the killing of Herbert Lee, an NAACP worker who was shot dead by a state representative, E. H. Hurst. Hurst claimed he killed Lee in self-defense, and at first Louis Allen backed him up. Then his conscience got him, and he talked to the press and to John Doar, who was prepared to prosecute. Allen had been warned to keep his mouth shut, but he still talked. Then someone killed him.

In this case, like so many others, there was no suspect, and no arrest. There would never be a trial.

On Saturday morning, with the jury fresh after a night's sleep, Waller began to introduce the highly technical evidence he would need to tie the murder weapon first to Thorn McIntyre and then to Beckwith. He called Francis Finley, the Memphis-based FBI agent who had collected fifty-three empty cartridge cases from Thorn McIntyre's farm on June 24. He called Richard Poppleton, an FBI ballistics expert, who worked in the FBI laboratory in Washington. Poppleton had test-fired the Enfield and then compared the microscopic markings on the test casings with the shells retrieved from McIntyre. He testified that thirty of McIntyre's casings had been fired by the rifle in evidence.

Poppleton's most important job was to link the bullet that had killed Medgar Evers to that same rifle. He had first examined the six live rounds recovered from the chamber and found that they were factory-loaded Winchester .30/06 180-grain soft point bullets. They could be bought at any hardware store.

When Poppleton had received the bullet, the lead tip was squashed like a mushroom, and the sides of the copper jacket were folded back along the lower half of the base. Poppleton had to smooth back the sides — basically try to reconstruct the original contours of the bullet to examine it. Two fragments of the jacket had broken off when he unfolded it.

Poppleton could say for certain that the spent round that had killed Evers was the same type and manufacture as the bullets in the chamber of the Enfield. Then he ran into a problem.

The basis of ballistic comparison is the supposition that every gun has a signature: microscopic markings that are etched into a bullet as it passes through the barrel. No two barrels are exactly the same, and each leaves a distinctive "fingerprint" on the bullet jacket.

Poppleton was clearly proud of his skill in ballistics. He spoke lovingly, endlessly, of riflings and grains and land-and-groove impressions. But for all his expertise and precision he could not do the one thing Waller needed: he could not put that bullet back in the rifle.

The FBI man testified that the bullet that killed Medgar Evers was so mutilated that there were not enough identifiable markings to associate it with any particular gun. He could tell it had been fired from an Enfield, and he had found "some similarities" with other bullets test-fired from the rifle in evidence, but not enough to justify a scientific match.

It was a blow for the prosecution, and with it the first breeze of reasonable doubt wafted through the courtroom. Waller was able to get Poppleton to say that there was nothing about the bullet to suggest it had not been fired from the rifle, but Hardy Lott was ready to pounce.

In cross-examination Lott got Poppleton to admit that it was "remotely possible" that the spent round could have been fired from a different type of rifle fitted with an Enfield barrel. He had him testify that two million of this type of American Enfields had been manufactured during World War I and later sold as surplus. These rifles were now scattered around the country in the hands of private gun owners.

"And this spent bullet, Exhibit 18, in your firm opinion, could have been fired from any one of those rifles?" Lott asked.

"That's correct."

During breaks in the testimony Beckwith made a point of hounding Waller. Once he slipped a cigar into the astounded prosecutor's breast pocket. Waller numbly handed it back. The little fellow was always trying to put his hands on his adversary, and Waller had to stay alert to keep out of reach. Beckwith sometimes managed to pat Waller on the back as he left the courtroom. Waller ignored him as best he could.

Beckwith just couldn't keep still. He once walked over to the jury box and started to chat with the jurors before the bailiff herded him back to his seat.

After lunch John Fox took over the examinations. He called to the stand John W. Goza, known to folks around the Delta as "Duck" and proprietor of Duck's Tackle Shop on Highway 8 East in Grenada, Mississippi. Duck did not seem happy to be in court. He said he knew Delay Beckwith well; the salesman would come by the shop every month or so to trade guns.

Goza told the court that Beckwith had telephoned him at his shop on May 12, 1963, to tell him that he was coming over to do some trading. Beckwith was calling from Greenwood, and he wanted to know how late Duck would be open that night. Goza told him eight o'clock.

Beckwith drove the thirty miles to Grenada that night. Duck traded Beckwith five dollars' worth of .22 cartridges for an inoperable .22 rifle. There were other trades as well.

"I traded a nice .45 automatic for a lesser grade automatic, and I got four or five clips to boot. And then I — I wanted to go home. He said he had another trade to make, and I traded him a six-power scope, telescopic sight."

"And what did you trade with him for the six-power scope?" Fox asked.

"A .45 automatic. . . . I was trying to run him out. I wanted to go home. He said, 'I've got one more trade to make,' said, 'What will you give me for this .45 automatic?' And I wanted to go home. I just noticed this scope laying there in the showcase, and I told him I'd trade him even."

"Did you run him out of your shop?"

"I wanted to go home."

Fox produced an invoice from United Binocular Company showing that Goza had received one Golden Hawk six-power scope on September 12, 1962. Goza testified that it had been the only one of its kind in his shop. It was the scope he had traded to Beckwith.

Stanny Sanders took the cross. He got Goza to say that Beckwith was just like any other gun trader who came into the shop — that he would come in and handle things, pick them up. Goza also agreed that when he had traded the scope, there hadn't been anything unusual or secret about the deal.

The Court adjourned early that afternoon.

The trial of Byron De La Beckwith resumed Monday morning, February 3. The state was still making its case.

Ralph Hargrove was called to the stand to describe the fingerprint he had found on the Golden Hawk scope. This was crucial testimony for Waller, the very cornerstone of his case against Beckwith.

Hargrove, the captain in charge of the Identification Division, described his training. He had been on the force for twenty-three of his forty-three years. He described himself as a graduate of the Institute of Applied Science in Chicago.

When Hargrove dusted the rifle, he said, he found a number of smears on parts of the weapon, vestiges of fingerprints and palm prints, typical of the surface of a gun. In his opinion the weapon had not been wiped down after it was last handled.

Hargrove found only one clear, identifiable print. He said that latent print "practically jumped up" when he spread the powder over the right front section of the scope. Charts and diagrams and photos were produced on an easel for the jury to examine. Hargrove droned on about what a fingerprint is, how it is made.

Then Waller asked, ". . . do you have an opinion as to the age of that fingerprint, based upon all circumstances?"

Lott objected. He was overruled, and Hargrove was allowed to answer.

"A latent fingerprint will last according to its surroundings. It — the life of a print cannot be pinpointed, although a print will last, as I said, according to the things that come in contact with it. . . . I believe that the print is not over twelve hours old."

Hargrove then compared Beckwith's fingerprint card, taken at the time of his arrest, with the latent print lifted from the scope, and said he found a match with Beckwith's right index finger. He marked fourteen points of comparison; he said he could have marked more.

The prosecution set up a slide projector to show the two prints side by side. Hargrove compared them, ridge by ridge, whorl by whorl, bifurcation by bifurcation, through the fourteen comparison points. He also pointed out a small scar visible in both prints. He said that the identification was "positive."

Hardy Lott needed to destroy this testimony in a bad way. So he began chipping away at Hargrove's expertise. He mocked Hargrove's "degree" from the formidable-sounding Institute of Applied Science in Chicago. It was a correspondence course, the kind advertised on matchbooks and in detective magazines. Lott read from a magazine advertisement for the school: "Blue Book of Crime free! Given to men who want to get into crime detection — fingerprint identification — train at home — spare time . . . learn fingerprint identification — crime investigation — police photography — other subjects vital to qualifying for good-paying, secure, interesting jobs."

Then Lott referred the captain to the slide projection of the two prints. The print taken in ink at the jail included the whole terminal joint of the right index finger and part of the second joint. Lott made much of the fact that the latent print taken from the rifle was of a smaller section of the fingertip, roughly between one-third and one-quarter the size of the jailhouse print. He referred to it from then on as a "fraction" of a print, while Hargrove insisted that it was a "large, plain impression" with more than enough information to make a comparison. It was simply narrower, showing only the natural contours of a fingertip as it would touch an object without rolling from one side to another.

Lott tried to inject skepticism into the minds of the jury — there were bits missing, smudges. And Lott tried to discredit Hargrove's evaluation of the age of the print. He got Hargrove to admit that fingerprints can last indefinitely — months, even years — under certain circumstances.

Lott then asked whether Hargrove knew for a fact how long the rifle had lain in the honeysuckle, whether it had been in a case just before that or been wrapped in cellophane — something that would preserve a fingerprint just like new. Hargrove said he didn't know.

Lott asked Hargrove if the dew that had collected on the hot, humid night of the murder might have destroyed the latent fingerprint. Hargrove countered that the dew was light, and he took that into consideration when he aged the print. But Lott had planted his seed: couldn't the weapon have been placed there in the hours after the murder?

After lunch George Edward Goodreau, an FBI fingerprint examiner, took the stand to tie the prints to Beckwith's Marine records. As with Hargrove, Hardy Lott tried to inject doubt that a man could be identified with only part of one fingerprint.

After hours of droning technical testimony, Waller decided to pick up the pace with something more dramatic. He called Herbert Richard Speight, the first of two cabdrivers who had said they saw Beckwith in Jackson the weekend before the murder.

Speight testified that he was sitting in his White Top cab outside the Trailways bus station around 4 P.M. on the Saturday before the murder, when Byron De La Beckwith had walked up and asked him "if I knew Negro Medgar Evers, N-double A-C-P leader." Speight said he didn't, so Beckwith walked back into the bus station, went into a phone booth, and came out with a map.

"He came back to my cab, and . . . he asked me if I knew where Lexington Street was. I told him I did, but that couldn't be where the colored fellow lived because it's an all-white section."

"All right. What did Mr. Beckwith do then?" Waller asked.

"He turned around and went back to the bus station. He came back with another address on Buena Vista, if I recall right, and I told him that couldn't be it, because that was a white section."

Beckwith came back again with an address on Poplar, again a white neighborhood. He was, Speight remembered, "very calm." He said another cabbie named Lee Swilley was sitting in the cab with him at the time.

After that Speight got a radio call to pick up a fare in North Jackson, and he pulled out of the bus station. He didn't think about it again until Beckwith was arrested.

Stanny Sanders took the cross. He reminded Speight of the time when he and Hugh Cunningham had gone to Speight's boardinghouse to talk to him. Although the prosecution didn't have to reveal its witnesses, Speight had accidentally been served a subpoena, so Beckwith's team had gone by to check him out. The conversation had lasted some forty-five minutes, and in that time Speight had told them he "guessed" he had been subpoenaed because he saw Beckwith "about a week before Evers was shot." Speight told them he'd had a "general conversation" with Beckwith he didn't really remember.

"And we asked you specifically, did we not, if the name Medgar Evers was mentioned, didn't we?" Sanders asked.

"You did."

"You told us no, didn't you, Mr. Speight?"

"Yessir. I don't talk to two parties at the same time."

The courtroom broke up in laughter, and the sheriff was called in to keep order. Speight continued to admit that he had misled the defense lawyers.

"As I say, when I talk to one attorney, I don't talk to another." Speight also had lied about being alone in the cab when he saw Beckwith.

Speight then testified that he had been taken down to the police station for a lineup and had identified Beckwith among six or eight men. "I never forget a face if I ever see it once," he said.

Speight said that he just didn't know whether Beckwith was the only man in the lineup who wasn't wearing a coat and tie, didn't have a belt on, and happened to be wearing a shirt with the monogram BDB. "I didn't pay that much notice," he said. He just knew the face.

Waller, he testified, had told him not to discuss the case with anyone. Speight was sputtering and tongue-tied when Sanders got through with him.

"Were you acting under the instructions of Mr. Waller when you misrepresented yourself to us?" Sanders asked.

"I — uh — uh . . ."

The judge wouldn't let Sanders ask it that way, but Sanders already had what he needed. The witness was dismissed.

After a brief recess Lee Swilley was sworn in and repeated the same basic story Speight had told. Beckwith was looking for Evers and had wanted to know whether he lived on Poplar, Lexington, or "Arbor Vista." He added that Beckwith had told the cabbies, "I got to find where he lives in a couple of days."

Swilley said he called the Jackson police on June 13 about the incident, and gave them a statement. He too picked Beckwith out of a lineup.

Waller then called W. T. Lee, a telephone company executive, to testify that Medgar Evers had had an unlisted number and was not in the phone book of 1963. This would show that Beckwith would not have found his name and address in the phone booth at the bus station.

Lott attacked the whole scenario. He handed Lee the phone book and asked him to read the names and addresses of every Evers in the directory: "Dr. Carl Evers, 4325 Azalea Drive; David W. Evers Jr., 505 Witsell Road; James E. Evers, 344 Culley Drive; and Mrs. Mary L. Evers, 4233 Chennault Avenue." There was no Evers on Poplar or Buena or Arbor Vista. Why, then, would Beckwith have mentioned those streets? This made the cab drivers seem less credible.

Dewitt Walcott, president of Delta Liquid Plant Food and Byron De La Beckwith's employer, testified that Beckwith worked for him since February 1963. Walcott said that the white Valiant in Beckwith's possession in June of 1963 belonged to the company. It had a broken speedometer, he said, so there were no records of its daily mileage, but Beckwith was allowed to take it home and use it for personal business.

All Waller wanted Walcott for was to establish that Beckwith drove a white Valiant. But as it turned out, Mr. Walcott was a bit of a time bomb for the prosecution.

Sanders used his cross-examination to discuss Beckwith's work habits. He was, according to Walcott, hardworking. In fact the week of June 10 was extremely busy, as every customer needed soil and tissue tests. Walcott also slipped in a few other points. He had seen Beckwith with a rifle in his car on Monday morning, June 10, and he had seen a fresh, quarter-moon-shaped cut over Beckwith's eye. Also, the doors and the trunk of the Valiant didn't lock real well. In other words, it would have been easy to steal something out of the car. Like a rifle.

Bill Waller next called Leroy Pittman, who lived with his wife next to their small grocery store on Delta Drive, just south of Joe's Drive In. Pittman and his wife both testified that early one evening the week before the shooting, probably that Thursday, they saw a stranger dressed in a business suit strolling around the field behind their property. Since those vacant lots were for sale, they assumed he was looking at real estate. He paid them no mind, but he was staring toward Guynes Street.

They thought it was strange that the man was wearing dark glasses, and it was almost night.

The Pittmans had not been around on the night of the murder. They had left for a trip to the Gulf Coast on Sunday. Their son, Robert, told the court that he also saw a man get out of a white Valiant and walk around the vacant lots. He said that the man was wearing a hat, sunglasses, a dark suit, and white shoes.

Robert Pittman, who was seventeen, said that he had seen that white Valiant on other occasions. At about eleven o'clock on the Saturday night before the shooting, he saw a white Valiant backed into a secluded spot next to the grocery store, facing Delta Drive. He noticed a whip-type antenna lashed to the back bumper and a Shriners emblem dangling from the rearview mirror. Robert was certain that the car was a '62 model.

He saw the car again the night of the murder. He and his friend Ronald Jones were minding the store. Just after 9 P.M. on Tuesday, June 11, Ronald and Robert closed the store and started throwing model airplanes out back. One plane landed on the roof of the store, and Robert climbed up to get it. That's when they saw the white Valiant with the big antenna cruising by the place, real slow. They thought it was a police car.

The teenagers were asleep when they heard the first shot. They looked out toward Joe's, saw nothing, and then heard the screaming. They ran in the direction of the screaming and found a hysterical Myrlie Evers in her front yard. She shouted something at them, like they were the ones who killed her husband, so they ran back home.

Jones testified that another shot was fired, maybe at them, while they were running home. Both boys were awakened by the police at four o'clock that morning, taken to the station for questioning, and then released.

The trial had everyone's attention now. On Monday the gallery was standing room only. The Negro neighborhoods were tense, particularly the area around the Jackson State campus.

That night a twenty-year-old student named Mamie Ballard stepped out into the traffic that passed through the campus. A white motorist hit her, breaking her leg. The crowd of students who surrounded the accident soon broke into a wild, angry demonstration. Jackson police came in to chase them off and got a chance to roll out their new riot wagon: a baby-blue armor-plated troop carrier they called the "Thompson Tank." Dogs were set on the students, and police fired buckshot at the crowd. At least three were hit.

The next day Charles Evers stopped two hundred students from marching to the Hinds County Courthouse in protest. They were demanding that the city erect a traffic signal at the dangerous intersection.

"If you are such heroes that you want to die for a traffic light, then go ahead," he told the crowd. "They will shoot you. They showed that last night."

The students stayed on campus.

On Wednesday morning Bill Waller called Martha Jean O'Brien to the stand. The sixteen-year-old carhop had been working at Joe's Drive In on the night of the murder. She was small and pretty, with shoulder-length brown hair. Her job was to go out to cars when they blinked their lights, take the customers' orders, and bring them their food.

Sometime between 8:30 and 10 P.M. on June 11 she saw a dirty white Valiant pull into the parking lot. She later identified it as Beckwith's car.

O'Brien said a man got out of the car without blinking the lights for service and walked to the rest room. She remembered he was very tall, dressed in dark clothes, and in his early twenties. His hair was dark and combed back, and he "walked straight."

When Hardy Lott cross-examined the witness, he asked her how many statements she made to the police. She remembered signing two statements — one taken two days after the murder and another taken on June 24. Waller had referred only to the latter statement and could not produce the first. But Lott seemed to know what was in it.

Didn't she say she noticed the man because he was exceptionally tall and good-looking and in his early twenties? She had. In fact, didn't she pick a six-foot-four policeman out of a lineup as someone who was the same height? She had.

Barbara Ann Holder testified next. She was twenty-two and had recently stopped working at Joe's after six years as a carhop. On the night of June 11, she said, she had been driving around and had stopped at

Joe's on an impulse. She saw Jean O'Brien, and while having a cup of coffee between 8:30 and 8:45, she saw a car pull in and park next to a pile of asphalt.

"I thought it was a police car," she said.

Waller asked her to describe it.

"It was white, and it had a radio aerial on the back, and it was a Valiant, and it was dirty. It looked like it had been out on a dirt road or something."

"Did you see the man in it?"

"Yes, sir. He got out of the car and went in the rest room. . . . I would say he was between five feet seven and five feet nine and a half, and he was slim, and he had on dark clothes. He walked straight, because most of those people out there don't walk straight, but he walked erect and real straight."

She said she left and came back again, around 11:30, and the car was still there.

The judge disallowed one statement she made. She said it was her "opinion" that the man in the lot was Beckwith, based on the pictures she saw in the papers.

Waller wrapped up testimony with a string of official witnesses. FBI agents Lee Prospere and Sam Allen described approaching Beckwith at his home on June 21, the day before his arrest. He refused to talk to them.

Waller called an FBI firearms expert, who testified that a scar over Beckwith's eye and a gash in the tree bark at the sniper's nest could have been caused simultaneously by the recoil of a rifle and scope.

The last witness was the pathologist Dr. Forrest Bratley, who had gotten a good look at Beckwith after his arrest. He described the vivid pink scar, which he determined was between ten and thirty days old and was consistent with the contours of a rifle scope. This was the image Waller wanted to leave with the jury as he rested his case.

In the end Waller and Fox felt they had put on the best possible case. Waller was proud of all the scientific evidence, and he felt that part had gone well. But despite all the circumstantial evidence, he knew the case wasn't a strong one. He never could put the defendant at the scene beyond a reasonable doubt, never could put the gun in his hands at the moment the shot was fired.

Waller also was troubled by how well the defense was prepared for his witnesses. It wasn't much of an ambush when the defense attorneys seemed to have an answer for everything Waller threw at them. Someone was feeding information to the defense team, but Waller could never be sure who was doing the leaking.

He was sure that he would need a break to win the case. He needed the other side to make a mistake, something that would give him an opening.

17

The Varmint Hunter

ALL HARDY LOTT had to do was plant some reasonable doubt in the minds of the jury. He began with a young white woman who lived on Missouri Street, near Medgar and Myrlie Evers.

Willie Mae Patterson had been standing in her parents' kitchen, by the refrigerator, when she heard a loud shot. She ran to the front door and looked through the glass at the house across Missouri Street and she saw "the guy," Medgar Evers, fall in front of his doorway. Everything was still, and then about a minute later she saw three men in light clothes running in front of her house. She didn't recognize them. After the men ran by, she heard two more shots.

When Waller cross-examined Patterson, he read her the statement she had made to police at 4:25 A.M. on June 12. It was very different. She said then that she had waited longer before looking out the window and that the "men" were just walking fast. It had all happened after the second shot was fired. She said that she also saw "three white boys standing next to the fence" across from her house. Waller wondered whether she could have seen young Ken Adcock and Betty Coley, who was wearing slacks, hurrying by.

Next was Lee Cockrell, recent owner of Joe's Drive In, who wasn't having much success getting people to call it "Lee's Drive In." On the night of the murder he pulled into his lot at about 11:30 P.M. He recognized several cars belonging to employees or regular customers. There was no Valiant.

The Drive In shut down at midnight, but the employees were still inside the building at 12:30, closing up. Cockrell said he didn't hear any shots, since he was in front of the restaurant, by the cigar counter. But Eloise Cooper, the "colored girl" who worked as a cook, came running up from the kitchen, saying there had been "some shooting" going on outside. He "immediately" ran to the back door, the one facing east and the houses on Guynes Street, to see what was going on. He stayed maybe two, less than five, minutes. Did he hear or see a man running? He did not. Did he see or hear a car pull out of the gravel lot? He did not. He didn't stay long, he said, because there were two customers up front who had been drinking all day and he was afraid they were about to start fighting.

Waller asked Lee Cockrell if he knew how long Eloise Cooper had waited before running back to tell him there had been a shooting. He didn't know. Waller asked him if it was true that he had told police that he had no idea what had gone on that night because he was so distracted by the fighting drunks. In fact couldn't a car have pulled out of the lot while he was so distracted that he didn't even hear the shot before Eloise Cooper told him about the shooting?

Lee Cockrell didn't think so, but by the time Waller was through with him, Lee Cockrell was not so convincing.

Doris Sumrall, a bookkeeper who worked part-time as a waitress at Joe's, heard the shot. She testified next, saying that she was standing by the cash register at the carhop window when she heard gunfire — one shot, then two or three pistol shots, sounding far off. After the last shots Eloise Cooper came running up, saying, "Someone is shooting out here!" Doris Sumrall, who had a good view of the parking lot, neither saw nor heard a man running, and never saw a car pull out of the lot.

The next witness, Ansie Lee Haven, was another waitress at Joe's who had put in a long day of work — she started at 5 A.M. — when she finally got off at 11 P.M., the night of the murder. As she walked through the parking lot to get her car, she noticed a blue Ford parked in a dark corner, and next to it a white or cream-colored Dodge with no aerial. When police showed her a picture of the Valiant, she was sure it was not the car she saw.

Then Bill Waller cross-examined her, holding her police statements in his hand. Didn't she tell Officers Luke and Turner on the day after the shooting that the car she saw was either a Dodge or a Plymouth? And on June 24, didn't she tell the detectives that she had seen a white Valiant that night, with a big aerial on the back? She denied this. She also denied the statement she made to police only a few weeks earlier, on January 7, saying that the car was either a Valiant or a Dodge.

Alpha Mae McCoy was the owner of Smith's Bait Shop out on Delta Drive, next door to Pittman's Grocery. She was reading in bed when she heard the gunshot. Alpha Mae said she had a good view of Joe's parking lot in the minutes after the shooting, and that she didn't see anybody running or any cars pulling out.

The next two witnesses were friends of Beckwith, Mary Branch and her son Bo, both from Sidon, a small town near Greenwood. Together they reconstructed an odd event on Sunday night, June 9. As they drove together to the bus station in Greenwood at ten o'clock that night, they both testified, they saw a man they didn't know getting out of Beckwith's white Valiant. After Bo ran into the station to find Beckwith, Delay came out and talked to the man, who had hurried over to a pickup. That was all that was said. Bo Branch testified that he saw a cut over Beckwith's eye that night.

The defense later produced four more of Beckwith's friends and co-workers who swore they saw a cut over Delay's eye prior to June 11. One was Fred Conner, a college student who worked at the bus station. He said that he saw Beckwith that same Sunday night, and noticed a "fresh" cut over his eye.

Conner also saw Beckwith the night of the murder. They had dinner together at the Crystal Grill in Greenwood between six and seven in the evening. Fred said Beckwith seemed "normal, just as calm as he always was."

The defense now brought out its own expert witnesses to dispute the state's most solid physical evidence: the fingerprint on the Golden Hawk scope. First up was C. D. Brooks, a chemical engineer and former employee of the Alabama State Department of Toxicology and Criminal

Investigation. Brooks made the point that it is almost impossible to determine the chemical composition of a fingerprint — it depends on what the finger touched beforehand.

"Now, from your work in the field I will ask you whether or not it is possible to determine the length of time that any fingerprint has been in existence?" Lott asked Brooks.

"It can't be done without knowing what the substance is."

"In other words . . . there is no way to determine how old it is?"

"No, sir."

After lunch L. B. Baynard, a former investigator who was briefly director of the Bureau of Identification for the Louisiana State Police, also testified that there was no way to tell the age of a fingerprint.

Roy Jones, the defense's first alibi witness, said he had known Beckwith by name for about three years and could recognize the man. Jones was a thirty-three-year-old small-time entrepreneur from Greenwood who had three kids, a neon-sign business, some real estate interests, and a well-known segregationist point of view. Like many with his beliefs, he had joined the Greenwood auxiliary police to boost the force in those troubled times of Negro agitation.

On the night of June 11, Roy Jones was just learning his new job, and he was eager for all the lessons he could get. After he checked off duty at 11 P.M. he stuck around the Greenwood Police Station to learn about arrest techniques like how to use a nightstick, how to lead a man around by his finger. He then drove to Short's Café for a sandwich and a glass of milk, and he lingered there for about twenty-five minutes. That's how he estimated, as he testified in court, that he saw Byron De La Beckwith around 11:45 near the Billups filling station in Greenwood the night Evers was killed in Jackson.

"When you left the café you were by yourself?" Lott asked.

"I was by myself."

"What did you do then?"

"I proceeded to go home."

"Now, when was it then that you saw Mr. Beckwith?"

"Just as quick as I got in the car and started turning to the left, he was sitting right there on the right, with his lights on, just like he was waiting for a car to pull out, I mean to go on by so he could pull out."

"Did you get a good look at him?"

"Yes, sir."

"Are you positive that was him?"

"I know it was."

Bill Waller pounced during his cross-examination. He had to demolish any alibi witnesses, or at least make them seem confused or biased. He began by asking why, if Jones had knowledge that Beckwith was in Greenwood the night of the murder, did he let him sit in jail for eight months before coming forward with his story. Jones said he didn't know.

"You didn't see fit to notify *anyone?*" Waller asked incredulously.

"That's right, because I hadn't been on the auxiliary police but for four or five months. I didn't know which way to go."

"In spite of the fact you have only known Mr. Beckwith for three years you are good friends of his in the sense that you want to help him out in the trial?"

"I don't know what you mean by good friends."

"Well, you had seen him enough to recognize his automobile at midnight with the headlights on . . ."

"Yes, sir."

". . . at a right angle to the street?"

"Yes, sir."

"To see him in it and know he was driving?"

"Yes, sir."

"Was that a dark night or was it moonlight?"

"It was a dark night."

"Had it been raining?"

"No, sir."

"You want to tell the jury it was a pitch black night?"

"That's right . . ."

The jury may have remembered that other witnesses in the trial testified that it was a bright moonlit night.

Waller picked through the rest of Jones's testimony. How could he see in the car when the headlights were shining at him? Was he sure he hadn't seen Beckwith on the tenth? The ninth? Could he pinpoint any other time he saw Beckwith except at 11:45 on a black night with his lights on? He could not.

On redirect Lott established that there were floodlights shining around Billups service station, making it easy to identify Beckwith in his car as he waited to turn onto Highway 82. He also asked Jones whether he had told anyone about seeing Beckwith that night. He said he had told a Greenwood policeman, who told him to report it to Beckwith's lawyer. So he called Hardy Lott.

In those days of trial by ambush, all Waller and Fox knew was that Hollis Cresswell and James Holley were alibi witnesses. They had no idea what they were going to say.

Cresswell was fifty years old and a lieutenant with the Greenwood police, where he had worked for the past fifteen years. Holley was his partner. Cresswell said that he had known Beckwith casually for some eight or ten years and he could recognize him easily, along with the white Valiant he drove.

On the night of June 11, Hollis Cresswell and his partner, James Holley, were on patrol, "mostly in the colored section of town, and part uptown." Their shift ran from 11 P.M. to 7 A.M. Cresswell swore that he had seen Byron De La Beckwith at the Shell service station in Greenwood at 1:05 A.M., June 12. That was just over half an hour after the shooting, ninety miles to the south. There was no way Beckwith could have driven fast enough to get back to Greenwood by that time.

Lott asked the policeman where he had been right before he saw Beckwith. "We had just pulled into Billups service station, which is an adjoining station and which is just south of the Shell station and Mr. Holley had bought a package of cigarettes," Cresswell replied.

"I see."

"Then I pulled on out from under the station and had started up on the Main Street at the time we saw Mr. Beckwith."

"All right. Now, how close was he to you?"

"Approximately seventy-five to a hundred feet, hardly that far," Cresswell said. The station was all lit up; he could see clearly. "He was sitting — his car was sitting in the driveway of the Shell service station. At that time there was being some gas put in his car. Mr. Beckwith was standing beside of his car, on the left-hand side of his car, and his front door was open at that time."

"Now what way have you got of fixing that time that you saw him in the Shell service station?"

"Well, the reason I remember what time it was, usually at night, when we are patrolling around, a lot of times we stop over at a little grocery store there on Main Street and eat something. . . . That's Bracci Danton's. And as we were sitting under the station where Mr. Holley bought the cigarettes, he asked me, said, 'Are we going to eat anything tonight?' I said, 'Well we might as well, if we got time.' He said, 'What time is it?' And I looked at my watch and I told him it was five minutes to one o'clock, I mean, after one o'clock, at that time. He said, 'Well, we had better go on over before he closes up.' "

Cresswell said he had been listening to an all-night radio station from Nashville when he heard that Medgar Evers had been shot in Jackson. He said it had been about 4 A.M.

Bill Waller's cross was short. All he wanted to know was whether or not Hollis Cresswell had come forward at any of Beckwith's hearings or had spoken to the Jackson detectives to try to clear Beckwith with an alibi. Cresswell said that he had told only a few officers at the Green-wood Police Station and Beckwith's lawyers, and that was all. Waller didn't bother asking him why. He would let the jury decide for themselves.

Hardy Lott then called thirty-six-year-old James Holley to the stand. Like Cresswell he said he knew Beckwith by sight. His story about seeing Beckwith at the Shell station matched Cresswell's exactly, except he reckoned that the distance between them was thirty or forty, instead of seventy, feet. He testified that he had mentioned the sighting to several other cops and to Beckwith's lawyers after they called. They advised him not to mention it to any investigators unless he was asked. None of them asked.

Waller performed another brusque cross-examination, hammering home the uncomfortable fact that Holley had held his tongue until the trial. He also questioned Holley's specific memory of Beckwith. Could he say who else he saw that night and when?

"Who did you see at 1:10 on the morning of June the 11th?" asked Waller.

"I don't know, sir."

"Who did you see at 1:15?"

"I don't recall seeing anyone."

"Do you know of anybody you saw that whole night on that whole shift?"

"Not specifically, no, sir."

"That's all."

Judge Hendrick excused the witness and then turned to the defense table. "Who do you want, Mr. Lott?" he asked.

"We call the defendant, Mr. Beckwith."

Some people gasped. A man who had coughed continuously all day stopped coughing. The courtroom was silent as Beckwith's fingers fluttered over his tie and pulled straight his suit coat. Then he strode to the witness stand.

Waller and Fox sat, stunned, for a moment. Then Fox hurried out to retrieve a large file from the D.A.'s office. Waller leaned forward, his massive bulldog head over the wooden table, watching closely as Beckwith was sworn in.

By now Waller knew he could lose this case, badly. The three alibi witnesses were hard to impeach. This was the break he was hoping for.

Beckwith carefully crossed his legs and shot his French cuffs and shifted around to face the jury as Hardy Lott began the questioning. Beckwith answered rapidly, with an odd military precision.

"How old are you?" Lott asked.

"Forty-three, suh!"

"You married?"

"Yes, suh!"

"Do you have any children?"

"One son."

Beckwith beamed amiably at the jury, conjuring all his nervous salesman's charm for this moment in the spotlight. He told them that he was a marine, that he "got the business" at Tarawa, and informed them that he was a gun lover and trader.

"I trade guns like I might trade dogs or stamps . . . ," he said.

"Now, Mr. Beckwith, did you shoot Medgar Evers?"

"No, suh!"

"Were you in Jackson, Mississippi, when Medgar Evers was shot?"

"No, suh!"

Beckwith then denied speaking to the cabdrivers, ever going to the bus station in Jackson. He denied parking next to the grocery or going to Joe's Drive In or even knowing where those places were.

He got the scar above his right eye, he explained, on Sunday afternoon before the murder. He was target shooting with a rifle and scope out on the police range in Greenwood, practicing in a prone position. "And I got my eye right up in that scope and I got it up a little too close and I squeezed that trigger and that heavy recoil came back and cut a hole, cut a gap in my head!" Beckwith said.

Lott asked him if he was a hunter. The man on trial for his life couldn't help finding the humor in the moment. "I am the worst hunter in the world. I've had guns all my life and if I have ever killed anything besides time we haven't been able to cook it at home!"

Waller stared at him from the distance of his table.

Beckwith clearly delighted in this gun talk. He boasted about the guns he kept and traded, how it was his habit to keep thirty or forty pistols in suitcases in the trunk of his car, ready to trade, and rifles and shotguns under the front seat, "so I can feel down there and see if they are there."

Beckwith admitted having owned a few Enfield 30/06 rifles in his time. He admitted trading with Duck Goza for a scope. He also admitted trading with Thorn McIntyre for a .30/06, although he had taken only the barrel and bolt action; he had put his own wooden stock on it. Then he'd had a local gun dealer put Goza's stock on the rifle. He had hoped, he said, to trade it to a deer hunter.

Hardy Lott picked up the jet-black rifle from the evidence table and walked toward his client. Again, the rifle's dark, heavy presence seemed to suck the energy from the air around it. Every eye in the room followed it to Beckwith's outstretched hands.

"I will hand you a rifle with a scope — State's Exhibit 21 — and ask you to examine it."

Beckwith ran his eyes over it with the attention of a connoisseur. Then he sited it over the heads of the jury, and peered into the empty breech. "There's a little dust in it," he grumped.

"Looking at it, do you see any difference between the rifle and scope you have just testified about that you had and that one?" Lott asked.

"There is much similarity between this weapon and the weapon — several weapons that I possess — much similarity between them."

"Do you know whether or not that is the rifle and scope that you had that you have just testified about?"

"No, sir . . . I don't know that it's my rifle or one that I have ever had but it is similar to it."

He said all of his rifles had slings on them, and this one didn't. He narrated a story about his Enfield rifle, the one he had fired the Sunday before the murder, the one that cut his eye. He said he took it home that night to clean it thoroughly and wrap it up and put it in the bathroom closet "where nobody would be picking it up and fooling with it."

He had spent the next day in the field with John Book, his instructor at Delta Liquid Plant Food, learning about crop fertilization. They drove all over the southern Delta in Book's car. Beckwith's Valiant, he testified, was parked, unlocked, in front of the office in Greenville all day. When he got home after dark, he noticed the rifle was gone. He hadn't been able to find it in his car with his other guns or upstairs when he'd checked. He wasn't sure whether the gun was missing from the car or the house.

By now Beckwith's mouth was running away with him, and the judge had to remind him not to argue with himself and not to ask questions on the stand.

He said he lived in the house alone.

"What about your wife?"

"My wife and son, they . . . were in an apartment because the house was in such a fearful state of repairs, it wasn't hardly fit to live in. . . ."

"Were you and your wife separated at that time?"

"Only by geography. She was living in another part of town in a comfortable apartment, and I was living in that old house until we could make better arrangements."

The old house was never locked, he said, unless they went away for a week or two.

Now the defense offered an explanation as to why Beckwith's fingerprint should be on the scope. Was it Beckwith's custom to handle shiny objects such as guns and scopes in gun shops? Yes. Including the objects in Duck's Tackle Shop? That was correct.

Finally he was asked why he refused to speak to the FBI agents who came to talk to him before his arrest. Beckwith told the whole story, complete with dialogue on both sides.

"And they said, 'We want to talk to you about a scope.' And I said 'Gentlemen,' I said, 'I don't have anything to say to you, don't have any comment to make to you and you have my permission to leave.' "

He explained that he did this as a matter of routine, since the LeFlore County Bar Association had advised the citizens of Greenwood not to speak to FBI agents for any reason. There were articles about it in the *Commonwealth*.

One such article was produced and entered into the record. It was the only piece of physical evidence the defense would offer.

Hardy Lott turned his witness over to the prosecution.

Bill Waller stood up slowly. The courtroom was very quiet. "Mr. Beckwith, I will ask you whether or not, sir, if you have been rather public in your pronouncement of your ideas on segregation and what forces should be used to maintain segregation?" Waller asked.

Beckwith answered snappily, "I have been very pronounced on my ideas in regard to racial segregation and constitutional government and state's rights. Yes, sir, very pronounced. In fact I have written many articles to many newspapers and a lot of them have published the articles. And I don't write under a pen name!"

Since Beckwith himself had opened this door, Waller fished a piece of newsprint from his files and read from a letter to the editor of the Jackson *Daily News,* April 16, 1957: " 'I believe in segregation just like I believe in God. I shall oppose any person, place, or thing that opposes segregation.' Did you write that?"

"I sure did write that. You are reading it just like it was written."

Waller continued, " 'I shall combat the evils of integration and shall bend every effort to rid the U.S.A. of the integrationists.' Did you write that?"

"I sure did write that, suh."

"Do you still feel that way?"

"As it is written, you read it."

"Do you still feel that way?"

"Of course I feel that way, sir."

"And you mean any force, when you say any force you mean . . ."

"Within *reason,* you understand, *reason,*" Beckwith said, pouring syrup over the vowels as he uttered them. "And moderation. I won't say moderation. I say within reason, civilized reason. Reason within civilized and organized society."

Waller kept reading. " 'And further, when I die I will be buried in a segregated cemetery. When you get to heaven you will find me in the part that has a sign saying — quote — "For White's Only" and if I go to Hades I am going to raise hell all over Hades until I get to the white section.' Did you say that?"

No answer.

"Anyway, Mr. Beckwith, that's your letter and written by yourself and mailed to the editor?"

"Mr. Waller, I want you to understand and where there is humor intended I want you to laugh and smile and where it is serious I want you to be serious and so you have read the letter about like I intended for it to go to the press."

If the jury, up to this point, had been wondering what might cause this quirky little salesman to shoot a man in the back from ambush, Waller intended to use this opportunity to provide the motive. With any luck he could hound Beckwith and make him crack on the stand. Already it was hard to shut him up. He was like a wind-up toy with a taut spring — he couldn't seem to control his own mouth.

"I have a letter here dated January 26, 1963 [to the] National Rifle Association, Washington DC. 'Gentlemen: For the next fifteen years we here in Mississippi are going to have to do a lot of shooting to protect our wives, children and ourselves from bad niggers.' Did you write that?"

"I don't know. Let me look at it and see. I probably did if you say so . . ."

If it was Waller's intention to make Beckwith lose his temper on the stand, it was Beckwith's intention to spar with Waller and goad his tormentor as best he could. When Waller showed him a picture of the white Valiant, Beckwith would only say that it "sure looked" like his car, until the judge prodded him to answer directly. It was the same thing with the rifle: "I couldn't say that it is or that it is not my gun."

There was no use in badgering the witness; it wasn't getting them anywhere. So Waller dug back into his files and produced another letter to read to the jury. Beckwith had written it to the editor of *Outdoor Life* only a week or so earlier.

"Mr. Beckwith, let me read you this part of the letter, sir: 'I have just finished an article on garfish hunting at *night*' — which you underscored — 'which is sure to be of interest to the reader along with several ideas I have on shooting at night in the summertime for varmints.' Those are your words on January the 22nd."

Beckwith eyed the prosecutor with disdain. "Do you know what a varmint is?"

"No, sir, I thought maybe you did."

"I do."

"What is it?"

"A varmint is game, disagreeable game, game that does no good, for instance, a crow or a hawk. Well, a hawk may do some good, but — well, you might even call a squirrel a varmint, but we don't refer to squirrels as varmints, but down in the Natchez area you might call an armadillo a varmint. . . . It's wildlife that contributes nothing to the welfare of other animals and it's a, it's a great sport to varmint hunt."

Waller ignored the contradiction in Beckwith's earlier testimony, that he wasn't a hunter. Instead he threw out some bait: "Are you talking about . . . would you say an integration leader is a varmint?"

Beckwith wouldn't take it.

"Oh, that's a human being," he cooed. "But we're talking about varmints. I'm talking about crows and things like that."

Waller tried another tack. Of the 150 letters Beckwith had written from his jail cells since his arrest, had he once denied killing Medgar Evers?

"I don't imagine I said much about killing Medgar Evers in all of them. . . . The only mention that I can imagine that I would put in a letter regarding this case is that I am not guilty of . . . any crime," Beckwith replied.

"And you don't believe that killing an integration leader is a crime, do you, Mr. Beckwith?"

"Oh, that's a crime. But I say I believe I am guilty of no crime."

"Yes, sir. Now in four months' time and a hundred and fifty letters, I'll ask you whether or not you have referred frequently to the fact that you are making sacrifices for the cause?"

"This is a cause, yes, sir."

"All right. Now I'll ask you further if you have not referred to the fact that you have written a book about the subject matter of which you are being tried now, you have given it a title, and you have offered it to publishers to print, is that not so?"

All in all Beckwith was on the stand for two hours and twenty minutes, with only one short break. For someone with Beckwith's temperament he controlled himself reasonably well. But for some reason this line of questioning, about the book he was hoping to see published, touched something in him, and the jury got to see something in his eyes they hadn't seen before.

"I have made mention of it many times as a book, but it is not a book. It is a compiling of literature and facts and background material."

"What is the title of the book, Mr. Beckwith?"

"The title," he snapped. "The book has ten titles . . ."

People who were there say they saw an odd glint in Beckwith's eyes, and a change came over his face as the lawyers argued back and forth over whether the book should be mentioned in court. As Beckwith testified about the book, his choice of words seemed mild enough, but his demeanor projected, as one reporter put it, a man on the verge of hysteria.

"Mr. Beckwith, could I refresh your memory and give you one title to your book that you have used in your correspondence to various editors and people in reference to your book?" Waller asked.

"You certainly may, sir."

"Is it, *My Ass, Your Goat and the Republic?*"

"You say that's the only title you have seen?"

"Well, other than *Varmint Hunters.*"

"Oh, that's not a title to a book or to anything. That's just a matter of expression."

"That's another subject, but I want to talk to you about your book now."

"That is one of ten titles now," said Beckwith. "*My Ass, Your Goat, and the Republic.*"

"Would you explain that to us?"

"It is thus explained, by the left-wing forces riding my donkey!" Beckwith sputtered. He was breathing hard now, his eyes blazing. "They intend to aggravate the public and continue on with their method of destroying state's rights, constitutional government, and racial integrity!"

Stanny Sanders jumped in to stop it. "If the court please, we are not here to discuss philosophy," he said.

Lott rose to object again to the questioning. Judge Hendrick said he would allow the witness to continue, but the spell was broken, and Beckwith gathered up his composure.

Waller tried getting at him from another angle. Based on his philosophy, and all that he had said in his letters about using force and about sacrifices, did it mean — yes or no — that he would do "whatever is necessary and use whatever force you deem best to stop integration?"

"No, sir. I am not going to go that far."

"How far will you go?"

"To do whatever is morally, legally, and spiritually right to preserve the wholesome forces in this nation and in this republic. To do whatever I can in a small way with a pen. I am a writer."

Another tack: "Do you hunt?"

"I wouldn't admit to any such thing as that, sir."

"Do you hunt?"

"Of course, I hunt moderately and haven't done much hunting in many years. . . . I shoot at tin cans, snakes, and turtles, things along the side of the road."

"You are accurate at two hundred feet with a .30/06 Enfield rifle with a six power scope, too, aren't you?"

"I should do better than that. I ought to hit something at a range better than two hundred feet, sir."

Waller then asked about Beckwith's gun collection. He had boasted of having many guns. So why had the police, when they had searched his house, found only three guns — a rifle, a shotgun, and a .25 automatic pistol — but several hundred rounds of ammunition? Beckwith told the court that he had been selling off his gun collection before his arrest "to stay alive," because he was running out of money.

If he was so strapped for cash, why had he traded an expensive handgun for a useless scope a month earlier? How could he justify going out to the rifle range and firing off rounds that cost thirty cents each? And when he fired off those rounds that Sunday, he had the rifle sighted real good and then he wiped it down real good? Beckwith said he had. And then he put it in his closet, where he kept his guns? Yes. So why, when the police searched his house twelve days after the shooting, were his guns "setting in your bedroom by the bed?"

"I always keep my guns around me."

As hard as he tried, Waller never caught Beckwith in an obvious lie. There were no major breakthroughs except for one: Waller had shown the jury the face of a fanatic.

After five days of testimony both sides rested their cases.

On Thursday morning, February 6, the house was packed to hear the closing arguments. John Fox, looking eager and collegiate, asked the jury to recall Beckwith's demeanor throughout the trial. "Has he in any act or utterance behaved like an innocent man? Does this man come and say, humbly: 'I'm innocent'?" Fox asked.

"I have never before been so hypnotized by the testimony of a witness. . . . It became embarrassing for me to look at him. He sat upon his throne of glory and reveled in it. . . . He is a fanatic, pure and simple." Fox asked the jurors to "take the conscience of Mississippi" with them to the jury room.

Bill Waller spent his time summarizing the case. The murder weapon belonged to Beckwith; the fingerprint on the scope was his. He had a cut over his eye that matched the contours of that scope. His white Valiant had been seen near Medgar Evers's neighborhood in the days just before the shooting and in the parking lot of Joe's Drive In on the night of the murder. Two witnesses said they saw Beckwith there that night. And the supposed alibi witnesses who could place Beckwith in Greenwood around the time of the murder hadn't come forward until "the eleventh hour" of the trial, even though they could have testified at three preliminary hearings. The two Greenwood policemen could not be believed.

"Lo and behold," Waller said. "Their old buddy Beck was down there getting some gas, the same place he was an hour ago. I wonder if it wasn't 2:30 A.M. and Mr. Beckwith had just rolled in from Jackson."

Beckwith was far more subdued this morning and sat glumly at the defense table while Waller tried to send him to the gas chamber. The D.A. told the jury that Beckwith got "a real big kick out of being a martyr." The murder of Medgar Evers, a human being, said Waller, "was the most cold-blooded killing I have ever heard about. He did not come to Jackson to get Medgar Evers. He came to kill evil, and get the number one man."

Stanny Sanders and Hardy Lott hammered on the obvious weaknesses in the state's case. "There's not a single, solitary person who can identify Beckwith as the man who did it," Lott said. It could not be proved that the bullet that killed Evers came from the weapon found at the scene. No one saw the shot fired. There was no way to prove how old a fingerprint was. And three men saw Beckwith in Greenwood at the time of the shooting.

That wasn't all. The defense lawyers had some buttons to push, and they made sure they hit them all. "We believe that this jury is not going to render a verdict to satisfy the Attorney General of the United States," Sanders said. Just invoking the image of Robert Kennedy was enough to make most white southerners bristle.

"If anybody had a motive, it seems to me it would be the people of Jackson," Lott said. "The motive is non-existent. If you're going to bring up everybody in Mississippi who believes in segregation, lots of us better leave. I might be guilty!"

It was something to think about. What Hardy Lott was saying here was that every white man in Mississippi had a reason to kill Medgar Evers. And, by inference, maybe he needed killing.

The judge sent the jury into deliberation after lunch on Thursday. To everyone's surprise by 9:30 that night they still hadn't reached a verdict. It had only taken an hour to acquit Emmett Till's accused killers, and that wait was just for show. Folks were wondering what was taking so long in there.

On Friday morning, after eleven hours of deliberation and twenty ballots, the jury reported they were hopelessly deadlocked. Later some people would say that things got so hot in the jury room that fistfights nearly erupted. One told an Associated Press reporter that it was "hell in there." The final vote was an even tie — six for acquittal and six for conviction.

Beckwith sat soberly as the bailiff polled the jurors. Then he kissed his wife and was led back to jail.

This was not what anyone had expected. Beckwith was so sure he'd be freed that he was writing letters during the trial saying he expected to "win with honor." He was asking for donations to help pay off his lawyers.

The Evers family was equally shocked by the mistrial. Myrlie Evers had prepared a statement about the outcome, but she held on to it. "The fact that they could not agree signifies something," she said.

Charles Evers wouldn't comment until the second trial.

Outside the courthouse Waller spoke to the news crews. "We felt we put on a good case," he said in his abrupt, north Mississippi accent. "The evidence amply justified a guilty verdict." Folks couldn't help but notice the eruption of canker sores on his lower lip. It had been a long couple of weeks.

Out in the blustery February day, in front of the cameras, Waller maintained the public attitude that the state would adopt for the next thirty years. "There has been nothing peculiar, unusual or different about this case," he said, just like it was true.

What would he do now? "I plan to try another murder case Monday," he replied.

18

The Second Trial

TORRENTIAL RAINS pounded Mississippi the weekend before Beckwith's second trial. Three and a half inches fell in Jackson, ten inches in Meridian. Rivers jumped their banks, roads washed away, and people had to climb trees to be saved from high water and floodborne snakes. When jury selection began on Monday, April 6, 1964, the Pearl River was eleven feet above flood stage, and the temperature was eighty-two degrees and rising.

There weren't as many reporters this time around, mainly the stalwarts from the wire services and the local papers and a few offbeat freelancers. There were other trials to cover that spring: Jack Ruby for the murder of Lee Harvey Oswald, Jimmy Hoffa on racketeering charges, the kidnappers of Frank Sinatra, Jr. Byron De La Beckwith was becoming old news.

Once again jury selection dragged on for days and bored most of the spectators right out of the courtroom. That process was, however, of crucial interest to the attorneys present. Some believe a case is won or lost by the time the jury is seated.

This jury selection didn't seem unusual to Fox and Waller, but in fact there was something very different about it. A jury pool of three hundred men was assembled. The prosecution accepted its first twelve jurors, and the defense could challenge or accept them. One of the potential jurors was Durward L. Hopkins, and Stanny Sanders wondered whether he was related to Andy Hopkins, the Sovereignty Commission investigator. So Sanders called him. Hopkins wasn't sure whether he was a cousin or not, but he offered to check. That same day the investigator told Sanders that Durward was indeed a distant cousin; moreover he would make a "fair, impartial juror."

Anyone knows that lawyers don't really want jurors to be fair and impartial. They want jurors to be predisposed to favor their client's position — if they can get away with it. A defense attorney wants a juror who can empathize with his or her client, who hates putting anyone in prison, who is skeptical of the police. Prosecutors want to pick the coldest, most merciless jurors, people with a rigid respect for authority and the ability to make hard decisions. Certain types of people, it is thought, are predisposed to vote certain ways. A Roman Catholic, for instance, isn't as likely to sentence someone to death as, say, a Baptist, although lawyers are supposed to swear up and down that this never affects their choices. It's a little charade they all play.

The best way to find out how a juror might vote is to question him in court and investigate his background. The latter takes time and money. Lucky for Beckwith the Sovereignty Commission offered its services for free.

Years later this obscure episode would make banner headlines in Jackson. Erle Johnston, who in 1964 was director of the Sovereignty Commission, would say that what happened might have been unethical but not illegal (which turned out to be true). One state agency had simply volunteered to subvert the efforts of another state agency, the district attorney's office.

Andy Hopkins offered to investigate the rest of the potential jurors, Erle Johnston gave his approval, and by the end of the day the defense team had an interesting list on its desk. In the short time he had to work, Hopkins didn't learn all that much. Mostly just addresses and employment — things anyone could get from the city directory. In some cases he made some phone calls or visits to learn more. For instance, Hopkins reported that John T. Hester was "an analyst for the State Hi-Way Department and formerly lived in Jones County. He has a good reputation with people that work with him, would probably be a fair and impartial juror." Hester got on the jury.

Another man on the list was Joseph S. Harris, noted to be "president of J. H. Harris, Inc. . . . He is a contractor and believed to be Jewish." Beckwith's lawyers struck him from the jury.

By midnight Wednesday a twelve-man jury had been selected. They appeared to be solid citizens, businessmen and executives, more educated than those in the first trial. Seven had college degrees, and two were actually Yankee born. There was a bookkeeper, a food broker, an IRS employee — guys who might be Lions Club tail-twisters or have country club memberships. All were Protestants, and, of course, all were white.

Once the testimony started, the crowds came back to the courthouse. John Herbers, who dropped in to cover the case for the *New York Times,* noted that the Ku Klux Klan seemed to be making its presence felt at the trial. He wrote that about seventy-five "tough-looking" men from Greenwood, some "linked with the Klan," showed up in court and stared intently at Ralph Hargrove as he testified.

Herbers also noted that the Klan, which had been quiet in Mississippi for many years, seemed to be undergoing a revival. There had been cross burnings in southern Mississippi and the Greenwood area. And literature was being passed out by a new organization, something that called itself the White Knights of the Ku Klux Klan of Mississippi. On Thursday night, four days after the trial began, ten crosses were burned in and around Jackson.

Bill Waller and John Fox both remember the second trial as smoother, shorter, and more efficient than the first. Each side knew better what the other had in its hand and what the judge would allow into evidence. But the trials were not carbon copies of each other. Although apparently nobody ordered transcripts of the second trial and the stenographer's notes were later lost, newspapers of the time reported some interesting new testimony.

For instance, the prosecution again called Herbert Speight, one of the cabdrivers who had identified Beckwith as the man who asked him for directions to Evers's house days before the murder. At the second go-around Speight suddenly couldn't be positive the man was Beckwith. He now said on the stand that he "couldn't swear to it."

"Have you been threatened in any way?" Waller asked him.

"Yes, sir."

"Since you testified before, have you been assaulted?"

The defense successfully objected to this line of questioning. Later, during noon recess, Waller told reporters that Speight "got the hell beat out of him" and had received threats since his first testimony.

That afternoon Lee Swilley, the other cabbie, took the stand and more or less stuck to his story. In cross-examination Hardy Lott asked him whether he told a coworker that he wasn't going to testify because he was not going to lie. He denied it. Lott asked him if he was mad because he wasn't paid for his testimony. He denied that too. The defense later produced that coworker, Sam Warren, as a new witness. Warren swore that Swilley, who was working at the time at the state mental hospital, had told Warren that he wasn't going to "tell 'nary 'nother lie."

Another new twist in this second trial was the defense's attempt to discredit a key witness who could place Beckwith near the crime scene on the night of the murder. Hardy Lott produced three witnesses to dispute Barbara Ann Holder's testimony that she saw a white Valiant at Joe's Drive In at 11:45 P.M. on June 11. John Turner, the owner of a redneck nightclub, the Club Kathryn, testified that Holder was definitely at his establishment, just up Delta Drive from Joe's, at the time she said she was at the drive-in. He remembered the date, he said, because he was raided by the police and arrested that night for selling beer after hours. The raid was at 12:10 A.M. Turner said Barbara Holder was there and she had been there all night. Two of his employees backed up his story.

Martha Jean O'Brien, the young carhop, also testified that she couldn't remember seeing Holder at Joe's Drive In on the night of June 11.

If things were looking bad for Bill Waller after this testimony, they got worse when the defense called a surprise witness named James Hobby. He was a thirty-seven-year-old truck driver from Memphis, Tennessee, who had been living in Jackson in June 1963. Hobby testified that he owned a 1960 white Valiant and had been at Joe's Drive In between 12:10 and 12:30 A.M. the morning of Medgar Evers's murder. Hobby, who was the same height and build as Beckwith, said that he had gone to the rest room at Joe's and then ordered a cup of coffee. He had been on his way to work, he said. He also said that he had been in the neighborhood in his Valiant that weekend, watching drag races.

To Waller's relief Beckwith again took the stand on the eighth day of the trial. This time Beckwith chose a more casual look: a striped sports jacket and gray tie. He fidgeted in his chair and pulled at his face, but he calmly answered Hardy Lott's questions, disputing each of the state's witnesses in turn. For the first time he gave an account of what he was doing on the night of the murder. He said he had dinner at about 7:00 P.M. in Greenwood, and then he went home to his house on George Street. It was so hot he couldn't get to sleep.

"I got up, put on my clothes and drove around some," he said. "I thought I'd get a bottle of beer."

Waller's cross-examination went about the same as before. This time he felt that Beckwith did a better job for himself. Somebody obviously had told him to shut his mouth. He didn't run on as much as the first time. Still there were moments.

Waller produced another letter that Beckwith had written during his first trial — even though he knew all his mail could be used against him. "We shall soon engage the enemy in mortal combat. . . . We will surely win . . . combat will always bring a few casualties," the letter read. Waller asked Beckwith what he meant by "mortal combat."

"What it means to you, it wouldn't mean to me," Beckwith snapped.

Waller combed through Beckwith's story about finding his Enfield missing right before Evers's murder. "Did you or did you not report it missing?" he asked.

"I don't have any recollection of reporting it or not reporting it."

Waller hadn't been able to make this point in the first trial.

Waller was making an effort to stay out of Beckwith's reach. He didn't want to be ambushed with any cigars. But as Waller closed in to show Beckwith a picture of the car the state said was used by the killer, Beckwith patted him on the shoulder. Waller jumped back as if he had been stuck with a cattle prod. Beckwith grinned, saying, "I'll say anything you want me to about that car, Mr. Waller."

Hardy Lott and his team had a more direct closing argument this time: the theme was that Beckwith had been framed. He was the victim of a plot to make it look like he had killed Evers. Someone must have planted that gun in the bushes. And besides how could you hear the testimony of three fine alibi witnesses and not have a reasonable doubt?

The jury began deliberation just after noon on April 15. More than two hundred spectators remained in the courtroom, waiting. Beckwith sat with his lawyers, chatting softly.

Again the jury had four choices: innocent, guilty as charged, guilty as charged with life sentence as punishment, guilty as charged but with no agreement on punishment.

By midday of the seventeenth, they reported they were deadlocked. Judge Hendrick declared another mistrial. This time the vote was eight to four in favor of acquittal.

Bill Waller could have asked for a third trial date. The law would allow it, but another trial seemed pointless. Waller felt he had presented the best case he could. He had made the most of the evidence he had, but he apparently needed more to get a conviction. So when Judge Hendrick set bond for Beckwith at ten thousand dollars, the D.A. did not object.

Beckwith would remain on bond until the judge ordered a new trial or until the court voided his indictment. That could take months, even years.

When Byron De La Beckwith made bail that afternoon, he was not technically a free man. He was still an accused killer, and he could be hauled back into court at any time.

Beckwith slipped out the back of the courthouse sprawled on the backseat of Sheriff Fred Pickett's car while the huddle of newsmen waited out front. An hour later, when Beckwith's small police convoy coasted out of the hills and down into the Delta along Highway 49, Beckwith spotted a sign that read "Welcome Home DeLa." Another homemade banner hung from an overpass just south of Greenwood with the same slogan. Some people waved Confederate flags as he passed. At a brief meeting with reporters at the LeFlore County Courthouse that afternoon, a joyful Beckwith remarked that the sight of the signs "brought tears to my eyes." He had been in jail for ten months.

That night Delay and his wife, Willie, ate a steak dinner, on the house, at the Hotel LeFlore, where Beckwith's supporters had been lodging his family during Beckwith's imprisonment.

Hardy Lott had told the press that Beckwith would not be making any statements, but that was of course not the case. The next day he discussed his plans with a UPI reporter.

"I'm not bitter against anyone," he said. "The Beckwith family does not hold bitterness. We have been inconvenienced and aggravated but we have only been hurt financially."

Willie added, "This thing has about wiped us out."

The couple discussed their relationship.

"I'm as happy today as the day I married Delay," Willie cooed. Beckwith said they were even happier than that, because "all the pleasant moments we have had have been multiplied by this incident in our lives."

They divorced again, for the third and last time, the next year.

Meanwhile Delay was eager to get back to work, to get back to "normal." He was going to take a couple of weeks on the Gulf Coast to do some fishing and relax.

His fertilizer job was waiting for him. He was given a new company station wagon. The little Beckwith family moved into a mobile home at the Rebel Court Trailer Park in Greenwood.

Beckwith's friend and admirer Gordon Lackey lived just across the street. Gordon was very tall and skinny, with Elvis-black hair and eyes the color of pond water. He was in his late twenties, married, and he worked in his parents' café when he wasn't fixing and selling motorcycles or flying crop dusters over the cotton fields. Gordon used to keep a chimpanzee in the café, with a sign around the ape's neck saying, "I am a man." That was Gordon's sense of humor. According to government reports and most other sources (except Lackey himself, who always denied it), his other job was as a kleagle, or recruiter for the Ku Klux Klan. In fact Gordon, who had been in and out of college over the years, was said to have written the White Knights' constitution.

The White Knights were a fast-growing group. To celebrate Beckwith's release from jail and demonstrate their widespread appeal, members had burned crosses in nearly half of the eighty-two counties in Mississippi on the same April night.

White supremacists hadn't been very organized in Mississippi until the trouble at Ole Miss. The first real modern Klan had crossed the border from Louisiana at Natchez back in 1962 or 1963. They called themselves the Original Knights of the Ku Klux Klan. They were a nasty, violent group, but not much different from other Klans across the South. Like the others they held some public rallies and bickered among themselves over the usual things: money and power.

In February of 1964, while Byron De La Beckwith was still in jail, a hard-nosed group of Klansmen broke away from the Originals to form a new, secret Klan. Their aim was to act instead of talk. They called themselves the White Knights of the Ku Klux Klan of Mississippi. There were two hundred to three hundred men at the first meeting. By the end of the year there were somewhere between six thousand and ten thousand Klansmen in the state.

The imperial wizard of the new, secret Klan was a peculiar man from Laurel named Sam Bowers. Most rank-and-file Klansmen fit the stereotype of ignorant, sadistic, redneck laborers with a grudge against anyone who might be different. Bowers was an exception. He was the grandson of a four-term Mississippi congressman with a distinguished social pedigree. He had studied engineering at the University of Southern California and Tulane before joining the navy during World War II.

Bowers was thin, sandy-haired, ferret-faced, smart, charismatic, and crazy. He was a religious fanatic with a swastika fetish who had been observed in his living room saluting his German shepherd dog with a stiff-armed "Heil Hitler." He never seemed to date women. The wizard lived with his business partner in the back room of their vending machine enterprise, Sambo Amusements, across the street from the Masonite plant in Laurel.

Sam Bowers was Beckwith's sort of person, an archconservative soul mate. If they hadn't known each other before the murder trials, there are people who will tell you they became close associates soon afterward. According to government sources, Byron De La Beckwith was officially sworn into the White Knights of the Ku Klux Klan of Mississippi in a secret ceremony in Gordon Lackey's living room in the summer of 1964.

19

The Long Summer

AFTER THE TRIALS had ended and the school year was over, Myrlie Evers moved with the children to southern California. She brought only her car, clothes, a few pieces of furniture, a Cable and Nelson piano, and a trunkload of letters and photographs and other mementos of her life with Medgar. She told friends that she chose the Los Angeles area because Medgar had once said that if he ever left Mississippi, that was where he would go.

Althea Simmons, the West Coast NAACP field secretary, had found a nice little beige-and-pink stucco house in a quiet neighborhood in the suburb of Claremont, thirty miles south of Los Angeles. The three-bedroom ranch had a low-slung roof with an Oriental flare, a eucalyptus tree in the front, and a lanai in the back. There were six colleges in the town. The public schools were excellent. The NAACP bought the property for $26,500 out of proceeds from the Evers Trust Fund, which had grown to $60,000, and turned the deed over to Myrlie.

The Everses were the only blacks in the neighborhood. In fact there were only five Negro families in the entire town of Claremont. Myrlie knew none of them, or anyone else in Claremont.

But even before she arrived, Myrlie had received congenial handwritten notes from some of her new neighbors. An editorial in the Claremont *Courier* singled her out for a hearty welcome.

The two older children enrolled at the previously all-white Mountain View Elementary School. Myrlie registered at Claremont College. She would get the degree that she had given up when she married Medgar Evers.

Myrlie found it ironic that she was now surrounded by white people. A hatred still smoldered in her even though she knew it was wrong. That was not, she told herself, what Medgar would have wanted. So she quietly began to shed her bitterness.

Just as Medgar would not abide her hatred, she knew he would not want her to grieve forever. He would want her to get on with her life. But that was something she could not yet do.

Sometimes, when she could no longer take the pressure at home, she would drive out into the peculiar dry desert air, up into the San Bernardino Mountains to a chaparral-covered ridge. She could see a long way from there. She could be alone and think about Medgar and cry without the children seeing her cry. Then she could go back down the mountain and start another day.

A few months after the second mistrial Bill Waller told a reporter from the *New York Times* that he would not attempt to try Byron De La Beckwith for a third time without new evidence. The case remained open but dormant. Gloster Current suggested, in a memo to Roy Wilkins, that the NAACP should "not let this go by the boards without some effort on our part to have this man put under peace bond to prevent him from doing further damage to the Negro cause." But nothing was done. All the prosecutor could do was watch and wait for a new witness to come forward or for Beckwith to make a mistake.

Every working day after Medgar's murder, Charles Evers went to the NAACP office on Lynch Street and sat at his brother's desk, trying to think what to do. The tempting old idea of a Mississippi Mau Mau still circulated in his brain from time to time. It was a guaranteed way to get the white man's attention, and it fit Charles's general strategy in dealing with them: always give back to the white man what he gives you. If he smiles, meet him with a smile. If he kills, meet him with a rifle. Charles went so far as to stockpile some weapons. He thought about knocking off the biggest white racists in every county in Mississippi. It was a long list. But when Charles sat at Medgar's desk, sitting below a large framed portrait of his brother, something would tell him, "That's not the way."

So instead of seeking revenge, Charles Evers carried on Medgar's work. He drove around the state visiting NAACP branches. He encouraged voter registration. He schemed economic boycotts that would hurt the white man in his most sensitive place — his pocket. Charles put himself out front and took risks he shouldn't have taken, such as driving alone at night and talking back to cops who were just looking for a reason to hurt him. He later said that he was hoping someone would try to put a bullet in him and that would be his excuse to take some of his enemies down with him. He had the survivor's guilt.

Charles Evers did not work well with the national NAACP staff. He was accustomed to being his own boss, and he could never tolerate a New Yorker telling him how to run Mississippi. Roy Wilkins and Gloster Current, with their nearly religious attachment to procedure, were driven to bemused distraction by their renegade field secretary. Still there was no way to get rid of him without causing a scene. Charles had name recognition and power in Mississippi.

Charles also had cultivated a warm relationship with Robert Kennedy, who had stayed on as attorney general for Lyndon Johnson after John Kennedy's assassination. The two men had met at Medgar's funeral in Washington, and they formed a powerful, inexplicable bond. Bobby Kennedy called Charles often that summer, and when his brother was killed in November, Charles Evers went to his friend's side. Charles backed Kennedy's U.S. Senate campaign, even when the NAACP endorsed Kennedy's opponent.

Charles Evers's irascibility and essential conservatism surfaced frequently during his early days as field secretary. He clashed with other civil rights groups from the outset. Evers didn't like the long-haired, scruffy college students who had taken over SNCC and were now dominating COFO. He was offended by a man who wore dungarees when he could afford better. The SNCC style of consensus leadership clashed with Evers's authoritarian streak. And like the NAACP leaders, he didn't want outsiders coming into the state and stirring up trouble they couldn't handle. Charles knew what he was dealing with in Mississippi, and he knew what was going to happen when COFO announced a huge voter education project for the summer of 1964.

Dave Dennis and Bob Moses also knew what it meant when COFO invited more than a thousand fresh-faced and eager white college kids to Mississippi. The object of Freedom Summer, as it came to be called, was more than literacy classes and registration drives. It was to get the attention of the whole country and to involve the federal government in the civil rights business. Folksingers and governors' sons, white boys and white girls ready to change the world, preferably from the best schools and the most prominent families, would attract attention the way no black Mississippians could. The organizers knew some of them were going to get hurt or worse. But the strategy worked in a way that would haunt Dennis for the rest of his life.

The state of Mississippi hired seven hundred extra highway patrolmen in anticipation of the summer "invasion." Jackson's mayor Allen Thompson responded with typical panic. He hired another hundred policemen. "This is it," he said. "We are going to be ready for them. . . . They won't have a chance."

Like so many white boys in the South, Delmar Dennis grew up hearing the stories about the "good" Ku Klux Klan of Reconstruction and how it saved the southern way of life from the evil Yankees. At his father's knee he learned about the "second Klan" organized in the early twentieth century to fight back against the waves of immigrants and Catholics who seemed to be overrunning the country.

In the spring of 1964 Dennis was a twenty-four-year-old Baptist preacher with a wife and two children. He had what he felt was a healthy interest in politics. He believed in God, country, and a segregated Mississippi. The Klan was still a shadowy, romantic outfit to him. And so, when a friend from the local Masonic Temple asked Delmar if he wanted to come to a real-life Klan meeting, he was curious.

Three dozen men sat on folding chairs in an old army barracks outside Meridian. The meeting started when three robed Klansmen came in and led the group in the Pledge of Allegiance. The new men were sworn to secrecy, then one of the Klansmen gave a lecture explaining what the

Klan was all about. It was pro-American and anti-Satan — a fine Christian organization sworn to destroy communism and uphold segregation and the U.S. Constitution.

Nothing wrong with that, Dennis thought. All it took to join was a ten-dollar bill. Everyone seemed to be signing up. Delmar's friend nudged him. "C'mon. Let's do it." He even loaned Dennis the ten dollars.

And so Delmar Dennis was sworn in as a citizen of the Invisible Empire, a White Knight of the Ku Klux Klan of Mississippi. After the oath was over, the robed leader said, "All right, all you old members sit down."

Only Delmar and three strangers were left standing. His friend grinned up at him.

The kleagle at the front of the room took off his mask and looked Delmar Dennis in the eye. "I want you to know," said Edgar Ray Killen, a rawboned man nicknamed "The Preacher," "that you ain't joined no Boy Scout group."

Even though he suspected it was a bad outfit, Delmar agreed to go to a meeting of the local Klan unit, or klavern. It was held at night down a lonely dirt road near the little town of Chunky. There were ten Klansmen in full white robes. The "exalted cyclops," or klavern leader, was there with news from the imperial wizard. He had ordered a "number four" on Michael Schwerner, the CORE/COFO organizer in Meridian. What that meant, Dennis learned, was that the young, bearded New Yorker the local Klan boys called "Goatee" was marked for assassination.

On the night of June 16, 1964, a group of White Knights raided a church meeting in the Longdale community in Neshoba County, where COFO had arranged to set up a freedom school that summer. Several people were ambushed on the road and savagely beaten. Later that night the Mount Zion Methodist Church was burned to the ground.

The next Sunday, June 21, Mickey Schwerner and two other civil rights workers named James Chaney and Andy Goodman drove from Meridian to Longdale to visit the church and talk to the injured parishioners. On their way back to Meridian Deputy Sheriff Cecil Price pulled over their station wagon and arrested Chaney, the driver, for speeding. All three boys were taken to the Neshoba County jail in Philadelphia, where they were locked up and fed a hearty home-cooked supper by the jailer's wife. At about 10:30 P.M., after Chaney paid a twenty-dollar fine, they were released and told to get out of the county. For some reason they never made a phone call.

Deputy Price followed them out of town. He pulled them over again, threw them in his patrol car, and delivered the boys to a gang of Klansmen on a deserted back road. Mickey Schwerner was the first to die. He told his killer, "I know just how you feel," right before the man pulled the trigger and shot him in the heart. Goodman was next. James Chaney, who was black, struggled to get away, but he didn't get far.

When Schwerner did not phone the COFO office at the usual time, the duty staffer alerted headquarters in Jackson that Goodman, Chaney, and Schwerner might be in trouble. By Monday morning the three missing civil rights workers had become a national news story. Pressure was brought to bear in Washington and in Jackson. Everyone seemed to want this case solved quickly, from J. Edgar Hoover to Lyndon Johnson to Mississippi's commissioner of public safety.

At the same time white Mississippians started speculating out loud that the disappearances were probably a hoax, a publicity stunt. Governor Paul Johnson suggested that the boys might be hiding in Cuba, for all he knew.

On Tuesday afternoon, June 23, Choctaws living on a reservation north of Philadelphia reported seeing a torched car mired in the Bogue Chitto swamp. The FBI pulled it out of the muck. It was the missing station wagon, but Goodman, Chaney, and Schwerner were not in it.

The next day three buses full of sailors from the Meridian Naval Air Station arrived to drag the snake-infested bog. They found nothing. Meanwhile federal investigators poured into the state to look for what were now assumed to be the killers of Goodman, Chaney, and Schwerner.

Later that week a letter, dated June 24, arrived at Governor Paul Johnson's office. It began,

> Dear Wonderful Friends,
>   *Hooray, Hooray* for our Mississippi and *all* like states that destroy the "Enemy," saboteurs, that *invade* your state to *destroy* all you have. . . . When the stinking, Odious, nauseous "nigger-lovers" come there this summer . . . give them "what is coming to them"!!!!

Why doesn't LBJ, nauseous, sickening as he is . . . investigate the "nigger" murders of innocent white victims that have taken place? Doesn't he realize we white citizens will *fight* for our *lives*, will fight to the hilt to protect our *rights*, our *homes*.

The letter asked the governor why he was letting those "nigger-lover college students" into the state at all. It suggested "they ought to be publicly stoned, to say the least, 'strung up & quartered' as any other enemy of the people." The letter was signed "a group of northerners who love you!"

If anyone had looked closely at the penmanship of the handwritten inserts crawling along the margins of the page and then compared it to samples of Byron De La Beckwith's hand, they may have found a marked similarity. But apparently nobody did this.

The governor simply filed the letter away in a folder marked "Klan," where it stayed, unread, for two decades.

With the specter of a third trial hanging over him, Beckwith kept a reasonably low profile all summer. He was still living in the Rebel Court Trailer Park with Willie and their teenage son. On that front things were going from bad to worse. The couple still drank too much, and when they drank they fought. Pistols were fired, and the police came. During their drunken brawls Willie would sometimes call Delay a murderer.

"Did you kill him?" she would scream.

He'd scream back, "He's DEAD, ain't he?"

Willie later told a nephew that she was convinced that her husband shot Medgar Evers. She was in the hospital drying out after a binge on the night Evers was killed, so she didn't know for sure. Beckwith never confessed it to her, but she felt it in the way he acted and the spooky things he would say. Once Little Delay and some other teenage boys were caught stealing and butchering a pig to barbecue. Beckwith was furious. "If you're going to kill something, kill something important," she remembered him saying.

That summer Beckwith rode around with his friends in the Greenwood police force. He carried a pistol and billy club while they patrolled the Negro neighborhoods. He sometimes stood with the mob of whites who harassed patrons of the newly integrated LeFlore Theater.

Beckwith trained his flashlight in the faces of patrons as they left the movie.

If one thing aggravated the Klan even more than the invasion of summer volunteers it was the recent passage of the 1964 Civil Rights Act. The new law made segregation illegal in all public places — restaurants, bathrooms, theaters, hotels — even if they were private property. President Lyndon Johnson signed the act into law on July 2. It was the package that President Kennedy had proposed the night Medgar Evers was murdered.

Soon after Charles Evers, Aaron Henry, Gloster Current, and a few other NAACP officials made a quick tour of central Mississippi to test the new law. Most establishments offered little resistance, but one landmark in Jackson, the Robert E. Lee Hotel, closed its doors forever rather than integrate. A sign hung on the door read, "Closed in Despair."

The NAACP group also took a side trip to Neshoba County to keep up the pressure to find the missing workers. They had a tense meeting with Rayford Jones, the county attorney, in the Philadelphia courthouse. No one had forgotten that this was the town that hounded Charles Evers out a few years back when he tried to register voters. A mob of hectoring white men gathered in the courthouse square while the meeting degenerated into a shouting match.

"Are Negroes allowed to vote in Neshoba County?" Evers demanded.

"Now Charlie," Jones said. "You know damn well niggers can vote here!"

When the NAACP men objected to that kind of language, Jones just looked at them in astonishment. "Well, if you aren't niggers, what are you?" he asked.

The group walked out. Deputy Cecil Price spotted Evers leaving and shouted, "Get out of town!" while the mob closed in behind him. Charles was ready to go for Price, but Current and Henry wrestled him into the car and raced back to Meridian. Current was sure they were about to be lynched.

The NAACP soon issued a report charging that Mississippi was a virtual police state that hadn't changed in a hundred years. "Negroes are still in slavery in the state," the report said. Among other recommendations it called for the federal government to take over the administration of the state.

Dick Gregory returned to Mississippi to see what he could do to find the missing COFO workers. He brought twenty-five thousand dollars in cash and made it known he would pay anyone who had information about the crime.

The FBI also was flashing money around, big time, in the streets of Philadelphia and Meridian. Once the FBI decided to jump onto the bandwagon, the fight against the Klan became a growth industry. For the first time since World War II the FBI opened an office in Jackson. J. Edgar Hoover himself came down to cut the ribbon. By the end of the summer the FBI presence in Mississippi had increased from a handful to hundreds of agents.

Late in July an informant told the FBI where they should look for the bodies. The man was paid thirty thousand dollars for the tip. His name has never been revealed.

On August 4 the FBI got a warrant to dig up the new earthen dam on Olen Burrage's farm, a few miles southwest of Philadelphia. By nightfall they found the three bodies buried under fifteen feet of Mississippi clay.

Mickey Schwerner's family wanted to bury him next to James Chaney in Meridian, but that proved impossible. Even the dead were segregated in Mississippi.

It was a powerfully hot evening when James Chaney was buried in a Negro cemetery in his hometown. Later, at the memorial service, the mourners sang "We Shall Overcome," and the cameras rested on the face of Ben Chaney, the eleven-year-old boy who had idolized his big brother. Sheets of tears ran down his cheeks, and his face was the face of utter, uncomprehending human grief.

Dave Dennis got up to say a few words of eulogy. Dennis had been Mickey Schwerner's supervisor. He had approved the freedom school in Longdale, and he was supposed to have visited the Mount Zion Church with Goodman, Chaney, and Schwerner the day they were murdered. A case of bronchitis had kept him in Jackson.

Dave Dennis planned to talk about nonviolence. The head office of CORE wanted him to encourage people to keep cool and calm. But when he looked down at the face of Ben Chaney, something hard and bitter inside him cracked open. He couldn't lie to that boy. His eyes were glazed, almost wild. The cords in his neck bulged, and his already thin voice choked into a dry wail.

"I'm sick and tired of going to the funerals of black men who have been murdered by white men!" Dave Dennis shouted. ". . . I've got *ven-*

geance in my heart tonight, and I ask you to feel angry with me. The white men who murdered James Chaney are never going to be punished. . . . We've got to stand up! If you go back home and sit down and take what these white men in Mississippi are doing to us . . . if you take it and don't do something about it, then God damn your souls!"

He was hoarse, actually screaming his final words: "Don't bow down anymore! We want our freedom NOW!"

This moment, rarely remembered in the history books, was perhaps the precise juncture in time when the civil rights movement turned the corner into a dark and uncharted territory. It foreshadowed the atomization of COFO and SNCC and the end of the black-white coalition. So much goodwill had been spent and hope squandered. A new kind of child was being born, and it would travel the road to black power and black separatism and beyond, although it would be years before anyone would know its name. Not Charles Evers, or Roy Wilkins, or even Martin Luther King could change its course.

COFO recorded hundreds of acts of violence against black Mississippians and civil rights workers that summer. For two solid months the spotlight of media attention was trained on the state, and gradually the bayous and back roads began to yield their secrets and their ghosts.

It was shocking, for instance, to anyone except black Mississippians that as soon as the authorities started dragging the rivers and swamps for the two white New Yorkers and their local colleague, they stumbled on other bodies. A back channel of the Mississippi River gave up dismembered pieces of an Alcorn student named Charles Moore and his friend Henry Dee. It turned out the two men had been kidnapped and beaten to death by some Natchez Klansmen. Their disappearance would have probably gone unnoticed under different circumstances — just two more local boys gone missing, never to be found. Before the end of the summer another body surfaced in the Big Black River. All that remained was the torso of a thirteen- or fourteen-year-old black boy wearing a CORE T-shirt.

By the end of the summer the FBI had recruited several informants in the Klan, and they put together a roster of White Knights. Sooner or later most of the members got a house call.

When FBI agents Tom Van Riper and John Martin knocked on Delmar Dennis's door in September, 1964, Dennis said, "Come in. I've been expecting you."

The FBI men convinced Delmar Dennis that not only could he save his own neck from conspiracy charges, but he also could serve God and his country by going undercover for the FBI. For his services he would get one hundred dollars per week in expense money.

Delmar agreed to do it. Before long, based on information provided by Dennis and others, the FBI knew who was behind the murders of Goodman, Chaney, and Schwerner. They just had to keep their informants alive long enough to get the case to court in Mississippi.

The first batch of twenty-one indictments came down in early December 1964. The Justice Department had no faith in the local courts, so the crimes were handled under the U.S. Code. Murder is not a federal charge unless it takes place on government property, so the accused killers were charged with conspiracy to deprive the victims of their civil rights, a federal crime. The stiffest sentence available was ten years in prison, but it was better than nothing. Lawrence Rainey, the sheriff of Neshoba County, his deputy Cecil Price, and the Klan kleagle, or recruiter, Edgar Ray Killen, were among the first group of defendants. Sam Bowers, the Klan's imperial wizard, was not. It would be three years before the case came to trial.

After the FBI agents had their talk with Dennis, he had gone right out and paid his dues to rejoin the White Knights. Dennis had an amazing memory, and without using a tape recorder he was able to recall, almost to the word, what was discussed at meetings.

Since Dennis was a smart, presentable, respectable person, he stood out from the usual rabble that the Klan attracts. Sam Bowers spotted his talent right away. Only two months after the minister went undercover, Bowers named Dennis province titan for his sector of Mississippi. He reported directly to the imperial wizard. He was hot-wired right into the center of the White Knights.

During the three years Delmar Dennis spied on the Klan, he was able to give the FBI a clear picture of the White Knights' inner workings. He knew their leaders and their heroes. He even got Byron De La Beckwith's autograph. The occasion was a statewide Klan meeting and "kleagle school" on the banks of the Pearl River near Byram, south of Jackson, in August 1965.

Fifty to seventy-five Klansmen had gathered that day at L. E. Matthews's fishing camp, but nobody was talking about fish. There were seminars on how to make bombs and the best ways to blow up churches.

After dark Beckwith, a big Klan hero, gave a motivational speech. He stood on the back of a flatbed truck while the headlights of parked pickups lit the makeshift arena. As Delmar Dennis remembered it, Beckwith encouraged the group to kill their enemies "from the President on down." Dennis also heard him say this: "Killing that nigger gave me no more inner discomfort than our wives endure when they give birth to our children." Dennis knew that Beckwith was talking about Medgar Evers, and he reasoned that so did everybody else standing in that field in the hot Mississippi night.

As always Delmar Dennis reported what he had heard to his FBI handler, Tom Van Riper. Even though the agent knew Beckwith was still under indictment for the Evers murder, he and his superiors decided not to share the information with Bill Waller. As Van Riper saw it, Delmar Dennis was much too valuable an informant to risk blowing his cover on a state trial. At the time nothing was more important than the case the FBI had labeled MIBURN, for "Mississippi burning."

20

White Knights

IN LATE 1965 the House Un-American Activities Committee (HUAC) decided to make a big show out of investigating the Ku Klux Klan. The usual suspects from various Klans across the South were called to Washington. Subpoenas went out to dozens of reputed White Knights from Pascagoula to Petal, Mississippi, including Sam Bowers, Gordon Lackey, and Byron De La Beckwith.

The White Knights were questioned in January 1966. None said anything useful to the committee. Sam Bowers was so adamant that he pled the Fifth Amendment when asked his name. Beckwith appeared relaxed. He was polite, willingly providing the personal information the committee requested. But he held up the U.S. Constitution when the committee asked him if he even knew Gordon Lackey.

"Sir, I respectfully decline to answer that question and invoke as a defense the privilege granted to me by the Fifth, First and Fourteenth Amendments to the Constitution of the United States," Beckwith said.

Did Lackey recruit him into the White Knights?

"Sir, I respectfully decline . . ." On and on it went.

Did Beckwith, on March 5, 1965, throw eleven quart beer bottles filled with gasoline and stuffed with lit rags at the house of Laura McGhee of Greenwood?

Same answer.

On August 8, 1965, did he attend a state klonvocation held off Eldon Road in Jackson? At that same time was he appointed a kleagle in the White Knights?

Same answer.

A congressional investigator asked these questions. Then, oddly, Chairman Edwin Willis broke in. "The chair announces that it is the committee's view that it would not be proper to go into matters in which this witness might have been involved as a principal, but which have not been finally resolved."

Beckwith said, "I certainly appreciate that courtesy, thank you sir."

Willis looked at the witness. "The chair was referring to criminal matters and I must say to the witness that we appreciate his expression, but we have taken that attitude because of our own determination of the propriety of our inquiry. The witness is excused."

Beckwith left the table.

The only criminal matter before Beckwith at the moment was the still-open case of Medgar Evers's murder.

If the HUAC hearings were meant to have a chilling effect on Klan violence in Mississippi, it didn't work. While the hearings were still going on, a gang of White Knights firebombed the home of Vernon Dahmer, a civil rights leader in Hattiesburg. When he ran through the flames firing his shotgun to protect his family, Dahmer gulped fire and burned his lungs. He died a few hours later.

Here was another ghost in Mississippi, another man for Charles Evers to bury. Evers went to Hattiesburg the next night to lead a march and a prayer service for Dahmer on the steps of the Forrest County Courthouse. He couldn't let this act go unanswered, let the Klan think they were afraid. Evers told the three hundred demonstrators that this killing should make them all go out and pay their poll tax. He called for a boycott of Hattiesburg businesses.

The FBI was all over the case within hours, and it didn't take long to compile a list of suspects in the Dahmer case. By the end of March fourteen Klansmen, including Sam Bowers, were arrested on federal warrants and charged with the now-familiar charge of conspiracy to deprive a man of his civil rights by killing him. They were all released on bond.

By now the Ku Klux Klan was shot through with FBI informants. While investigations focused on Sam Bowers and his immediate circle, the bureau was also keeping an eye on Beckwith and his Klan buddies in Greenwood.

The Evers murder case was still open, and the FBI kept tabs on the Hinds County district attorney's investigation.

An FBI memo dated June 19, 1966, reported that Bill Waller had advised the bureau that there had been no new developments in the case against Beckwith. The indictment was still outstanding, but Waller had said he wouldn't pursue a prosecution unless additional evidence came to his attention.

Less than one month later, the FBI office in Jackson received an intriguing new piece of potential evidence: a "reliable" informant reported to his FBI contact that Gordon Lackey had bragged about how he and Beckwith had murdered Medgar Evers. The informant said that the conversation had taken place sometime before Beckwith's first trial. The informant, Lackey, and one other man had been drinking at a lakeside clubhouse when Lackey allegedly told them this story:

Lackey and Beckwith had made two or three reconnaissance trips to Ever's neighborhood in Jackson before the night of the killing. Lackey and Beckwith had been hiding in some bushes when Evers came home late one night. According to the informant, Lackey boasted, "They got the wrong man. Beckwith did not do the shooting."

After the shot was fired, Beckwith and Lackey started to run out of the bushes, but they saw someone coming and dropped back. Eventually they split up; Beckwith ran to his car and Lackey hid in the bushes until it was safe to move. Beckwith picked him up "some distance from the area." Lackey told the informant that he was late getting back to the National Guard camp where he had been training and had almost gotten caught.

The Jackson FBI office forwarded this information to Washington in a memo dated July 13, 1966. The memo noted that Gordon Lackey had been questioned about the Evers murder in June 1963, and that he had said he was at Camp Shelby near Hattiesburg, Mississippi, on the night of June 11, 1963. Lackey's alibi was supported by two National Guard buddies from Greenwood who both said they had been out drinking with Lackey on the night of the shooting and had not been near Jackson.

J. Edgar Hoover quickly replied with a memo instructing Roy Moore, the SAC, or special agent in charge, of the Jacksonville office, to personally interview the informant and to do everything possible to convince him to testify in the Evers murder case. Moore replied on July 21, 1966, that the informant refused to come forward because he "loved life." He had said there was not enough money in the world to make him testify. The SAC suggested to Hoover that the only thing they could do was to urge the informant to introduce Beckwith to another person who would be willing to testify, hoping that Beckwith would brag to him about the killing.

The FBI never passed any of this information to the Hinds County district attorney.

In early 1967, Byron De La Beckwith moved from Greenwood to an apartment in Jackson to launch his latest venture. His ex-wife, Willie, had by then moved back to Tennessee. Beckwith's only employment was as a salesman for the *The Southern Review*, the White Knights' unofficial organ, edited by Elmore Greaves. For this he earned five hundred dollars per month.

Beckwith had meanwhile decided it was time to get into politics. On Valentine's Day he announced his candidacy for lieutenant governor of Mississippi.

In those days Mississippi was essentially a one-party state, and the Democratic primary was the only important election. The November race against the Republican candidate was just a formality.

Beckwith took to the campaign trail, apparently unconcerned about the indictment still hanging over him. He was walking around the Hinds County Courthouse one day when he spotted one of the Jackson detectives who had tried to send him to the gas chamber for killing Medgar Evers.

"Fred Sanders!" he called across the hall. Beckwith ran up to Sanders like an old friend, grabbed his hand and pumped it.

"What are you doing?" Sanders asked.

"I'm running for lieutenant governor of the fine state of Mississippi,"

Beckwith said cheerfully. He hoped for Sanders's support, he said, "because, suh, you of all people *know* that Byron De La Beckwith is a straight-shooter!"

Sanders just looked at him with amazement. The detective later learned that "He's a Straight-Shooter" was Beckwith's unofficial campaign slogan. It made Sanders wish he had been able to build a stronger case against the guy.

A month before the August primaries the *Review* published an interview with candidate Beckwith. He said that among his "chief qualifications" for the job was that he was "conscious of a diabolical international conspiracy against states' rights and racial integrity." Although Beckwith professed interests other than segregation, such as an unspecified "Highway Casualty Reduction Program," the subject inevitably turned to race. He urged all "sane" Negroes to reject revolutionaries such as Stokely Carmichael and Charles Evers and to accept benevolent white rule in the interest of their own material well-being and "safety."

It was during this campaign that Delmar Dennis met Beckwith for a second time. Sam Bowers had told Dennis to take care of Beckwith when he showed up in the area and introduce him to some other Klansmen.

Dennis recalled how Beckwith seemed to enjoy campaigning. He wore a white suit and white bucks; he kissed babies and hugged grandmothers. Beckwith scared the bejesus out of Delmar. The man had the remorseless eyes of a reptile.

In the primary Beckwith came in fifth in a field of six, with thirty-five thousand votes. For years he would boast that he did not finish last. After his political defeat Beckwith moved back to Greenwood, to a rented room in an old couple's house in an unfashionable part of town.

By 1967 there were as many as 260,000 blacks on the voter rolls in Mississippi, about 29 percent of all voters. In 1964 the figure had been less than 5 percent. The change was a result of the 1965 Voting Rights Act that finally eliminated the literacy test and poll tax.

In 1967 108 black candidates ran for office statewide, although only 22 of these won their elections. Robert G. Clark from Holmes County became the first black in the state legislature since the 1890s. That same year Bill Waller, whose main claim to fame was his prosecution of Beckwith, made an unsuccessful bid for governor.

That fall, Delmar Dennis ended his long career as an informant to testify at the trial of the accused killers of Goodman, Chaney, and Schwerner. More than three years had gone by since the bodies of the civil rights workers had been found in Olen Burrage's dam. Now Sam Bowers and sixteen codefendants sat in the federal courthouse in Meridian on federal conspiracy charges. Dennis was only one of several Klansmen and informants who testified against the plotters. But Dennis's testimony was the key to tying Sam Bowers to the killings.

After a ten-day trial, seven men were acquitted, including Sheriff Lawrence Rainey and Olen Burrage. The jury was deadlocked over three other verdicts, and it found seven defendants guilty as charged, including Alton Wayne Roberts, a Meridian klansman who had pulled the trigger on Goodman and Schwerner; Cecil Price, the deputy who had set them up; and Imperial Wizard Sam Holloway Bowers.

Price and Bowers were sentenced to ten years each; Roberts was given six. They were set free on bond during their appeals.

Beckwith remained loyal to his friends. He even sent out a fundraising letter for their defense.

"Five years ago I found myself completely uprooted from the normal pursuits of life and transplanted in the Hinds County Jail under an artificially concocted Federal charge of conspiracy . . . ," he wrote. "I was also charged with murder. . . . Today in Mississippi, there are over forty patriotic, white, Christian soldiers now standing before local state or Federal Court of injustice on charges as trumped-up as was mine."

The point of the letter was a plea for help for "those who fight your battles for you." Beckwith urged supporters to send money to a defense fund administered by L. E. Matthews, who FBI sources said was the Klansman slated to take over for Bowers when he went to prison.

In March of 1969 a new Hinds County district attorney named Jack Travis quietly dropped the murder indictment against Byron De La Beckwith. Beckwith's bond was refunded, and the case passed into a legal limbo known as nolle prosequi, which means "a discontinued prosecution by the authorized attorney for the state." Under nolle prosequi, in cases where a statute of limitations has not run out, the defendant can be reindicted and reprosecuted. And there is no statute of limitations on murder.

*   *   *

As the 1960s wore on and the various cases against Sam Bowers and his White Knights worked through the courts, the Mississippi Klan made a tactical error. They started blowing up Jewish targets. It was the outcome of a shifting ideology within the hard-core Klan, and it coincided with the growth of "Swiftism" and the Christian Identity Movement.

Sam Bowers was a "Swiftian." Byron De La Beckwith was introduced to Wesley Swift's virulent anti-Semitism when a friend gave him a set of Swift's taped lectures shortly after his mistrials. Swift had founded the California-based Church of Jesus Christ, Christian, which would later be known as the Aryan Nations, to promote the Identity Movement.

There are many forms of Identity "faith," but basically its followers believe that Caucasians are God's chosen people — the true Israelites. Jews, along with blacks and other nonwhites are the "mud-people," mongrels, not even humans, the offspring of Cain, who was born from the seed of Satan. The Jewish imposters, out of jealousy, want to destroy the white race. The blacks are merely their pawns.

Swift taught that white men were destined to be God's enforcers, using "weapons of war to destroy the powers of darkness and the forces of evil" — namely, the Jews. Gradually the White Knights lost interest in most black targets and set their sights on the small but influential Jewish community in Mississippi.

Since early 1967 a spate of bombings had plagued Jackson. It had started with the dynamiting of a real estate company that sold houses to blacks in white neighborhoods. It progressed to more potentially deadly, and more specific, targets. First it was the new synagogue on Old Canton Road, then it was the rabbi's house. He and his wife were sleeping when the bomb went off and were nearly killed.

A group of Jewish businessmen, led by a Jackson lawyer named Alvin Binder, decided to put an end to these outrages. With the help of Adolph "Bee" Botnick, head of the regional Anti-Defamation League (ADL) based in New Orleans, the Jewish group worked out a shadowy arrangement with the FBI. They supplied money to pay informants to put a stop to the bombings. And they, particularly Binder, developed their own paid sources.

With the heat on in Jackson, the Klan started targeting other cities. On May 26, 1968, two young Klansmen named Tommy Tarrants and Danny Joe Hawkins planted a huge dynamite bomb in a doorway of the

Temple Beth Israel synagogue in Meridian. The explosion shook houses three miles away, but, incredibly, no one was hurt.

Two of the most valuable informants the FBI and the Jewish group developed were brothers from Meridian, Raymond and Alton Wayne Roberts. They were able to supply amazingly detailed information, since they were trusted White Knights. Wayne Roberts was, at the time, appealing his conviction for depriving Mickey Schwerner and Andrew Goodman of their civil rights by murdering them. He was such a Klan hero that he was beyond suspicion. But in fact his conviction motivated him to cooperate with the FBI, and so did the seventy-five thousand dollars raised by the Mississippi Jewish community.

It's not easy to catch a bomber in the act. Timing is everything. The Robertses' FBI handlers, acting with the Meridian police, told the brothers to set up the time and place of the next bombing. That way the law could be waiting.

On June 29, 1968, Raymond Roberts called his contact at the Meridian police department: Tommy Tarrants was going to bomb the house of a prominent Meridian Jew named Meyer Davidson. Just after midnight Tarrants finished the final procedures to arm a bomb attached to twenty-nine sticks of dynamite. He set the timer for 2 A.M.

At 12:45 a green Buick without its headlights on cruised quietly up Davidson's street and parked fifty feet away from his driveway. Davidson and his family were not home. Instead dozens of Meridian policemen and FBI agents were positioned around the house, waiting.

Tarrants carried the bomb in one arm and a Browning automatic in his right hand. Depending on who's telling the story, when he reached the driveway, either the cops shouted "Halt! Police!," Tarrants fired twice with his handgun, and the cops opened up — or the cops simply opened up. The result was the same.

Tarrants was shot and captured after a fierce gunfight. His companion, a young schoolteacher and secret Klanswoman named Kathy Ainsworth, was killed by a bullet as she sat in the getaway car.

Three days later Byron De La Beckwith was on the road, carrying messages from Sam Bowers to other White Knights. The word was to lay low. There was a traitor among them.

The Meridian shootout marked the end of the Klan's reign of terror in Mississippi. The bombings stopped and the remnants of the White Knights drifted apart, retired, or started serving jail sentences.

Beckwith had been continuously monitored by the FBI since his mistrials. His name appeared from time to time in intelligence reports that certain agents in the Jackson FBI office shared with Al Binder and other Jewish leaders in the region. Beckwith seemed to be a minor actor in the Klan drama of the late sixties. According to informants, he was mainly a messenger and recruiter who traveled across the South visiting fellow fanatics. Beckwith had a big mouth and a reputation as a loose cannon. The FBI believed that although he had access to Sam Bowers's inner circle, he was not trusted.

When Sam Bowers finally went to prison for the Neshoba County murders in February 1970, the Mississippi Klan seemed moribund. A few radicals were, however, still on the loose and willing to strike. L. E. Matthews and Danny Joe Hawkins were among them. These were Beckwith's friends.

After a long period of quiet, word began to percolate through the paid informants still active in the vestiges of the White Knights that another job was being planned. This time the bomber would be Byron De La Beckwith. The target was Bee Botnick, the New Orleans ADL leader, to avenge the ambush of Tarrants and Ainsworth.

The FBI still had at least one informant deep within the Klan. He was a respectable sign painter and printer named Gordon Clark, who was very close to Matthews and Beckwith. He was so close, in fact, that he traveled down to New Orleans with Beckwith to help scope out the target.

At first Beckwith was going to blow up the ADL headquarters downtown. He even walked up to Botnick's office and tried to get in to see him. The ADL secretary told him that Botnick wasn't in. Beckwith decided it would be easier to bomb Botnick's house.

L. E. Matthews was a prosperous electrician and expert bomb-maker. Together he and Beckwith plotted the attack. According to the informant, Beckwith boasted to Matthews that it had only taken four or five weeks to set up the Medgar Evers murder. Matthews criticized him for bungling the job by leaving his rifle at the scene. Beckwith apparently brushed that off and asked Matthews for money to set up the job. As usual Beckwith was broke.

As the plans took shape, Clark reported regularly to the FBI and to Al Binder, who was apparently paying him for the information in an arrangement similar to the Tarrants operation. Binder later said it had cost his group ten thousand dollars to find out when the Botnick bombing was going to take place.

Agent Thompson B. Webb, who was in charge of the operation, says he knew nothing of Binder's alleged relationship with Clark. On September 18, 1973, Webb alerted the New Orleans FBI office, which in turn notified New Orleans police intelligence about the bomb plot. Sergeant Bernard Windstein, who was acting chief of the subversives unit, was briefed by an FBI agent. They knew Beckwith would be driving an Oldsmobile, tag number 42D4112 or 42D412. The FBI man added that the subject usually carried a loaded .45 automatic on his person and a .30-caliber carbine in his car. The agent told Windstein where Beckwith planned to enter the city and what route he would take. They just didn't know when.

It occurred to Windstein that this sort of tip was out of the ordinary. It's pretty rare that a federal agency will turn over a bust to local police, especially if there's some glory to be had. But there it was. He wasn't about to question it.

So Windstein chose John Evans, the biggest, toughest cop in intelligence, to be his partner. He put the special units on alert and prepared to intercept the bomber.

On Wednesday morning, September 26, Byron De La Beckwith turned his Oldsmobile onto Highway 49 and headed down to Jackson. He got there just before noon. He went to the Mayflower Cafe, a modest old Greek seafood place in the downtown business district and one of the city's most popular lunch spots. From there he made several phone calls. One was to Elmore Greaves, who wasn't in. Then he called L. E. Matthews and Gordon Clark.

Al Binder later told many people that he had been tipped off that Beckwith was going to be given the bomb at this meeting. He said he was watching from another booth in the restaurant when Clark and Matthews joined Beckwith for lunch. Binder said he was so nervous that sweat dripped into his plate of fish. He saw Matthews hand Beckwith a large paper bag. Beckwith got up and carried the bag to his car, which was parked out front, and drove off.

This story has passed into local legend, but it seems unlikely that even dolts from the Ku Klux Klan would pass a large sensitive time bomb in a crowded restaurant frequented by cops and agents.

According to FBI sources, Beckwith drove to Matthew's house in Florence on the rural outskirts of Jackson. Matthews assembled the bomb in his shed and gave Beckwith a lesson in how to arm it after he arrived at his target. Clark, who was at the scene, called Webb as soon as he could get to a phone.

At 5:30 P.M. the FBI contact called Windstein and told him that Beckwith was on his way. Bee Botnick and his family had been warned of the plot and had gone into hiding. Windstein was told that Beckwith would be carrying a powerful dynamite time bomb in a black wooden box measuring 8 by 9 by 22 inches. He was due in New Orleans between 11 P.M. and midnight, and he would be entering the city from Slidell, traveling west on I-10, and taking the Twin Bridges across Lake Pontchartrain.

Windstein briefed the intelligence officers, then alerted the Headquarters Tactical Unit, the bomb squad, the emergency medical services, and whoever else might be useful. By 10 P.M., they were all in place.

It was decided that the bomber would be arrested right after he came off the bridge. But just in case Beckwith changed his route, snipers and other specialists were positioned around Botnick's neighborhood to take him there.

At 10:15 P.M. Dick Huth at intelligence headquarters radioed an update. The subject was driving a 1968 Oldsmobile 98, white over dark blue, with two antennas on the rear fender, one a whip type fastened down. The car had a different — probably stolen — set of Mississippi plates: 61D2390. The driver was alone.

When Beckwith's car was spotted crossing the Louisiana line, two unmarked units pulled up behind him and fell back, blocking both lanes of the highway and slowing traffic, so that by the time he hit the five-mile span across Lake Pontchartrain, he would be isolated. At the same time, traffic was diverted from the eastbound lanes.

Windstein and Evans waited in a patrol car just beyond the bridges. The lights of New Orleans glowed softly to the west. It was a perfect spot. There were no houses, no commercial buildings. Just miles of lonely swamp and landfill that had been prepared for a development that was never built. Instead there were a series of turnarounds — "no-name exits," they were called — leading to nowhere. The turnarounds were ideal for hiding squad cars.

Nobody knew what Beckwith would do, but they figured that he would stop for a patrol car and uniformed officers. That's where the psychology came in. According to his FBI profile, the subject was a law-and-order type. He liked cops. He would think that it was an ordinary traffic stop and he could talk his way out of it. Windstein and Evans were wearing navy blue summer uniforms as they sat beside the loneliest stretch of highway in New Orleans, waiting to grab a man with a bomb.

Windstein and Evans had nothing to do but sit and wait. They talked about their families. Evans was thirty-three and Windstein was thirty-seven. They had grown up in Catholic, working-class neighborhoods on opposite ends of Carrollton Street in New Orleans. Their fathers had both been firemen. They both liked country music. They had rarely worked together before this night.

They went over what would happen if Beckwith didn't stop when they tried to pull him over. They would have to give chase. There were cars lined up in every no-name exit along the way. They would ram him, if necessary, to keep him from getting to the city. It was a kamikaze move, and they knew it.

"I just want to tell you that if that guy makes a move, either for his car or his gun, I'm gonna shoot him, Benny," Evans said. "I just want to know now if you have a problem with that."

Windstein shook his head. He had no problem.

The detectives saw the glint of headlights skimming across the lake. "There he is."

It was 12:02 A.M.

The blue-and-white Olds whizzed by, not speeding, not too slow, just driving steady down the blank, empty highway. Evans pulled out behind it, followed the car for about a mile, and then flipped on the blue lights. Sure enough, Beckwith pulled right over. As soon as they stopped, the subject was out of the Olds and jogging toward the patrol car along the edge of the highway.

Evans jumped out and stood behind the door with his shotgun pointed at a skinny little guy with rimless eyeglasses. "Stay where you are! Put your hands on the hood!" he shouted.

Beckwith did what he was told. He was dressed in gray trousers and a yellow sports shirt that hung loose over his belt. He said nothing. While Evans covered him, Windstein came around and patted him down. When he reached Beckwith's waist, he stopped and pulled up the shirt for Evans to see. There was a Colt .45 automatic, nickel steel, tucked into his pants behind his left hip.

"What are you doing with a gun?" Windstein asked.

"I always carry a .45," Byron De La Beckwith answered amiably in his rich Mississippi drawl.

Windstein checked it. Fully loaded.

"You're under arrest for carrying a concealed weapon," Evans said.

While Evans read Beckwith his rights, Windstein swept his flashlight beam over the Oldsmobile. He peered into the windows, careful not to touch the car — or to breathe on it too hard. On the front seat he saw a photocopy of a map of New Orleans with a route marked in red. In the well of the passenger seat he saw a black clothing bag covering all but one corner of a black wooden box.

A warm, damp breeze stirred the swamp grass. The back-up units and bomb squad hadn't arrived yet. There was no one else around.

It was a routine question, so Windstein asked it: "Have you ever been arrested before?"

"Yessuh, I was arrested before," Beckwith said mildly. "They say I killed a nigger in Mississippi."

Within a minute or two a marked unit pulled up, and Evans loaded his handcuffed prisoner into the backseat for the ride to central lockup. Windstein waited with the Oldsmobile.

Beckwith was sweating in the backseat with the windows up, but he was calm, even chatty. Evans could hardly believe how friendly this guy was for someone who had just been jumped and handcuffed. Most guys would be screaming bloody murder. Beckwith made small talk.

Evans later said Beckwith set the tone for the evening. He behaved liked a gentleman, so Evans and Dennis DeLatte, the other officer in the car, treated him like one. Evans wanted to relax him, draw him out, get him to talk. Instead Evans ended up telling Beckwith about his relatives in Mississippi and how he liked to hunt up there. Beckwith invited him to come up sometime; he would show Evans some good squirrel hunting.

It went like that right through booking at central lockup. Beckwith said only one thing that night that could later be used against him, something the prosecution called a "spontaneous declaration." He seemed to tell Evans and DeLatte that he didn't hold a grudge over the arrest. "You have a job to do, and I have a job to do," he said.

Beckwith later claimed he was misunderstood. All he meant was they were all workingmen.

When the men from the bomb squad got the black box in Beckwith's car open, they found a very large bomb: six sticks of regular stump-blowing, construction-quality Hercules dynamite and one five-pound cartridge of Trojan Seismograph dynamite, the kind oil companies use to find underground oil reservoirs. The police estimated that the bomb was big enough to blow up Botnick's two-story house and take out both next-door neighbors for good measure. Who knows what would have gone up if the bomb had ruptured a gas line.

It was a sophisticated bomb, as the police bomb expert Glenn Keller would later testify, built by someone who knew what he was doing. A Westclox alarm clock — ticking and set for 4:30 A.M., with a mercury switch on the back — was attached to blinking flashlight bulbs and an Eveready battery. A blasting cap had been inserted in the dynamite. All that would be needed was a few twists of wire to complete the circuit and fully arm the bomb. Keller disabled it and carted it away in the bomb pot.

Windstein had a look in the car. He placed into evidence the photocopied map marked with a route to Bee Botnick's neighborhood.

The car itself was cluttered with Beckwith's possessions, like a capsule of the narrow concerns of his life. In the front seat, along with the bomb, were a steel hatchet, brown work gloves, a King James Bible, four seven-round clips for a .45 pistol, a six-inch Buck knife, and a first aid kit.

The backseat contained, among many other things, a .30-caliber M-1 carbine; a thirty-round clip for it, fully loaded; ammunition for the rifle; a Polaroid Swinger camera; enough clothes for a week, including five sets of Jockey shorts, black and brown shoes, and a few foreign coins from Guatemala and Holland.

The trunk, once they got it open, offered up a small arsenal of various ammo and gun parts, including the barrel of a .50-caliber machine gun and the barrel and action of a Royal Enfield rifle. There was also a box of blue-and-white antique china, packets of letters and photos describing the antiques, letters from the wife of Jefferson Davis to Beckwith's grandmother, an umbrella, a black wooden walking stick, several boxes of personal items such as little lapel pins (one in the shape of a gun), Massey-Ferguson sales materials, a silver dollar, and twenty-three copies of a book titled *None Dare Call It Conspiracy* by Gary Allen.

Although the car was equipped with a tape player, the detailed police report did not mention any box of eight-track tapes.

Beckwith was held in lockup overnight, then taken to the parish jail to wait for arraignment. Word had gotten around that the man accused of killing Medgar Evers had been arrested with a time bomb. Beckwith was met by reporters and managed to answer a few questions.

He told them that he had been coming to New Orleans to sell some antique china. When he was asked about the dynamite bomb, he replied, "I'll just say a lot of dynamite is used in the Delta to blow up stumps." The Associated Press reported the quote, adding that "he would not say if he planned to blow up any stumps in New Orleans."

Somebody asked if he was a member of the KKK.

"I've been accused of it," he said softly. Then he snapped, "Thank you for your interest."

Beckwith was finally charged in both federal and state courts. Some leading citizens in Greenwood vouched for his eligibility for bail, including the mayor, a former sheriff, and a justice of the peace named Curtis Underwood. A Greenwood businessman named Z. A. Prewitt put up his $36,000 bond. Beckwith told the *Greenwood Commonwealth* that another rich planter had flown him back from New Orleans in his private plane, since his Oldsmobile had been impounded.

Now Beckwith had a more direct answer to give about the bomb in his car: he had no idea who could have put it there. "I was astounded to find out about it," he said. He praised his jailers in Louisiana, and even the inmates, who were "very courteous with few exceptions." Ever the gentlemanly guest, he even complimented the prison food as "very good, ample, wholesome and well-prepared." He was still, he said, trying to sell his china.

Within weeks a fund-raising letter was circulating among the usual Christian patriots. "This is Urgent!" it began. Beckwith begged that money "in any amount" be sent to his son's address in West Point, Mississippi. They were after him again. "Because of who I am, I have the right type of enemies." They were in "high places." He was the victim of "a plot to Abolish Beckwith."

In every way Beckwith was back where he felt he belonged. He was once again the center of attention.

Beckwith was tried in federal court in New Orleans in late January 1974. The charges were straightforward: possessing an unregistered handgun and an unregistered bomb. For the first time in his life Beckwith was up before an integrated jury, including three women, a black man, and a black alternate. His court-appointed attorney, Wayne Mancuso, was an Italian Catholic.

There had been a number of pretrial skirmishes. The most dangerous to the government's case had been the defense motion to suppress evidence found in the arrest and search, which would effectively end the case. Where was their probable cause to stop Beckwith and search him and his car?

What the defense wanted to know was who tipped off the police to the time bomb. How could the informant know the exact dimensions of the bomb unless he or she constructed it? And if the informer made the bomb, then he or she was a coconspirator and not subject to special protection. In the end the court ruled that the search had been proper, and the informant's identity was kept secret.

The delicate matter of the informant hamstrung the prosecution. The government couldn't get directly into the motive for the crime without producing him. But the FBI was not willing to sacrifice the informant's identity — and, possibly, his life — for a conviction.

This didn't prevent the prosecution from trying to paint a picture of the larger crime for the jury. For instance, Bee Botnick's secretary, Lorraine Treigle, testified that Beckwith had come to the ADL office on Gravier Street on September 14, 1973, asking about her boss. Botnick himself took the stand to corroborate her account. But the judge threw out their testimony. It wasn't relevant to the charges.

The defense strategy was to convince the jury that a bomb was planted in Beckwith's car either to frame him or to kill him. Beckwith took the stand to offer his version of events that day in September. He had decided, he said, to take a few days off and head to New Orleans to try to sell off his family's antique china. He said there was a black wooden box filled with music tapes in his car when he left Greenwood. He said he stopped in Jackson to visit friends and business acquaintances, leaving his car parked and unguarded.

Shortly before dark he left Jackson for New Orleans — a three- or four-hour drive to the south. Feeling tired, Beckwith pulled off the road for "a nice long snooze." Then he continued on to New Orleans.

The next thing he knew, he was under arrest for some reason. He collected guns, and he carried a loaded pistol for self-protection. He had a permit to carry it, he said. Beckwith said he never saw the map of New Orleans on the front seat of his car. He had no knowledge of a time bomb. He read in the paper that a bomb was found in his car.

Assistant U.S. Attorney Dennis Weber was sarcastic in his cross-examination. "You have no idea who put that device in your car?" he asked incredulously.

"No sir," Beckwith said. "I'm just as curious as you are, and believe me, I'm going to find out."

The jury went out at 1:40 on a Friday afternoon. They stayed out all evening. By noon on Saturday they had reached a unanimous verdict: not guilty on all counts.

Reporters who interviewed the jurors later learned that what bothered them most was that they felt they weren't getting the whole story. They wanted to know why Beckwith had a bomb in his car. Where did he get it? They were a cautious group, and if they couldn't get all the facts, they weren't taking a chance on a conviction. They wouldn't even convict him on the handgun charge.

The U.S. attorney was dumbfounded. The judge seemed livid.

"You were arrested under most suspicious circumstances," the judge lectured Beckwith. "You have literally walked through the valley of the shadow of death."

Beckwith delighted in his victory. He immediately announced his intention to run for office again in Mississippi. Maybe try for Congress this time. There was just the little matter of the Louisiana state charges against him that were still pending.

That fall New Orleans elected Harry Connick, Sr., as its new district attorney. Connick brought in his law partner, Bill Wessel, as his first assistant. Wessel was a reform-minded lawyer. He had worked on civil rights cases in Mississippi. He wanted to send out a message that the new D.A. wasn't going to conduct business as usual. He searched through the stacks of pending cases from the departing Jim Garrison's docket and found the one he was looking for.

Louisiana has strange laws, a mélange of British common law and Napoleonic Code from the state's origins as a French colony. Although the laws have been changing, back in the 1970s a person could be tried by a five-member jury for certain misdemeanors. Beckwith, who was still charged only with illegally transporting dynamite into Louisiana without a permit, qualified for the small jury.

Beckwith was put on trial in May 1975. This time, despite the loud protests of the defense, the jury consisted of five black women.

The second trial was much like the first one. The prosecution was allowed to use crucial testimony from the federal trial, including the hearing to suppress evidence obtained in the search of Beckwith's car. It was, all in all, not a favorable situation for the defense.

Again Beckwith took the stand. He narrated his version of events on the day before his arrest in September 1973. It was a now-familiar performance. Beckwith argued with his own lawyer, he interrupted and asked questions, and he sparred with the prosecutor on cross-examination, leading the judge to admonish him again and again. He offered to sell his china to Wessel or anyone in the gallery who might be interested. He seemed to be enjoying himself thoroughly.

The outcome was rather different this time around. It took the jury thirty-five minutes to find him guilty. He was given the maximum sentence of five years in prison. Beckwith was allowed to remain free on bond while his lawyers filed an appeal.

A few years earlier Beckwith had bought a dilapidated old house deep in the woods of Carroll County, just south of Greenwood. He returned there to await his appeal. The old Melton place, as it was called, had no heat or electricity or running water. The roof leaked when it rained, and a family of skunks resided in the foundation. In good weather Beckwith slept outside or under a mosquito net on the veranda. What it had was privacy and good hunting for his son. Beckwith took up reading as his main hobby, and by most accounts his fanatic philosophies grew more and more elaborate.

Sometimes FBI agents would hazard a trip down the rutted dirt road to drop in on Beckwith, if only to remind him that they were still watching. Mostly he kept to himself. The press was not welcome.

A reporter and photographer from the New Orleans *Times-Picayune* managed an audience with Beckwith before he began serving his sentence. He was still working for Ricks Motors tractor dealership. While the photographer, Jim Miller, snapped away in the fluorescent office light, Beckwith quietly terrorized the writer. He was describing how he could tell the differences between a black man and a Chinese man by cutting off their heads, boiling them down to the bone, and comparing the skulls side by side.

"You can do the same thing with a white man's skull," Miller remembered him saying. "But I wouldn't want to cut the head off a white man, unless he made me *real* mad."

According to Miller the shaken reporter tossed his notebook in the trash as they left the building. The story never ran.

Beckwith kept busy while he waited out his appeal. In the spring of 1977 he traveled to Washington, D.C., to stay with Pauline Mackey, a friend from the ultra–right wing Liberty Lobby organization. He was trying to sell some sort of oil filters to the Pentagon through the office of his hero and distant relative, Senator James O. Eastland.

While he was there, Beckwith's appeal was denied. But since he was out of the state, he missed his appointment to report to prison.

Late one night in May a dozen or so armed officers appeared at Mackey's house and rousted Beckwith from his bed. Among them was Ben Windstein, who carried a fugitive warrant from the state of Louisiana.

Beckwith spent the next three years at the Louisiana State Penitentiary in Angola. He served his time in a solitary cell, often just off death row, where guards could keep him away from the general population. It was well-known that the man who was supposed to have shot Medgar Evers was a prisoner at Angola. He would not have lasted long in the yard. So he took his meals in his cell, and he exercised in the corridor while the guards watched.

Beckwith was by then an experienced prisoner. He made the best of a bad situation. He was allowed a radio, reading matter, and limitless access to the commissary. To fight the drabness of prison life he managed to customize his jail togs: he cut the sleeves and sewed them with mattress buttons to give himself French cuffs. He continued his regimen of compulsive reading and letter writing.

One of his correspondents was the new, self-proclaimed leader of the Identity Movement. Richard Butler was a disciple of Wesley Swift, whose tapes had proved so inspirational to the Klan and who had died in 1970. Butler would soon establish a white separatist compound near Coeur d'Alene, Idaho, to be headquarters for his own group, the Aryan Nations.

Beckwith wrote Butler a long letter in March 1978, which was promptly printed in Butler's newspaper, *The Tribal Chronicle,* organ of the Identity Movement. Beckwith's reason for writing was to complain loudly that he had been booted out of the Masons for being a convicted felon. He wanted fellow travelers to answer a question for him: was Jesus Christ a Mason? It seemed to be an important point to him in his appeal to the lodge.

Never one to pass up the chance to talk about himself, Beckwith provided some background about his life and his legal troubles. "In 1963 I was accused of murdering Mississippi's mightiest NAACP nigger Leader named Medgar Evers. . . . I got two hung juries." he wrote. "In 1973 I was accused of coming to New Orleans, La., to put a bomb in the lap of a top Jew of the ADL or B'nai B'rith. In 1974 I was tried and found TOTALLY innocent . . . In 1975 I was retried before an all nigger jury made up of 5 nigger women and in 5 minutes I was a convict!"

Just in case some of the readers might miss his affiliations, he rolled out his Klan pedigree: "I was carried to Washington, D.C. (in 1966) as one of the top super secret (ACCUSED) White Knights of the KKK of Mississippi. . . . We (thanks be to Yahweh) came home with honor and our scalps, too! Now a White Knight looks at all other KKK groups as Boy Scouts or Cub Scouts or John Birchers at the most — I think — I really don't know. Ha! But I mix and mingle with all KKK groups."

Beckwith then sent out a plea for donations: "I am really hurt and need help running into thousands of dollars."

Richard Butler printed a flamboyant reply: "My very being is racked with vexation that our manhood has sunk so low that an abomination of Justice such as your case reveals, could exist. I salute YOU, a great Warrior for Christ."

The rest of the front page was devoted to inspirational quotes from

Adolf Hitler and an all-purpose slogan: "Get rid of the Jews and all of your troubles are ended!"

After three uneventful years in Angola Beckwith was released in 1980, with two years scratched from his sentence for good behavior. Broke and jobless, he returned to Mississippi to live in a trailer on the old Melton property.

21

Homecoming

BEN CHESTER WHITE was a sixty-seven-year-old farmhand who never got involved in politics and went out of his way not to upset the white man. His luck simply ran out one hot spring night in 1966 when he had the misfortune of entering the dim consciousnesses of Claude Fuller, Ernest Avants, and James Lloyd Jones when they had a mind to "kill them a nigger." Anyone would do. At least that was the testimony of Jones at his murder trial a few months later.

In spite of his confession the all-white jury couldn't agree on a verdict for Jones. He was never tried again. Charges against Fuller, the alleged ringleader in the killing, were dropped. Avants was tried and acquitted.

Lane C. Murray first met Charles Evers at the end of Jones's trial. Evers was leading a big civil rights demonstration around the courthouse in Natchez after the Jones jury had hung up. Murray and E. L. McDaniel, both ranking members of the United Klans of America (UKA), showed up to heckle them.

The UKA was an interstate Klan group that had evolved alongside the White Knights, although the UKA was far less secretive. McDaniel, a former White Knight, was the UKA grand dragon for Mississippi. Murray was his right-hand man.

Evers knew most of the Klansmen in this part of the state, and he knew all about Murray. When Evers would lead a march in Natchez, Murray would be out in his sound truck, blaring his favorite tune from the Klan hit parade: "Move Them Niggers North."

Tonight it was Evers's turn to harass Murray. "We gon' make sure this case is tried again," Evers bellowed. "And this time old Lane C. Murray ain't going to be sitting at the lawyers' table like some big dee-fence attorney or somethin'."

Murray looked over at Evers and gave him the finger.

By now Evers had moved his base of operations from Jackson to the tiny town of Fayette, not far from Alcorn in the river lowlands. He opened the Medgar Evers Shopping Center, then organized crippling boycotts of white-owned businesses in the surrounding counties. This further enraged the Klan.

Murray and McDaniel would sometimes show up on Main Street in Fayette in their robes to taunt Evers and try to scare the people. Evers and his security crew would meet the Klansmen in the dusty street, and everyone would be posturing, growling, and shouting, calling each other "nigger" and "peckerwood."

Then one day Evers started talking to the Klansmen, really talking, and they listened. He told them they weren't enemies, that it was the rich man who kept them both down, poor whites and blacks, kept them fighting each other. Something clicked, and they started talking some more.

Evers said, "Lane, you got to look back to those sharecropper days, and even today, the rich folks, their priority is to make that money. They made it off the blacks, and they make it off the whites. A poor black family and a poor white family could never get ahead. They'd sell you a mule, and if it died before you paid for it, you'd be paying for two."

Murray will tell you that Evers helped put him on the right road. It didn't happen overnight, but eventually he quit the Klan, and so did McDaniel.

Murray found his calling in state politics. He found work as a behind-the-scenes political operative, vote getter, and general campaign organizer. For a while in the seventies he, Evers, and McDaniel, along with some other characters from the state's colorful recent history, teamed up to promote a "redneck-blackneck" coalition to form a voting block of the state's working poor.

*   *   *

By the end of the 1960s Charles Evers was the runningest politician in the state of Mississippi. In 1968, when Congressman John Bell Williams became governor of Mississippi, he left a vacant seat in the Third District, which included the capital city. Evers ran and beat six white men in the Democratic primary. He lost the runoff to Charles Griffin by a two-to-one margin, but even that meant that forty-three thousand people — most of them new black voters — were willing to come out for a black candidate. After the returns were in, Evers bounded over to Griffin's campaign headquarters to congratulate him and call for unity. The startled politician accepted his outstretched hand. The white crowd applauded. Evers's political career was launched.

Evers was an old-fashioned Mississippi rogue politician in the Bilbo tradition — ruthless, charismatic, more than a little shady, and almost comically Machiavellian. Evers called himself an independent Democrat for most of his career, but he was always a Republican at heart. The eldest son of James Evers hated the welfare state, and that's what the Democrats represented to him. They gave you handouts and kept you weak. At least the Republicans let a man stand on his own legs. The racism of white liberals, Evers figured, was just more subtle than the racism of the old rascals. It was easier to deal with something if you could see it and fight it in the daylight.

For a while he was the black Democratic standard-bearer in the state. He helped lead the breakaway Mississippi Freedom Democrats in a successful challenge to the state delegation at the Democratic National Convention in Chicago in 1968. The all-white, pro-Wallace delegates were thrown out and replaced with the new, integrated "loyalist" group.

Evers was elected mayor of Fayette in 1969. It was another benchmark in a decade of firsts. He became the first black mayor of a racially mixed town since Reconstruction.

Next he set his sights on the Governor's Mansion. It was the beginning of the end of his rising stardom. He began to squander his power. Even though he could depend on the backing of the loyalist Democrats, Evers decided to sit out the all-important primaries and run for governor as an independent in November 1971.

Worse, he encouraged blacks to vote for Jimmy Swan in the Democratic primary. Swan was a redneck populist country singer whose political views put him in the same class as Byron De La Beckwith. Evers explained his reasoning to the press: if Swan won the primary, Evers would be running against such an outrageous racist that even conservative white Democrats would have to vote for him in the election. It was the only way to win.

Liberal whites were outraged.

It was a raucous, mudslinging campaign. Swan cruised the back roads in his Cadillac, with American and Confederate banners flapping in the slipstream and a country band in tow. Evers stumped in cities and backwater settlements, his entourage of protection men, advance men, soul singers, and reporters leapfrogging across the state.

One scalding-hot afternoon the show pulled up in Decatur, Evers's hometown. Two hundred nervous blacks gathered in the town square, the white man's part of town, where they had once been forbidden to drive a car. Now, while a few dozen local whites stood across the street, watching silently, they came out to hear their own Charlie Evers make a political speech. Evers spoke on the courthouse steps, the same spot where he had heard Bilbo speak forty years earlier, and he reminded folks of how it had been.

"Medgar an' I watched him spit that ole racist fire," he said to the transfixed crowd. ". . . But look out, Bilbo, we comin' at you!"

Evers looked over the familiar faces in the crowd.

"Yeah, Decatur! I'm your prodigal son! This black man went off to Chicago, but when Medgar died, I said it's time to come back and change all this ol' hate, all that racism got to change it into love."

The people cried, "Amen."

Evers's campaign slogan was "Don't vote for a black man, don't vote for a white man. Vote for the best man. Evers for governor!"

In 1971 Mississippi had 671,000 registered white voters and 268,000 registered blacks. Of the seven candidates in the Democratic primary, Swan came in third with an astonishing 129,000 votes. More astonishing, he carried Evers's mostly black Jefferson County.

In the runoff primary, the contest was between an old-time politico named Charles Sullivan and Bill Waller, the man who had prosecuted Beckwith. Waller was campaigning as a reformer, champion of the common man and foe of the Capitol Street gang. "This time, let's take on the machine!" was his rallying cry. It was somewhat ironic that he had the backing of James Eastland and Ross Barnett, who arguably *were* the machine.

People say that Evers's baiting of Sullivan cost Sullivan the race. It was Evers against Waller in the November election.

Evers reportedly asked Swan to throw the Klan vote his way. It was the first test of the redneck-blackneck coalition.

Evers never expected to win, but he was thrashed, receiving only 172,762 votes to Waller's 601,222. Fifty blacks were elected across Mississippi, although most of them were in low-level positions.

Still, Evers put a positive spin on the election. In a gracious concession speech he declared, "Whites and blacks are going to look at each other differently now, as citizens. I've proved that a black man can run for office in Mississippi without getting shot, without getting killed."

Although the power and money still rested in the hands of white Mississippians, things were certainly changing. The Ku Klux Klan had been more or less emasculated by the FBI, and its leaders had been bought off or imprisoned.

Bill Waller's administration was a turning point in Mississippi politics. He appointed blacks to positions in the state government for the first time in this century. He also engineered the demise of the Sovereignty Commission by simply cutting off its funding.

But white racism persisted in a more elusive form. Ever since Congress had passed the 1965 Voting Rights Act, whites had looked for ways to hold on to their power. In the old days they had used poll taxes, literacy tests, harassment, and murder to keep blacks away from the polls. Once the federal government had stepped in, making all these practices illegal and invoking federal oversight of state and local elections, the white majority had embarked on a state-sanctioned program of "massive resistance."

Like a virus that mutates to elude every medicine, white racism adapted to the times and worked around each new law passed to overcome it. Voting districts were merged and gerrymandered to prevent black majorities; qualifications for elected officials were stiffened. Private all-white academies sprouted like mushrooms on the outskirts of towns across Mississippi, drawing students from the underfunded public schools.

White conservatives learned the value of stealth. Racist rhetoric had no place in campaigns anymore. The militants came out only when needed, to quietly terrorize the countryside, to steal elections if necessary. Pressure was exerted beneath a surface of conciliation. The face of racism had changed from a grimace to a friendly smile. The xenophobic cabal of big-time planters and moneymen who ran the state was slowly supplanted by a new generation of businessmen, a more urban, less traditional set who favored expansion and industry. By the seventies segregation and hatred had become unfashionable and very bad for business.

A new breed of moderate progressive leaders was coming up in the South: Jimmy Carter in Georgia, Reubin Askew in Florida. There were new slogans to go along with the new mood. The South was now "Too Busy to Hate." Dixie started calling itself the Sunbelt.

One sweltering June night in 1975, twenty-five hundred people squeezed up against the stage at the annual Medgar Evers Homecoming celebration in Natchez. Charles Evers had a surprise in store for the crowd.

"Well we've come a long way!" he shouted into the microphone.

"Tell it, Mayor!"

"We've come a lot farther than some of you know . . ."

"Tell us about it . . ."

The homecoming had started in 1973, when Governor Waller set aside June 12 as a day to honor Medgar Evers. It had since become a tradition, both as a celebration of Medgar's life and as a gauge of Charles's political clout. Charles still wielded considerable power in Mississippi, and in early June every year celebrities, ministers, and white politicians flocked to his side.

Ten thousand people had come to the barbecue in Fayette that afternoon in 1975. That evening Evers filled the auditorium in nearby Natchez for a B. B. King concert and a round of speeches. Evers read telegrams from Vice President Nelson Rockefeller and Governor Bill Waller. He introduced NFL quarterback Joe Namath to the crowd.

"We've got some other guests here tonight, and y'all don't know they're here," Evers crooned into the mike. "But you know 'em! It's E. L. McDaniel, grand dragon of the Klan in Mississippi!"

The crowd was oohing and aahing as McDaniel nervously made his way toward the stage.

"It took a lot of guts for him to come out here tonight, so let's give him a welcome!" Evers shouted.

The mostly black crowd cheered and clapped.

"And we've got another one, even worse!" Evers said. "Lane, where you at?"

Lane Murray joined McDaniel and Evers onstage. They clasped hands, and Evers put his arms around them both for the cameras. He said, "If anyone wants to get elected governor, they've got to come by us!"

There were hoots and hollers, and then everyone, even the Klansmen, sang "We Shall Overcome."

"Never no more will Mississippi have the image she has had in the past!" Evers shouted.

This bizarre tableau was stirring to some; to others it seemed just another cynical cabaret event in the long line of Evers's productions. In any case it was a high point in Evers's career. He was, in fact, standing on the edge of a cliff, looking down at harder times ahead.

A few days later he was tried in federal court for criminal tax evasion. The IRS accused him of concealing more than $52,000 in income between 1968 and 1970, much of it looted from his 1968 congressional campaign. Evers denied the charges, and his case ended in a mistrial. Never an agency to give up, the IRS pursued a civil suit against Evers and more or less hounded him for the next two decades.

Throughout the seventies Evers's behavior placed him increasingly at odds with the new black political mainstream. He openly embraced Richard Nixon and Gerald Ford (and reaped generous federal grants for Fayette projects). He praised George Wallace. He voted against Jimmy Carter at the 1976 Democratic convention.

Evers became a full-blown pariah in 1978 when he made a play for the U.S. Senate seat vacancy left by a retiring Jim Eastland. He ran as an independent, brought in Muhammad Ali to campaign for him, and siphoned off 133,646 votes from the Democratic candidate, Maurice Danton. That threw the election to Thad Cochran and gave Mississippi its first Republican senator since Reconstruction.

People started grumbling out loud that Evers was in the Republicans' pocket. Owen Brooks, a black leader and director of the Delta Ministry, wrote a scathing open letter to Evers, calling him "the black prince of political opportunism."

"Your behind-the-door closed meetings with some of the worst racist elements in this state are part of your sordid history," Brooks wrote. "Eastland was too much for black folks to have to swallow, so for a price you will run the interference for Cochran by splitting up the black vote."

Naturally Evers endorsed Ronald Reagan in the 1980 presidential election. He was also tried for tax evasion again that year for the old debt plus charges of unreported income from his Fayette operations. Charles by now owned a lion's share of the land and businesses in town: along with the Medgar Evers Shopping Center there was Sheila's Restaurant and Lounge, Carolyn's Grocery, Eunice's Washeteria, and the Evers Motel, Restaurant and Lounge. But his base of support was eroding. He ran Fayette more like a king than a mayor, and people were starting to resent him.

As the town judge he was accused of throwing his enemies in jail without trial. Charles responded by saying that "when you break the law, there are no such things as civil rights."

In 1981 Evers was unseated as mayor by Kennie Middleton, a young black attorney. Middleton's campaign slogan was "We've seen what this town can do for one man, now let's see what one man can do for this town."

There had never been any love lost between Myrlie Evers and her brother-in-law. In fact by the time Charles lost his seat as mayor, they were barely speaking to each other. He had ignored her and her children over the years, never visited them in California, and never helped them when they were in need. He still hadn't forgiven her for marrying his brother; she never forgave him for pushing her away.

After she moved to Claremont, it never occurred to her that she should do anything except go back to college, start a career, support her children. It was a family tradition. She came from a line of capable, educated women, teachers who taught her to value learning. An education was the one thing nobody could take away from you.

While she went to school and reared her children, she still made appearances for the NAACP. She also took paid speaking engagements when she could get them, and she collaborated on a book about her life with Medgar titled *For Us, the Living*. All of this related to the central project of her life: to keep Medgar Evers alive in memory. She admitted that everything she did during those years was based on what she thought he would have wanted her to do. He was in her head every day.

Myrlie graduated from Pomona College in 1968 with a BA in sociology, and went to work as director of planning and development for The Claremont Colleges. It was a big job, but it was not enough. Medgar had never gotten a chance to run for office; Myrlie ran instead. In 1970 the painfully shy woman from Vicksburg became the Democratic candidate for a congressional seat from southern California.

The campaign almost broke her, but she kept on. Charles refused to give her any money and wouldn't help with the campaign. But his ex-wife, Nan, slipped Myrlie five hundred dollars to pay the household bills in the last month of the race. She lost in the heavily Republican district but got 38 percent of the vote.

The children eventually adjusted to the shock of leaving Mississippi. After the family moved to California, Darrell slowly came out of his grief. The boy named for Jomo Kenyatta grew up in white schools, with white friends, listening to the Beatles and the Rolling Stones. Like his father he was an athlete, a star football player, a runner. He always wondered whether if he'd had a father around — someone to work with him and train him — he might have played professional ball. Instead he focused on art, where he found his other talent. He was always searching, never sure where he was going.

Darrell had a dream when he was a child, even before his father's death. He must have been seven or eight, and he dreamed he was at the United Nations, and all the delegates were screaming at each other in different languages. He couldn't be heard himself, because he was just a kid. Then he saw another young boy walk up to the podium, and slowly the voices stopped and the room fell quiet. The boy radiated a beautiful light. He said, "Why can't you just love one another?" Everyone started crying.

Darrell never forgot the dream and always wondered whether the boy in the dream was him or someone else he had to find.

Between her children, her job, and her politics, Myrlie didn't have much of a social life. Even the idea of dating seemed repugnant to her. Then she met Walter Williams.

Walter was almost fifteen years older than Myrlie. He was a handsome six-foot-four longshoreman and union activist who had an idea to market playing cards with the images of civil rights leaders. He needed Myrlie's permission to use Medgar's likeness, so he looked her up. Although she gave her consent, the project never got off the ground.

Myrlie didn't see Williams again until a couple of years later, when she was serving on Los Angeles mayor Tom Bradley's task force on gang violence. One day she spoke to a group of gang members, and Walter was there. He was a childhood friend of Bradley's and active in the community. After the speech he asked her for her phone number. She gave it to him to get rid of him; she was still not interested in dating.

But Williams eased his way into her life. He became a friend. He would drive through a pounding rainstorm from Los Angeles to Claremont just to cook dinner for the kids when Myrlie was having one of her difficult days. He was there to hold her when she felt as if she couldn't go on.

Although he is a modest man and would be pained to admit it, Walter Williams had a lot in common with Medgar Evers. He loved the outdoors; he loved to hunt. He was soft-spoken and strong, and he had spent his whole adult life fighting the bosses and the unions to open up jobs for minorities in the port of Los Angeles. At least three of his friends had been killed in the struggle, and he had gone to work every day of his life prepared for a fight. Like Medgar he had chosen a public, political life, and he had many friends.

Walter had been married three times, and he had five children of his own. By now he knew who he was and what he wanted. He was not intimidated by Medgar Evers's ghost or Myrlie's devotion to his memory. If her life would be a shrine to Medgar Evers, Walter Williams was willing to be a part of it. She called him her "best friend," her "rock of Gibraltar." He was, she said, the wind under her wings.

When they were finally married in 1976, Darrell and Van gave Myrlie away, and Reena, then twenty-one, served as her maid of honor. Myrlie said that she felt Medgar's presence in the room, as if he was telling her "this is right." Walter didn't mind that she chose to keep Evers as her professional name.

Myrlie was still hearing Medgar's voice in her head, pushing her to achieve. She became a founding member of the National Women's Political Caucus. She moved on to a high-powered job with a public relations firm and later Atlantic Richfield, where she was vice president for advertising and publicity. The honors and awards for her political work and social activisim piled up in her cabinets and filled her walls. And yet she still felt as though she had some unfinished business in Mississippi. All her achievements were dedicated to one man's memory, and she never gave up hope that someday his killer would pay for what he had done to Medgar, to her, and to their children.

In 1987 Myrlie ran for Los Angeles City Council. She lost the race but not her taste for politics. Mayor Bradley appointed her to the Los Angeles Board of Public Works.

This was a big job. She was one of five people in charge of the infrastructure of Los Angeles. They supervised six thousand employees and administered half a billion dollars in contracts. She loved the work and the leverage her position gave her to promote her social causes.

The children were grown now. Darrell was an artist. Reena was married, had children, and worked for an airline. Van was developing a reputation as a professional photographer.

Myrlie had long ago stopped attending Charles's homecomings in Mississippi. But every year, as the anniversary of Medgar's death approached, she sank into a sadness, deepened by a sense of incompleteness, of unfinished business.

She thought maybe the time had come to put it all to rest on the twenty-fifth anniversary of the assassination, at a ceremony at Arlington National Cemetery. She brought a special guest with her: her grandson, Reena's eleven-year-old boy, Daniel Evers Everett.

There were a thousand people in the crowd, and Danny got up to make a speech. Myrlie was nervous for him. She had delicately suggested that he show her a copy of his speech, perhaps she could help him with it? He told her he didn't need any help. She quickly realized he was not reading his speech at all.

"I don't know that much about my grandfather because I wasn't really there," he said, then paused, as if remembering suddenly. "I wasn't there at all."

The crowd chuckled, and Danny grinned. He had them in his hands.

"If we didn't have those like Malcolm X, Martin Luther King, Jr., and Medgar Evers we wouldn't be free today," Danny said. "We wouldn't be able to go anywhere we want to. We wouldn't be able to do anything we want to."

When he was through, Myrlie beamed at Danny. He was the image of his grandfather. Back in Los Angeles she would sometimes go out to his school and watch from the stands as he ran around the track. The long, lean strides and the way he held himself were so familiar. It was as if she were watching Medgar run.

Myrlie's younger son, who called himself Van Evers and was twenty-eight years old, also accompanied her to Arlington. He had unfinished business too. Van had never visited his father's grave.

Later that day he followed his mother to the quiet, grassy spot where Medgar was buried. They stood there for a long time, and then Van started to cry. Myrlie wrapped her arms around him and rocked him against her, as she had when he was a child. She was thinking, *No, it's not over.*

There were signs that Byron De La Beckwith intended to lead an obscure and quiet life after he got out of prison. First he went off to a "retreat," rumored to be the Aryan Nations compound of his good friend Richard Butler, out in Idaho. Then he returned to the Melton place in Cruger, Mississippi, the only home he had. It took a bulldozer to clear a path in the kudzu that had grown there. He kept to himself and seemed generally forgotten in his home state. Once in a while, usually on an anniversary of Evers's death, one newspaper editor or another would wonder what ever happened to Beckwith and then would send a reporter out to find him.

That happened on the twentieth anniversary of Evers's death, in June 1983. Jim Ewing from the Jackson *Daily News* got directions to the trailer in Cruger. Neighbors warned that Beckwith wanted to be left alone and that he was always armed, which, if true, would have been illegal, since he was a convicted felon. Ewing maneuvered his car down a rough dirt track through the tangled backwoods of Holmes County, past the posted signs, and up to the door of the "rural retreat." Beckwith "politely, but firmly" refused to be interviewed. He said he would just be misquoted by the "Jewishly owned" press. The headline for Ewing's story read "Byron De La Beckwith lives quietly in the Delta."

Before he went to prison in 1977, Beckwith tried to get back together with his ex-wife, Willie. He wrote her long letters, telling her about his continuing interest in radical politics and begging her to remarry him.

She was living a sober life in Knoxville, Tennessee, and, sensibly, turned him down.

Around the same time a close friend from the Liberty Lobby introduced him to Thelma Lindsay Neff, a retired nurse in Chattanooga, Tennessee. She was ten years older than Beckwith, but they had a lot in common. They both believed in the Identity faith and the Jewish conspiracy. She was every bit as racist and outspoken as he was, and she was deeply committed to right-wing causes. The first thing Beckwith said to her was, "Honey, your phone's tapped." For her it was "love at first sight."

Neff was a small, garrulous woman with wispy hair the color of old lace and hard blue eyes. She had been a local beauty queen in her heyday and had once dated the crusading Tennessee senator Estes Kefauver.

She had been married and divorced, and she had a grown son living nearby. Her family had deep roots in this part of Tennessee, and her voice carried the flinty edge of her mountain home.

Once Beckwith got out of Angola in 1980, he began to court Neff in earnest. They were married in June of 1983, and soon after Delay moved into Thelma's little bungalow on Signal Mountain. He took over the breezeway as an office and hung a full-size Confederate battle flag over the front porch. He helped take care of the string of rental apartments on the property.

Thelma and Delay pursued their fanatic crusades as a couple now. To them the world was a dangerous, frightening place controlled by their enemies, the Jews — all communists — who sponsored one-world government and fluoridation, among other things. They believed, for instance, that the Holocaust was a hoax and that Jews kidnapped Christian children for human blood sacrifices.

They campaigned to get fluoride out of the water supply. The chemical, they said, was used as a form of mind control to make the people docile. They collected all their drinking water from a spring in Georgia. They tried to grow and can their own food, preparing for the race war they knew was coming. They were fixtures at local political meetings. Walden, the community where they lived on Signal Mountain, was essentially segregated. Beckwith compared the foggy, rustic hill to heaven. He joked that whenever any blacks or Jews tried to move in, their houses mysteriously burned down. "You know how niggers are careless with their cigarettes," he said, chuckling.

Beckwith tried to start a business selling stoves and water filters. He ordered up new stationery, identifying himself as a "wholesaler." His personal motto was printed at the bottom of every page: "On the White Right Christian Side of Every Issue."

Once he was settled, Beckwith couldn't seem to resist calling attention to himself. He mounted a campaign to be pardoned by the governor of Louisiana (he was turned down). He and Thelma had their picture taken at cross-burning ceremonies. He even allowed himself to be interviewed by an "inquiring photographer" from the local newspaper. The reporter asked, "What stance do you believe the U.S. should take in the future to combat terrorism?"

"The best thing I know that we could do is to drop a bomb on Israel," Beckwith replied. "That would stop terrorism."

Beckwith kept up ties in Mississippi. He took Thelma to Greenwood and introduced her to Gordon Lackey and other close friends. By now Beckwith's only child, Little Delay, had been in and out of the marines, a new family tradition, and had married. He and his wife, Marianne, had two children, including yet another namesake: Byron De La Beckwith VIII. Like his father Little Delay was a traveling salesman, flogging retreads and used tires in northern Mississippi. He was short and blocky; he favored spiky cowboy boots and wore his hair in a buzz cut. His father was always welcome in his home, and so was Thelma. Little Delay never talked about his mother, Willie, who had by this time changed her name.

The elder Beckwith's health started to fail him during these years. He suffered from high blood pressure and had surgery to replace a blocked renal artery. As the eighties wore on, he seemed increasingly determined to take his place in the pantheon of patriotic heroes. He contacted writers to ghost his autobiography. He considered running for office and continued to fight to clear his felony record. Mainly he wanted to be able to own guns again.

Beckwith showed up at a big political rally in Blackhawk, Mississippi, right before the 1987 primaries, in which Bill Waller was making another run for governor. While Waller and other candidates glad-handed over the smoking barrels of barbecued chicken, Beckwith caught the ex-prosecutor's eye and flagged him over. He wanted to introduce him to Thelma. A stunned Waller graciously shook hands.

Later Beckwith told reporters, "Mr. Waller tried to put me in the gas chamber twice. I told Mr. Waller back then I had a sinus condition and that smelly gas would upset my sinuses."

The meeting made front-page news in Jackson. Before long people were wondering out loud whether Beckwith should be tried again for Evers's murder.

Myrlie Evers was contacted in Los Angeles. She told the *Clarion-Ledger* that she wanted the case reopened, that she "had never given up hope."

A Jackson civil rights attorney asked the Hinds County district attorney, Ed Peters, to reopen the case. Peters said too much time had passed; it couldn't be done.

In the old days that would have been the end of the discussion. The call for a new trial would have died out as it had in the past. But the old days in Mississippi were over. Or so it seemed.

22

Mississippi Turning

THE CASE against Byron De La Beckwith was brought back not because of any one event, but by a confluence of many events in a slow tide of change. That slow, exasperating, but undeniable change led to what social scientists term a "new political reality." In this new reality Mike Espy would, in 1986, be elected Mississippi's first black congressman in this century, with 52 percent of the vote in his Delta district, including 12 percent of the white vote. By the end of the 1980s blacks, who accounted for 35 percent of the population of Mississippi, would make up nearly a third of its registered voters. There would be more than six hundred black elected officials, the highest number in any state.

In 1987 a handsome thirty-nine-year-old Harvard lawyer from Ackerman, Mississippi, named Ray Mabus was elected governor. He ran as a reformist and won with 90 percent of the black vote and 40 percent of the white vote. Mabus was fond of saying, without irony, that "the civil rights revolution freed us all." Mabus called for a new state constitution, computers for every school, and catfish farms in the Delta. He swore, with a fervor that reminded his critics of Scarlett O'Hara, that "Mississippi would never be last again."

Those critics predicted, correctly, that Mabus and his reforms were doomed to crash on the rocks of the immovable and unreconstructed state legislature. But for a time Mississippi, never a place for half measures, was giddy with change. Although true Mississippians would never admit that they cared what anyone in New York thought, it was significant that Mabus and his young white cronies were featured on the cover of the *New York Times Sunday Magazine* with the headline, "The Yuppies of Mississippi: How They Took Over the Statehouse."

This secretly pleased members of the rising young white professional class, who were increasingly embarrassed by Mississippi's backward, racist image. Lawyers and legislative aides, who congregated nightly at the George Street pub or an upscale fern bar called 400 East Capitol Street to sip their chardonnay and complain about the Yankees who thought they still went barefoot in Jackson, were pleased by the PR potential of the new Mississippi. The state was still hovering around last place in per capita income and first in teenage pregnancy, but its backward image was fading.

Margaret Walker Alexander, the author and scholar who had been the Everses' neighbor on Guynes Street, gave a memorable speech at the beginning of the eighties: "I believe that despite the terrible racist image Mississippi had in the past, despite her historic reputation for political demagoguery, despite racial violence and especially lynching, despite all the statistics about being on the bottom, Mississippi . . . offers a better life for most black people that any other state."

The real changes were subtle; the cosmetic changes were dramatic. In 1987 Miss Mississippi was a black woman. In 1988 the city of Vicksburg elected a black mayor. Pollsters noted a sharp difference in attitude between the older and younger generations. For instance, 80 percent of whites under thirty favored integration, as opposed to fewer than 50 percent of whites over sixty.

At its core Mississippi was still a segregated society, with separate schools and churches and neighborhoods, just like most of the rest of America. But now blacks and whites could at least eat lunch together, work side by side, and live in armistice, if not peace.

Myrlie Evers returned to Mississippi in the summer of 1989 to mark the twenty-fifth anniversary of the Goodman, Chaney, and Schwerner murders in Neshoba County. She usually felt sick to her stomach whenever she came back. This time she felt merely suspicious. And hopeful. She was astonished by the young white politicians who stood up to condemn the killings of the past. During a ceremony at Mount Zion church Governor Mabus recited the words to "Lift Every Voice and Sing," the anthem of African-Americans.

Myrlie marveled. She didn't think Medgar Evers could have done it better. She remembered that Medgar used to tell her how Mississippi would one day be the best place to live, and she hadn't believed it. Now she began to wonder if she might live to see the day his prophecy would come true.

The climate of hope in the late eighties coincided with an upwelling of memory and regret. The twenty-fifth anniversary of so much sorrow brought on a period of self-examination. At the same time the local newspaper started publishing extracts of dozens of secret files from the Sovereignty Commission, which brought the names Medgar Evers and Byron De La Beckwith out of the past and onto the front page.

When the state legislature voted to abolish the Sovereignty Commission in 1977, the politicians wanted to destroy all the agency's records. When they couldn't get away with that, they settled on keeping them sealed for fifty years. The ACLU and a number of other plaintiffs, including John Salter, who was a professor of Indian Studies at the University of North Dakota, and Ed King, who was teaching in Jackson, sued to open the files. The presiding federal judge, none other than Harold Cox, threw out the case. After years of appeals and depositions the case landed with a more reasonable U.S. justice, William Barbour. In 1984 Barbour allowed the ACLU plaintiffs to read and copy the files for purposes of research. They were barred from revealing the contents. Naturally the contents of the files started leaking to the press.

Former governor Paul Johnson died the next year and his papers were donated to the University of Southern Mississippi. The papers, ordered by a local judge to be opened to the public, contained copies of hundreds of Sovereignty Commission files from his years as governor in the mid-sixties.

It looked for a while as if the whole fetid heap of scandal and dirty tricks and character assassination that had been the business of the Sovereignty Commission was about to be dumped, in all it's vileness, right into the laps of Mississippi's citizens. Then Salter and King broke away from the ACLU suit and appealed to restrict access to the files. They had read through the eight filing cabinets full of press clippings, informers' reports, and other raw intelligence, and they had concluded that most of it was a pack of lies that would only hurt the people mentioned if the files were made public. There were reports of drug use and sexual perversion, family secrets and financial information — most of it uncorroborated or invented — that had been used to pressure and discredit antisegregationists. Salter and King wanted the victims of these investigations to decide whether to release these reports and asked that the files be opened under guidelines similar to those set forth in the Freedom of Information Act.

Among some liberals and left-wingers in Mississippi, Salter and King went from being regarded as civil rights heroes to being cast out as pariahs overnight. "What were they trying to hide?" asked ex-state senator Henry Kirksey, the perennial protest candidate for public office. The rift further weakened Mississippi's already fractious and quarrelsome left-wing coalition.

Meanwhile the news business in Mississippi had gone through a sea change. The oldest Jackson TV station, WLBT, had been shut down by the FCC for bias during the civil rights years. It had been taken over by a community board of directors, including Aaron Henry and other black leaders.

The *Clarion-Ledger* had been inherited by a new generation of Hedermans. The morning daily, which was once called the "Klan-Ledger" for good reason, actually won a Pulitzer Prize in 1983 (for a series on education) under Rea Hederman, who went on to be the publisher of the *New York Review of Books.*

That same year the Gannett chain bought the *Clarion-Ledger,* ending a regional monopoly on newspapers in Mississippi. By this time the state could no longer claim to be a hermetically sealed backwater, the closed society of the recent past. More and more native sons and daughters were going to colleges outside the state and coming back with new attitudes. The Sunbelt boom had drawn in Yankee businesses and foreign notions. And all anyone had to do to see another view of the world was to switch on the television.

Oddly the *Clarion-Ledger* became more cautious and superficial once it was owned by outsiders. Gannett did, however, bring in a black managing editor named Bennie Ivory and increased minority hirings. And the paper hit hard on a few selected stories, most notably ones connected with the civil rights movement of the sixties. Critics say it was safer to dwell in the past than to deal with the present predicament of corrupt public officials and intractable poverty. In any case the new, improved *Clarion-Ledger* led the charge to dredge up some old, unpunished civil rights murders, including that of Medgar Evers.

At the head of the pack was an ambitious thirty-year-old reporter named Jerry Mitchell. It was the sober, red-haired Mitchell who kicked open the doors to Mississippi's moldering basement of nightmares.

It began with the imbroglio churning around the release of the film *Mississippi Burning* in January 1989. The movie, based on the Goodman, Chaney, and Schwerner murders, managed to offend almost everyone who'd had anything to do with the Neshoba County case or Freedom Summer, except for a few retired FBI agents who liked being portrayed as idealistic good guys.

Civil rights activists said that the script downplayed the role of blacks in the struggle and whitewashed the FBI's basic indifference to racial violence. Nobody was about to forget how the agents stood by and took notes while cops and Klansmen beat demonstrators to the ground. That wasn't in the movie. Nor were the COINTELPRO operations used to spy on black leaders such as Martin Luther King, Jr., and Malcolm X and to harass and intimidate others.

Conservative whites lambasted the movie for what they said was an exaggerated depiction of Klan violence and southern racism. Ordinary citizens shrugged and said it was just another black eye for Mississippi.

The *Clarion-Ledger* covered the controversy, and when the twenty-fifth anniversary of the murders came around that June, it sent a team of reporters, including Mitchell, to track down as many participants in the case as they could find. The coverage reminded everybody that only a few of the original conspirators had been sent to federal prison and none had faced state murder charges. The newspaper duly published an editorial calling for a reopening of the case.

Before long Mitchell got a tip that some secret Sovereignty Commission papers had been accidentally misfiled in federal court. That led to a story, cowritten with another reporter, about how a Sovereignty Commission spy had infiltrated CORE headquarters during Freedom Summer and copied some stolen documents.

Other leaks followed, until one source gave Mitchell about seven hundred pages of key documents. Despite the wrath of Judge Barbour and an FBI investigation, the *Clarion-Ledger* went ahead with a lengthy series on the Sovereignty Commission papers.

Among the leaked files was a thick folder titled "Medgar Evers: Race Agitator." It confirmed that Evers had been kept under surveillance for years by the Sovereignty Commission and state and local police.

There were huge gaps in the Evers file, but one very important document found its way into Mitchell's hands: the report that Sovereignty Commission investigator Andy Hopkins had prepared on the background of potential jurors in the second Beckwith trial.

The banner headline across the front page of the *Clarion-Ledger* on October 1, 1989, read "State Checked Possible Jurors in Evers Slaying." The files showed that at the very least the Sovereignty Commission had tried to subvert the efforts of another state agency, the district attorney's office. At worst the report pointed to possible criminal jury tampering.

Mitchell called Myrlie Evers at her office in Los Angeles to get her comments on the story. Evers remembers the moment clearly. It was as if a little light turned on inside her, and it caused a shudder of recognition. Could this be it?

She told Mitchell what she had said many times before, that she wanted the case reopened if evidence was available to get a conviction. But this time it felt different. She said she would be coming to Jackson before the end of the year to see what could be done.

The district attorney's office was lodged on the fifth floor of the Hinds County Courthouse in a maze of cubicles and hallways that, before renovations, had been part of the county jail. In the old days condemned prisoners had been hanged on the fifth floor. In fact when a visitor stepped up to Clara Mayfield's desk, just left of the elevator, to ask for an appointment with the district attorney, Ed Peters, the floor often emitted a queasy creak where the trapdoor to the gallows had been imperfectly covered.

This was, however, one of the few grim notes in a surprisingly sunny and lighthearted office. Despite the rumors circulating about the goings-on in the district attorney's office, most of them focused on the D.A. himself, anyone who wasn't a stranger could wander freely through the hallways. Even a stranger might think she'd walked into a friendly faculty lounge instead of a death-belt prosecutor's headquarters.

Peters was tall and lanky, with wavy white hair and wire-rimmed glasses. Although he looked and sounded a lot like Andy Griffith, Peters was the most feared prosecutor in the state. In private conversation he was a soft-spoken, avuncular, pleasant man. In the courtroom he was a wolverine. His scathing cross-examinations of witnesses were so relentless that any defendant took the stand at his or her own peril.

In the fall of 1989 Peters had been the district attorney of Hinds and Yazoo Counties for seventeen consecutive years. He would be up for reelection for his sixth term in 1991.

Peters inspired extreme reactions; you loved him or hated him. After so many years in office he had many enemies. The talk around town was that he was a ruthless machine politician with his sights set on higher office, maybe the Governor's Mansion. People who knew him disputed this.

Peters was forty-nine years old. He had married well. He was already rich, and he didn't seem to want to be anything other than what he was. He already held down one of the most powerful jobs in the state, since Hinds County includes Jackson, the capital, where the governor and the state legislators dwell at least part of the year. That gives the district attorney jurisdiction to indict, or not indict, every state politician who might get caught in behavioral or financial indiscretions.

There were a lot of indiscretions. The peccadilloes of elected officials offered a limitless supply of entertainment in the capital. They were open secrets, fuel for conversation among people who loved to talk. People whispered about the prominent politician who was supposedly shot by his wife during an argument over his mistress. Or the former governor who allegedly solicited male prostitutes on Farish Street. (The prostitute who snitched on him reportedly said, "I didn't know he was the governor! I thought he was just another legislator.")

Peters's office concentrated on violent felonies and avoided political prosecutions, leaving that to the state attorney general and U.S. Justice Department. His office was staffed with talented prosecutors who won their cases and made do with few resources. This conviction record helped win him elections, but it had not quieted his enemies. In the Byzantine world of Mississippi politics and rampant rumor, Peters had figured into just about every conspiracy theory of corruption and influence peddling making the rounds.

Depending on who was talking, Peters was either a power-hungry government stooge or a dope-smoking racketeer who sold protection to Mafia-types and who used the Jackson Police Department and the Ku Klux Klan to terrorize his critics. This was the view — usually whispered and sometimes printed — of some of Peters's political rivals as well as a cabal of activist black leaders. It is interesting to note that the local klansmen and their sympathizers were equally certain that Peters was controlled by international communist banker Jews and *their* pawns, the FBI. They were particularly unhappy about Peters's prosecution of a bunch of partying brownshirts who got into a shooting match with a black gunman during a racist picnic in Jackson one summer.

As with all conspiracy theories, there were enough factual elements to keep the rumors alive: the little grains of truth in the oyster of paranoia.

There had been attempts to convict Ed Peters of one thing or another over the past two decades. Back in the seventies he had been investigated by the state attorney general's office for allegedly taking payoffs to protect a prostitution ring. Jack Anderson, the syndicated columnist, made it a national story. Peters was cleared. He had been reprimanded by the state bar for negligence for his role in a securities-fraud scandal when he was in private practice. But Ed Peters has never been found guilty of any crime, which must be a record in the state, where fifty-seven county supervisors were recently indicted on corruption charges in an FBI sting, and a federal district court judge was impeached and sent to jail for perjury.

Since what Peters's office did best was to prosecute violent criminals and send them to prison or to the gas chamber, the D.A. was popular among law-and-order voters. This record also made him a target for anti–death penalty activists. And that is where Peters got in his worst trouble with the black community.

On May 27, 1987, a headline in the *Clarion-Ledger* read, "Hinds DA Says Race Is Factor in Jury Selection." The article was about a federal court hearing in the case of Leo Edwards, a black man sentenced to death for murdering a clerk in a Jackson convenience-store hold-up. His lawyers argued that Edwards deserved a new trial because his rights had been violated when, in 1981, he was convicted by an all-white jury. Ed Peters had used his peremptory, or automatic, strikes to keep blacks off the Edwards jury. In fact, a study by an American University professor showed that Peter's office used peremptory strikes to exclude 80 percent of potential black jurors in capital murder cases.

Peters was asked, under oath, why this happened, and the D.A. admitted that he favors whites over blacks for death penalty juries. The reason, he said quite candidly, was that blacks are less likely to vote for executions. As a group, Peters said, blacks have "been discriminated against, they've been subjected to much crueler treatment at the hands of law enforcement [and are] more likely to be against the system."

All criminal lawyers know about this theory, and many would agree it is true. The U.S. Supreme Court, however, has ruled that you can't strike jurors based on racial stereotypes. Peters's admission caused a minor uproar in Jackson. It did not go over well with black leaders, many of whom were looking for a way to get rid of him anyway. There was talk that there might be an African-American challenger for Peters's job in the next election.

The grumbling, in fact, was still going on when the *Clarion-Ledger* articles on the Beckwith jury appeared in October 1989, and the Jackson City Council voted to urge the district attorney to reopen the Evers murder case.

In the fall of 1989 there were eight assistant D.A.s working under Ed Peters and three full-time investigators. No matter how long they knew him, everyone called the D.A. "Mr. Peters" in public, the way a diplomatic staff might say "Mr. Ambassador." An outsider would pick up right away their fierce loyalty to and respect for Peters, who was himself a spectral figure in the office. He would dart in and out at appropriate times, either to advise someone on a case or, if it was a big capital murder trial, to help out in court. His style was to give all of his A.D.A.s as much freedom to make decisions as possible. But if they screwed up, Peters would be right on them. John Davidson, a young Texan and the newest member of the staff, remembers the first time a jury of his came back with an acquittal. Peters passed Davidson in the hall and without looking at him muttered, "Loser," and kept on walking.

There were two black lawyers on Peters's staff, Linda Anderson and Glenda Haynes, who specialized in trying robberies and abuse cases. The most serious violent felonies were handled by Cynthia Hewes and Bobby DeLaughter, Peters's first assistants.

Hewes was the daughter of a judge, a Tri Delt, an Ole Miss Law School graduate, a Junior Leaguer, and an utterly lethal prosecutor. On court days she wore trim suits and short skirts and tied her chestnut hair in a French twist. Her laugh carried from one end of the office to the other. The cops all loved her. In fact few people in town had anything but good things to say about her, even the defense lawyers she regularly beat up in court.

Her office door was plastered with clippings and cartoons that reflected her unusual view of the world. *The Far Side* comics and funny tabloid headlines ("Woman Sets Husband on Fire for Eating Chocolate Bunny!") were posted right next to a prized memento: the execution order for Greg Davis, a serial killer who had preyed on old ladies.

DeLaughter stood over six feet tall, but he looked shorter, probably because he walked fast and with his head down, as if weaving through a field of unseen linebackers. DeLaughter, pronounced "dee-lawter," had piercing dark eyes and heavy black eyebrows that almost met at the bridge of his nose. His hair was straight and of medium length. The only really remarkable feature about him was the thick, dark mustache that completely covered his upper lip. He projected the earnestness of a kid who had decided to become a prosecutor in the ninth grade and had carried a briefcase ever since.

DeLaughter's office was right next to Hewes's and was as sloppy and dark as hers was neat. In one corner an ancient, dried-up fish tank was a museum of mold species. An old, rusted Browning shotgun rested against another wall, the souvenir of a diving expedition in the Pearl River. Diving for evidence was one of DeLaughter's few hobbies. His main hobby, he would tell you, was the law.

So it only made sense that a headline about jury tampering in the *Clarion-Ledger* would get his attention. He read about how the Sovereignty Commission had helped pick the jury in Byron De La Beckwith's second murder trial. He showed the article to Peters, who shrugged and muttered something about looking into it. Then he showed it to Doc Thaggard, one of the investigators. They started talking about it in a casual way.

That's how Thaggard remembers it all started for him, just as a curiosity. He and DeLaughter wondered how many people were still living among those who had sat on the Beckwith juries and how long it would take to find them. Thaggard was real good at finding people. It was a specialty of his, something he had been known for since he was a homicide detective. The other thing he was known for was his . . . calm. As in, one morning he called Hewes to tell her he was going to be late.

"How come, Doc?" she asked.

"Well," he said mildly. "Last night our house burned down."

That was Thaggard. He used that sort of patience to search for missing persons. He figured chasing down the members of a thirty-year-old jury might be a challenge.

The clerk's office came up with a list of people who had served on the two Beckwith juries. Just names. No addresses. So Thaggard started by opening up the Jackson phone book.

By the end of October the reopening of the Evers murder case had become a political cause. The Jackson City Council had voted to urge Peters to reopen the case, and there was pressure from the County Board of Supervisors and the NAACP. On Halloween Peters announced that he was calling together a grand jury to investigate the charges of jury tampering in the second Beckwith trial.

Thaggard and DeLaughter did the investigating. Naturally Thaggard found the Beckwith jurors, dead and alive. Some still lived in Jackson, or their widows did. Others he had to track down all over the South.

Thaggard interviewed each living juror, asking them if they'd had direct contact with a Sovereignty Commission investigator, or anyone else connected with the case. Not one had. Some knew that someone had been asking friends and associates about them, but that was all.

Andy Hopkins, who had checked out the jurors for Beckwith's defense team, was dead. So Thaggard and DeLaughter drove out to Forest, Mississippi, to talk to Erle Johnston, who had been the director of the Sovereignty Commission at the time.

Johnston was an unusual character. After he left the commission in 1968, he went into publishing and local politics. He had always considered himself a moderate in the segregation wars. He felt he had served his state well. Now retired he spent his time reaching out to his former enemies. He kept up a lively correspondence with John Salter, who had written an endorsement for Johnston's new book about the Sovereignty Commission called *Mississippi's Defiant Years*. Johnston also was friendly with Charles Evers and Aurelia Young. He had even been named cochair of the Committee on Preservation of Civil Rights Papers at Tougaloo, a college he had once tried to destroy for its student activism.

When Thaggard and DeLaughter visited Johnston at his pine-shaded house, he told them that he remembered giving Hopkins permission to help Beckwith's defense. He didn't see anything wrong with it since there had never been any personal contact with the jurors.

"It wasn't ethical," Johnston admitted. "But it wasn't illegal."

They agreed, and so did the grand jury. The eighteen-member panel concurred that there was no evidence of criminal jury tampering. The grand jury did, however, recommend that the district attorney look for another way to reopen the Evers case.

Meanwhile Myrlie Evers decided that it was time to fly to Jackson to find out what was going on. Benny Bennett got the assignment to pick her up at the airport and bring her to the district attorney's office. Bennett was a Jackson police detective assigned to the district attorney's office as an investigator. Because he was six-foot-two and 240 pounds and had special skills — he was an expert marksman, and a connoisseur of defensive arts — Bennett usually pulled special escort duty.

He had spent time in police intelligence, some of it semiundercover as a "Klan sympathizer" and later as a leather-jacketed, Harley-riding wanna-be Bandito (Mississippi's version of a Hell's Angel). Frankly Bennett looked the part. And now that he was cleaned up and shorn and squeezed into a sports jacket, he still wore a silver skull ring and carried a rattlesnake-head key chain to remind him of the old days.

Bennett was thirty-nine years old, the son of a Jackson detective who, in fact, had worked on the Beckwith investigation almost thirty years earlier. He had some old-fashioned attitudes about police work, and he was not what you would call a liberal. But if he decided to be your friend, he was your friend for life.

All Bennett knew about Myrlie Evers was that she was the widow who wanted the old murder case reopened. He wondered whether she wouldn't be hostile, an in-your-face Angela Davis type, so he prepared himself for that. He was pleasantly surprised when she greeted him with a warm smile and a handshake. She was a good-looking woman, well dressed and friendly, and she put him at ease. Like most cops, Bennett made fast judgments about people. He liked Myrlie Evers right off.

"Miz Evers," which is what he called her from the moment they met, and would never call her anything else, had a good sense of humor, which was another big plus. At the time, Bennett was learning to use a new weapon — a butterfly knife that flipped open like a switchblade. After he had escorted Evers to the D.A.'s office, he was walking around the hallway, snapping it open and shut, trying to get the hang of it. He rounded a corner and almost walked into Miz Evers. She just laughed and said, "Well, I knew things had gotten rough in Jackson, but I didn't realize it had gotten THIS bad." That really cracked him up. She had a lot of class.

Unfortunately, Evers's first encounter with Peters was not as pleasant. She didn't want to go into this meeting alone. She wanted advice and she wanted a witness, so she had asked her friend Morris Dees to meet her in Jackson. Dees was the cofounder and head of the Southern Poverty Law Center in Montgomery, Alabama. He had made a big name for himself by suing Nazi and Klan hate groups and bankrupting them out of business. He had a memoir about to be published, and Corbin Bernsen was going to play him in a television movie.

Peters had no idea who Dees was, but Peters took an instant dislike to him. Dees reminded Peters of the bleeding-heart "death squad" lawyers who harassed him and his office just about every time they tried a capital murder case. The Southern Poverty Law Center sounded like one of those outfits.

It didn't matter when Morris Dees, a man of considerable charm, assured Peters that his organization was prosecution-friendly and that he would help them out, making sure that the case was properly investigated and prosecuted. At least that's how Peters interpreted the offer, and it didn't set very well with him. Peters never blamed Myrlie Evers for what happened. He assumed she had been told bad things about him by his enemies. But the meeting with Evers and Dees started off chilly and got worse.

Peters never liked this case, just as he had said back in 1987, after an earlier move to reopen it. Peters told them that the case couldn't be reopened, that they could never get around the speedy trial problems. It just wouldn't stand up. The murder weapon was missing, along with all the other physical evidence and most of the court records. DeLaughter had located part of the old police report, which he carried into the meeting in a legal envelope. Peters pointed to the file: That was all they had to go on.

It seemed like so little to Evers, but she knew there was more. She had the transcript of the first trial, information she would keep to herself for the time being.

Evers informed Peters that she did not want to hear why the case could not be reopened. She wanted to hear how he was going to reopen it. Peters told her that they would keep trying to locate court documents and evidence to see if the case could be revived, but he didn't offer her much hope. That's how the meeting ended.

DeLaughter said very little. He just listened and watched. Afterward he and Peters talked. DeLaughter wanted to do some more research to see whether they could find a way around the speedy trial issue. As usual Peters told him that it was his bone and he could run with it.

Myrlie Evers impressed Bobby DeLaughter. She was smart and personable. DeLaughter sensed Evers was truly interested in reopening the case, but only if it could be successfully prosecuted. She didn't seem to have a political agenda, just a desire for justice. He could relate to that. It made him want to find a way to do it.

DeLaughter felt personally offended that a state agency like the Sovereignty Commission would try to undermine a prosecution. But to him the case wasn't about politics, or ghosts, or revenge. It was a cold-blooded, back-shooting sniper ambush assassination, and there was no statute of limitation on murder.

The problem was, if the case was to be reopened, DeLaughter would need something different, and something solid. He could do a lot with evidence, but he couldn't create it.

23

The Case

BOBBY DELAUGHTER got his first taste of the law when his ninth-grade civics teacher took the class to watch an actual trial at the Hinds County Courthouse.

It was a murder case, and the victim was a prominent lawyer named Millard Bush, whose wife, Peggy, had shot him in their daughter's bedroom. She claimed it was an accident.

DeLaughter sat in the balcony of courtroom number three, entranced, while Bill Waller, who was in private practice then, defended the small blond widow. DeLaughter begged his parents to let him return all week to watch the rest of the trial. By the time the jury came back with a verdict — not guilty — DeLaughter had decided to become a prosecutor. Like a man who marries his high school sweetheart and never loves another, DeLaughter never considered doing anything with his life other than practice law.

His first afternoon at the Hinds County Courthouse provided De-Laughter with more than a career path. So many characters at the trial would play leading roles in his life, it was almost as if a tableau of his future was arranged in front of him.

The law partner of Millard Bush, the shooting victim, was Alvin Binder, who would be DeLaughter's first boss and mentor. The defense attorney, Bill Waller, who had prosecuted Byron De La Beckwith in that very courtroom, would one day consult with DeLaughter on the most important case of his life. The presiding judge was Russel Moore, whose stepdaughter, Dixie Townsend, Bobby DeLaughter would marry. And Moore, as it turned out, held the key to a crucial piece of missing evidence in DeLaughter's own prosecution of Beckwith.

While you might say DeLaughter was destined to inherit the Beckwith case, he was not, on the surface, the most likely candidate to drag Mississippi through its most turbulent civil rights trial of the modern era.

DeLaughter was born in Vicksburg in 1954. His mother, Billie, came from a big political family with roots in rural Issaquena County. Her uncle was Buddie Newman, Ross Barnett's right-hand man in the state legislature. His father, Barney, was a commercial artist who worked for a newspaper. He moved the family to the capital when Bobby and his younger brother were little.

DeLaughter grew up in South Jackson's white middle class. It was a world apart from the boycotts, demonstrations, and fairground stockades just a few miles north. Like most white boys his age, he was interested only in sports, school, family, and church, the parameters of his sheltered universe. He never heard the name Medgar Evers when he was growing up and would not hear it for many years.

DeLaughter's first real encounter with the dramas of the civil rights movement came when his family moved to Natchez for a year. When he went home for the Christmas holidays in December of 1969, there were maybe two or three black students at his high school. When he returned to school in January, the teachers and students from black and white schools had been shuffled like a deck of cards. He now attended an integrated public school. He remembers it was strange because it was different. But the adults took it a lot harder than the kids. DeLaughter's interests had expanded to include girls by now, but the parents and white school administrators, fearing riots, rapes, and whatever, threw a wet blanket over school activities. They would no longer allow proms, dances, or pep rallies where students could mingle socially.

The situation was the same when he came back to Wingfield High

School in Jackson the next year. DeLaughter was an active and popular kid. He played varsity football even though he was too tall and skinny to do much more than get knocked around. He played basketball, joined a high school fraternity, and was sports editor of the yearbook. He was president of the honor society and the student council. He was even elected "Mr. Wingfield," which got him a full-page picture in the *Wingspread*. DeLaughter just couldn't see the point of going to high school and joining all these things if you couldn't have proms and pep rallies. So he decided to return fun to high school. Twenty years later he would still be bragging about organizing the first integrated senior prom in Wingfield's history.

Bobby went to college at Ole Miss and graduated from its law school. By then he had married Dixie. One day his father-in-law brought him around to Al Binder's office and recommended him for a job. Binder put him to work on legal research. Binder would later say that he'd never met anyone as talented as DeLaughter when it came to finding the law.

DeLaughter concentrated on personal injury cases. In one case involving a tractor accident he was able to find an angle nobody thought of that earned the firm a $700,000 fee. With another young and hungry lawyer named Bill Kirksey, DeLaughter helped Binder put together research for his most famous client, Wayne Williams, defendant in the Atlanta child murder case.

In 1983 Kirksey and DeLaughter left the firm, amicably, to start their own practice. They were supposed to make their money on divorce and personal injury cases, but they ended up defending accused killers, rapists, and dope dealers. They won their cases but lost their shirts in the process.

By 1987 DeLaughter had three kids and a troubled marriage. He wanted out of private practice. One afternoon during the Christmas season he stopped by the district attorney's office on his way home. Ed Peters was the only one left in the office, so he invited DeLaughter to come in and talk. Peters remembers that DeLaughter said something about how tired he was of defending all those criminals; how it was driving him crazy.

So Peters said, "Why don't you come over and be on the other side?" DeLaughter accepted the offer, and Peters hired him.

Bill Kirksey, who loves DeLaughter like a brother and feels as if he could just about read DeLaughter's mind when they tried cases together, had no idea DeLaughter wanted to be a prosecutor.

DeLaughter doesn't brag much, but his self-confidence is formidable. At the same time he is an intensely private, introverted man. Even people like Kirksey who count him among their best friends will pause from time to time, stumped by one question or another about him, and admit that they really don't know him that well.

When DeLaughter chooses to reveal himself, it is like the sun coming from behind a cloud. Myrlie Evers, who instinctively understands the quiet in people, recognized this in DeLaughter when she first met him in Peters's office. She liked him, and she saw past his reserve. Morris Dees liked him too. From then on her contacts were with DeLaughter instead of Peters. DeLaughter made a point of calling Evers in Los Angeles every week or so to fill her in on his progress with the case.

DeLaughter had some long conferences with Bill Waller, who was in private practice in a building across from the courthouse. While De-Laughter was putting the facts of the case together, a sergeant in the police identification unit found an envelope of old negatives while cleaning out an old filing cabinet. They turned out to be the crime scene and evidence photos from the Medgar Evers murder case. DeLaughter had them printed up. Meanwhile the FBI turned over some records of the Beckwith case, including blow-by-blow accounts of both trials and the names of the witnesses. Beckwith's fingerprint records were located in Washington. DeLaughter's file was slowly growing.

When something new turned up, DeLaughter would generally let Myrlie Evers know about it. When he saw that she was keeping the information to herself, he stopped worrying that she would leak material to the media, and he began sharing even more of the investigation with her. He felt he could call her at any time of the day or night; she insisted he wake her up if he needed a name or a source in the black community to develop new leads.

Evers was astonished to find herself starting to trust this white man, whose job once symbolized everything she hated about southern justice. She felt she had made a friend in DeLaughter. But for the first months of the investigation, they kept a professional formality between them. She still called him Mr. DeLaughter, and he called her Mrs. Evers. During one late-night phone call they used each other's first names.

"Hello, Bobby," she said.

"Hello, Myrlie."

There was an uneasiness, she recalls, as if they had crossed an invisible line into the forbidden.

"Good night, Mrs. Evers," he said when they were through talking.

Charlie Crisco always wondered whether some kind of fate had brought him to the Beckwith case. Why, for instance, should it fall in his lap the month he started work as an investigator at the Hinds County D.A.'s Office?

Crisco retired from the Jackson Police Department twenty years to the day after he joined the force on September 29, 1969. He had spent his first few years on the job riding around in a patrol car, then he got into investigations. Ten years after he'd started the job, he'd made it to homicide, where he'd spent the rest of his police career.

Crisco was of average height, thin, almost wiry, with thick brown hair that brushed over his collar in back. He wore aviator glasses. You could tell Crisco was a cop because he looked at things longer than other people; he didn't avert his gaze. When Crisco was feeling friendly, relaxed, his eyes were a warm brown. When he was suspicious or ticked off about something the eyes turned black right in front of you, like twin holes in space.

Crisco took his job in homicide seriously. He liked the big cases and the moment of discovery, when everything fit into place and he knew he had a suspect nailed. During his last couple of years in homicide some cases had given him satisfaction. He went out on a roll.

First was the case of Greg Davis, Jackson's serial killer. Crisco had set up a war room, with charts and psychiatric profiles. He had ended up following a hunch, caught a burglar, and gotten the guy to confess. And there was Kenny Davis, who had killed an off-duty cop in a hold-up. That had been a satisfying bust. Crisco had tracked him down through the murder weapon. Another long story.

Every morning Crisco worked a crossword puzzle or two to get his mind going and because he enjoyed it. Solving the puzzle. That was the interesting part of the job. So he wasn't unhappy when his first major assignment in the district attorney's office was to help DeLaughter piece together a thirty-year-old murder case.

Crisco had been fifteen years old in 1963 and going to high school in Jackson. He remembered the Beckwith case and being sorry somebody had gotten killed. But he also remembered when segregation was just something you grew up with. It was a way of life, and you never questioned it any more than you questioned going to school or to church.

DeLaughter was that much younger. Since he knew almost nothing about Medgar Evers and the climate in which he had been killed, DeLaughter gave himself a history lesson. He read books. He interviewed old folks. He poured over yellowed press clippings from Beckwith's trials. The more he learned about the case, the more it mesmerized him.

DeLaughter thought that he knew the facts of Mississippi's segregated past. He knew what he had learned in schoolbooks. Now he had to feel the facts, to crawl inside them as he absorbed the murder case. He came to know Medgar Evers and to understand his life, how hard it was to fight for something when everyone, even your friends, thought your cause was hopeless.

What surprised DeLaughter was how high a price had been paid for so little. Evers and the NAACP hadn't been asking for a separate nation or billions of dollars in restitution for the evils of slavery. All Evers had been asking for was the right to be treated like a man, to be called "mister," to send his kids to a good school, to vote — things we take for granted now. A good man could be killed for that thirty years ago.

Meanwhile there were other cases to try in the D.A.'s office. DeLaughter and Crisco worked on the Beckwith file when they had time.

At the end of February 1990 a few black leaders in Jackson called a press conference on the steps of the Hinds County Courthouse to protest the inaction of the D.A.'s office. Aaron Henry, who was still the leading voice of civil rights in Mississippi, still president of the state NAACP, and a state legislator, lent some weight to the protest. The old pro urged the prosecutors to keep on looking for evidence. "Whenever we don't want to do something, we find reasons not to do it," he said.

DeLaughter insisted that he didn't have enough evidence to go on. Not that he would make it public if he did. This was a criminal investigation, after all, not a campaign.

The state attorney general's office had helped come up with a strong legal argument to get around the speedy trial problem. DeLaughter had decided it was possible to bring Beckwith to trial again, but he wasn't sure he could win it. The physical evidence was still missing. Most important, the rifle could not be found. He could try the case without the fatal bullet or the autopsy report, which also were missing. Theoretically he could even try it without the murder weapon, but there wouldn't be much hope of success.

A trial is a piece of theater, and you have to have some props, particularly in the TV age. There wasn't a juror out there who didn't watch television, and few of them could say they hadn't seen *Perry Mason*, *Matlock*, or some other fanciful courtroom drama. On television, the prosecutor always seems to have everything he or she could possibly need to try a case. Like fingerprints. Jurors don't realize how rare it is to lift a clear fingerprint from a crime scene and especially from a gun. They had Beckwith's fingerprint but still no gun. That fact could derail the case. DeLaughter had to find that Enfield rifle.

Researching this case brought back a lot of memories, things DeLaughter hadn't thought about at the time. One of those things went back fifteen years, to when he and Dixie were first married. They had been visiting her folks when DeLaughter found a rifle in Russel Moore's bathroom closet. That wasn't unusual. Moore, like a lot of men in Mississippi, kept guns all over the place. DeLaughter was interested in firearms, so he'd asked the judge about the bolt-action .30/06. All he remembered Moore telling him was that it was a weapon used back in an old civil rights murder. That was it.

Moore had died a few years back. One night when DeLaughter got home from work, he called his mother-in-law and asked if she still had the gun. She did. He drove over that evening, and they fetched it down from a shelf in a different closet, where some of the judge's things were stored. DeLaughter never expected it to be the murder weapon. It was just a nagging memory he had to check out.

He pulled down the heavy black-barreled Enfield and held the serial number up to the light. He had written the missing murder weapon's serial number on a scrap of paper from the office. The hair raised up on the back of his neck as he read off the numbers etched into the metal beneath the fat black telescopic site and compared them with his notes: 1052682. It was a match.

The next day DeLaughter sat down in Cynthia Hewes's office and told her the story. He was a religious man, and he did a lot of praying. But even he couldn't believe that every time he needed something in this case, it would just show up. The photos, now the gun.

Hewes looked hard at DeLaughter over the top of her spotless desk and said, "I think Mr. Beckwith is in big trouble."

DeLaughter got the next thing he needed later that spring when a colleague handed him a copy of *Klandestine,* an obscure book that told the story of Delmar Dennis and his years spying on the Klan for the FBI. The author was William H. McIlhany II, a writer, professional magician, and John Birch Society member who had met Dennis on the right-wing speaking circuit. On page 38 was a curious passage about a Klan meeting in the summer of 1965, near the old swinging bridge at Byram: "The accused killer of Jackson NAACP official Medgar Evers is reported to have fully admitted his guilt in that crime." Dennis quoted Beckwith as saying, "Killing that nigger gave me no more inner discomfort than our wives endure when they give birth to our children."

This was exactly what Bobby needed. But he had a problem: where was Dennis? DeLaughter was thinking about where to start looking when the phone rang in his office.

It was the reporter Jerry Mitchell, calling to bug him about the Beckwith case. Mitchell wanted to know if there was anything new. Why was it going so slowly? DeLaughter lost his temper and blurted out, "Well, I'll tell you what. We'll probably make some kind of headway if I can ever find a guy named Delmar Dennis."

There was a short pause on the other end of the line, and then Mitchell said pleasantly, "Why, I've got Delmar's number."

It turned out that Mitchell had interviewed Dennis half a dozen times for the project the *Clarion-Ledger* had done on the twenty-fifth anniversary of the Goodman, Chaney, and Schwerner murders. He was living in Sevierville, Tennessee, in the Great Smoky Mountains.

DeLaughter called Dennis, and the man told him yes, he had heard Beckwith talk about "killing that nigger," and he knew he'd meant Evers. Dennis told him he had no interest in testifying, but if he wanted to come up and visit, that would be fine.

As soon as he got off the phone, DeLaughter called Benny Bennett and Crisco and told them to get packed. While he was clearing off his desk, he started to wonder about something: Beckwith lived near Chattanooga, and that was only a couple of hours from Sevierville at most. Beckwith was running his mouth with every reporter who showed up at his door. Maybe he'd talk to DeLaughter too.

The phone rang again. It was Mitchell.

"So, I hear you've reached Delmar," he said cheerily.

Of course Mitchell wanted to do a story about this, but DeLaughter tried to convince him to hold off for a while. He hadn't interviewed Dennis, and the man was nervous. He didn't want to spook a potential witness or put Dennis's life in danger. He did not tell the reporter that he wanted to visit Beckwith.

When the conversation ended, DeLaughter had the impression that Mitchell was going to cooperate. So he placed a call to Signal Mountain.

"Why Miz Thelma and I would be tickled to have you come on up here," Beckwith said in his thick Delta drawl.

DeLaughter couldn't believe his luck. The man was trying to charm him. He was all syrup and smiles. DeLaughter told Beckwith he just wanted to clear some things up, hear Beckwith's side of the story. De-Laughter was playing stupid.

"Well, you know we're getting a lot of pressure down here, you know, to at least look at the situation," DeLaughter said. "You certainly don't have to talk to me, or if you want a lawyer present . . ."

Beckwith was trying to pick him for information too, but he had one condition. "Now you know I don't allow nobody on my property except white Christian folks," Beckwith said. "Now, you don't sound like you're anything but white . . ."

"I am white."

"Are you Christian?"

"Yeah, yeah I am."

"You know, I don't allow no Jews up here!"

"I know."

"Well, who else is coming?"

"I'll be bringing at least one investigator. They're all white, and as far as I know they're Christians."

DeLaughter ran home to pack. Just as he walked through the door, his wife, Dixie, handed him the phone.

"Beckwith's on the telephone," she whispered.

This time Beckwith's attitude was belligerent. He was suddenly afraid that he would be kidnapped if an investigator came along with De-Laughter.

"I don't want anybody with arrest power up here," he said.

DeLaughter felt a sinking in his gut, but he tried to turn it around anyway.

"We're not going to be able to arrest you, Mr. Beckwith. We don't have the authority," he said. "Number one, if you were indicted, we'd have to go through the governor's office and get an extradition order. We can't just come up there and kidnap you."

It didn't work. Beckwith called off the meeting. Before he hung up, he said, "I'm going to tell you something, you know. When you see old Delmar, you tell him that I'm very aware of what's going on."

How could he have known about that? DeLaughter pondered for a moment. The only way he could have found out was if Mitchell had called him. That burned him. Here was a newspaper leading the charge to reprosecute Beckwith and accusing him of dragging his feet. Then Mitchell goes and blows the best break DeLaughter's had.

He was fuming when he saw the next day's paper. It carried a picture of Dennis alongside the headline "Ex-FBI Informant Agrees to Cooperate."

It got worse. The wire services picked up the story, and by the time DeLaughter, Crisco, and Bennett pulled into Sevierville, the whole country knew that Dennis was talking to the prosecutors.

Naturally Dennis was a bit jumpy. He insisted that they rendezvous in a crowded Cracker Barrel restaurant near Great Smoky Mountains National park. Then he got in his pickup, and they followed in their car as he led them deep into the woods, past perfectly good picnic benches and rest areas to a spot he had chosen to talk.

Dennis told them how he had joined the White Knights and spied on them for the FBI. After his testimony in the Goodman, Chaney, and Schwerner murders, his life had been in ruins. His wife had left him, and he had been threatened and harassed. Someone had put metal shavings in his car engine; someone had blasted a hole in his house with a shotgun. Eventually Dennis had left Mississippi and settled in Tennessee. He had been a speaker for the John Birch Society, even run for president on the anticommunist platform he still endorsed. He had remarried and had more children. One of his sons was named Andy, after Andrew Goodman.

Dennis saw his life as a continuous struggle. He felt underappreciated and overlooked for the risks he had taken in helping bring down the Klan in Mississippi. The FBI, he felt, had all but abandoned him. He tried to keep on preaching, tried different businesses, but none of them was successful. He kept hoping to make some money by selling his story, but that had never worked out. He ran a small press from his mountain home. He was trying to keep a low profile because whenever his neighbors found out about his past, they would shy away. Now this had happened, and he wasn't too happy about it.

Still he didn't shut the door on the possibility of testifying against Beckwith if the district attorney's office ever made a strong enough case to bring the man to trial. He'd just have to wait and see.

It was a turning point. The investigation seemed to take off after Dennis appeared. Crisco tracked down Thorn McIntyre, who had traded the murder weapon to Beckwith. He found him in Montgomery, Alabama, leading a new life as a real estate developer. McIntyre said that he would be willing to testify again if it came to that.

Soon another witness came forward when she heard about the investigation. Her name was Peggy Morgan, a woman whose husband had been a friend of Beckwith's in Greenwood. She said she needed to get something off her chest; it had been bothering her for years. Beckwith, she said, had bragged in her presence that he had killed Evers. It had happened while she and her husband had been giving Beckwith a ride up to Parchman prison sometime in the late sixties — she wasn't sure of the year.

None of these developments was made public. This was a murder investigation, and DeLaughter was not about to tip his hand before he even had an indictment. It would have been tempting to blast his evidence all over the press to show how much work he was doing. But that would just blow the case.

The national media were getting interested by now. *PrimeTime Live* was the first to go public with a story that at least four witnesses were willing to testify that they had seen Beckwith at the New Jerusalem Church the night of Evers's murder. In fact the old Jackson police reports in DeLaughter's file showed that the rumors of Beckwith's supposed appearances in Jackson had been checked out during the initial investigation. But he kept that information to himself.

DeLaughter was getting a crash course in modern media. The television people were asking him and Peters pointed questions, such as "The murder weapon is still missing?"

"That's right," Peters said during an on-camera interview, looking the correspondent directly in the eye with all his handsome sincerity.

DeLaughter sat there nodding. He figured it was too late to back out of the story now. Lying about the rifle, he thought, was the lesser of evils. He didn't want Beckwith to get spooked and clam up, or maybe even leave the country.

The *PrimeTime* story aired on June 14, 1990. Five days later the *Clarion Ledger* ran the banner headline "Gun Used in Evers Slaying in D.A.'s Hands."

The accompanying article, cowritten by Mitchell, charged that the prosecutor's office had found the rifle "months" earlier. DeLaughter admitted he had the gun and tried to explain his dissembling as a strategic ploy. He said that he hadn't wanted the "target of the investigation" to know that they had such a crucial piece of evidence. As it appeared in print, his explanation sounded feeble. What made it look worse was that the gun had been found in his late father-in-law's closet. It was the kind of coincidence fiction writers would throw out of a novel because nobody would believe it.

To those who were inclined to distrust the district attorney's office, the blundering lie reconfirmed their worst fears. Peters and DeLaughter were "hiding" evidence to avoid a new prosecution. It was the same old business from the same old boys.

By the next day black politicians, led by a city councilman named Louis Armstrong, were calling for a federal investigation of the "cover-up." Myrlie Evers felt betrayed. It was one thing DeLaughter had not confided in her. She wondered what else she didn't know.

"I am surprised, I am stunned, I am speechless," she told the paper, then added icily, "I certainly hope that more 'missing' information will surface."

The trust Evers and DeLaughter had built over the months was badly damaged. This was still Mississippi, Evers thought. No matter how much she liked this young man who seemed so sincere, she had to remember that this was still Mississippi.

*   *   *

There was a federal probe and a lot of hollering in the community. Bennie Thompson, a rising black politician who represented Evers's old neighborhood on the Board of Supervisors called the concealment of the evidence a "crisis of confidence." Charles Evers weighed in with a defense of the prosecution. "I'm sick and tired of these politicians politicizing off my brother's name," he said. He said he was confident that Beckwith would be indicted. By the end of July the Justice Department investigation was over; they could find no evidence of a cover-up.

Myrlie Evers extracted a promise from the district attorney's office that there would be no more surprises, no more "missing" evidence that suddenly reappeared without her knowledge. She had no choice but to cooperate with these prosecutors. They were all she had, and she was willing to deal with the Devil himself to get this case to court.

In mid-October, Evers made the final gesture of trust. She walked up the steps of the Hinds County Courthouse and handed over the single most important element in the reprosecution of Beckwith: the original transcripts of the first trial, which she had kept locked in a safe deposit box for two and a half decades. After a short hearing circuit court judge Breland Hilburn ruled them to be authentic, which meant that, under Mississippi law, they could be used in a future trial. All that stood in the way of an indictment was the grand jury.

By now the prosecution had an impressive stack of evidence: the transcript, a big chunk of the police report, the crime scene and some autopsy photos, the murder weapon, the fingerprint files, a surprising number of living witnesses from the first trials, and some new witnesses, including Delmar Dennis, Peggy Morgan, and Mary Ann Adams, another woman who had come forward with a story of Beckwith's bragging about the murder.

Another grand jury was convened that December. DeLaughter and Peters made the unusual decision to present part of the defense case as well as the prosecution. They wanted the panel to have as much information as possible before they made the decision whether to indict. In a way it was a dry run for an actual trial.

The grand jury summoned James Holley and Hollis Cresswell, the two surviving alibi witnesses who said they had seen Beckwith in Greenwood the night of the murder. They also presented Myrlie Evers, who told her story with such dignity and sorrow that, according to one grand jury member, "there wasn't a dry eye in the room."

That afternoon Byron De La Beckwith was again indicted for the murder of Medgar Evers.

"He's not here!" Thelma Beckwith shouted from behind the front door of her bungalow on Signal Mountain.

"Ma'am, we've got a warrant," the deputy said. "Please open up."

Beckwith was in fact home on the afternoon of December 17, 1990. He was shaved and showered and had a fresh set of clothes ready. He knew they'd be coming for him. Finally Thelma let the officers inside.

"I'm ready to go, boys," Beckwith told them. "I'm not guilty."

He even joked as they led him away to the Hamilton County Jail. "You want to search my pockets to see if I've got a bomb?"

The old man's mood had soured by the time he showed up in green jail togs for his hearing in Chattanooga the next day.

"How many Jews are among you?" Beckwith snapped as he peered at the mob of reporters. "I see one nigra man."

Inside the courtroom Beckwith told the judge that the murder charge in Mississippi was "nonsense, poppycock and just something to . . . incite the lower forms of life to force and violence against the country club set." Beckwith vowed that he would fight extradition to Mississippi "tooth, nail and claw."

The judge released him on fifteen thousand dollars bail. He was hastily rearrested on a governor's warrant and returned to his cinder block cell while he fought extradition.

Beckwith adjusted quickly to the jail routine. By now he knew how to do his time. He kept up his frantic correspondence with friends, donors, and journalists, writing twenty or more letters a day. He said he was a political prisoner.

He had a slick court-appointed lawyer named Russell Bean who fought off the extradition and tried to keep reporters away from his client. Beckwith never minded being interviewed, but he decided he would now put a price on it. Five thousand dollars, cash or check, in advance, no exceptions. In all the time he spent in jail, only a BBC documentary crew managed to interview him on tape. They wouldn't say how they'd persuaded him to do it.

In that interview he denied the new allegations against him. He had not attended any NAACP meetings in Jackson, he said. He had never seen Medgar Evers.

"You ought to have enough sense not to ask such a damn fool question," he told the interviewer. "I am not going to waste my time going to a nigger meeting. When I want to know something from a nigger, I tell the nigger to come to me!"

Beckwith denied bragging about the murder in front of Delmar Dennis at a Klan meeting in 1965. "Sounds like a fabrication to me," he said. He started to say something else, then stopped himself, chuckling. "You see, the only time . . ." he paused. "I'll just save that for the courts. Because you see, heh, heh, if Delmar's still living, heh, heh, I'm goin' drop one on him."

"You'll drop one on him?"

"Verbally. . . . He'll know that he has fizzled around and blown the lamp out and he will have found himself in the dark!"

Dennis, who also was interviewed for the show, took that as a threat. By now he had written to DeLaughter to inform him that he would not testify at the trial, and he had informed the media of his decision. Privately he said it was a ploy to throw the assassins off his trail. The Klan had already left a calling card in his mailbox. Someone wanted him to know they knew where he lived.

Back in Mississippi DeLaughter and Crisco were taking advantage of the delay to strengthen the case against Beckwith. Among the many items still missing from the first trial was Evers's original autopsy report. That was a big problem, almost as bad as not having the murder weapon. They needed a new autopsy, but that meant exhuming the long-buried body.

Myrlie Evers was horrified, and at first she refused to allow it. She couldn't put herself or her family through it. But she changed her mind when her younger son, Van, offered to go to Washington in her place.

DeLaughter and Crisco flew to Washington to oversee the exhumation and autopsy. They met Van for the first time at the grave site. There wasn't much time to talk. It was a warm, sunny morning, and the backhoe was standing by. They all watched as its blade cut through the thick turf, uncovering a perfectly dry grave and a well-sealed casket. That was a good sign. But nobody knew what they might find inside. The casket was raised up and placed in a hearse. Van got in with the driver, and they set out for Albany, New York. DeLaughter and Crisco followed in another car.

DeLaughter had arranged for the autopsy to be performed by Dr. Michael Baden, New York State's chief pathologist. Baden was probably the best-known and most respected forensic expert in the country. He specialized in old cases. He had reviewed the autopsy reports of both John F. Kennedy and Martin Luther King, Jr., for the House assassinations investigation in the late 1970s. Baden would soon be heading to Russia to examine what were said to be the bones of Czar Nicholas II and his family to help solve one of the century's great murder mysteries. DeLaughter wanted someone with Baden's credentials to do this autopsy and testify at the trial. He wanted the historic weight of Baden's résumé. And Baden, who was a very expensive expert witness, had volunteered to do the work for free.

The somber little convoy arrived at the Albany medical center before dark. DeLaughter and Crisco finally had a chance to talk to Van. Like Myrlie, Van was warm and friendly and put them at ease.

The coffin was opened the next morning. Since they had no idea whether the body would be dust and bones, or whatever, Van stayed outside the room. Crisco recorded the procedure with a camcorder as Baden pried open the box. Everyone in the room gasped. Evers's body was perfectly preserved. His burial suit was still neat and dry; his face was only slightly altered from dehydration, as if he had been dusted with a thin coat of ashes. Medgar Evers looked as if he were sleeping, certainly not like someone who had been dead for almost thirty years.

Baden said he had never seen anything like it. Crisco remembered a feeling of awe in the room, as if they had stepped back from 1991 and were again at the wake in 1963. DeLaughter slipped out of the room and brought in Van. Then DeLaughter, Crisco, and Baden withdrew for a while to give Van a chance to be alone with his father.

Crisco, the homicide cop who had seen just about everything you need to see in this life, recalls that he was "moved" by the moment. It was emotional, almost spiritual.

After Van was finished, the autopsy team removed the clothing and opened up the body. Crisco took pictures as Baden prepared for X rays. No X rays had been taken back in 1963. Forensic science was a lot more sophisticated now. When the chest X rays were developed, Baden slapped them on a light screen, and everyone got the second surprise of the day. Although the part of the bullet that had passed through Evers's body was still missing, the X ray showed that fragments of that bullet remained in his chest. Enough to present as evidence.

24

The Statue

All the others, where are they now? The ones who didn't have patience, they lost their minds, or disappeared. I saved part of myself, always held something in reserve. I didn't give it all away while the others did. That's why I'm still here.

— *Charles Evers, 1991*

CHARLES EVERS was bankrupt and divorced, and the IRS was still chasing his tail, trying to collect back taxes. He had lost another race for mayor of Fayette, and he was living in an apartment behind the radio station, WMPR, just off the Tougaloo campus. His job was general manager of the nonprofit blues and gospel and talk station. He wasn't allowed to own anything, at least not on paper, until the IRS and his many creditors were satisfied.

His office at WMPR was a shrine to his better days: There were pictures of Evers with every Republican president from Nixon to Bush. There were photos from his campaigns and pictures of him with Bobby Kennedy, famous pictures of Kennedy riding in an open convertible through an ocean of people, all of them reaching out to him and him reaching back. Evers's dark, serious face is in the foreground, along with those of Rosie Grier and Jim Brown, Kennedy's unofficial bodyguards. Evers was walking behind Kennedy the night he was killed in Los Angeles. After that Evers shut down his heart.

He kept mementos of everyone who had mattered to him. There was an Asian sculpture in one corner. He said it reminded him of the Philippines and Felicia, his one true love. There was a picture of James and Jessie Evers, seated in their clean parlor, and a publicity shot of B. B. King. If you asked, Evers would tell you that B.B. was his best friend. "But we're not too close," he'd say.

Above and behind him, dominating the room, was a large oil painting of Medgar Evers seated at his desk, looking over Charles's shoulder. "I'll never let anyone get close to me again," he said.

By the fall of 1991, he had stopped talking about "the case." Myrlie Evers, for one, had told him to keep out of it. But that wouldn't be enough to quiet him if he wanted to speak. He seemed pained by the whole thing, too weary to hope for a conviction.

He was spending more and more time down in Jefferson County, because he was running for office again, this time for chancery clerk. Evers would tell you that he was campaigning out of a sense of obligation to "his people." He was old and should be retiring, but "the people" had asked him to run and to fix the place up.

It was true that Jefferson County was having hard times. The two factories Evers had enticed to open there had closed and moved to Mexico. The roads were full of potholes. The swimming pool at the Medgar Evers Community Center in Fayette was cracked, with a foot of green slime festering on the bottom. The lawns were unmowed. The courthouse and jail had burned years ago and had not been rebuilt.

Skeptics said that Evers was running for chancery clerk because that was where the money was. He would be in charge of the county payrolls and get a percentage of every contract filed in his office. Some chancery clerks made more money than the governor. Others said that Evers just lived to run. He needed the action.

And so on a balmy autumn day in downtown Fayette, Evers kicked off his tenth campaign for office.

"Bro' Willie!" Evers called.

"Okay," a voice squawked on the CB radio.

"You be on the end, and I be on the front!"

"Ten four."

"Okay. We gone," Evers said.

It was about ten thirty in the morning. It would be eleven before the motorcade set off. Everyone had to get gassed up at Mazique's, had to get posters, had to find each other. Evers drove his Ford van around the Fayette Plaza, home of the Dude Burger and Bill's Discount Store, waiting for Willie, his security man, to check in again.

"Politics is never organized," he explained to a passenger. "You just go 'round in circles."

Finally they were off, crawling out of town at twenty-five miles an hour, the strictly enforced speed limit. Cars and pickups bobbed along the bumpy, potholed macadam like slow-moving barges on a choppy current.

The first stop was a country store in Harriston, a community just east of Fayette. Evers leaped from the van, a handful of flyers in his fist. He was the vision of an expert politician at work, of someone who had been on the campaign trail for thirty years.

He shook the first hand he saw, which belonged to a black man in farm clothes climbing from a pickup. "Please vote for me. I sure need your support," Evers said heartily, pressing a flyer in the man's hand.

"How you feeling?" Evers called to an old woman on her porch.

"Fine, fine, Mayor," she replied. Although he hadn't been mayor for years, that was how folks remembered him.

He moved quickly but stepped carefully down the paths to the small frame houses, looking for dogs. "Campaigning in the country is hard work," he said. "A lot of walking, a lot of bad dogs."

Dogs were Evers's bane. They scared him, but everybody in the country had one.

Out behind the store he spotted a young white man and his small towheaded son fiddling with the hitch of a livestock trailer. Two brindled mutts lay in the shade of the trailer, watching Evers walk by.

"Don't you bite me now," Evers muttered to the dogs. "I appreciate your support now, you know I don't want to kill no dogs. You just stay put."

Killing a man's dog would lose a vote, Evers reasoned. He didn't want to mess with them. The dogs stood up warily as the candidate walked up to their owner, hand outstretched. The white farmer in the red cap seemed slightly stunned but took Evers's hand. His smile was friendly if not warm.

"I sure could use your vote," Evers said with all his considerable charm.

The county was 80 percent black, with just over six thousand registered voters. The whites tended to vote for Evers. He said he had been promised 95 percent of the white vote in this race. It was, ironically, the African-Americans he had to sell himself to.

Evers jumped back into the van and tore off down the two-lane highway, beeping his horn as he passed homes, driving fast to make time. The route was lined with fields of goldenrod, southern pine, oak, and sweet gum thick with road dust.

At a former filling station a group of young white men gathered around the back of a pickup. Since it was squirrel season, two of them wore camouflage fatigues. One held an empty quart of Jose Cuervo. There were rifles on the rack. Evers pulled over to talk to them. By now he had put some distance between himself and the rest of the motorcade. He had no backup.

Twenty years ago men like this would have been likely to take a shot at Evers. Now they recognized him and shook his hand.

Lou, a wiry little fellow with short blond hair and a ruddy face, told Evers that he thought he had been the best mayor Fayette ever had. He'd get Lou's vote. The others nodded in agreement.

"People gonna elect me for one reason — I'll make life better for them," Evers said as he pulled away. "They don't give a damn about Charles Evers."

The two-way radio crackled with static. Bro' Willie's voice faded in and out. It seemed the motorcade was ready to roll into Red Lick. Evers drove faster now, weaving off the road and recovering as he fiddled with the radio. A little plastic Garfield ornament bounced on a string attached to the rearview mirror. The van was awash with empty soda cans, campaign flyers, and one copy of Evers's eponymous autobiography, which had been published in 1971.

The book had been placed carefully on the dashboard, facedown. The whole back page of the dust jacket was a photograph not of the author, but of the author's brother, Medgar, positioned to look out the windshield. Because of the angle of the window and the afternoon light, Medgar's face was reflected in the glass. For the rest of the trip Medgar Evers hovered just ahead of Charles, a disembodied face with eyes turned to the driver, floating over the wide fields of Jefferson County.

On a September afternoon Myrlie Evers looked out her kitchen window and studied the colors of the high desert at her hideaway in Oregon. Green, yellow, lavender, tan. It was so different from the landscape she knew best, the muted shades of the Vicksburg bluffs and, later, the smoggy hills of southern California. This was a good, clean place to be.

She had retired, reluctantly, at age fifty-eight from her job on the Los Angeles Board of Public Works. She had injured her back when a chair collapsed. She could no longer sit at a desk all day and she was in almost constant pain. Now that she had left her job, her first priority, after her family, was the case against Beckwith.

The phone had been ringing all morning. Reporters wanted a comment on the latest news. Beckwith had lost his appeal in Tennessee. He was about to be extradited to Mississippi, but his lawyers had slapped down a writ of habeas corpus. Another delay. But it was close; DeLaughter almost had him. She felt like kicking something, she was so frustrated.

She was surprised at how emotional she could get after all these years. For a while life had seemed almost normal: marriage, a job, grandchildren.

Her husband, Walter Williams, was with her, and that kept her together. He never complained when she was distracted by the case.

But now the old fears were back, along with the anxiety of hope. At least something was happening with the case. But she was riding an emotional roller coaster, and it was ruining her health. The bad back was worse now. Her stomach was acting up again.

Sometimes all she wanted to do was disappear. But then she would hear Medgar's voice. Not literally, she would tell you with a laugh. She wasn't crazy. She would feel him, though. He was saying, "Speak, girl! Speak your mind. You can do this thing."

*   *   *

On Thursday, October 3, 1991, a federal judge in Tennessee cleared the way for Beckwith's extradition. Tim Metheny and Sammy Magee from the Hinds County Sheriff's Department were standing by in Chattanooga when the ruling came down. They dressed Beckwith in his pinstriped suit, cuffed him, and whisked him into a waiting car before his lawyer could file yet another appeal.

Thelma Beckwith got to the courthouse too late to say good-bye. It was hard to tell who was angrier, Beckwith or his wife. Thelma shouted at the gathered media, "He may die anytime! I hope you all are happy." She told anyone she could corner that she knew the true identity of the man who had killed Medgar Evers: it was Lee Harvey Oswald.

Beckwith was fuming as he sat in the backseat of the sedan. He told Metheny and Magee that they'd never make it out of Tennessee. There would be roadblocks. "They" would never let him go. The deputies knew the old man was just blustering. Still they didn't relax until they'd left Tennessee, Georgia, and Alabama behind and crossed the state line into Mississippi.

By the time they pulled up to the Hinds County Detention Center, a small herd of cameramen and reporters were waiting. Beckwith's eyes flashed angrily behind his glasses as the reporters shouted questions.

"Did you kill Medgar Evers?"

Beckwith wheeled and glared into the television cameras.

"Did *you* kill Medgar Evers?" he snarled, mocking the question. "I didn't kill him, did you?" He raised a gnarled, handcuffed hand and pointed a finger at one red-bearded reporter.

"Are you a Jew?" he hissed before the deputies hustled him away.

The next morning Beckwith was arraigned before circuit court judge Breland Hilburn. Jackson didn't have a public defender at the time, so two experienced local defense attorneys were appointed to represent Beckwith. He was confined to a private cell in the hospital unit of the jail while his court-appointed attorneys, Jim Kitchens and Merrida Coxwell, drew up a motion for bond.

Beckwith probably couldn't have found better lawyers in Mississippi if he'd had a sack of money to spend. Kitchens had been district attorney for the counties south of Jackson in the seventies. He was a seasoned, white-haired, country-style lawyer, the defense counterpart of Ed Peters.

Coxwell, whose friends called him Buddy, was one of Jackson's rising young stars. He was a junior partner at an old, established downtown law firm. Coxwell was something of an oddity in Jackson, a city so conservative that a woman who didn't wear stockings in August or a businessman with a beard was considered eccentric. Coxwell was thirty-five years old and he wore his sandy hair trimmed on top and long in the back. He bombed around town in a not-yet-vintage Mercedes with Jimi Hendrix or James Brown blasting on the speakers. Coxwell was divorced, living out in singles paradise in a condo on the reservoir. He didn't eat meat. He was good-looking and painfully thin, with high cheekbones that made his features seem both fragile and tough.

Before Beckwith he was best known for taking on the most difficult death penalty cases, usually for indigent black defendants who ended up costing him a fortune in lost billable hours. But he did it out of a sense of obligation, because he was good at it, and because he flat out believed that everyone was entitled to the best defense. Even, his friends noted, a raving seventy-year-old racist who couldn't keep his mouth shut.

Coxwell took his job seriously, and he fought to win. Up until now, he and DeLaughter had been fairly good friends. Even though they were so often on opposite sides of the table in court, they could usually put that aside and see each other at parties and hang out together. Not now. This case was a war. After the arraignment, Coxwell walked up to De-Laughter and shook his hand. "I'll see you when this is over," he said.

The skirmishes began at Beckwith's bond hearing a month later. First DeLaughter laid the foundation of his case. Beckwith looked like Scrooge, forced to confront the ghosts of his Christmases past, as De-Laughter called witness after witness from the defendant's earlier trials. Ralph Hargrove, the old crime lab chief, identified the physical evidence: the fingerprint cards, the crime scene photos, and the Enfield rifle. Ben Windstein was called out of retirement in New Orleans to tell the judge how he'd had to fly to Washington, D.C., to arrest Beckwith as a fugitive after his Louisiana bomb conviction. And DeLaughter called an agent from the FBI's domestic terrorism division to talk about the hate groups to which Beckwith had been linked, including a new, shadowy outfit called the Phineas Priests.

Coxwell pointed out that his client should get bond because he was not charged with capital murder. The rules had changed since Beck-with's first trials. The death penalty was reserved for killings in which there was an underlying felony, such as rape or robbery. Beckwith's alleged crime was, in modern jurisprudence, a "simple murder." Cox-well reminded the court that unless it was a death penalty case, some sort of bond had been granted to every other accused felon who had passed through this courthouse. That included suspected drug smug-glers and gang killers.

To show the court that Beckwith was not dangerous and would not be a flight risk if released, the defense called some character witnesses to testify. One of them was Gordon Lackey.

Lackey was fifty-five years old. He was a tall, hearty man with steel-gray hair combed back from his forehead. He wore plastic aviator glasses and his sun-hardened face was set in a look of righteous determination.

Lackey made his living selling irrigation systems and spraying fields — he called it "aerial application" — from his own crop duster in the summer months. He had a teenaged son in private school, kept a collection of a hundred or more guns in his house and had a clean record with the law.

When Jim Kitchens asked Lackey the nature of his acquaintance with Beckwith, Lackey replied that he had known Delay most of his life, and that they'd had "many different relationships," including business, so-cial, and "fraternal" relationships. They had been fellow Masons and Shriners.

Lackey assured the court that Beckwith was a man of his word and was not a danger to the community. "I have never seen a single act of violence from this gentleman," he said in his deep Delta voice.

Ed Peters rose to question the witness. "You've managed to tell us all the organizations that you belong to with this defendant," he said. "You've omitted one, haven't you?"

"What might that be, sir?" said Lackey.

"The Ku Klux Klan."

Lackey appeared to be indignant. "I am not a Klansman, sir," he said.

"You deny that you swore this defendant into the Ku Klux Klan?"

"How can a person that's not a Klansman swear a person into the Klan?" Lackey said.

"So you deny that?"

"Oh, yes, sir."

"Thank you."

When the hearing ended, Judge Hilburn decided to keep Beckwith locked up until his trial date, which he set for February 1992.

Nobody expected that date to stick. But few suspected that the case would drag on for two more years.

Meanwhile there was an election in Mississippi. Charles Evers made his political comeback when he won the job of chancery clerk for Jefferson County.

Peters was reelected for his seventh consecutive four-year term as Hinds County district attorney. Since he had been unopposed, this was no shock.

The big surprise on November 5 was that the incumbent governor, Ray Mabus, was defeated by an unknown conservative businessman from Vicksburg named Kirk Fordice. No one was more stunned than Mabus himself, who quickly went into seclusion. The black voters, who had put him in office and whose support he'd apparently taken for granted, did not go to the polls for him. The state that was barreling headlong into a decade of change had suddenly slammed on the brakes.

Almost overnight the mood in Mississippi turned as hard as the dour new governor-elect. Some columnists made unkind comparisons between Fordice and David Duke, the baby-faced ex-Klansman who ran for governor of Louisiana on the Republican ticket. Duke lost his race, but some of his stands sounded uncomfortably like Fordice's platform — anti–big government, anti–affirmative action, antiwelfare — the modern code words for keeping black folks down.

Fordice was fifty-seven years old and had thinning white hair and a craggy, weathered face. He smiled with his lower teeth. His abrupt, seven-minute inaugural address covered the usual topics: fiscal responsibility and cooperation among people. His new motto, "Together Forward," was as blunt and graceless as the man himself.

He quickly set the tone for his administration. His favorite book, he told a group of elementary school students, was Machiavelli's *The Prince*. At a meeting of the Mississippi Press Association, Fordice vowed to fight the Supreme Court–ordered equalization of funding to traditionally black and white state campuses. "We may have to call out the National

Guard," he said. In the uproar that followed, Fordice said he regretted his choice of words, but grumped, "C'mon people, if you can't use a metaphor . . ."

Kim McGeoy was upset, just ticked off in general. The more he thought about it, the more it tortured him that his cousin Delay was still in jail.

McGeoy was twenty years younger than Beckwith, a distant cousin on Beckwith's mother's side. His full name was Morgan Kimbrough McGeoy, a nod to three old Mississippi families. He had grown up in Greenwood knowing the scandal surrounding Beckwith. But McGeoy had always liked Beckwith; he thought he was funny. And as ugly as Beckwith could act sometimes — such as calling a young boy "nigger" to his face, which was ungentlemanly behavior — McGeoy couldn't believe that Beckwith was a killer.

Ever since this new trouble had started, McGeoy had visited his cousin in jail at least once a week. He did it out of kinship and loyalty, and because the old man was so entertaining.

McGeoy cornered patrons at the Dutch Bar on weekday afternoons and tried to get them to chip in for bail. He called Beckwith's lawyers to push them to keep trying. He called Judge Hilburn to complain. To his surprise Hilburn invited him to come down to the courthouse and make a formal statement on the matter.

On January 14, 1992, McGeoy met with Hilburn in his chambers. He started off by reminding the judge of Beckwith's war record and that he deserved bond "due to the fact that the man has never run" from his previous charges. McGeoy reminded Hilburn of Beckwith's good family name, of how he was descended from the founding families of Mississippi, and that he had "three or four hundred" relatives in LeFlore County alone.

Finally he got around to what he really wanted to say. "We're letting one man stand alone, just like Jeff Davis stayed two years in manacles for the sins of us all. . . . We're letting one man pay for the sins of people like Ross Barnett, people like Paul Johnson, who stood up for us at Ole Miss."

This situation reminded McGeoy of the movie *Spartacus* that he had just watched on television. He told the judge about the crowd scene in the movie, where the soldiers wanted to arrest Spartacus and the slave leader stepped forward and turned himself in, saying, "I'm Spartacus."

Then all the other slaves stood up and said, "I'm Spartacus." The scene reminded McGeoy of the case against his cousin.

"Well, there were a lot of people, actually in my feeling, killed Medgar Evers," he said. "Who pulled the trigger, I don't know."

"I understand," the judge said. But he didn't seem to. He suggested that McGeoy advise Beckwith's lawyers to ask for another bail hearing.

That was just what the lawyers had in mind. Coxwell had drawn up fill-in statements for friends who would attest to Beckwith's character, his ties to the community, and the unlikelihood of his flight.

On February 24, Coxwell submitted to the court eighty-eight completed affidavits. Most were filled out by old friends from Greenwood, but some signers had interesting political associations. Two were Mississippi sheriffs. Robert Patterson, the aged founder of the Citizens' Councils, wrote Beckwith a recommendation. More than a dozen others were reputed members of the White Knights of the Ku Klux Klan.

Although Sam Bowers did not fill out a character reference for his old friend, he did take an active interest in the case. One day he showed up, unannounced, at Coxwell's office. He handed the receptionist a business card that said his name was "Mr. Bancroft," apparently one of his aliases. Coxwell recognized him and invited him in to talk. Bowers came several times to offer Coxwell long treatises on legal strategies to defend Beckwith. Coxwell listened politely.

Other old-time radicals also showed up to tell Coxwell how to run the case. Finally he banned them from his office unless they had some evidence for him.

Beckwith's health problems had been acting up since his return to Mississippi. He had been hospitalized twice for minor heart attacks. Up in Tennessee Thelma was not in good shape. She had been declared legally blind, and she needed an operation to remove colon polyps.

There had been rumors all week that Hilburn was going to release Beckwith. By Friday it was a done deal. The bond would be $100,000. It was already arranged. There would be a hearing on Monday, just as a formality. DeLaughter told a reporter from the *Clarion-Ledger* that he had given up hope of keeping Beckwith in jail.

This was news to Myrlie Evers. She knew that if Beckwith was released, he might try to hold up the trial with motions and appeals into the next century. She had to do something.

So she made some calls to Jackson. She wrote a long telegram to Judge Hilburn, reminding him — courteously — of how bad this looked and how she hoped that Mississippi's "image will not revert back to the days of hatred and injustice." She also reminded him that a number of Beckwith's character witnesses were known Klansmen.

The *Clarion-Ledger* conducted an informal phone-in poll, asking readers whether they thought Beckwith should get bond. Seventy percent of the callers favored his release.

To the apparent surprise of the district attorney's office, and to the obvious shock of Beckwith's lawyers and family, Hilburn changed his mind again after a brief hearing. He said there was not enough evidence to reverse his original ruling. Beckwith's murder trial was now scheduled for June 1992.

Myrlie Evers, from her Oregon retreat, told reporters that she was "relieved." She was not going to speculate about what had happened, but she wondered privately if this trial was ever going to take place.

She realized it was up to her to keep the pressure on. Some black politicians supported her and kept pushing for a trial. Old NAACP stalwarts such as Aaron Henry, Sam Baily, and Doris Smith backed her up. But many other voices in Jackson society were telling her, "Leave it alone; it's too old. You'll never win. You're just stirring things up." In a way it was like the old days, when Medgar had tried to get black teachers and ministers involved in the movement and so few would join him.

The most pressing thing that Jackson's black community seemed to be doing for Medgar Evers's memory was raising funds to erect a statue in his honor. In almost every courthouse square in the state of Mississippi there is at least one monument to the Confederate Civil War dead. Some blind stone soldier poses in an attitude of defiance and undefeat, on foot or on horseback if the county could afford it, and always as proud and enduring as the memory of the lost cause. But in Mississippi in 1992, in a state where the symbolic gesture is as important as the real thing, there was still no monument to Medgar Evers.

Finally, after five years of fund-raising, the Jackson community coughed up the $55,000 needed to pay for a life-size bronze statue. The unveiling ceremony was set for a Sunday in June. Myrlie was sick with an infected throat and couldn't attend, so Darrell came in her place. It was his first public appearance in Mississippi since his father's funeral.

Darrell was thirty-eight now and a good-looking man, tall and slim and stylish with his hair pulled back and twisted into a small knot at the nape of his neck. A fund-raising dinner was held the night before the unveiling in the Masonic Temple, in the same auditorium where Medgar had spoken and Lena Horne had sung, and where Medgar had lain in state.

For years it had made Darrell sick, physically ill, to return to Jackson. Like his mother he had too many bad memories.

It was hard enough to be the son of a martyr back in Los Angeles, where Medgar was a legend few people knew as a man. Sooner or later someone would say to Darrell, "You're Medgar Evers's son. What do *you* do?" Reena and Van always felt the pressure of being Medgar's children, but not as much as Darrell, the first son, the boy his father had named Kenyatta, "Burning Spear," long before African names were fashionable.

What could Darrell say? He was an artist whose conceptual pieces were freighted with political content: the Rodney King beating, the invasion of Panama, South Africa. He spoke out through his art and in an even more subtle way. His activism, he would try to explain, was on a spiritual level. He had been a follower of the Indian guru Mahara Ji for almost twenty years. He had received "knowledge," he said, in a way that could not be described in words.

Darrell had been searching for this knowledge all his life. As soon as he met the Mahara Ji, Darrell realized that his was the face of the child in his dream, the boy who had spoken to the United Nations and made the audience weep.

Tonight it was Darrell who spoke. He stood up and gave a speech without notes. He had inherited Medgar's charisma.

"I don't know what to say, except that you all are my immediate family," he said. "That's the way I feel about everybody, no matter what race, color. 'Cause inside, we're all the same color . . . We are human beings that love, that's all we want."

There were three hundred people at the banquet tables, and some of them started calling back to him. "Say it!" a woman shouted. "All right!"

Darrell described for them the night his father had died, how he felt Medgar's spirit rise up and enter his own body. He said there "was a feeling in my soul that was more powerful than anybody else had put in my head. That was his soul!"

This was slightly different from the usual after-dinner fare in Jackson. But folks continued on with him. "Tell it!" they cried.

When Medgar's spirit had risen out of his body, Darrell said, "his mission was accomplished. It was time for him to go. . . . It brings tears to my eyes that people still see that my father's name is kept alive. Sometimes people forget about that other 'M': Malcolm, Martin, and Medgar."

The next day Darrell attended the formal ceremonies dressed like a Nigerian oil tycoon. He wore gold-and-white robes, a tall hat, and dark shades. He had spent the morning with his Uncle Charlie. They just drove around Jackson. It was the first time they had ever really talked. Darrell wanted his uncle to know that he didn't hate him, that they were family.

Charles sat in the front row for the afternoon ceremonies, wearing his blue seersucker jacket and looking proud of his nephew. When someone asked him if he was going to speak, he said, "Naw, naw," as if that were the last thing he wanted to do. He sat there alone while the speeches were given and the names of Mississippi's great civil rights heroes were recited as if in a litany: Medgar Evers, Fannie Lou Hamer, Aaron Henry. Nobody mentioned his name. It was as if he had been erased from the books.

He didn't care, he said. He was happy being chancery clerk of Jefferson County. Things were moving down there. He had contracts out to build a new jail and courthouse. And he had plans to bring jobs and tax revenues to the county: he wanted to start a big landfill out in the woods and charge out-of-state companies huge fees to dump there.

"We got nothing else to sell," Charles said. "If Detroit is the Motor Capital of the World, we're going to be known as the Garbage Capital." If the landfill was a success, Charles hoped to expand the business to include toxic waste, maybe even nuclear waste. The government paid good money to take care of that.

When the unveiling ceremony was over and the television crews had left, a few people stayed behind to stare at the statue. It seemed so small, dwarfed by the wide green field. A car pulled up, and a couple got out, walked over to read the inscription, stood quietly, and then left. Medgar Evers looked, with his hand in his pocket and a serious expression on his tired face, as if he was in a deep, deep studying, gazing out over the hill in the direction of Capitol Street.

25

Hurricane Season

Here's latest mailing — going out over Mississippi like shingles on your roof! Gee those niggers had a ball in L.A. As you know, I'm a native son of Calif. — but it will be hotter than that here in Jackson — you'll call it chimneyville #2 — Remember your Confederate history. The damned Yankees did it 1 time. But this will be a Peters DeLaughter NAACP Jew Burn Out! Yep. Lot's of real estate bargains when it cools off.

Ta Ta. De La IV.

A DOZEN OFFICERS guarded Judge Breland Hilburn's small courtroom on the morning of August 3, 1992. A nervous police captain muttered into a walkie-talkie and hassled journalists who tried to bring briefcases past the sign-in desk. Inside two rows of polished wooden benches, like church pews, were loosely filled with reporters and assorted friends and relatives of the defendant.

Beckwith marched in wearing a dark navy suit, soft gray leather shoes, a white shirt with French cuffs, and gold cuff links. He sat at the defense table and seemed chipper, laughing and flirting with a female legal assistant until Merrida Coxwell finally turned to him and said sharply, "Mr Beckwith! Shhhh!" Beckwith pouted, and Coxwell went back to his papers.

The point of this hearing was for the defense to argue that the charges against Beckwith should be dismissed before he went to trial. When you hear editorial writers and man-on-the-street interviewees complain about all the crooks getting off on "technicalities," these loopholes more often than not can be found in the U.S. Constitution. The technicalities that could free Beckwith were in the Bill of Rights, specifically the Sixth Amendment, which says the following:

> In all criminal prosecutions, the accused shall enjoy the right to a speedy and public trial, by an impartial jury of the State and the district wherein the crime shall have been committed . . . and to be informed of the nature and cause of the accusation; to be confronted with the witnesses against him; to have compulsory process for obtaining witnesses in his favor, and to have the assistance of counsel for his defense.

Any reasonable person could see how trying a man for murder twenty-nine years after the fact might raise some doubts about the speediness of his trial. Then there was that other clause about a defendant's having the right to confront witnesses — a problem here because so many of them were dead. If that wasn't enough, there was also the Fifth Amendment to deal with, the one that guarantees "due process of law." Dozens of court cases over the years had bolstered a defendant's rights to due process and "fundamental fairness," concepts that Coxwell and Jim Kitchens were arguing had been trampled by the prosecutors of their client.

The still-missing evidence, the lack of a transcript of the second trial, dead lawyers, and absent witnesses were just a few points of prejudice the defense planned to bring up. Worst was the problem that Beckwith couldn't seem to remember enough about his first two trials to help defend himself.

Coxwell and Kitchens had tried to talk Beckwith into claiming diminished capacity to avoid the trial. They'd wanted to order a psychological profile of their client to use as evidence. Beckwith had been insulted. "What do you think I am, an idiot?" he had shouted.

There were times when Beckwith threatened to fire his attorneys. He and Kitchens couldn't stand each other. But Coxwell usually could calm him down. Coxwell knew how to handle Beckwith's tantrums, but no-body knew what Beckwith was likely to do next.

At 9:20 A.M. the bailiff said, "All rise," and Judge Hilburn flapped through the door in his black robe. The state announced that it would call no witnesses. This seemed to surprise the defense lawyers, who conferred for a moment. Then Kitchens stood up and called Beckwith to the stand. Two dozen people gasped. This was not expected.

Beckwith seemed composed and alert when he took his seat to the left of the judge. He shot his French cuffs, arranged his hands on one knee, and offered the spectators his three-quarter profile.

Kitchens wore a boxy blue suit that looked slept in. His white hair was perfectly combed into a slight flip above his left brow, which he smoothed with his hand as he questioned the witness.

"Mr. Beckwith, have you ever been prosecuted on this same charge before?" Kitchens asked.

"I have, sir."

"Can you tell the court how long ago that's been?"

"It's been quite a while ago, 1963 and '4. In those years."

As the questioning continued, Kitchens established that Beckwith couldn't remember more than 50 percent of what had happened at his first trials, that two of his previous lawyers were dead, and that another of his lawyers, Hardy Lott, was eighty-three and unable to help out with the defense. Beckwith himself was now seventy-one and in bad shape.

"How would you describe your level of energy or stamina at this time, Mr. Beckwith?" Kitchens asked.

"Well, for about a year every morning when I get up I walk around my room, and I am exhausted and I have to go back to bed and sleep until . . . I have enough strength to do my reading, writing and arith-metic. . . . I just seem to be going down all the time."

Beckwith was so clearly enjoying the chance to talk that Kitchens had trouble getting in his questions.

"Mr. Beckwith, how is your ability to concentrate at this time?"

"It's diminished mightily."

"Now, sir, I want you to compare these several infirmities that you have described —"

"May I interrupt you, sir?" Beckwith interrupted.

"No, you may not," Kitchens answered curtly.

"I will hush," said Beckwith, chastened.

It went on like this for some twenty minutes. Beckwith claimed he had dim memories of some of the old witnesses. Except for Delmar Dennis, he didn't recognize any of the new witnesses, and he couldn't recall making statements to any of them.

Kitchens handed over his witness.

Ed Peters looked like a hungry man stepping up to his meal. He didn't waste any time.

"Did you know an individual named Cecil Sessums?" he asked.

Beckwith raised his chin and leveled a scornful stare at the district attorney.

"The name is familiar, and I do know a man named Cecil Sessums," he said with almost comic haughtiness. "And I do not —" he stopped himself, as if remembering instructions. "Go ahead. What's the next question."

Peters moved closer to Beckwith. "Go ahead, you can finish answering," he said.

"You've got the floor. I'm listening."

"How did you know Cecil Sessums?"

"I can't recall, but I do know Cecil Sessums."

"Did you go visit him in the penitentiary?"

At his seat behind the prosecutors' desk, Charlie Crisco stiffened. He had been trying for months to pin down this information, and he hadn't had much luck.

"I went to the penitentiary to visit some people," Beckwith said. "And I would say that they were men that are accused of being to the far right, but I don't know who or what persons or what day it was or anything about it."

Peters let him ramble on and then asked, "If in fact you went to visit him with Peggy Morgan . . . would you say that you don't remember that?"

"I don't remember any Peggy Morgan. I remember a woman or a girl, a wife of a man, and that's all I remember," Beckwith replied.

Crisco let out his breath. He had been trying for months to verify that Beckwith had driven to Parchman with Morgan, one of the witnesses who said he had bragged about killing Medgar Evers.

"Don't [you] recall going to see Cecil Sessums who had been convicted of a civil rights slaying?" Peters asked, moving closer still. Peters's voice, which could be so soothing in private conversation, took on a wheedling, annoying cadence in the courtroom. It never took him long to rattle his witnesses.

"I just told you that I went to Parchman penitentiary in the company of some other people," Beckwith snapped.

"And if —"

"That's how blank my mind is, sir!"

Peters abruptly changed course.

"If I recall correctly what you told your attorney, you told him that this was quite an embarrassment for you to have been even charged with having killed Medgar Evers, is that correct?"

"You just going to have to go all over that again, please, sir!" Beckwith said coldly. "Make it — just talk slow and distinctly and loud and *look at me* when you talk to me and I will, I will answer your question."

Peters repeated his question again and again, and Beckwith got angrier and angrier, until Coxwell objected. The judge ordered Peters to rephrase.

"You are saying that this was an embarrassment to you and your family," Peters said. "I am asking you if it was a badge of honor to you, if it was something that you were proud of that you had been charged with that."

"Well I don't think it's any badge of honor to be charged with murder. . . . I am very *enraged* over it."

"And you were enraged over —"

"And I am still mad about it, and I will remain mad about it. I am indignant about it."

"You were enraged over —"

"And I will not look with kindness upon those that attack me and, and those that are supporting me" — Beckwith was staring hard at the prosecutor — ". . . all of this heinous, scandalous, ridiculous charge!"

Peters kept baiting Beckwith, and the old man kept swallowing it. Beckwith even argued while his lawyers voiced their objections. At one point Kitchens had to yell, "Be quiet, Mr. Beckwith!" to stifle his client.

The cross-examination went on for the rest of the morning, until Judge Hilburn called a recess for lunch.

*   *   *

Bobby DeLaughter and Crisco walked off the elevator and onto the fifth floor like football buddies who had won the big game. "I couldn't *believe* they put him on the stand!" DeLaughter kept saying. "I smiled at him the whole time."

They had ordered sandwiches for lunch, and they sat at the little table by receptionist-secretary Jeanie Stewart's desk and reviewed the morning, play by play. They chuckled over Beckwith's admission that he had been to visit Parchman with "the wife of someone."

"I spent so much time trying to nail that down, putting him at that jail," Crisco said. "And he gives it to us!"

What Beckwith revealed on the stand that day set up the prosecution for the day his case would come to trial. Assuming there would ever be a trial.

Beckwith seemed more in control of himself when he resumed his testimony after lunch. Peters kept trying to shake him. At one point the two men nearly ripped an exhibit — the photocopy of an old letter — in a childish tug-of-war right in front of the judge. Beckwith kept addressing Peters as if he were a buck private in boot camp: "Look at me when you talk to me!" he would say.

By the end of the day Beckwith had proved to his lawyers that he was a very risky witness to put on the stand.

In spite of Beckwith's petulant performance observers felt that the defense team had made a strong case of prejudice against their client in their legal arguments. At the same time the defense had quietly scored a tangible victory in another state. Coxwell had filed an appeal to vacate Beckwith's Louisiana dynamite-transport conviction. Since his release from prison, the U.S. Supreme Court had ruled that five-member juries were unconstitutional in such cases. Based on that ruling a Louisiana judge retroactively set aside Beckwith's guilty verdict. He now had no criminal record, and the bomb incident could not be brought up at his murder trial. If there was one.

It was only eight-thirty in the morning, and the August heat was already building in the concrete sidewalks along Tombigbee Street as DeLaughter ducked into the back of the courthouse. He was taking big strides, walking much too fast for someone who had grown up in Mississippi and ought to know better. He was dressed in one of his dark gray murder-trial suits, with shiny black brogues to match his overstuffed briefcase.

He punched the elevator button in the cool courthouse basement.

Crisco was already working in his roomy corner office. The case files for the week were neatly stacked on his desk. Crisco was hunched over the Selectric, pecking at the keys with his two crooked forefingers, typing up another sheaf of subpoenas.

Crisco was already prepared for the murder case DeLaughter was suddenly scheduled to try that morning. When DeLaughter walked through the door, Crisco handed him the fact sheet and the witness list.

"Just tell me — when did the murder happen and where?" DeLaughter asked his investigator. He hadn't had time to get ready for the case.

Crisco pointed to his sheet, and DeLaughter was scribbling the details down on a legal pad when Jeanie Stewart came quietly to the door.

"Bobby, there are reporters and a news crew waiting for you. They want to talk to you," she said.

Crisco looked at DeLaughter's face — is there something else I need to know? — but DeLaughter was still concentrating on copying the fact sheet as he said, "Okay, tell 'em I'll be right out."

Both men knew that Judge Hilburn was going to make his decision on the Beckwith case today. It was the unspoken tension behind every move anybody made. You could feel it in the way Jeanie tiptoed around, her southern-breeze voice even breathier than usual; the way Bobby tightened up when he was worried, closed up his face so even his mother wouldn't know what he was thinking. Beckwith seemed to follow him today like a dark shadow.

Crisco leaned back in his chair and crossed his arms over his stomach. He was going to have to see a doctor about this pain in his gut.

When Crisco was working homicide, he used to carry a pack of Rolaids in his pants pocket wherever he went. Always had a roll. He used to eat them by the handful. He ate his last Rolaid the day he took this job nearly two years ago. Not that working in the D.A.'s office didn't have its own brand of stress. There were literally hundreds of violent felonies to try every court term and only two judges and two prosecutors to handle them. Doc Thaggard had suffered from ulcers for years. Cynthia Hewes had them. DeLaughter seemed to be the only one in the office with an iron stomach. He would joke that all he ever got was a bad attitude. Give him time. Crisco could feel the twinges of a return performance of his own bad stomach.

The Beckwith case had been with him as long as this job. Now two years of work could crash and burn with one ruling if Breland Hilburn decided that Beckwith's constitutional rights had been violated.

The whole city seemed on edge this week. People had been calling all morning: Have you heard anything? Are they gonna let him go? A rumor was percolating through the white community that the blacks would riot if Beckwith was set loose. Someone called to see whether she should cancel her evening yoga class.

Only a few months ago the city of Los Angeles had gone up in flames because of an unpopular court case. Nobody was forgetting Rodney King in this part of town. The Board of Supervisors had already approved $31,315 to buy riot gear and gas masks for the sheriff's department. The Jackson Police Department had taken the old Thompson Tank out of mothballs, tuned it up, and painted its armor with shiny black lacquer. The SWAT team had nicknamed the personnel carrier "Darth Vader," it looked so wicked. Even the young cops knew that the tank had made its first public appearance in 1964, the week of Beckwith's first mistrial.

Crisco drained his mug of decaf, then reached in his drawer for the bottle of Riopan. As he turned back to his typing, Cynthia Hewes poked her head in the door. "Hear anything?" she asked.

Crisco shook his head.

Hewes, who was getting ready to try a rape case, wore her own version of the serious-felony suit: a slim black dress-and-jacket combination and drop-dead black heels. She spotted the Riopan on Crisco's desk.

"I swear, Crisco," she said. "We ought to set out a candy dish full of Tagamet for the office."

Crisco laughed. "It'd help if they'd just get this trial over with," he said.

Hewes had heard the rumors about the impending riot, just like everyone else. She blamed it on the media, particularly the *Clarion-Ledger*, which had been running helpful headlines such as "State NAACP Chief Calls for Calm If Beckwith Acquitted."

"Now there's a thought!" Hewes said, chuckling. "It's like, WHATEVER you do, DON'T think of an elephant!"

*   *   *

Late that afternoon, without fanfare, Judge Hilburn issued a written statement denying the defense motion to dismiss the charges against Beckwith. Hilburn allowed the defense to appeal his decision to the state supreme court but refused to delay proceedings while awaiting the outcome of the appeal. He set a new trial date for September 21.

At the same time Hilburn announced that the trial would be moved from Jackson to Hernando, Mississippi. Two weeks earlier the judge had presided over an eight-hour hearing to decide Beckwith's request for a change of venue. The defense showed how obsessive local media coverage of the Beckwith story had become: 188 broadcasts on WLBT alone; 150 stories in the *Clarion-Ledger*. Coxwell and Kitchens had then paraded witness after witness, including three private investigators who had, rather unscientifically, polled the county, asking whether they thought Beckwith could get a fair trial in Jackson. Their conclusion, naturally, was that he could not.

The district attorney wanted the trial to be held in Jackson. The judge, in an unprecedented move, ruled that the jury would be selected from Panola County, in north-central Mississippi. Of the county's thirty thousand residents, 48 percent were black — close enough to the Hinds County ratio to satisfy the judge. Once the jury was chosen in Panola, it would be moved to Hernando, the seat of neighboring DeSoto County, where the trial would be held. It was a confusing arrangement, and, as it turned out, only the judge was satisfied.

Coxwell and Kitchens were howling before the ink dried on the decision. "We think it's grossly unfair to Mr. Beckwith," Kitchens told the *Clarion-Ledger,* which, as usual, gave the story front-page coverage. "I can't imagine a situation where you are carting jurors around from one county to another that doesn't heighten the seriousness or the heinousness of the case." Kitchens, incidentally, wanted the trial held on the Gulf Coast, where most people were white.

The fathers of Hernando bayed even louder than Beckwith's defense team once the news had sunk in. It soon occurred to them that Hinds County was about to deliver them a huge, steaming gift-wrapped package of horse manure disguised as a celebrated murder trial.

It was only a coincidence that at that moment the best-selling paperback in America was John Grisham's *A Time to Kill,* set in a town very much like Hernando, where Grisham used to practice law. The novel centers on a racially freighted murder trial that sparks a series of bombings, fatal beatings, Klan demonstrations, and race riots in the picturesque town square.

To seal the deal, squads of Jackson television crews and print journalists descended on Panola and DeSoto Counties, shoving microphones in the faces of shoppers at the feed store, asking if they were worried about a riot.

Quietly the city attorney for Hernando began exploring ways to worm out of the agreement the county had made with Judge Hilburn. Within a month he would have the courthouse declared a fire hazard in a desperate move to push the trial out of town.

As it turned out, Beckwith himself handed DeLaughter the opportunity to try the case on home turf. On the weekend after Judge Hilburn's decision mysterious packages appeared in the driveways of houses in white neighborhoods in Panola and DeSoto Counties. Each contained a signed letter on Beckwith's stationery and a small fifty-page booklet produced by the Liberty Lobby titled *Citizens Rule Book*.

In the letter Beckwith described himself as a "political prisoner presently being held . . . on the politically motivated charge of the 1963 assassination of the Mississippi NAACP president [sic] for that period, of which I am innocent."

A note in Beckwith's hand in each booklet directed the reader to the chapter titled "A Handbook for Jurors." Basically it was an instruction manual on how to hang up a jury with one vote. It pointed out that a juror is not obliged to follow the written law if he doesn't like it: "If you feel the statute involved in a criminal case being tried by you is unfair, you must affirm that the offending statute is really no law at all and that the violation of it is no crime at all."

DeLaughter immediately filed a motion to return the trial to Jackson, since Beckwith had attempted to poison the jury pool in the new venue. The judge did not change his ruling.

DeLaughter concentrated on his pending felony cases for the rest of the term. He rarely came out of his office, rarely had lunch with the staff. He seemed lost in himself, brooding, while everyone else was buoyant, optimistic that there might be an end to this saga after all.

When DeLaughter went into a dark mood, nobody could crack it. Not even Hewes, who left a note on his sloppy desk one day, telling him a mutual friend of theirs had been interviewed by a national newspaper for an article profiling DeLaughter. "She told them you were boring and had no hobbies!" Cynthia wrote. No response. Everyone gave him a wide berth after that.

Crisco spent his days on the phone, arranging logistics for the trial in Hernando, trying to track down all the witnesses. There were more than sixty names. Some of them had moved; some had left no forwarding address. A couple of the old Jackson policemen had suffered heart attacks since the case had been reopened. Crisco tried to talk personally to everybody, to reassure them and give them an update on how the case was going. Some of the witnesses, particularly Delmar Dennis, were blowing hot and cold. Will they testify or won't they? Sometimes Crisco felt like a cowboy with a nervous herd and storm clouds on the horizon.

Meanwhile DeLaughter dealt with the state supreme court appeal, which should have been the last legal hurdle to the trial. Beckwith's lawyers submitted a forty-nine-page brief, citing eighty-nine cases to support their arguments that Beckwith was being denied his rights to due process and a speedy trial. DeLaughter filed his response on Friday, August 21. After that all anyone could do was wait.

That weekend the first storm of hurricane season plowed into Miami. Hurricane Andrew flattened southern Florida in a few crazy hours, then headed out into the Gulf of Mexico. By Monday morning the big, heaving monster storm was sucking in humid air from all directions, gaining strength by the hour, and churning north, heading straight for the Mississippi coast. The last time a storm of that size had hit the Gulf Coast was 1969 and hurricanes were still named for women. Camille had killed hundreds, most of them people who had ignored the weather reports.

By Monday afternoon the radio stations in Jackson were playing disaster sets: "Bad Moon Rising," "Who'll Stop the Rain?" A steady stream of refugees was trailing up I-55 from New Orleans and Biloxi.

That night Crisco turned on the ten o'clock news to hear the latest on Andrew, and that's how he learned that the Mississippi Supreme Court had stayed all circuit court proceedings in the Beckwith case. The justices wanted new written arguments submitted, and they wanted to hear oral arguments on October 15, 1992. So much for the trial schedule, and all the witness arrangements, and all the plane tickets and hotel reservations and bodyguards lined up and all the rest of it. All Crisco could do was laugh at the television set because he didn't feel like crying.

The next morning Crisco wasn't laughing anymore. In fact he was walking around the district attorney's office like a man in a daze, wondering who to call first. Nancy Lee noticed him walking across the short hall between the coffee machine and the reception desk with a full mug of coffee, lost in thought and sloshing big spills all across the floor.

"Charlie! You're spilling your coffee," she said as she ran to mop it up for him. Normally she wouldn't have done that; she would have made him go get a rag, scolding him like a child. He would have wiped it up, laughing, and this would have been one of the small jokes of the day: Crisco spilled his coffee. But today he seemed so forlorn and distracted that nobody even wanted to tease him.

"I am not a happy camper," he said in his flat cop voice as Nancy Lee handed him another cup of decaf.

Then the elevator doors parted, and out stepped DeLaughter. It was one of those suspended moments — the pause after the sheriff walks into the saloon — as everybody turned to read DeLaughter's expression.

This was the two-week break between court terms, so DeLaughter was wearing his civvies: Dockers khakis, brown deck shoes, a green polo shirt. His eyes looked strained with fatigue, but they revealed a wicked amusement.

"Can you believe it!" he shouted at Crisco in his big courtroom voice. "It's crazy! There's no logic to it!"

DeLaughter grabbed his pink message slips, and the two men walked down the hall. DeLaughter was pouring it out, like a dam bursting. He was saying that dismissing the case would have been one thing — that would have made him mad, but at least it would have been over. This was just crazy, having to resubmit the arguments he'd already submitted, going through this schedule that forced them to put the trial off yet again, when both sides were ready to make their oral arguments today if they had to!

He was still railing about it an hour later, throwing pieces of paper around his office, trying to clear a work space.

"Meanwhile we delay this thing and the witnesses are fading. Dying!"

He tossed a pink message slip into a file drawer. "Look at this — Betty Jean Coley died! We found that out this week."

This had gone on too long. The case had already lasted one full term in the D.A.'s office.

"A whole career," DeLaughter said, shaking his head.

He flopped back in his chair and stared at the fresh stack of papers on his desk, his share of the 930-something cases coming up next term. He and Hewes were expected to try or settle every violent felony in Hinds and Yazoo Counties. His whole load had been cleared for Beckwith, and now all this work had come back at him and Crisco. All these other cases needed to be scheduled for September.

"If it wasn't for all this work," he said, half serious, "I'd just go to the beach and get drunk!"

Someone pointed out that the beach might not be there tomorrow, and he laughed harder.

"Right! There's that storm coming! The beach won't be there!"

It seemed as if everything in DeLaughter's world was spinning out of control, like he was caught up in a whirlwind of bad omens. The only thing to do was to have lunch.

Hewes, Crisco, and Doc Thaggard appeared in Bobby's doorway.

"Where do we eat?" said Hewes.

"How about across the street?"

They gathered DeLaughter up in a tight little scrum of friends, closing ranks around each other as they always did in times of crisis, and walked him to the restaurant. They were raucous and loose as mourners at an Irish wake. It was the kind of nerve-charged laughter you might hear after a battle, or before a hurricane.

Outside the atmosphere itself felt different, as if all the air had been replaced with something unfamiliar. There was a tropical mildness to it, and a tension, like something was coming in on an invisible, evil wind — felt but not seen. The sky was bright turquoise, with two layers of clouds in it. There were thick, dark swaths in the stratosphere; wispy low clouds, like puffs of gray smoke, skimmed just overhead, as quick as Learjets.

As DeLaughter crossed Pascagoula Street, he glanced hard over his shoulder at the blank face of the county jail. Beckwith was in his basement cell, just a few yards away. He turned to Crisco, who was walking next to him.

"Well, even if this case gets dismissed," he said, "I can say one thing. That mean old son of a bitch spent more time in jail this time around, just waiting for his trial, than he did for the last two trials combined."

That night Hurricane Andrew veered west and struck a glancing blow in southern Louisiana. By the time it swung north and hit Jackson, the storm was a tropical depression, and it spent its dwindling fury in a deluge of hot summer rain.

In the summer of 1992 Dave Dennis left his personal injury law practice in Louisiana and moved back to Mississippi. He still had trouble talking about the old days. He avoided publicity, dodging most interviews and all political events. His strange, sea-green eyes filled with tears whenever he talked about his friend Medgar Evers and all the others who were dead, or gone missing, or gone crazy. He would tell you he had been among the missing. He was lost, unsettled; he hadn't been whole since the summer of 1964. He had spent thirty years looking for himself, and he had to come back to Mississippi to be complete again.

The reason he had come back was Bob Moses. They had met at a symposium to refute the premises of the movie *Mississippi Burning* in 1988. They hadn't seen each other in twenty-four years. Before long they knew they had to somehow finish what they had started with Freedom Summer. Annie Devine, the tireless old COFO activist, was there, and she lit into Dennis for abandoning Mississippi. She told him that he and Moses were like men who had fathered a child and then left it without any support. That stung, because they knew it was true.

Moses had returned from his exile in Africa and was quietly revolutionizing the teaching of math in Cambridge, Massachusetts, where he had earned his doctorate. With the help of a MacArthur Foundation "genius" grant, Moses had set up the Algebra Project, a holistic approach to teaching children who sorely needed a grounding in math. Dennis got excited about the possibilities of expanding the Algebra Project to the Mississippi Delta.

Now Dennis was coordinating the project full-time in Mississippi and across the South. He had no intention of attending Beckwith's trial, if it ever happened, or of getting involved in Mississippi politics again, and neither did Moses. That part of their lives had ended.

Dick Gregory also was staying away from the Beckwith scene. He had returned to the state from time to time as a paid inspirational speaker and supporter of various causes. He had left show business back in the seventies to promote nutrition and fasting. He was a purveyor of vitamin powders and radical diets. Recently he had been waging a campaign against drug abuse. Gregory was constantly on the road, and he answered his phone calls in hotel rooms with the words "God Bless You!" He had become an oddity on the fringe of politics, a casualty of an old war.

Ed King still bore the scars of the car wreck that had almost killed him the week Evers was murdered. He faithfully attended the functions and fund-raisers for civil rights causes in Jackson. But his lawsuit to limit access to the Sovereignty Commission files had distanced him from some of his former allies, and he was involved in other, less than progressive causes, such as Operation Rescue, the antiabortion project. King would tell anyone who asked him that he thought the Beckwith case was a sham and a smoke screen to cover up the real problems in Mississippi such as crime and poverty and indifference.

John Salter was now chairman of the Indian Studies department at the University of North Dakota. He had remained true to his social causes after leaving Mississippi and had spent many years working with the poor and disfranchised before settling in Grand Forks. He still considered himself an activist and maintained his considerable network of contacts across the country. He had written a thoroughly researched and well-received book on the Jackson Movement, and he was a thoughtful and helpful interview subject for any writer who was interested in the era.

He was surprised that DeLaughter had never called to ask him about the case. He could have told him that Beckwith had not been in the church the night Evers was killed, because Salter had been there the whole time and would have seen him. But Salter might have a credibility problem in a court of law. He now taught a university course on the UFO phenomenon. He had written articles about it and had appeared on television recounting his personal experiences as someone who had been abducted many times by friendly visitors from space.

Salter and King had had a falling-out over the UFO business. They were no longer speaking.

The room where the Mississippi Supreme Court hears cases is shaped like an egg. Justices sit at a long, semicircular desk, spectators are arranged in three ascending rows on the opposite side, and a podium stands in the middle, where the yolk would be.

On October 15, 1992, every last seat in the spectator gallery was filled. It was the biggest crowd yet for any of the proceedings in the Beckwith case. Curious lawyers, family members, old Klansmen, and black city council members sat side by side. A passel of community activists and NAACP leaders showed up. The message, in case the justices missed it, was: You are being watched.

For the first time Beckwith skipped a court appearance. It was not the custom for a defendant to appear in these chambers, no matter how badly he might want to be there.

Myrlie Evers was not expected either. But for the first time since Beckwith had been indicted, she came to court. Heads turned and people murmured as she walked into the hall. Klansmen squinted and strained to get a better look at her.

She wore a dark gold suit and a cheetah-print scarf. She sat in the front row of the gallery, right behind the prosecutors. She had a notebook and pen in her hands.

Evers studied the seven justices carefully as they entered wearing their flowing black robes and took their seats. Fred Banks, the one African-American justice, had recused himself because he had known and admired Medgar Evers, and so had one white justice, without giving a reason. There was one woman on the court, Lenore Prather, who wore her hair in a stiff honey-blond froth and seemed perfectly in place among the elderly men who radiated whiteness and grim decorum. Evers's heart sank. They were all nearly Beckwith's age. Looking at them she saw the face of the Old South. Then she saw something else in the stern, dyspeptic expressions and wattled necks emerging from robes like black, folded wings, and she suppressed an inappropriate giggle. Arranged in a patient semicircle in front of her the justices looked like vultures surrounding a fresh kill.

"Only God can make you do the right thing," she thought to herself as the hearing began.

Merrida Coxwell wore a European-cut suit, and his trademark long hair flowed over his collar. His skin was so taut you could bounce a quarter off his cheeks.

He had so much to say and only fifteen minutes to say it in. He began by pointing out that the delay in his client's prosecution had been the longest he could find on record in Mississippi or anywhere else. He outlined how this delay had prejudiced Beckwith. His strongest argument was not the twenty-eight-year lapse between the first trial and the current proceedings, but the fact that Beckwith's indictment had been open and on the books from 1964 until the nolle prosequi in 1969. Coxwell argued that Beckwith could have been retried at any time during those five years, while his lawyers were alive and well, memories were fresh, and witnesses available. But he hadn't been.

DeLaughter rose to respond. There was no statute of limitations on murder, he said, and a murder case that has been dismissed can be retried in good faith, as in the case of Jeffrey MacDonald, the Green Beret doctor convicted of murdering his family. He challenged Coxwell's claim that the delay between 1964 and 1969 prejudiced Beckwith's case because Coxwell could show no evidence that the open indictment had been a hardship for Beckwith. DeLaughter also pointed out that Beckwith could have had another trial if he had asked for one. According to the law in those days, the burden was on the defendant to demand action.

The justices asked each side a few questions, and then it was over. The decision would be announced later.

Among the lawyers in the audience the smart money was on the defense. Most of them felt that the case would be dismissed.

After the hearing was over Myrlie Evers faced the mob of cameras and tape recorders in the foyer. "I cannot deal with the idea that Medgar may be assassinated all over again in the courts," she said. "I have no tolerance for people who say that it has been so long and, for that reason, this case should be dropped."

Little Delay, the defendant's forty-five-year-old son, edged into the crowd of reporters, straining to hear what Evers was saying. "Do people criticize when the German war criminals are pursued for those injustices they did to people? Why is this different?" she asked.

A few feet away Little Delay began holding forth to his own crowd of journalists. "Both families have suffered," he said. "I would like to hear the truth as much as she would like to hear the truth. We are just going about it in different ways."

Evers continued, finding her stride. She spoke with the extraordinary eloquence that she could sometimes muster in interviews, so that it was hard to believe she wasn't reading a prepared statement. A trial, she hoped, would open the door to more investigations and prosecutions of other unpunished crimes of the past. "We have to settle these dastardly acts of old," she said. "If we don't, we will live with ghosts that will haunt us forever."

Evers soon flew back to Oregon to wait for the decision. She hadn't been home for a long time. Her husband, Walter Williams, was in Los Angeles for some medical tests. The houseplants were somehow all right, the ivy and the Christmas cactus and the two gardenia plants that she had nursed from tiny sprouts, that weren't supposed to live in that climate, had somehow survived a month of neglect. The cactus was blooming.

She learned from her neighbors that the house alarm had gone off twice in her absence — both times in the early-morning hours. The police had come and found nothing.

The police had been on alert ever since someone had planted a bomb in Myrlie's mailbox a few months earlier. It was a crude bomb, and luckily the heat had melted its detonation device. If it hadn't, the bomb could have blown her hand off, or perhaps her head, when she opened the box. No one had claimed responsibility for the package. The FBI wasn't sure whether the bomb had been put there because of the Beckwith case or simply because Evers and Walter Williams were the only black people in the neighborhood. This was no consolation as she bolted the doors.

Evers spent that first night in her own bed with an array of items on the nightstand: a heavy flashlight, a pipe, an aerosol can of antispider spray (good to spray in somebody's face), and the gun that she knew how to use and would use without hesitation.

Her injured back was acting up again, and she was worried about Walter and frazzled by all the waiting, feeling absolutely helpless while the supreme court took its time deliberating. It could be days or months before they handed down a decision. She was so weary it hurt to breathe.

There wasn't a columnist in Mississippi who thought the state supreme court would allow the Beckwith case to proceed. Every pundit seemed to have just had lunch with one of the justices, and they knew for a fact that the case would be dismissed over the speedy trial issue.

Then, on December 16, the court punted. In a 4–3 decision, they decided not to decide until after the trial. "While Beckwith's indictment, arrest and anticipated trial may raise serious and troubling constitutional questions, he clearly has no constitutional or statutory right" to appeal before trial, the majority ruling said.

At the same time the court reversed an earlier decision and recommended that Beckwith be granted bond unless the circuit judge could prove he was a danger to the community.

Myrlie Evers expressed relief that the way had been cleared for a trial. "It's been a long, emotional roller coaster," she told the *Clarion-Ledger*. The ruling softened the realization that Beckwith might soon walk out of jail. If that happened, DeLaughter told the press, he doubted that Beckwith would ever return to Mississippi to stand trial.

Meanwhile Coxwell and Kitchens appealed the state supreme court ruling to the U.S. Supreme Court in a last-ditch effort to get the case dismissed before trial.

One day before Christmas Eve, 1992, Beckwith was released from the Hinds County jail on $100,000 bond. John Branton had died that fall, and Beckwith needed another source for his bond. A "stranger" had appeared out of nowhere and handed Little Delay a check for $12,000 to secure the bond.

"The Lord works miracles," the son whooped.

A couple of white supremacists claimed credit for the deed, but the donor was — of all people — a Jewish lawyer from Jackson named Harry Rosenthal. He said he couldn't stand to see Beckwith's rights violated. As much as this irked Beckwith, he took the money anyway.

Judge Hilburn ordered Beckwith to remain in the state of Mississippi and to report periodically to the court. By nightfall a deputy sheriff had driven him north to Aberdeen and dropped him off at his son's doublewide mobile home out in the country, where he was installed in the second bedroom.

Beckwith's wife, Thelma, was still in Tennessee and not happy about it. "He hasn't called me!" she told Beverly Kraft of the Jackson paper, hinting at some previously unknown family rift. "Let him stay with his son. I'm going to die and I hope I die quickly!"

While Thelma kept her vigil on Signal Mountain, the Beckwith clan planned a quiet Christmas Eve in Aberdeen. The phone, however, would not stop ringing. One eager young reporter from the *Clarion-Ledger* named James Overstreet wanted an interview. Little Delay asked if he was willing to pay for it.

Overstreet called back and said no, the paper didn't pay for interviews. But by the way, he asked, where do you live?

"On Darracott Road, but you don't need to know because you are not invited," Little Delay replied.

The reporter tried to explain this to his bosses, but Overstreet's editors apparently told him to get that interview anyway. So he did what most reporters do if they are hungry enough. He went up and knocked on the door.

First he had to get through the gate. It was locked and chained. He said, later, at his trial, that a helpful neighbor had pointed to a hole in the fence and told him to go through. Nobody was home when he got to the trailer. He was walking back down the driveway when Little Delay and his father pulled up in a pickup.

"I asked him, 'Just what in the hell are you doing on my property and who are you?' " the younger Beckwith recalled at Overstreet's trespassing trial a month later. "I threatened to whip his young bee-hind!"

The father and son made a citizen's arrest of the shaken reporter. The younger Beckwith told their captive that he had three options: "Break and run, get in the vehicle with me or I was gonna put him in my vehicle."

Overstreet wisely got in the pickup, and Big Delay climbed in with him. Overstreet testified that the elder Beckwith told him, "Your options aren't too good. It's deer season and there are a lot of stray bullets flying around."

The judge in Monroe County found Overstreet guilty and fined him one hundred dollars for trespassing, plus court fees. Father and son Beckwith were photographed at the courthouse grinning gleefully at each other after the verdict.

When Big Delay was asked if he'd actually made that remark about the stray bullets, he coyly replied that he didn't remember saying any such thing. Not that it wasn't a true fact. "There *are* stray bullets in deer season," he said. "What would make you think I would want to threaten this young man? I didn't know him."

*　　　*　　　*

Months went by with no word from Judge Hilburn about a new trial date. The rumor going around Mississippi was that a decision had been made, "somewhere high up," that the case would never get to court, that "they" were going to drag out the process and wait for Beckwith to die. Nobody was saying who "they" were. Judge Hilburn, as always, would not talk about his reluctance to set a date.

Two and a half years had gone by since the case had resurfaced. The country had been through a war and elected a new president and Congress. Mississippi had a new governor and was about to get a new legislature.

The Hinds County District Attorney's Office also had changed. Ed Peters was still there but grumbling that this was definitely his last term in office. Peters was warring with both the mayor and the new chief of police, Jimmy Walker, a transplant from the Washington, D.C., force. One of the first things Walker had done in his new job had been to take away the two police detectives assigned to the district attorney's office as investigators. Benny Bennett had been transferred to a special anticrime unit, and Doc Thaggard had been sent to municipal court for bailiff's duty.

That left Crisco to do everything, with no time to spend on the Beckwith case. It took a lot of political clout, not to mention a few phone calls from Myrlie Evers, to correct the situation. Thaggard was brought back as a sheriff's investigator, and Max Mayes, a smart young black detective from the Jackson Police Department, was assigned to replace Bennett.

Merrida Coxwell had gotten married since the case had begun. So had Cynthia Hewes, who was now Cynthia Speetjens. She was still trying murderers and rapists, and there were a few new pictures on her office door.

Bobby DeLaughter had divorced his wife, Dixie, gained custody of the three kids (Bill Kirksey was his lawyer), and remarried a lovely dark-haired nurse named Peggy.

Every political observer in the state expected DeLaughter to run for Peters's job. It was a natural progression. But DeLaughter had other plans. A bill had passed through the legislature to reform the bottled-up appeals process in Mississippi, which had always been handled by an overworked supreme court. The new measure would create five new appellate judges to handle the first level of appeals. DeLaughter planned to run for one of those judgeships. But there was a problem. As the point man on the Beckwith case, DeLaughter had made a lot of powerful enemies. If it did come to trial and he lost, he might as well move to another state. His political career would be over before it began.

In March Judge Hilburn granted Beckwith permission to go back to Tennessee to take care of Thelma, who was legally blind and had developed colon cancer. The prosecution was almost back to where it had started more than three years earlier.

On June 11, 1993, a sign in the lobby of the Cabot Lodge in north Jackson said, "Welcome Heat Wavers." The weather was one thing that hadn't changed in thirty years. There were other things as well. But for now Myrlie Evers was noticing the superficial changes in the landscape: the friendly white face behind the desk welcoming her to the motel; the handsome African-American cashier behind the counter. These were the things Medgar had fought for, and he would be pleased. They were also some of the things he had died for, thirty years ago. And in a way Mylrie was here to finally bring him home.

This time she was coming to Jackson with a plan to donate their old house, and eventually their papers, to Tougaloo College.

On Saturday, June 12, thirty years to the day after Medgar's death, Tougaloo hosted a symposium at the Medgar Evers Library to discuss the meaning of his life.

The first speaker was Bennie Thompson, who had recently been elected to fill Mike Espy's seat in Congress after Espy was appointed secretary of agriculture. Thompson wore a well-cut, dark blue pinstriped banker's suit. His large head bobbed above his conservative tie, and his round, baleful face looked solemnly down at the thirty or forty people in the audience as he began to speak.

Thompson had been fifteen years old when Medgar Evers was killed. But his death, and his life, had profoundly affected the freshman congressman. "I believe I am here because of Medgar Evers," he began.

Myrlie, who was seated in the audience, looked up at the speaker and felt her heart slowly shift into place. She felt as if it had been off beat for a long time and now was settling into a comfortable, familiar rhythm.

Everything began to make sense to her. She watched Thompson with a new intensity.

"As most of you know, Medgar had a firm commitment to economic justice in the state of Mississippi," Thompson continued. He went on for a few minutes about that. He said that he did not want to be "confrontational," just "truthful," as he noted, "If Medgar came back today in this state he would be very disappointed. Because thirty years later we still haven't accomplished nearly the dream that Medgar had."

Thompson went on to name a few of the inequities in Mississippi and Washington. "One of the first realities I got when I arrived in Washington — they asked me which department did I work in? I said, 'Wha'd you mean?' Said, 'You're new, we haven't seen you around.' 'That's right.' 'So are you in the printing department? Or in housekeeping?'

"I said, 'No, I'm a member of Congress.' 'You ARE?' So that was my wake-up call."

There were other speakers that afternoon — doctors, lawyers, and politicians who all owed so much to Medgar Evers's legacy. When they had finished, Myrlie walked to the podium to thank them. "Medgar would have wanted to know that he helped make a difference in all of our lives," she said. "He also said that once we reach our goal, that we would have to work even harder to hold on to it."

She was visibly moved by what she had heard, and she spoke to the people in the room in a personal way, as they had spoken to her. "There is not one day since his death that Medgar has not been with me, that I have not thought of him, that I have not been guided by his life. And as I stand here now I can say that I love him, so much. Thirty years later, of course, it's not that romantic thing because I can't touch him. But it's a love that goes deeper than anything that we had in this life."

Myrlie drew a breath as she prepared to say something she had never said before. "He will live with me forever, and I think he will live with some of you," she began. "Today I still miss him. But I don't *mourn* Medgar anymore. What we are doing now is celebrating him, and we are also celebrating ourselves and our successes. For us, the living, he does go on."

With that, Myrlie released Medgar at last — not the pain of losing him, and certainly not his memory, but the weight of his legacy that she had carried, alone, all these years. She carried Medgar's life in her like she'd carried her boxes of letters and photographs from Mississippi to Los Angeles to the Northwest mountains. And now she was turning it over at last. She would now share with Tougaloo the house, and the trunks of papers, and the burden of Medgar's legacy. The weight passed from her hands lightly, like a wreath of dried flowers laid on a grave.

26

Batesville

ON OCTOBER 4, 1993, the U.S. Supreme Court refused to consider Byron De La Beckwith's motion to dismiss. This was the last legal barrier to a new trial.

October went by, and then November, without a word from Jackson. In December Judge Hilburn finally set a date, but he made the peculiar decision not to announce it to the public. The press found out after Charlie Crisco sent out the first batch of witness subpoenas. Jury selection was set to begin on January 18, 1994, in Batesville, Mississippi. Without offering an explanation the judge also ordered that the trial itself would be moved back to Jackson, with the out-of-town jury. It would be held in the same courtroom where the first trial had taken place, thirty years earlier, almost to the day.

A week before the start of jury selection, Beckwith was — against his lawyer's advice — answering the telephone in his house on Signal Mountain. Sometimes the reporter who called got a tongue-lashing on race, politics, and the profession of journalism. Sometimes Beckwith actually answered questions. In an interview with a local Chattanooga paper, he seemed to be anticipating the trial. He even made some coherent statements about the case.

Beckwith denied killing Evers, for instance, saying he had been in Greenwood on the night of the shooting. "That's ninety-three miles away," he said. "It would have been a mighty powerful rifle for me to have done it."

He offered an opinion of the pending court proceedings, which he called "a Roman circus to entertain the people. It's strictly political — money-squandering tomfoolery and tommyrot."

When Mike Riley of *Time* called, Beckwith told him that he was packing his seabag for the trial, ready to do battle again. "I feel just like I felt when I went down to Tarawa to fight the Japs," he said amiably. "I'm just as confident I'll come back with honor [he pronounced it "ahwunnuh"] and dignity and good health."

He told Riley he wouldn't be giving interviews once he was back in Mississippi. "If I talk to you down there, my lawyers'll take a stick and beat the hell out of me! Heh heh heh."

Did he plan to testify?

"What do YOU think?"

"Well, I would guess no."

"Well, I'm going to do whatever it takes to win this case with honor and dignity. But WIN."

He was confident he could win with the right kind of jury. "I plan to get a jury of my peers, you know," he said. "That's white and Christian. If there's anything else on that jury, we might have problems."

Riley asked him if he was innocent.

"What the hell kind of question is that coming from a white man!" he snapped.

Back in Mississippi the *Clarion-Ledger* was running ecstatic walk-up stories to the big trial. There were articles about Panola County, where the jury would be chosen, directions to the scene of the crime, and a story in which local psychologists analyzed Beckwith's writings. The newspaper had gotten its hands on the latest bill from Beckwith's court-appointed defense team. So far the lawyers' fees alone totaled more than forty-eight thousand dollars — a real bargain for two years of work, but enough to stir up resentment. Taxpayers complained that it was a waste of money over an unnecessary trial.

Despite all the hoopla in the media, it was hard to find a white person in Mississippi who thought it was a good idea to try Beckwith. In fact, you could talk to just about anyone — black or white — and hear at least one complaint: the trial cost too much, it was unfair to try a sick old man, it was a useless dredging up of unpleasant memories, it was a political maneuver, and it was futile symbolism — they'll never convict him, what was the point?

Symbolism was, in many ways, precisely the point to those who favored the trial. The intangible benefits of concepts such as "justice" and "retribution" were worth the price of admission. In Mississippi, where words are such valuable currency and so little is actually accomplished, symbolism takes on a special importance.

For instance, as the new year began — in the face of crushing poverty and crime, schools closing because the buses had no brakes, and teen pregnancy rates at an all-time high — the legislature prepared to debate whether or not to change the state song. Black legislators felt that "Go, Mississippi," a modified version of Ross Barnett's racist campaign song, was offensive.

"It would be good to remove all our racist images," said Aaron Henry. Henry and other legislators also were fighting to change the state flag, which still featured the Confederate banner in one corner.

In a way all these exercises amounted to a form of community exorcism. It was an act of cleansing, of rubbing out the relics of a shameful era. Although changing a song nobody knew anyway or sending Beckwith to prison wasn't going to solve the problems of racism, crime, or poverty, at least it was something that could be accomplished. It made some people feel more hopeful.

Meanwhile, in January 1994, five hundred summonses were being delivered to potential jurors in Panola County. In Jackson Bobby DeLaughter and Charlie Crisco were literally dusting off the evidence from the courthouse vault. Visitors to the D.A's office could find the two men huddled over a table where the Enfield rifle, the photographs, and the boxes of files were being laid out in order, as they would be presented at the trial.

What the visitors would not know was that Crisco was still hunting for new evidence to use against Beckwith. Specifically, he was trying to locate a certain letter that Beckwith had written to his ex-wife, Willie, ten years after Evers's murder.

*   *   *

Panola County, population thirty thousand, is a media dead zone suspended between Memphis and Jackson. Radio reception from both cities seems to drop off at the county line. The cable TV stations come from Tennessee and Tupelo, not Jackson, so the Beckwith trial had not been covered to such a degree as in the capital. In fact, as the assembled lawyers were soon to find out, most potential jurors — black and white — could argue convincingly that they knew nothing or next to nothing about either Beckwith or Evers.

The county is a microcosm of Mississippi. It is, like Hinds County, nearly half black and half white. It straddles the Delta and the hills. Rich white neighborhoods are neatly separated from poor black and middle-class districts by the Tallahatchie River, which runs east to west through the county. People joke that the football teams from Sardis, the main town in the wealthy north county, and Batesville, on the south side of the river, could never play each other peacefully because of a fierce and intractable class rivalry.

But whatever divisions of education, and race, and class separated the Panola Countians who trudged through the icy air to the courthouse on Tuesday morning, January 18, 1994, most all of them shared one unifying goal: to avoid jury duty at all costs.

Rumors abounded. The trial might last six weeks. If you got on the jury, it was said, the Klan, the black radicals, or the media would hound you and your family no matter which way you voted. It was a no-win situation.

Security was rigid around the courthouse. The state police set up a communications trailer in a nearby parking lot. Law enforcement officers provided by the state, town, and two counties, not to mention shadowy federal plainclothesmen and at least one hapless "undercover" detective took their positions around the building. A bomb-sniffing dog checked the premises before the doors were opened. A brand-new metal detector shrilled its warning all day as businesslike deputies demanded keys, belts, and loose change from spectators and media people.

There were perhaps twenty-five reporters and cameramen covering this phase of the trial. To the surprise of everyone except local Panolians, crowds of protesters and gawkers never materialized. The people of Batesville were underwhelmed by the spectacle.

To the disappointment of feature writers hoping for some local color, the Panola County Courthouse was a modern, industrial-style building, the kind of soulless box that has replaced the grand old courthouses that once graced the squares of every county seat across the South. The austere main courtroom, which held about two hundred people, was decorated in dark wood veneer paneling and pea soup–colored walls.

DeLaughter and Ed Peters, both dressed in their matching, dark gray murder-trial suits, poured over stacks of paper at the prosecution table. Beckwith, who had arrived that morning wearing a curious old-fashioned fedora, wore his Confederate gray suit with his signature white French cuffs, a wide red paisley tie with a diamond stickpin (a gift from Thelma), and a little Confederate battle flag pin on his lapel.

He was sensitive about the pin. Later, when a courtroom artist asked what kind of flag it was, Beckwith stomped over to her and said, "If you don't know what a Confederate flag looks like you'll go to hell in Africa!"

Judge Hilburn was somber and pale, and he looked, with his dark hair and full beard, more like a Civil War colonel than a circuit court judge. The only clue to his hidden, playful nature was a red tie festooned with cartoon drawings of Tasmanian devils carefully tucked under his black robe.

The first 140 or so potential jurors filed in, nervous and cold, and took seats on the hard wooden pews. The winnowing process, called voir dire, began immediately.

Right off five blacks disqualified themselves from the jury for not being able to read or write. Then Hilburn asked whether anyone was physically unable to sit through a long trial. Within seconds the courtroom started looking like Lourdes as people — mostly white people — hobbled up the aisles on walkers and canes, limping, shuffling, wheezing, and waving notes from their doctors. Soon only fifty-eight potential jurors remained. Most of them were black.

"The only people getting on this jury are the ones who haven't figured out a way to get off of it," mused Joe Reid, the county clerk, as he sucked on an unlit cigar during a break.

Beckwith seemed subdued during the first hours of jury selection. As the morning wore on, he brightened visibly, craning his neck and looking around the room for people he recognized. Thelma had arrived on his arm, wearing a hot-pink coat, a fresh honey-blond wig, and open-toed platform shoes. She sat in the front row throughout the proceedings, mostly quiet but sometimes shaking her head in her hands and spouting tears, particularly when the lawyers were talking about the penalties for murder.

The potential jurors were given numbers, and the first thirty or so took seats for some questions.

Peters stood up and introduced himself. He spoke slowly and gently, and he moved with an aw-shucks gawkiness that put country people at ease. Jury selection is an act of seduction, and Peters played the perfect suitor. It was agreed that nobody could pick a jury like Peters, and DeLaughter happily took a backseat during this crucial phase of the trial.

Although Peters often repeated his contention that this was not a "racial" trial, race and racial attitudes were on everyone's mind. Peters's unstated goal was to get as many white people off the jury as possible.

Meanwhile Merrida Coxwell and Jim Kitchens were going to do everything they could do to get a white jury for the trial. They would have to come up with excuses for removing blacks.

Peters asked the potential jurors to search their hearts and confess whether they had already made up their minds in the case, whether they thought it was too old, it was about politics, or they couldn't convict the old man no matter what evidence was presented.

"If you feel that way," Peters said, "don't put yourself in the position of lying under oath before God. Just put your hand up!"

Three white arms shot up and one black one. The potential jurors were taken into chambers and interviewed privately. Before long most of the whites in the first group of jurors had excused themselves, and the count was ten blacks to five whites.

At Beckwith's first trials the district attorney, Bill Waller, had brought the race issue right out in the open, asking whether the jurors thought it was a crime to kill a "nigger." Peters was more subtle. Did they send their children to private school? Did they feel times were "different" thirty years ago?

Peters knew his Mississippians. Instead of asking the religion of each panelist, he simply asked everyone who wasn't a Baptist to raise his or her hand. There were very few.

By the time Kitchens took over the voir dire, there wasn't much left to ask. Kitchens looked for all the world like Peters's stockier brother, right down to the flowing white hair. He was just as folksy and smooth, but there was something annoying about him, something bulldoggish that got on your nerves.

Mostly the process was excruciatingly boring. The main event every day was lunch, which took on a surreal cast, since there was only one place to eat on the town square.

At noon break the sheriffs went through the elaborate ritual of escorting Delay and Thelma to the beige Suburban that was used to transport them to and from court. A deputy drove it, and another veteran sheriff was assigned to their protection. The small, polite knot of photographers was kept at bay until the truck pulled away. Then everybody — press, prosecutors, lawyers, defendant, deputies, and bodyguards — disembarked at the homey little Bankery café to line up for the $3.99 plate lunch.

The Bankery had never done so much business. Local motels were enjoying an off-season boom. While the prosecution team and the out-of-county cops stayed at the modest Ramada Express, Beckwith and his team, along with most local TV people, were bunking at the equally modest Comfort Inn on Highway 6.

Right from the start there was a problem with Delay and Thelma's room. It was something about no heat or no water, and complaints were lodged with one of the managers, who happened to be an immigrant from India. The manager had figured out that Beckwith was some sort of VIP, but it was unclear whether he knew more than that. He was mortified that his most famous guest was unhappy with the room, so to make it up to Beckwith he personally brought over a complimentary tray of lunch meats. Beckwith eyeballed the dark-skinned man as he carried in the tray.

The manager muttered something about his unworthiness. This must have appealed to Beckwith because he looked the man in the eye and told him he could tell he was really a white man. He then proceeded to quote Scripture and lecture the Indian about the origins of the white race, and this seemed to impress the manager. When Beckwith asked him how he could repay his kindness over the cold cut tray, the manager asked to be blessed. To the astonishment of the others in the room, Beckwith drew himself up to full height and placed his hands on the manager's head while reciting all manner of Identity Movement gibberish and, perhaps, a few lines from the Koran and Omar Khayyám. The hotelier left, apparently satisfied that he had been anointed by some sort of holy man.

Beckwith was keeping quiet in the courtroom, and under the watchful eyes of his attorneys he was no longer giving interviews. However, he was temperamentally unsuited to silence, and during breaks he was often overheard making comments to his lawyers or family members.

For instance, after the first group of mostly black prospective jurors took their seats, Beckwith was overheard in the hallway saying in a stage whisper like a buzz saw, "Why I thought I was looking up a stovepipe! All I could see was black!" Another time he announced, "I didn't know whether I should smile at them or throw coconuts!"

DeLaughter and Peters did their best to steer clear of him, but sometimes the man cornered them in the corridor. Once Beckwith was carrying a copy of his paperback biography, and he walked up to DeLaughter and said, "You can buy this now for only eighteen dollars." DeLaughter looked at him in astonishment as he added, "It'll be twenty-two dollars after the trial!"

DeLaughter extracted himself and hurried down the hall.

On Friday afternoon Crisco crouched over his desk in Jackson like an army general preparing his battle plan. Papers and charts were stacked around him. He had neatly printed the name of every state witness and highlighted in green the ones who were from out of town and needed to be put up in hotels.

DeLaughter and Peters were keeping him up to date from Batesville while he put the final touches on the case. He had sent out subpoenas to thirty-seven state witnesses; seventeen of them had testified at the first trial. There were two new names to add to the witness list. Reed Massengill, a writer who happened to be Beckwith's nephew by marriage, had just published a nasty biography of his uncle. Crisco had tracked him down and convinced him to fly down from Knoxville, Tennessee, to read some incriminating documents on the stand. And there was another former FBI agent whom Crisco had located through Massengill's book who could back up Delmar Dennis's story.

It put Crisco in a good mood. The only surprises he liked in a trial were his own.

*   *   *

Myrlie Evers came down with the flu and missed the first week of jury selection. By the weekend she felt well enough to travel to Batesville, but then her husband, Walter Williams, got sick, so she came alone.

Evers was relieved when Benny Bennett picked her up at the airport in nearby Memphis. She liked him, and he made her feel safe. But when she was shown her room at the Ramada, something close to panic welled up in her. Every room was on the ground floor, where a car could pull up to the door. Her room, like all the others, had a picture window looking out on the parking lot. Anyone who wanted to could just drive up, blast through that window, and be done before anyone, even Bennett, could react. A wave of fear passed through her. She could hardly sleep that night.

On Monday morning she took a seat, alone, in the back of the courtroom. Even though she was expected to testify, the judge had given her special permission to witness the trial. She had a yellow legal pad in her lap, and her hands were steady as she quietly took notes, but inside her heart was jumping. At the front of the room was the man she had pursued for thirty years. It was the first time she had seen him since 1964.

Beckwith was particularly agitated that morning. He could not seem to stay in his seat. He paced around and sat next to Thelma. Both of them craned their necks and peered myopically at the back of the room. If Beckwith could not see Evers, he seemed to sense her presence. She was like a force field, drawing the focus of the press and the sheriffs, pulling the center of attention away from Beckwith. Whenever she was around, Beckwith seemed gloomy and distracted.

When she finally met his gaze and looked into those cold gun-barrel eyes, she felt strangely liberated. She had done it. She had faced Medgar's killer one more time, and now she could dismiss him from her mind. He was a nonperson, like a gnat she could casually brush away from her face. She shook off his stare and returned to her notes.

During a break Bennett saw Evers sitting by herself and walked over to talk with her. They chatted pleasantly, then Bennett told her something he had never mentioned before. "You know, Miz Evers, my daddy was one of the detectives who came to your house the morning your husband was shot."

Evers looked at Bennett with wide-open eyes, then said in a hushed voice, almost apologetically, "Oh, Benny. Do you know that I must have hated your father?"

Bennett told her that was all right. "In your position, I would have felt the same way," he said.

The jury was finally selected on Wednesday morning, January 26. Both defense and prosecution were allowed to strike twelve names from the panel and two from the list of alternates. Just about any reason would do. Kitchens removed a few potential jurors who had glared angrily at Beckwith and another one because she looked like Myrlie Evers. Peters rejected one elderly World War II veteran because he seemed like a "clone" of the defendant.

When it was over, Peters and DeLaughter were smiling. It was their jury to lose. The tally was eight blacks to four whites. The ages ranged from thirty to seventy, but only four black jurors were old enough to remember Evers's murder. It was a working-class jury, a panel of Wal-Mart shoppers of all complexions. Half of them hadn't finished high school. There were factory workers, truck drivers, a cook, a maid, a secretary, the white comanager of a Wendy's restaurant, and a black minister. When they went home to pack their bags for what was now expected to be a two-week trial, many of them didn't own suitcases. When they disembarked from the bus that night at the hotel where they would be sequestered in Jackson, several jurors trundled their clothes into the elegant lobby of the Edison-Walthall Hotel in laundry baskets and plastic garbage bags.

27

The Testimony of Ghosts

TO CONVICT Byron De La Beckwith, Bobby DeLaughter and Ed Peters had to resurrect Medgar Evers, then kill him all over again. They had to make people care about Evers and show that his death mattered as much today as it did thirty years ago. They also had to transform Beckwith from the addled old gray-headed grandfather at the defense table into a fanatic racist and a black-hearted, cold-blooded killer. There was only one person who could do all these things for them.

"Call Myrlie Evers," DeLaughter said.

The out-of-town jury was seated next to the judge's bench. Some jurors craned their necks to watch Evers walk through the door. She wore a simple gray jacket over a black skirt. Her face was solemn and composed as she settled into the witness chair. It was an eerie moment: the same teak-paneled courtroom in Jackson; the same wooden pews filled with a smattering of friends, supporters, and college students; the same defendant with his arm draped over his chair, the dim light from the art deco chandeliers glinting vaguely off the gold watchband on his wrist.

Beckwith had yawned elaborately during DeLaughter's opening statement earlier that morning. He sat quietly while Bobby outlined the case against him, promised the jury some new witnesses, and told them how for years Beckwith had gloated about beating the system. Now, finally, the state would be able to prove that the bullet that killed Medgar Evers was "aimed by prejudice, propelled by hatred and fired by a back-shooting coward," and the coward was Byron De La Beckwith.

Beckwith watched with some interest as Merrida Coxwell made his brief opening remarks. The defense, said Coxwell, would prove that it was physically impossible for the defendant to have committed this crime. He was ninety miles away at the time of the murder.

Some of the spectators were surprised at Coxwell's lackluster, narrow presentation. Where were the great conspiracy theories that had been hinted at for years? Where was the FBI plot, the list of other suspects, the sabre-rattling of previous hearings that this was a political trial and nothing more?

Dozens of reporters were covering the trial from the courtroom balcony, a place that had once been reserved for "colored" spectators. As much as the television stations and Court TV lawyers had pleaded and threatened lawsuits, Judge Hilburn refused to allow a video camera in the courtroom. As usual Mississippi was years behind the rest of the country in this practice, and Hilburn didn't want to set any more precedents than necessary with this trial. Besides nobody in government wanted to inflame the masses. Every law enforcement officer in the area was on alert for the duration of the trial.

The reporters in the press gallery whispered and wrote notes to each other until Myrlie Evers entered the courtroom. Then everyone fell silent and stayed that way. Nobody even cleared his throat as she spoke.

"State your name please," Bobby DeLaughter said.

"My name is Myrlie Evers."

She glanced over at the defense table just once, and she gave Beckwith a long, cool look. Then she turned her eyes away from him and focused on Bobby.

Her testimony began with who she was now. She was married to Walter Williams, and was a retired public works commissioner of the city of Los Angeles. She resided in Los Angeles and Oregon.

Then, slowly, Bobby walked her back into the past.

Yes, she had been married before, she said. Her first husband's name was Medgar Wiley Evers, and they were wed on December 24, 1951. They had met "the first hour" of her first day at Alcorn College.

The jurors watched her carefully. Some of them leaned toward her, as if to hear better. But her voice was strong and mellifluous as she recalled the landmarks of her life with Medgar: his rejection from law school because of his race, his job as the first NAACP field secretary in Mississippi, his role in James Meredith's enrollment at Ole Miss, his work to change the way things were in the state.

The defense objected when DeLaughter asked Mrs. Evers what her husband was "trying to change" in Mississippi. Kitchens was overruled.

"He wanted to integrate the schools," she said. "To open swimming pools, use libraries, go to department stores, and to be called by name instead of just 'boy' or 'girl.' "

A few of the younger members of the jury looked surprised. The older black folks nodded softly. That was what you could die for thirty years ago.

She told the jury about the last time she had seen Medgar, how he got into his car that morning and then came out again and hugged her "in a very special embrace" and told her to take care of herself. How he called from work that day.

Then Myrlie Evers told the jury what happened in the early morning hours of June 12, 1963. She told them the story she had repeated so often before, but her face showed them she was seeing it and hearing it all over again: the sound of the car motor, the slam of the door, the horrible rifle blast, her race to the front door, the sight of her husband lying in his own blood, the children screaming, "Daddy! Get up!" and her own screams.

DeLaughter pulled out a stack of black-and-white photographs and began showing them to her. There was her house on Guynes Street, this was Medgar's car, here was the thick pool of blood on the carport. Bobby entered each photo into evidence and passed them to the jury. Then he did something that Myrlie Evers wasn't expecting.

"Could you identify this please?" he asked as he handed her a snapshot-size color photograph.

Myrlie stared at the picture for a long moment, and for the first time her eyes filled with tears, and her voice cracked. "This is Medgar in his casket," she said.

Over the futile objections of the defense DeLaughter was allowed to

circulate the picture among the jurors. What was instantly clear to Myrlie, and quickly dawned on the twelve men and women in the jury
box, was that the picture they were looking at had not been taken at
Medgar's funeral in 1963. It was a very recent picture of an exhumed
body. The perfectly preserved features were those of a man who seemed
to be sleeping.

The crime of Medgar Evers's murder was no longer a distant political
act from a long-ago era. The peculiar alchemy of the testimony was
completed now. Medgar Evers had been brought to life, killed, and literally brought back from the dead in the course of one morning.

Beckwith, who at first seemed to be listening to the testimony,
cradled his head in his hands and looked down, as if he had a headache
or perhaps was falling asleep. All twelve jurors and both alternates sat
with their arms crossed over their chests. Some of them looked at Beckwith like he was a bug.

Bobby DeLaughter spent the rest of the day enhancing the spell. The
case against Beckwith would not only be recounted; it would be reenacted.

Houston Wells was much too feeble to testify at this trial. Bobby and
Crisco had found another witness from the murder scene who could
bring it to life. Willie Quinn was a very old man now. He seemed stunned
and somewhat confused as he ambled to the stand in his Sunday suit. He
couldn't hear the questions and couldn't recall most things about the
night Medgar Evers was shot. But he remembered one thing well, and his
voice was good and loud when he told it.

Quinn had been riding to the hospital in the back of Houston Wells's
station wagon when Evers had come awake and tried to sit up.

"Did he say anything, Mr. Quinn?"

"Yes, sir. He said, 'Turn me loose!' "

Charlie Crisco testified that he had been present at the exhumation of
Medgar Evers's body in Arlington National Cemetery in June 1991. He'd
accompanied the body to Albany, New York, where he had documented
the autopsy. Pictures and X rays had been taken, and lead fragments had
been removed from the body in Crisco's presence. They were entered
into evidence.

The fragments were too small to be of much use, except as a psychological anchor for the jurors. They were real; they had a physical weight. This was not just a case made from paper and words and memories.

DeLaughter next called Dr. Michael Baden, who had performed the second autopsy of Evers's body. DeLaughter lingered on Baden's credentials as the director of forensic sciences for the New York State Police. Baden stated that he had reviewed the autopsies of both John F. Kennedy and Martin Luther King, Jr., for the congressional investigations into their assassinations.

It didn't hurt the prosecution one bit to link Evers's name with Kennedy's and King's in front of a predominantly black jury. It telegraphed to every member of the jury that this was an important case indeed.

Baden was an articulate, animated witness. He spoke with a jackhammer New York accent that created a jarring counterpoint to DeLaughter's slow drawl. He was a tall man with glasses and thinning gray hair that curled over his ears.

Like a patient teacher Baden set up his X-ray charts, took out his pointer, and explained to the jury how he knew the man he had examined was Medgar Evers. Here, he showed them, was the old football injury in his left ankle. And here was where a bullet had exploded through his chest, fracturing two ribs.

The slug, he said, had left a "starburst pattern" consistent in every way with a high-powered rifle, such as a .30/06. He'd removed lead fragments that had splintered off the bullet as it had passed through the chest.

At this point DeLaughter tried to introduce several photographs from Baden's autopsy. Kitchens objected, and the judge removed all but three of the least gory photos to be shown to the jury. Some of them gasped as they examined the pictures.

Baden testified that Evers's corpse was the "most pristine" body he had ever seen in his many years of experience. "The body was as if it had been embalmed the day before," he said with some awe.

There was not much the defense could do to tear down such an obviously qualified witness. Kitchens made a stab at it anyway. He got Baden to admit that the rest of the fatal bullet was missing from evidence, that the lead fragments were not identifiable with any specific caliber bullet, and that bullets from other weapons, such as .357 Magnum pistols, can travel at the same velocity as those from a high-powered rifle.

The only point the defense lawyer managed to score off the famous pathologist was when Kitchens tried to trip him up about his knowledge of guns. He asked him whether a .38 was "like the guns the officers carry in this courtroom." Baden shrugged amiably and said he didn't know much about guns; he just knew what bullets did to bodies.

If Beckwith enjoyed Kitchens's sarcastic treatment of the city-boy Yankee who didn't know a .38 from a .45, he didn't show it. The defendant looked for all the world to be sound asleep.

The rest of the afternoon was devoted to the eerie encore performances of some of the witnesses of 1964.

Dr. Forrest Bratley, the pathologist who had conducted Evers's first autopsy, took the stand. The white-haired, bespectacled old doctor, who had retired in 1978 after fifty years of practice, repeated his findings that Evers had died of massive blood loss caused by a bullet wound in his right chest. He identified a black-and-white picture of the body showing the bloody exit wound, which was passed to the jury.

Next up was Kenneth Adcock, who had walked out of the courtroom the last time as a seventeen-year-old boy and reentered as a forty-seven-year-old man. He was tall and rangy and wore a bright orange shirt and blue pants.

Adcock told the court how he had been walking with Betty Jean Coley on the night of June 11, 1963, and how just after midnight they heard a loud boom right behind them. There was a lady screaming and then the sound of someone running in the bushes.

Coxwell had some questions for this witness. Had Adcock seen anyone running? He had not. Had he heard a car start up? No, he hadn't.

Betty Jean Coley was dead, but Bobby DeLaughter wanted her to testify from the grave. He asked that her testimony be read from the transcripts of the first trial in 1964.

Naturally there was a legal skirmish over this issue. Coxwell and Kitchens argued that introducing old testimony was prejudicial to their client. It denied him due process, since the rules had changed in thirty years. They pointed out that Beckwith's lawyers hadn't had access to the police reports that were now provided under modern discovery rules.

There was no way they could cross-examine the witness as effectively in 1964 as they could now.

DeLaughter argued that the procedure had been allowed in earlier criminal cases in Mississippi. There was no reason to disallow it now.

Judge Hilburn had apparently thought this one over already because he quickly denied the defense motion. Betty Jean Coley was permitted to testify through the voice of Mary Lynn Underwood, a bright, rosy-cheeked legal secretary in the D.A.'s office.

Underwood read the part with such feeling that she might have been trying out for a community theater production of the Beckwith trial. Merrida Coxwell added to the illusion by cross-examining her, each reading their part from the decades-old transcript.

When the state called retired detective John Chamblee to describe the crime scene, the defense had its first real opportunity to bring out the inconsistencies in the old police reports. Chamblee was tall and balding. He recounted his career for the court: a police officer for twenty-two years, then arson investigator for the state; he'd retired three years earlier.

O. M. Luke was too weak to testify, and Fred Sanders was in bed with a slipped disk. DeLaughter needed Chamblee to set the scene for the investigation and to testify that a bullet had been recovered from the kitchen counter. Chamblee also had seized Beckwith's car from a lot in Greenville after the arrest in 1963. He recalled seeing a Shriners emblem in the car.

Jim Kitchens rose to cross-examine Chamblee. "Is it at all difficult for you to remember?" Kitchens asked the old detective.

"I wish I could remember all of it," he said

"There's more that you don't remember than do?"

"Yes."

Kitchens asked him if he remembered that he had worked in 1972 as a probation officer in the district where Kitchens had been D.A. Chamblee laughed and said that was right. He'd forgotten to mention it. Kitchens made the point that it was hard to remember what happened twenty years ago, let alone thirty.

In his cross-examination Kitchens was able to make a number of points: Were there many suspects in the police reports? Yes. Have some of those written reports been lost? Yes again.

As he went along, Kitchens was able to insert some of those maddening, confusing early leads, tips, and dead ends that make a case look weaker in court. Wasn't there a bail bondsman in Jackson who'd had a gun just like this? Hadn't three men been seen sitting in a local hotel room with a rifle? Hadn't there been talk in town that the police had done this murder? Did the reports talk about a Shreveport man who had been a suspect?

Chamblee's memory wasn't that clear, but there it all was in the stack of police reports in Kitchens's hand.

Did you get a report of three men running by the house on Guynes Street? Kitchens got Chamblee to say that there had been a crowd of twenty-five to thirty bystanders around the Evers home when the detectives arrived. The home had not yet been roped off as a crime scene, although some uniformed officers had been deployed around the house. The gun was found in a two-acre lot of overgrown weeds more than two hundred yards from the house. The bullet that was found in the house could never be positively matched to that gun.

"Did it ever occur to you," Kitchens asked, "that the person who killed Mr. Evers had not fired that rifle?"

"No," Chamblee replied, "When you find evidence of that nature you go with it until you find something else."

While the job of a prosecutor is to create a logical scenario for the commission of a crime, the role of the defense attorney is to create confusion. He has to show the jury that a crime didn't necessarily happen a certain way, that there were all sorts of other characters lurking around and motives for the murder, and that the police didn't do as thorough a job as they say they did. Confusion leads to doubt, and doubt wins an acquittal, or at least a hung jury.

After nearly an hour of watching Jim Kitchens wave around sheets of paper and an old, not very spry detective rub his hands together trying to remember details from thirty years ago, the jury seemed adequately confused. How much doubt this created remained to be seen.

On Friday morning, January 28, Myrlie Evers took her place in the front row of seats, near the door and directly in front of the jury box. Nan Evers, Charles's ex-wife, sat by her side. The sheriff had assigned Myrlie two bodyguards, two veteran black officers, and they were always nearby.

On the other side of the aisle was Beckwith's entourage, an assortment of relatives and right-wing groupies. There was Thelma, Kim McGeoy, Little Delay, Delay VIII, a young man who published a hate sheet in northern Mississippi, and a smattering of curious old Kluckers.

The space behind the bar was crowded with security men, state VIPs, and various observers from the D.A.'s office. Benny Bennett, stuffed into a suit and tie and snakeskin boots, sat within easy reach of Judge Hilburn. He glowered quietly at the spectator gallery while he slowly kneaded a ball of plastic putty in his very large hand. From time to time Cynthia Speetjens, or Linda Anderson, or whoever wasn't in court at the moment would slip in the back door and sit with Bennett to watch the proceedings.

There were motions to deal with before the jury came in. The prosecution was asking to remove Beverly Perkins, one of the alternate jurors, after a *Clarion-Ledger* article suggested that her husband might be in the Klan. When the reporter, Grace Simmons, called the woman's husband and asked whether he was a Klansman, he seemed peeved.

"Yeah, I knew I was accused of being one," she quoted him as saying. "I ain't going to tell you yes or no. . . . I don't know whether you are black, white, yellow, green or purple. But it ain't no different. A white man's got the same right to be a member of the Ku Klux Klan as a colored man being a member of the NAACP."

This was alarming news to DeLaughter and Peters. They had always worried about getting a ringer on the jury. But they still didn't have proof that the man was in the Klan. If he was, the juror could be disqualified for lying to the court because one of Peters's questions to everyone had been, "Do you know anyone who is a member of the Klan?" What made things worse was that, unknown to any reporters, one of the elderly jurors had high blood pressure that was acting up. She was close to quitting the panel, and that would put the alternate in the jury box.

Judge Hilburn decided to delay any decision on the issue while the matter was investigated. For now the woman could stay. (There was never any evidence that the Klan story was true or that the juror lied.)

Doc Thaggard took retired detective O.M. Luke's part on the stand. He read from the transcript in his deep Neshoba County monotone, sounding exactly like, well, a homicide detective. With Bobby DeLaughter playing Bill Waller, Doc answered the questions where Luke had described finding the rifle stuffed into the honeysuckle vines the morning after the murder.

Later former captain Ralph Hargrove would appear as himself, now snowy-haired and walking with a slight limp, but sharp and lucid. He described lifting the fingerprint from the scope and later matching it with the print of Beckwith's right index finger. There was no talk this time about how "fresh" the print had seemed to Hargrove. Although Hargrove was an experienced and thorough investigator, in these days of DNA testing and computer reconstructions, the impressions of a local cop with a matchbook degree in fingerprint identification would not be too helpful to the state.

Times had changed, and that was never any clearer than when Kitchens, in his cross-examination of Hargrove, made one mild attempt to discredit Medgar Evers. He asked Hargrove whether he had ever fingerprinted Evers, and Hargrove said yes, for disturbing the peace.

You could actually hear the bodies stiffen in the courtroom, along with the outraged inhalation of breath. Kitchens quickly withdrew from this tactic, although he did attempt to explain, after the theatrical objections of Peters, that he was just trying to show that Beckwith had not been alone in his stance to uphold segregation, that others, even policemen, had felt the same way. It was Kitchens's only attempt to blame the victim, and it backfired.

It was midmorning when a slender, well-dressed man with trim brown hair and a neat mustache took the stand.

"State your name please," Bobby DeLaughter said.

"Thorn McIntyre."

Beckwith stared intently at his old accuser, but McIntyre barely gave him a glance.

Of all the free-flowing hatreds and resentments swirling around this case, probably more invective was flung in the direction of McIntyre than at any other party. If anyone talked to Beckwith's friends in Greenwood, and even some who were not his friends, he or she was likely to hear what a low-down dirty deed McIntyre had done selling out another white man for the reward money, and how the good people of Greenwood had shunned young Thorn and driven him out of Mississippi. Almost none of this was true. Since the reward had never been paid,

McIntyre never collected a dime. He hadn't been hounded out of town. He stayed on in Greenwood until 1972, until a car wreck, a divorce, and a new business strategy had pointed him in the direction of Alabama, and he started a new life there.

Now he was fifty-six years old and a successful real estate developer in Montgomery. If he was unhappy about having to go through another trial, he kept it to himself.

He sat stoically in the witness box and repeated his story while a number of white people who wished him ill glared at him from the spectator pews.

McIntyre said that he had traded the barrel and action of an Enfield rifle to Beckwith back in 1960.

Bobby picked up the rifle from under the defense table and walked it over to McIntyre. Was this the gun? Thorn had a good look and pronounced it almost identical to the one he had once owned. DeLaughter took the weapon back and held it up in front of the jury.

Beckwith was hyperalert. Throughout the trial, whenever the word "gun" was mentioned, Beckwith's head would shoot up like a napping dog hearing the word "bone." He leaned forward for a better look at the long-missing rifle.

The dull black gun metal of the long barrel and scope and the burnished mahogany stock seemed to suck all the light out of that corner of the room. The rifle radiated menace, just as it had thirty years ago. Bobby offered it to the first juror, who held it for a second and then passed it on, as if it were burning his hands. The second juror, a thirty-year-old unemployed black man named Frank Boyce, wouldn't even touch the gun. It was passed over him to the next man in the row. Most of the jurors looked as if they knew how to handle a rifle, and they examined it curiously. A seventy-year-old black minister named Elvage Fondren spent several minutes scrutinizing the weapon, running his hand over the smooth stock, holding the barrel to the light to read the serial number himself.

In cross-examination Kitchens asked McIntyre to look at the rifle. Weren't the serial numbers etched into a thin metal plate attached to the barrel below the scope? McIntyre said they were. Since Enfield parts are interchangeable, could those serial numbers on the receiver plate have come from a different rifle? Thorn said he supposed so.

When McIntyre stepped down from the stand, the rifle was still in plain view, resting heavily and upright against the dark wooden witness stand directly in front of the jury.

The fifth floor of the courthouse was humming like a hive during the two-hour lunch break that day. Sheriff's deputies stood guard by the elevator to eject unwelcome visitors. The long table in the conference room was laid out with plates of hamburgers and cold cuts and slices of homemade layer cake for the dozens of witnesses, law officers, and in-convenienced A.D.A.s.

Bobby DeLaughter wolfed down a sandwich then wandered back to Cynthia's office. He looked tired and pale, like a man who was fighting a bad cold and wasn't getting any sleep. All week long faxes, letters, and phone calls had been coming in to the D.A.'s office, most of them directed at him, some of them cursing him for persecuting an old man, some of them accusing him of wasting the taxpayer's money to advance his career.

Most alarming was a letter from a ranking legislator who had a direct effect on the prosecutor's budget. He let them know what a big mistake they were making in pursuing this prosecution and that there would be no safety net under them when they fell. The legislator told Peters not to bother replying to the letter; he didn't want to hear from him.

It made Bobby laugh when people accused him and Ed Peters of scoring political points by trying Beckwith. If anything, the trial was making dogmeat out of his political future, such as it was. Bobby flopped down in the chair across from Cynthia's desk.

She looked at him with a wry smile. "It's gonna be a tidal wave," she said.

"You think so?" Bobby said with a sigh. "I have no idea how it's going. I've been too busy to watch the jury."

"Tidal wave," she said again, and Bobby seemed happier.

Other news that day also made him happy, even hopeful. It was something that might turn out to be another of those out-of-the-blue miracles that this case had been built on.

The trial had been getting a decent amount of attention from the national news media. It might not have been as exciting as the story of Nancy Kerrigan and Tonya Harding, two Olympic skating rivals who were dominating the news these days, but the opening of the trial had put the Beckwith case near the top of every CNN news cycle.

The spot was still running every half hour on Friday morning when a communications manager in Chicago named Mark Reiley came down with the flu and called in sick. There was nothing for him to do but lie on the couch and flip on the tube. When he saw the familiar face on the TV screen, he thought about it for a while, then called information and got the number for the D.A.'s office in Jackson, Mississippi.

Jeanie Stewart took the call from Mark Reiley. The phone had been ringing off the hook for weeks now with cranks and complainers and Yankee reporters demanding all kinds of things she wasn't about to write down on those pink message slips that were spilling all over her desk. But there was something about Reiley's voice that told her she had better take this one seriously, copy down the number in Chicago carefully, and see that Crisco got the message right away. It wasn't every day, after all, that someone called saying they had new evidence.

Bobby was still talking to Cynthia just after noon when Ed Peters and Charlie Crisco poked their heads in the doorway. DeLaughter stood up to join them.

"Well, should we fly this guy down from Chicago?" Peters asked, smiling. "Or do you think he's hallucinating?"

Friday afternoon was cold and gloomy, the perfect setting for the testimony of ghosts.

John Davidson felt strange when he sat in the witness box and read the words of the long-dead Duck Goza. Davidson was a handsome young Texan, the newest addition to the D.A.'s office, and, like all trial lawyers, he enjoyed any opportunity to be in court. But this felt eerie, not quite right.

Davidson read Goza's version of how he had traded Beckwith a Golden Hawk scope one evening in May 1963 and that the scope was the one attached to the Enfield rifle in evidence.

The whole afternoon was taken up with a parade of "dead" witnesses, who were called back mainly to establish the chain of custody of the long-ago evidence. Davidson read the testimony of Francis Finley, the late FBI agent who had carried the rifle and bullet to Washington for testing. Crisco read the part of Sam Burdon, another agent who had handled the evidence.

Then Tommy Mayfield took the stand.

Mayfield also was an A.D.A. His job was prosecuting narcotics cases, but his avocation was clearly the stage. He was an accomplished blue-grass bassist, and he would sometimes gig around Jackson with some friends. He was known around the office as a storyteller and a mimic and a collector of obscure facts and figures. This was his moment.

Tommy started off reading the testimony of J. R. Gilfoy, the late Hinds County sheriff and a man Mayfield had known personally. Tommy captured the flinty accent just right.

Then came his reading of Herbert Speight, the cabdriver who had testified that Beckwith had asked him where he could find the house of Medgar Evers. Mayfield found the right accent for the country boy turned cabbie. He seemed not so much to be reading Speight's words as to be channeling him.

Mayfield led the jury through the scene at the Trailways station in Jackson and on through the lineup in which Speight had picked out Beckwith. But Tommy's finest moments came when Merrida Coxwell read Stanny Sanders's cross-examination of Speight. The defense attorney had grilled the petulant cabbie about how his story had changed since the defense team had interviewed him in his rooming house.

"We asked you, wondered why you had been subpoenaed, didn't we?" asked Coxwell, being Sanders.

"You sure did," snapped Mayfield being Speight.

"And you said you didn't know, you guessed it was because you had seen this man that you believed or identified to be Mr. Beckwith about a week before Evers was shot?"

"That's right."

"And we asked you specifically, did we not, if the name of Medgar Evers was mentioned, didn't we?"

"You did."

"You told us no, didn't you, Mr. Speight?"

"Yessir," said Tommy Mayfield in someone else's voice. "I don't talk to two parties at the same time."

At that the sixty or so spectators broke out laughing, and the judge chuckled and so did the jury, and even Beckwith smiled, which is just what had happened thirty years earlier, in the same courtroom, when the same words were spoken.

*   *   *

When the trial resumed on Monday, January 31, the black Enfield rifle was placed where DeLaughter had left it on Friday, leaning against the witness stand, always within the jury's sight, occupying the northern-most corner of their peripheral vision, which included the stoic widow to the south and, dead center, the dozing or fidgeting figure of Byron De La Beckwith.

Beckwith's attention was forever on the gun when it was in his line of sight. Once, when the jury was out of the room, he walked over to Henry Brinston, the deputy court clerk in charge of the evidence vault. "Could my grandson look at the gun?" Beckwith asked politely. "He hasn't seen it before."

Brinston could hardly believe what he was hearing: Beckwith wanted to see *the* gun? He said all right, go ahead. The little old man and his big, beefy namesake ambled across the room for a better look.

Brinston watched them closely. He was astonished that this trial was happening at all. He had been a kid when Medgar Evers was alive, but he remembered him well. He grew up in Jackson, and he remembered marching on Capitol Street in the days of the movement, being thrown in the back of a hot, stinking garbage truck, and then penned up like an animal in the stockyards. Brinston wasn't about to let himself believe that a Mississippi jury would convict a man like Beckwith. No matter what the members of the jury learned in this phenomenal trial, no matter what conclusion they reached with their hearts, their minds would tell at least some of them, *I've got to go home to my neighborhood and my job and live for the rest of my life with this verdict.* Brinston was sure it was going to be another hung jury. This was still Mississippi.

"I like this kind of rifle," Brinston heard Beckwith tell the boy. "It has less recoil."

Kitchens looked up and noticed what was going on. He hurried over to shoo them away from the murder weapon.

There was more technical evidence Monday morning about Beckwith's fingerprints and handwriting. Dr. Bratley returned to describe the livid bruise he'd noticed over Beckwith's eye and how it was consistent with the shape and size of the Golden Hawk scope. Witnesses old and new walked the jury through the chain of evidence: the rifle, the cartridges, the mutilated bullet. By noon Bobby DeLaughter had tied Beckwith to the murder weapon. Now he needed to put Beckwith at the scene and give him a motive for the killing.

DeLaughter started with Barbara Holder, the former carhop who had stopped by Joe's Drive In thirty-one years earlier. She was fifty-two now and overweight, with short gray hair. She was wearing dark glasses and walked with a cane. Her voice was surprisingly deep. She told how she had been "hanging out" with her friend Martha Jean O'Brien, a waitress on duty that night. She said that they had been talking over by the carhop booth around 9 P.M. when a white Valiant had come from behind the building and backed up into a dark corner of the parking lot. The car was muddy, and it had a long antenna on it, like a patrol car. She sounded like she knew all about cars and how they looked.

Holder explained that she had then left for a while but came back to Joe's just before the drive-in closed at midnight. The car was still there. Then she noticed it moving, pulling right up to the men's bathroom in the back, and a white man got out. She remembered he was five foot seven or five foot eight with dark hair, wearing dark clothes. Holder was shown a black-and-white picture of Beckwith's Valiant, the way it looked in June of 1963, and she said it was the car she had seen that night.

Coxwell stood up to ask a few questions in cross-examination. He tried to confuse Holder about where she had been standing and what she saw, and when. The more Coxwell tried to trip her up and challenge her memory, the more she dug in.

"I can't remember two weeks ago," she told him. "But I remember 1963."

A few jurors chuckled. They all seemed better attired today — sports jackets for the men, nice dresses for the women — as if someone had brought them good clothes over the weekend. They seemed to be trying to dress more like the lawyers and big-city secretaries they saw every day now. They dressed as if they knew this was serious business, as serious as a church service or a funeral.

Bobby kept up the pace. He was painting a picture for the jury of the world of Delta Drive and Guynes Street on a hot June night thirty-one years ago, and he brought back the people who had been in that world: the cops and carhops, cabdrivers and teenage lovers. Now he introduced two grown men who had been boys throwing a model airplane in the back lots along the strip when a white Valiant cruised by.

Just as he'd testified in 1964, when he was sixteen, Ronald Jones, now forty-six and wearing a tight blue suit, told the court how he and his friend Robert Pittman had seen what they'd thought was a police car circling the neighborhood on the night of June 11, 1963.

Ronald Mark Acy, who had worked in Pittman's Grocery when he was sixteen, was paunchy now and his hair was receding. He remembered seeing that white car on Saturday night, June 8, 1963. It had been parked in the little alley next to the Pittmans' house. When he had gotten closer to take a look, he'd noticed the long antenna and a Shriners emblem of a star and big sword hanging from the rearview mirror. He knew it was a Shriners symbol because his parents used to go dancing at the Shriners hall.

Robert Pittman testified last. He wore a pink button-down shirt, and his voice was middle-aged deep now. He was so nervous Bobby had to slow him down, but he recalled the details. On June 11 he had seen a white Valiant with a ten-foot aerial on the side, and it was driving slowly up and down the highway. Pittman saw it parked in the alley, the same as Acy, and he noticed the "Masonic or some type of emblem" hanging off the mirror.

Pittman then added something that he hadn't said in 1964. He had seen that same Valiant in the parking lot of Joe's Drive In that same night about 11 P.M. It had been just where Barbara Holder had said it was.

When Coxwell cross-examined Pittman and asked him why he hadn't said he'd seen the car in Joe's lot during the first trial, Pittman said, "I don't really believe anybody asked me about it at that trial."

Just as Bill Waller had done in the first trial, DeLaughter made a convincing case that a car just like Beckwith's had been in Medgar Evers's neighborhood the night he was killed and the weekend before that. What DeLaughter had that Waller hadn't had was the modern technique of photo enlargement.

DeLaughter showed the jury a photograph taken of Beckwith's Valiant the week of his arrest. You could see the aerial and the trailer hitch, but the interior was dark and indistinct. DeLaughter called an FBI technician, who had blown up a portion of the photograph twenty times. In the enlargement the sword and crescent moon of a Shriners emblem was clearly visible, dangling from the rearview mirror.

*   *   *

Reed Massengill's book publicist had been telling reporters that the author would testify at Beckwith's trial, so his appearance was not a complete surprise.

But the defense objected to his testimony and the letters that De-Laughter planned to have him read into evidence. Kitchens argued that letters from 1955 and 1956 were too remote, too prejudicial. The judge rejected that argument but disallowed one letter that Beckwith had written to his first wife while they were married. Massengill was allowed to take the stand.

Beckwith watched closely as Reed was sworn in. He stared at Massengill intently, as if trying to catch his eye. Massengill looked stranded and friendless. He was a tall, slender young man with carefully barbered brown hair and round, perpetually startled-looking eyes. He was wearing a good gray suit. He nervously rubbed his hands together, but when he spoke, he seemed surprisingly self-assured, as if the voice did not go with the body.

Massengill explained that Beckwith, his uncle, had approached him to write a book about Beckwith several years earlier. In the course of Massengill's research he had been given a number of letters, documents, tapes, and the manuscript of an earlier book by Beckwith. He'd also been supplied with dozens of letters that Beckwith had written to his ex-wife, Mary Louise "Willie" Williams Beckwith, Massengill's aunt. She was now dead. In one of those letters, written in 1976, Beckwith had written that he was "heavily involved in Klan work," the only time he was known to have admitted this.

Beckwith was on red alert for this testimony. He leaned forward eagerly and held up his hearing aid in Massengill's direction. But once his nephew started reading his letters, Beckwith testily pulled out his earpiece and tossed it on the table.

Another letter Massengill read to the court had been written by his uncle to the Jackson *Daily News* in 1957. "Believe it or not," he wrote, "the NAACP, under the direction of its leaders, is doing a first-class job of getting itself in a position to be exterminated!"

When it came time for cross-examination, Kitchens took a sarcastic tone with Massengill. Wasn't Reed writing about his uncle for money? Massengill allowed that he got paid to write. And his uncle never told him he killed Medgar Evers? He did not.

Kitchens tried to paint Beckwith as a harmless, loudmouthed eccentric. Wasn't he a talkative person? And someone who read the Bible a lot? And wasn't it true he drank only water he got in Georgia and carried with him to Tennessee? Reed agreed that Beckwith did all these things and that he had hired another author to write his earlier manuscript for him, that those weren't his words, although they were his thoughts.

Kitchens moved for a mistrial based on this secondhand testimony. His motion was denied.

Mary Ann Adams was a hefty, no-nonsense woman of fifty-one, a bookkeeper who carried her boxy tan handbag like a weapon. In 1966 she was twenty-four years old and working for the Holmes County Cooperative. She was having lunch with a friend in a small town near Greenwood one September day when her friend noticed a group of men at another table.

"That's Byron De La Beckwith," the friend told her, and he went over to talk to Beckwith.

After a while the friend brought Beckwith back to the table to meet Adams. He introduced Beckwith as "Byron De La Beckwith, the man who shot Medgar Evers." Beckwith reached his hand out to her.

"I refused to shake his hand," she told the court. "I wouldn't shake the hand of a murderer." She said Beckwith got "extremely agitated" and told her that he hadn't killed a man "but a damn chicken-stealing dog — and you know what you have to do when a dog has tasted blood."

Adams had never told anyone, she said, because she'd been under the impression that Beckwith could not be tried again. She came forward when she read that the Hinds County D.A.'s office had reopened the case.

Under cross-examination Adams admitted that she had changed her story somewhat. At first she didn't mention the remark about the "chicken-stealing dog" to the district attorney. She said she didn't trust him. "I called him later to tell him the whole truth," she said.

Next up was Dan Prince, a skinny, bearded middle-aged man who wore a light blue suit and dark blue tie. Prince was an alcoholic and an ex-con who had rented an apartment from Delay and Thelma on Signal Mountain back in 1986. Once, in a casual conversation, Beckwith had told Prince that he had been tried twice in Mississippi "for killing that nigger." According to Prince he'd said, "I had a job to do and I did it and I didn't suffer any more than your wife if she was going to have a baby."

Buddy Coxwell lit into this witness. He brought up Prince's alcoholism, the fact that he had sometimes been drunk when he'd lived on the Beckwiths' property, and that he was unhappy with the Beckwiths because they had evicted him.

"I had a drinking problem," Prince allowed, "but that's not why they evicted me." They had evicted him after police had come on the property to arrest him for vandalism, a charge later dropped. But Coxwell didn't want to get into that.

Coxwell pointed out that Prince hadn't gone to the police with his story but instead had gone to the local newspaper and gotten himself on the front page.

"Do you deny asking the paper for money?" Coxwell asked.

"I do," said Prince, who twisted around in his chair as he answered.

Prince might not have been Bobby DeLaughter's strongest witness, but his story fit in with the others, and it kept the momentum going.

On Tuesday morning DeLaughter was still playing the same theme when he called Elluard "Dick" Davis to the stand. Davis was a sixty-year-old small-press publisher from central Florida. During the late sixties and into the seventies he was in the construction business in Winter Haven, but his main job was as a paid FBI informant who had infiltrated the Ku Klux Klan.

In October 1969 Beckwith was a traveling boat salesman. He was introduced to Davis by a mutual acquaintance, and they met once for supper at a Lum's restaurant. The conversation was not just about boats.

"We discussed his arrest and his trials," Davis said. "He never admitted to me that he was guilty. He never denied it, which I thought was a little strange."

The defense lawyers objected. Davis was allowed to continue.

Davis said Beckwith had told him that "selective killings" were necessary to the right-wing cause. "He said he never asked someone else to do something he would not do himself," Davis testified.

Peggy Morgan, the witness who rode with Beckwith to Parchman penitentiary was up next. She wore a pink suit and pink stiletto heels and had frosted blond hair. Her thin face seemed pinched beneath large

dark glasses. She spoke haltingly, like a woman who knew the conse-
quences of talking too loud.

She told the court that she had lived in Greenwood with her now-
estranged husband, Lloyd, back in the sixties. One afternoon she and
Lloyd had driven up to Parchman to visit Lloyd's brother in prison.
They'd offered a ride to Beckwith. (The judge would not let her say that
Beckwith was going to see Cecil Sessums, who was doing time for the
murder of Vernon Dahmer.)

Peggy sat between her husband and Beckwith in the cab of the pickup.
During the eighty-mile drive Beckwith made conversation.

"He started talking about some bombings," she recalled. "He said that
he had killed Medgar Evers, a nigger, and he wasn't scared to kill again."

Kitchens challenged her credibility in his cross-examination. He used
his smoothest voice to try to grind her into confetti on the stand. She was
a vulnerable target. She couldn't remember exactly when the conversation with Beckwith had taken place, not even the year it had happened.
Kitchens dragged out her troubled family history, things she had told
him during their pretrial interview. She had accused her father of abus-
ing her, and he had later been murdered. Her mother had frozen to
death. Her husband had allegedly carried on an incestuous relationship
with her daughter. She had psychiatric problems and suffered from an
anxiety disorder for which she was treated with medication.

Peggy Morgan meekly conceded all these things. Kitchens's treatment of her only made her seem more sympathetic and somehow more
honest.

DeLaughter gently took over in redirect. "Tell the jury whether any
other traumatic thing happened before," he said.

"He [Beckwith] told me that this better not never get out," she said.

"What effect did this have on you?"

"It made me fear not to say anything."

She said that she had contacted the D.A.'s office after she heard the
case had been reopened because "there was evidence that should be
brought forward." She had no interest in becoming a witness at this trial.

She was encouraged to tell the jury that she was still married to Lloyd
Morgan, but he was now a drifter and she didn't know where he was. He
had contacted her recently, though, after he'd found out she had talked
to the D.A.'s office.

"He said I better not come here and testify," she said in a soft, calm voice. "I would wind up dead."

Later, after the court broke for lunch, the press ambushed Peggy Morgan in the hallway. She gave in to their questions and talked for the TV cameras. She had something she wanted to say. "I want Myrlie Evers to know that I'm sorry," she said. "I'm sorry I didn't come forward sooner."

After so much emotional testimony the long-awaited appearance of Delmar Dennis was somehow anticlimactic. Dennis surprised Crisco by showing up for court in a casual white pullover and slacks instead of a business suit. He wore his wire-rimmed glasses and a full beard.

His appearance in court lent a historical perspective to the case, to tying it to another one of Mississippi's notorious crimes; the Neshoba County murders of Goodman, Chaney, and Schwerner.

Dennis briefly told the story of his days in the White Knights, how he had been a titan responsible for ten Mississippi counties and had reported everything to the FBI. For his trouble, he said, he got one hundred dollars per week expense money. In his flat, nasal drawl Dennis told the jury about the meeting near the swinging bridge back in August 1965, when he had heard Beckwith talk about murder. "He was admonishing the Klan to kill the enemy, from the top on down," Dennis said.

Dennis had been telling reporters that for years. Then he came to the part about Evers. Dennis reported that Beckwith had said, "Killing that nigger did me no more physical harm than your wives have to have when they're having a baby for you."

A dozen heads shot up in the press section, and DeLaughter paused to look at Dennis for a moment. What happened to the part about "inner discomfort"? Was this quote, one that Dennis had repeated in exactly the same way again and again to anyone who'd asked him, only a paraphrase of what Beckwith had supposedly said? The jury, of course, wouldn't know that. This new quote did, however, sound just like what Beckwith had said to Prince.

Naturally Kitchens asked Dennis why he changed his quote, and Dennis just said that he'd he remembered it as best he could. He hadn't recorded the speech, and he admitted that he had never seen the quote written down in any FBI report, although he had told it to an agent.

Kitchens tried to make it seem as if Dennis was just saying these things to sell his books.

The prosecution then called another unexpected witness to stamp Delmar's testimony with the U.S. government seal of approval. Tom Van Riper had been one of Dennis's FBI handlers. DeLaughter and Crisco hadn't known he even existed until they'd seen him quoted in Massengill's book.

Van Riper was able to do what no one had done before: corroborate that Dennis said he had heard Beckwith brag about "killing that nigger." Dennis had, indeed, reported it to him, and they had discussed Beckwith.

Van Riper's testimony cleared up some nagging questions about Dennis's new evidence against Beckwith. In 1965 the Evers case had still been very much open. Why hadn't the FBI passed on this admission to the Hinds County district attorney?

Dennis, said Van Riper, had been the government's most important witness in the case code-named MIBURN, or Mississippi Burning, the one that was used to break the back of the White Knights of the Ku Klux Klan.

"That was the most important thing going at the time," the retired agent said. "The FBI would never have blown an informant as important" as Delmar Dennis. The unspoken coda to that statement lingered in the air: the FBI wouldn't have blown him on a state trial for the killing of a black leader, one that would probably not have ended in a conviction.

Van Riper said that he had written down Dennis's statements and passed them on to his FBI superior, Inspector Joe Sullivan. He assumed they were filed away.

On cross-examination Van Riper admitted that he had no idea what had become of those notes. No one had seen them in more than twenty-five years.

Kitchens and Coxwell fought hard to keep the next witness off the stand. So far the prosecution had produced a motley array of witnesses who had told the jury that Beckwith had bragged to them about killing, but none of them was unimpeachable. There were two FBI informants, one a former Klansman; a woman on Xanax; an alcoholic ex-con; and a bookkeeper who had changed her story.

Mark Reiley had no negatives. The man who had called the district attorney from Chicago in the middle of the trial seemed to be a stable, upstanding citizen. This surprise witness, who had once been a prison guard in Louisiana, had nothing to gain from his testimony against Beckwith.

Kitchens implored the judge to bar his testimony as inherently prejudicial, since it would mean telling the jury that Beckwith had been in prison. Barring that, he asked for a continuance to investigate Reiley's story. Judge Hilburn thought about it, then denied the defense motions. He said that the court could not "orchestrate" the creation of evidence just because it might put one side or the other at a disadvantage. He said he would allow the witness to testify as long as he didn't get into the reason Beckwith had been in prison.

Reiley was a big, red-headed Irishman with a trim mustache, aviator glasses, and a colorful tie. His years in Chicago had flattened out his Louisiana accent, but the southern inflections crept back into his voice as he spun his story for the jury.

He told them that he had decided to call the district attorney on Friday afternoon after watching a newscast about the trial. He told them that he had recognized Beckwith's face on TV and he remembered that when he was a prison guard in Louisiana in 1979, Beckwith had said that he had killed Medgar Evers. It wasn't until Friday that Reiley found out who Evers was.

Ed Peters, who was better at extracting emotional testimony from a witness, handled the direct examination. He urged Reiley to begin at the beginning. Reiley said he came from an abusive, broken home and had been raised by his grandparents. His grandfather had died when he was fourteen, leaving an aching gap in his life.

He had been twenty-one years old, working as a guard in a locked hospital ward for convicts at the Louisiana State Penitentiary in Angola, when he met Beckwith. "He seemed to give me a lot of attention," Reiley said. "He knew I was lacking a father-type figure."

Beckwith called Reiley "Youngblood" and had sat with him for eight to twelve hours a day, talking to him and indoctrinating him in his peculiar brand of religion.

"What did he tell you about black people?" Peters asked.

"Black people were beasts of the field, like animals or fishes. Pale white people were the chosen people to rule over beasts of the field." If they "got out of line," Beckwith had told Reiley, you could "kill them and not feel guilty about it."

The young guard began to lose his faith in Beckwith after he overheard an argument between the prisoner and a black nurse whom he wouldn't allow to touch him. Beckwith called her a nigger. She wouldn't take that talk from him, and soon both of them were screaming. That was when he heard Beckwith shout, "If I could get rid of an uppity nigger like Medgar Evers, I would have no problem with a no-account nigger like you!"

Peters asked whether Beckwith had said anything else about Evers. The young man replied that Beckwith had wanted to impress him with his power and influence in Mississippi. He'd bragged that if he was lying about his status, he would be serving time "for getting rid of that nigger Medgar Evers."

Soon Reiley had started questioning Beckwith's teachings, which enraged Beckwith. When Reiley told him he wasn't going to join his racist organization, Beckwith told him "he knew all along I was a communist nigger-loving bastard." That was the last time they had spoken.

Peters asked Reiley whether he had been pressured or paid in any way for his testimony. Reiley said that he hadn't.

"In fact all he'd gotten was a plane ride from Chicago and a sandwich for lunch?"

"I was lucky for that sandwich," Reiley said quite seriously. There were a few chuckles in the courtroom.

Jim Kitchens couldn't score any points off this witness, and he quickly released him from cross-examination.

It wasn't going to get any better than this. Peters and DeLaughter made a quick decision.

"The State rests," Ed Peters announced.

28

The Last Mile of the Way

On WEDNESDAY MORNING, February 2, the defense opened with another demand for a mistrial or a directed verdict of not guilty. Coxwell mentioned the denial of due process and a speedy trial. He also noted the unfairness of the jury selection process, because the change of venue had discouraged old people from sitting on the jury. Coxwell offered a long list of points in the prosecution's case that he considered unfair to his client, including the fact that the defense had not been given an opportunity to check out Reiley's story. By now Coxwell knew the motion was futile, but it had to go on the record.

Even though spectators had to answer a list of personal questions to get a visitor's pass, then walk through a metal detector and sometimes submit to frisks and handbag searches from unfriendly deputies, more and more of them showed up every day. By now the pews were nearly packed.

Myrlie Evers's coterie continued to grow. Her side of the aisle was the place to see and be seen for movers and shakers in the black community. Congressman Bennie Thompson dropped in. Bea Branch, the new state president of the NAACP, was there, as was William Gibson, chairman of the national NAACP board. Minister Charles X Quinn, local leader of the Nation of Islam, showed up, as did Sam Baily and other old NAACP stalwarts who had been waiting for this day for a long time.

Beckwith's corner was drawing a diverse crowd of relatives and radicals. Today the second row was packed with burly skinheads brought in by Richard Barrett, Jackson's resident neo-Nazi. They sat quietly, arms folded, watching the proceedings. Benny Bennett moved himself into their line of vision and stared at them while he squeezed his wad of putty, a look of grim imagination on his face.

After Judge Hilburn overruled Coxwell's motion, the jury filed in, and the defense of Beckwith got under way. From the beginning Coxwell and Kitchens had refused to concede that the transcripts from the first trial were an authentic and accurate record. They had fought hard to keep the prosecution from reading the testimony of sick or dead witnesses at this trial. This stance, however, did not prevent Merrida Coxwell from announcing that his first witness would be Roy Jones, a dead man, and that his testimony would be read from the transcript.

A private investigator played the part of Jones. Within a few minutes the first of Beckwith's alibi witnesses had told his tale from the grave. Jones, an auxiliary police officer, had sworn that he had seen Beckwith sitting in his white Valiant near the Billups filling station in Greenwood at 11:45 P.M. on the night of June 11, 1963.

Bobby read the cross-examination, selecting specific excerpts from the text to make the point that Jones had testified that the night was pitch dark (according to several earlier witnesses, there had been a bright moon) and that Jones couldn't remember seeing Beckwith any other night that month.

Even though Hollis Cresswell was still alive, Coxwell asked to have his testimony read because the man was in his eighties and in poor health. Ed Peters fought hard to prevent it. He held in his hand a list of eighteen of Cresswell's self-contradictions during his grand jury testimony back in 1990. He was ready to chew the man up in cross-examination. He had to. The alibi witnesses were the biggest problem he faced. If they were believable, he could wind up with another hung jury.

Judge Hilburn allowed Cresswell's testimony to be read. It was the first major blow to the prosecution in a trial that had, so far, been going its way.

Cresswell's testimony was read with feeling, but the jurors didn't seem particularly riveted by the performance. Some jurors actually covered their eyes with their hands.

The veteran Greenwood police lieutenant had sworn that he had seen Beckwith at 1:05 on the morning of June 12, 1963. Beckwith was having his car gassed up at a Shell station in Greenwood. The testimony touched on the details designed to make the story believable: Cresswell knew the time because he and his partner were about to eat a sandwich before a certain store closed; he had heard about Evers's murder on the radio later that morning.

Peters, in his cross-examination, restricted to the written text, made the point that Cresswell had not told his story to the Jackson police or D.A.'s office after Beckwith's arrest, even though the man had sat in jail for eight months.

At 10:30 Wednesday the first live defense witness was sworn in. James Holley was sixty-five now, overweight with a perfectly round, pink head covered with the translucent gray stubble of a military crew cut. When he raised his hand to take the oath, a roll of fat heaved over the collar of his tight maroon sports coat. He looked like a redneck cop from central casting, a young black male's worst nightmare. There were several young black males on the jury, and they eyed him soberly.

Holley seemed relaxed and jovial. He leaned back confidently in the witness chair as Coxwell led him back to a hot June night in 1963. He had been a young patrolman back then, riding with Hollis Cresswell on the graveyard shift.

He allowed that he could recognize Beckwith but didn't know him well and didn't remember how he had met him. Coxwell asked whether they had belonged to the same clubs or church or whether they had visited each other's homes. The answer was no.

Holley told the same story as Cresswell, that they had seen Beckwith at 1:05 A.M., a half hour after the shooting, outside a Greenwood filling station more than ninety miles from Jackson. Ten days later, when Beckwith was arrested for Evers's murder, Holley said he had "put two and two together."

"I knowed we saw him that morning and later that morning heard the man had been shot," he said.

Holley could remember the time he had seen Beckwith, he said, because "we always got a sandwich between one and one-thirty" at Bracci Danton's store and the store closed at 1:30 A.M.

The retired cop described how he had seen Beckwith standing in the lit parking lot of the Shell station while an attendant put gas in his car.

"After you saw Mr. Beckwith, what did you do then?" Coxwell asked.

"When we left, after we saw him gassing up, we went to the grocery store and got a sandwich."

Everyone seemed grateful when the judge called a two-hour lunch break.

At 1:45 that afternoon Ed Peters stood up to begin his cross-examination. As usual he began with a seemingly innocent question: how long had Beckwith and Holley been friends?

Holley was in an even brighter mood after his meal. He was loose and grinning. "Delay's been my friend ever since I've known him," he said. "Shortly after World War Two."

Peters had found an opening, and he was about to pop Holley like a boiled peanut.

Is that why he called him "Dee-lay," Peters asked. Didn't he say Beckwith wasn't his friend?

Holley was still smiling but not so hard. "Sure, he was my friend. Just like I hope you're my friend," he said.

Peters assured him that they were not friends.

Holley's face changed. He started working his hands together, fiddling with his tie. From now on Peters referred to the defendant as "your good buddy Dee-lay," until Kitchens objected and the judge stopped him.

Since Beckwith was his friend, Peters wanted to know whether Holley knew his views on segregation.

"He's outspoken," Holley said. "He speaks his mind. I've never heard him make a derogatory remark about anybody. I don't know if he's a segregationist. You'd have to ask him."

Peters stopped for a moment to let that sink in.

"Did you believe strongly in segregation in 1963?" Peters asked.

"Yessir," Holley said.

"Is that why you came here?"

"Nossir."

Peters kept the man on the stand for two more hours, picking apart every detail of his story. He got him to admit that Beckwith was more than just a casual acquaintance. He found discrepancies in Holley's often-repeated version of events, such as the fact that the patrolmen hadn't gotten a sandwich right after they'd said they'd seen Beckwith; they had patrolled uptown for a while. Peters got Holley to admit that he and Hollis Cresswell had "talked over" their story before testifying.

Peters seemed incredulous that Holley could have seen Beckwith standing with his leg up on the curb from the angle he described. The Valiant and the gas pump would have been in the way.

"Did you see through the car?" Peters demanded, almost yelling. "Over it? Under it?" Holley's big jaw jutted out, and he was getting flustered.

Peters hammered him the hardest over the fact that he had never told his story to any law officers until Beckwith's first trial. "Did you ever go to the police department and tell them what was going on?" Peters asked.

"No."

"Did you ever go to the FBI and tell them what was going on?"

"No."

"You let your buddy Delay stay in jail all that time and never told a single person investigating the case, 'Hey! You've got the wrong guy!'?"

"No police officer ever asked me."

By the time it was over, even some members of the press corps were starting to feel sorry for Holley. It seemed like Ed Peters was kicking a corpse.

It was nearly four o'clock when Peters asked his last question: "Think you and I are still friends?"

Kitchens leaped up to demand a mistrial, but the judge waved him down.

In his redirect Kitchens asked Holley whether he would lie for Beckwith or whether Beckwith had asked him to lie for him. "Nossir," he said to both questions.

Kitchens tried to soften Holley's image with the jury by asking him about his neighbors in Greenwood, who were mostly black. "And we don't have any problems whatsoever," Holley said. For whatever reason Kitchens did not bring up the fact that Holley had been elected to Greenwood's city council, representing a predominantly black district.

After a long and disheartening day, Holley was allowed to go home.

The defense next called John Book, who also had testified in 1964. He had been a senior employee with Delta Liquid Plant Food, and he had spent the day of June 10, 1963, driving around the Delta with Beckwith, testing soil samples from cotton farms. He'd noticed a wound on Beckwith's forehead.

"What kind of a wound?" Coxwell asked.

"A circular, half-moon cut over his eye."

Peters and DeLaughter had already decided that they weren't going to try to prove that the cut over Beckwith's eye had been made the night of the murder. It was good enough to show that he had been firing a rifle, sighting it perhaps, looking down the scope when it kicked and cut him. Peters managed to turn Book's testimony to his advantage.

Did Book remember whether Beckwith had said anything about segregation during that drive? Book didn't recall.

"Do you remember telling the police that you . . ." Peters read from the police report, ". . .'had a hard time keeping Delay's mind on the job because he was talking about segregation?' "

Yes, now Book remembered.

Crowds lined up to get into the courtroom on Thursday morning as word percolated through town that this was the day that Beckwith would take the stand. Thelma entered the courthouse on her husband's arm, wearing her flamingo-pink cape and sporting large, dark safety glasses to protect her eyes from the camera lights. Beckwith had chosen his maraschino-cherry-red blazer for the occasion. People wondered out loud whether his lawyers had picked his outfit to show the jury what a crazy old coot he was. He looked more like a retired carnival barker than a fearsome assassin. But for all his flaming menswear, Beckwith seemed glum and distracted.

The stress was showing on his family as well. Little Delay was snappish. He clumped down the hallways in his reptile-skin boots, toting a box of files, glowering and sometimes yelling at photographers to get out of his way. Thelma wandered about the courtroom until a friend led her back to her seat.

The case was clearly not going well for Byron De La Beckwith. It had not turned into a forum for his twisted beliefs, a platform on which to anoint him as patron saint of the last Confederate holdouts. The case was instead shaping up to be what DeLaughter had said it would be: a murder trial.

The day began with a calamitous setback for the defense. Coxwell had planned to call James Hobby, who had been a surprise witness at the second trial in April 1964. Hobby, who was a truck driver in Jackson at the time of the murder, was going to tell the jury that he drove a Valiant just like Beckwith's and that he had been at Joe's Drive In on the night of the murder.

His story was even more detailed thirty years later and was in some ways inconsistent with newspaper accounts of his earlier testimony. According to the defense, he was now prepared to say that he'd had a big antenna on his Valiant because he was a CB radio buff. He also was going to say that he was a regular customer at Joe's and that he had been there at closing time when a fight had erupted outside. He was going to say that he knew Barbara Holder and insist that he hadn't seen her there. He also remembered hearing the sound of the rifle while he was leaving the restaurant.

Hobby was a treasured witness for the defense. He was an oracle of reasonable doubt, someone who could smash every theory the prosecution had developed to tie Beckwith to the crime scene. There was only one problem: Coxwell had never notified the prosecutors — in writing — that he intended to call Hobby. In the heated arguments before the judge that morning, DeLaughter maintained that he had never heard Hobby's name until after the trial had started. Coxwell insisted that he had told him, orally, that Hobby was a potential witness.

Judge Hilburn had a serious dilemma here, with two prominent lawyers, friends, basically calling each other a liar in his court. He announced that he had to go with the strict interpretation of the law. Written notification was the rule. He denied the witness.

By now Coxwell was trying the case for the appeal. He knew that he could turn the trial into a free-for-all, could drive a whole garbage truck of dirt into the courtroom and dump it in front of the jury. He could rake up the FBI reports and set up all the other scenarios and other suspects — the mystery man from Shreveport at the bus station, the three men in the hotel room with the rifle, the blue pickup with the rifle in the gun rack that had been noted hanging around at a demonstration and was seen at Joe's Drive In the day of the murder. He could try all sorts of stunts, such as subpoenaing Beckwith's Klan friend Gordon Lackey, who had been tall, young, and dark-haired at the time, and asking him what he had been doing the night of June 11. But any of those things would just open up opportunities for Peters to bring up other FBI reports about Beckwith's political activities and suspicious associations. It would confuse the hell out of the jury, but it might end up putting his client in an even worse position, if that was possible.

Instead Coxwell chose to stick with the script. He felt so strongly that any higher court would find a sackful of reasons to overturn a conviction that he played it safe.

The next witness was Martha Jean O'Brien, a woman the defense could not locate. The missing witness had been a teenage carhop working at Joe's the night of the murder.

By now it was routine to have old testimony reenacted for the jury, and today a secretary read the part where O'Brien had said that she saw a man getting out of the Valiant who didn't look at all like Beckwith. She described a good-looking man in his early twenties, taller than six two, with black hair and dark clothes.

Bobby DeLaughter's cross-examination, taken from the script, was perfunctory.

At midmorning the moment everyone had been waiting for was at hand. Everybody knew that Beckwith needed to testify to explain certain things, such as how his rifle had ended up at the crime scene. He had to say that it had been stolen, and he was the only one who could do that.

But something unexpected was happening. With the jury out of the room, Kitchens and Peters were arguing about something called "Rule 804."

Coxwell and Kitchens wanted Beckwith to testify all right, but they could not risk Peters's cross-examination, or the probable outbursts from Beckwith. So they asked to invoke a rule to declare the defendant incapacitated. As Kitchens told the judge in the presence of his client, "Obviously Mr. Beckwith is here and alive, your honor. . . [but] in every sense of the Mississippi rules of evidence, Mr. Beckwith is unavailable to testify. We have spent hours talking to Mr. Beckwith, and he is less able to remember now than he was a couple of years ago."

The defense wanted Beckwith to testify through the transcripts of his first trial. Someone else would read for him.

The atmosphere in the main courtroom was increasingly tense. An overflow crowd had to be seated in the balcony behind the press. Klansmen, skinheads, and Jackson State students sat in close proximity, with a chemical volatility in their mingling breath that you could feel through your skin.

Cynthia Speetjens's husband, Joe, had come to watch the show and had ended up seated between the two camps. As the lawyers churned through their arguments, with Peters saying why he felt Beckwith should testify live and not as a living ghost, and Coxwell claiming that his client couldn't remember enough to defend himself, Joe experienced a strange bipolar commentary in stereo: The Klan youths muttered, "That's a lie," after every sentence Peters spoke. The old NAACP veterans on the other side whispered, "Praise Jesus."

Judge Hilburn offered what he felt was a compromise. He would not restrict Beckwith's testimony to the transcript, but he would allow the witness to keep it in front of him and refer to it during his testimony.

Peters and DeLaughter shifted in their chairs and straightened their papers expectantly. Then Merrida Coxwell rose from his seat. In that case, he said, Beckwith would not testify.

"The defense rests."

At that three hundred or more hushed and excited spectators let out a choked yawp of disappointment — like the sound of air going out of a small balloon.

Ed Peters threw his pen on the desk, then looked up for the judge to admonish him, though he never did. Peters had just been robbed of his finest performance. He had stayed in criminal law because he loved his time in the courtroom, like an actor loves the stage. But he was mostly a desk jockey now. This was a rare chance to do what he did best. He had two thick stacks of material in front of him. He was prepared to keep Beckwith on the stand for two days, to cut his alibis to ribbons, and to show the jury just what kind of a man this defendant was. He had videotapes of interviews Beckwith had given in recent years, where Beckwith had chuckled when he'd said he hadn't "killed the nigger, but he sure is dead." He planned to needle Beckwith until the man exploded in rage and showed the jury that his hatred was strong enough to lead him to murder.

Now, Peters thought, Beckwith had shown what he was. He was a coward. For perhaps the first time in his long and unquiet life, Byron De La Beckwith had nothing to say.

There were a few more orders of business before the end of the day. The prosecutors called former detective Fred Sanders as a rebuttal witness to dispute some things Holley had said. But the questioning was lackluster, the motions desultory. The air was heavy with frustration and a sense of anticlimax. DeLaughter walked around the courtroom as if his mustache weighed five pounds.

As the afternoon wore on, Beckwith sat crumpled up inside his large, loud jacket. He looked defeated. Nobody had taken the stand to sing his praises at this trial. Nobody had even said he was a good salesman. He had been betrayed again and again by people he considered his own kind. His own nephew had written a book that said he was an impotent drunk and then had taken the stand to condemn him by reading his own words back to him.

The man who had boasted that he shot down "the mightiest nigger in Mississippi" had to sit still and listen while his attorneys told the court that he was infirm, suggested that he was senile. The man who lived for an audience skipped his last performance. There would be no curtain calls.

It was all over by 2:30 that afternoon. Judge Hilburn scheduled closing arguments for Friday morning.

Myrlie Evers was visibly upset. After enduring Beckwith's taunts for so long, she wanted more than a guilty verdict. She wanted the whole horror show, with Beckwith howling and braying and Peters acting as her surrogate, the one who would slay the dragon for her and throw her the head.

She met the TV cameras at the elevator doors that afternoon with gloomy, distracted eyes. "I would have enjoyed immensely hearing the accused assassin of my husband," she said in a clipped, angry voice. "The fact that he didn't take the stand means — a lot. It's the first time in thirty years that he has not ranted and raved," she said.

Among the stunned people milling in the wide courtroom hallway was at least one woman who saw Beckwith's silence as a victory. Rosa Mitchell, a seventy-three-year-old NAACP veteran, was telling anyone who would listen that she was happy she hadn't had to listen to Beckwith this time around. She had sat through his first two trials, she said. "Now he can't be carrying on like a cobra, spitting out poison at our children. This poison and hate will end here, with this old man. It ends here, today."

It had been a peculiar, spooky case from the beginning, and it was not over yet. Early Thursday evening the phone rang in Kitchens's office. It was a woman who said she was Martha Jean O'Brien. She had heard on the news that somebody had read her testimony. She wondered why he hadn't contacted her, since she had been in touch with the prosecution. "I talked to Bobby DeLaughter the night before the trial started," she said.

"You're kidding me," the dumbfounded lawyer said. He'd had a private detective searching for her for months.

She told him her name was different now and she was afraid to come forward and testify in person. She wouldn't leave her number with him, but she said she had visited Charlie Crisco in his office. She repeated her story to Kitchens about how she had not been able to identify Beckwith, and she couldn't pick him out of a lineup. She had seen a much younger man at Joe's thirty-one years ago.

"Ma'am," Kitchens sputtered, "in the unlikely event that we would be able to reopen our case and put you on the stand tomorrow, would you be available?"

"I'm — I'm scared to do it," she said. Couldn't she just give a deposition?

Kitchens told her, regrettably, no. She ended the call without leaving her number.

Darrell and his sister Reena Evers-Everett flew into Jackson on Thursday night. Nobody expected the trial to be over so quickly. Darrell thought he could wait more time, at least another week.

Darrell came to give support to his mother, but he also was there for himself. He wanted to see Beckwith, and he wanted Beckwith to see him. Darrell was forty, slightly older than his father was when he died.

Darrell was taller, built slimmer than his father, but he had his father's face and his eyes. Later he would tell people that he wanted the assassin to see his face, his father's face, because all he had seen before was his back.

On Friday morning, February 4, Darrell took a seat on one side of his mother, and Reena sat on the other side. Darrell searched for Beckwith's eyes across the room. Beckwith glanced at him, recognized him, and met his stare. Their eyes were locked for ten, thirty, forty-five seconds. What Darrell saw in Beckwith's eyes surprised him. There was hate, of course, and plenty of attitude: the eyes said, *I'm right; I'm angry; I'm powerful.* But there was something else. Darrell thought it was fear, not of him or of black people, but of Beckwith's own beliefs, like they were choking him. Beckwith looked away first, and Darrell was satisfied.

Darrell wanted this man to pay for his crime. But this case wasn't a crusade for him as it was for his mother. He believed in karma, and he knew that Beckwith would be taken care of in the cosmic balance; he would get what was coming to him in this world or another.

On that spiritual level Darrell was cool. On another, more corporeal frequency he wanted like hell to see Beckwith convicted.

The first order of business was yet another call from the defense for a mistrial or for reopening their case. Coxwell and Kitchens accused DeLaughter of withholding information from them because he had never told them he knew the whereabouts of Martha Jean O'Brien. They wanted to subpoena her to testify.

Bobby argued that it wasn't his job to run down witnesses for them and that the prosecution had named O'Brien on their witness list as well. Besides, she had moved, and he didn't have a new number for her. Judge Hilburn apparently accepted this excuse, because the motion to reopen was denied.

There was also the question of Judge Hilburn's bizarre instructions to the jury Thursday afternoon. He had told them to pack their bags, that they should expect to go home Friday night.

Hilburn quickly rescinded that advice, but the defense team objected. It was as if the judge was telling the jury not to waste their time deliberating. The longer they were out, the better it was for the defense. Hilburn noted the defense motion and called the jury back in to hear closing arguments.

Bobby DeLaughter was up first. He had never been known for his rousing oratory, but to those familiar with his courtroom manner he was practically on fire that day.

This crime, he said, was an act of savagery, "the kind of murder every human being should be sickened by." He made sure he pointed his finger at the defendant, like the wrath of God was descending on him. "When he thought he had beaten the system, he couldn't keep his own mouth shut with people he thought would be impressed. His own venom has come back to poison him." DeLaughter said.

Beckwith, he said, had "danced to the music for thirty years. Isn't it time he paid the piper?" The murder had left "a gaping wound" on society. "Where justice is never fulfilled, that wound will never be cleansed. . . . Is it ever too late to do the right thing? I sincerely hope and pray that it's not."

Coxwell and Kitchens made their statements next. Coxwell reminded the jury of the alibi witnesses — the defendant hadn't been in Jackson and couldn't have killed Evers.

Kitchens played on a different, loftier theme. First he asked the jury to regard the defendant in the context of his era. "Just about every white person in this state was for segregation and I'm not here to say it's right," he said.

He invoked the names of Abraham Lincoln and Thomas Jefferson, pointing out that Jefferson had been a slaveholder and Lincoln had not been committed to black suffrage. Their views would not be accepted today, any more than Beckwith's views on race were.

"You're not here to decide whether you like Mr. Beckwith," he told the jury. "Or whether you want to take him home, or whether you'd like to join his organization . . . Judge this case on the evidence," he pleaded. "Forget it's Byron De La Beckwith. Forget you don't like him. Judge the case on the evidence because if the system doesn't work for everybody, it doesn't work for anybody."

Ed Peters was up last. Myrlie Evers was not disappointed. He slew the dragon and threw her Beckwith's head.

"By this defendant's own words shall he be judged," Peters began. He called Beckwith a "back-shooting, sneaking coward." He pointed a finger at the defense lawyers. "No wonder they don't want you to think about the defendant!"

Peters went on like this for half an hour, acting out the parts of the defense witnesses, mocking them, chewing them up so that Kitchens had to object to the theatrics. Peters told the jury what he thought about the alibi witnesses: "You know the way the cops felt back then . . . that's why they'd come down here and lie!"

He reminded the jury of the courage of the witnesses who had come forward at great personal risk to say that Beckwith had bragged to them. "Don't let him walk out of here and say 'I've got twelve more! They can't convict me!' "

"All we're asking you people to do is to give the Evers family some justice" Peters said, looking each juror in the eye. "Just justice after thirty years."

After that the jurors went to the back room to begin their deliberations. There wasn't a thing in the world for Myrlie Evers to do but wait, and pray.

Most times a Mississippi jury will be out for two to three hours if there is going to be a conviction. Few people overintellectualize their decisions in this part of the world. The judicial process reflects the society here, which is one of moral certitude. There is right and wrong, good and bad, heaven and hell, and Mississippians usually have no trouble telling the difference. So when 3:30 went by, and then 4:00, and then 4:30, the folks waiting it out on the fifth floor started getting nervous.

The most likely outcome, right from the start, had always been a hung jury. But the defense had been so hapless and the prosecution such a juggernaut of righteousness that everyone was feeling a conviction in the air. Besides there were eight black jurors in there. Still all it would take was one juror who didn't want to face the music back at the Pepsi-Cola plant or the feed store, one who would hold out and hang it up one more time.

A heavy storm hit in late afternoon, and the chandeliers in the courtroom hallways flickered a few times, then held steady. Thunder rumbled through the city and shook the heavy glass doors. It was Gothic weather, perfect for the occasion.

By six o'clock the bailiffs were whispering that they heard shouts coming from the jury room. That was not a good sign at all.

*   *   *

Up in the D.A.'s office, Myrlie Evers sat making small talk with Linda Anderson, Glenda Haynes, and Cynthia Speetjens in Anderson's office. Darrell and Reena chatted with the other lawyers. Darrell hadn't spent any time with the prosecutors before. He hadn't even met Ed Peters. But as soon as he saw them at work, he felt they were like family. It was another thing he hadn't expected, feeling this close to a bunch of Mississippi prosecutors.

Bobby was walking in a dark cloud of his own, pacing around, his black eyebrows knit together. He stood in Anderson's doorway, fretting.

"I hate this part," he said, looking at Myrlie. "I just can't stand the waiting."

Myrlie smiled up at him and said in a calm voice, "I'm a lot better at that than you are."

By the next morning the storm had worsened. Rain lashed the pavement and rattled the windows. It was close and dark inside the courthouse. At 10:20 A.M., Saturday, February 5, word began to spread that the jury had reached a verdict. They had only been back in deliberation for an hour and a half.

Nobody had expected this. The Evers family was still over at the Holiday Inn when the phone rang in Myrlie's room. It took fifteen minutes to get them to the courthouse.

The biggest, meanest-looking sheriff's deputies in Jackson stood shoulder to shoulder in the courtroom, facing the thirty-five or so early bird observers who had gathered that morning. As soon as the Evers family took their seats, the jury was called back to the courtroom.

They filed in and stood before the judge in a single line, their backs to the defendant and the spectators. Elvage Fondren had been elected foreman.

"Have you reached a verdict?" Judge Hilburn asked.

"We have Your Honor," said Fondren as he handed the judge a sheet of lined paper with some words written on it in ballpoint pen.

Beckwith sat so quietly that the D.A.s and bailiffs speculated that he was drugged. He never moved or even flinched when the judge handed the paper to Barbara Dunn, who read the verdict in her hard hill twang: "We find the defendant guilty . . ."

Myrlie clutched Darrell's hand and held her other hand over her mouth to keep from screaming.

". . . as charged."

"Yes!" Darrell whooped, and when that sound reached outside, to the crowd gathered in the hallway, a cheer of jubilation rolled though the old courthouse like the sound of a slow-breaking wave.

Since there was only one possible sentence available to the judge, he delivered it immediately. Beckwith rose to attention, squared his shoulders, and marched up to the bench. He was flanked by Coxwell and Kitchens, who seemed stunned. He kept his chin up when Judge Hilburn sentenced him to life in prison. He would not be eligible for parole for ten years.

Beckwith straightened his gray suit with the tiny Confederate flag pinned to the lapel and raised one hand dismissively, assuring the bailiffs that he could exit on his own steam. Then he strode out the door.

He was quiet on the way down the elevator to booking, except for a few words muttered to no one in particular. "They got what they wanted," he said.

As soon as Beckwith was out the door, Thelma started wailing: "He's not guilty and they know it! I don't care!" Finally Kim McGeoy put his arms around her to quiet her. Little Delay stood off to the side, looking at nothing, his arms folded across his chest.

As Myrlie left the courtroom, she finally broke down. She threw her arms around Darrell and sobbed into his shoulder as he gently led her to the elevators.

When they reached the fifth floor, the lawyers were there. Everyone was hugging everyone else like it was a reunion of long-lost family. Myrlie hugged DeLaughter, then walked over to Peters and wrapped her arms around him. She said the first thing that came to mind: "We've come a long way."

They sat around for a while and told stories, like soldiers after a battle: how it had all begun, how Peters had doubted and Myrlie had pushed and DeLaughter had found the way. Then DeLaughter and Peters went downstairs to the press conference.

The media center was set up in an empty courtroom on the first floor. Dozens of reporters and photographers were crammed into it. A bank of television cameras, more than anyone had seen in Mississippi in years, faced a makeshift podium for the press conference.

DeLaughter was nearly choked up. He said the first thing that had gone through his mind when he heard the verdict was a quote from the Bible: "To God be the glory for the things he has done." He thanked the people who had helped him, the witnesses with the courage to come forward.

Ron Smothers of the *New York Times* asked whether they thought the verdict would change public perceptions of Beckwith.

Ed Peters was blunt. "Well, he won't be bragging anymore," he said.

Had justice been done?

"Yes, I think justice was done," Peters said. "I'm sorry it took so long, but I'm glad that it was done."

One reporter wanted to know what had happened to all those witnesses who said they had seen Beckwith hanging around NAACP meetings back in 1963. Why hadn't they testified?

"Because we wanted to win," DeLaughter said flatly. He seemed relieved to be able to answer that, get it out of the way.

"We were not in this to cover our tails, but to win," he continued. "It would have been very easy to put on everything we had access to so in the event of a hung jury, in the event of an acquittal, we could have said 'we put everything on.'

"It was a strategic decision. Now that it's over we can comment on this. Those leads were tracked down by the police department during the initial investigation. They did not pan out." DeLaughter told them some of those witnesses could not identify Beckwith from a photographic lineup.

"We would have been ambushed if we had gone down that rabbit trail," he said. The defense had "any number of witnesses they could have put on including undercover detectives that would have testified that was absolutely not true. . . . We decided that any other case we would not run that risk, and we were going to win this and we wouldn't make any exception."

Some other reporters brought up the lack of support the D.A.'s office had enjoyed from the "black community."

Ed Peters answered that one. "I didn't want to say this, but since y'all asked, I was shocked and I was dismayed at the number of black jurors that said we shouldn't be prosecuting this case, and they didn't know who Medgar Evers was, and what in the world were we doing wasting money. I guess that was the last reaction I expected from black people."

Peters was saved from himself as all heads swung around for the arrival of Myrlie Evers and her family and bodyguards. Myrlie stood in front of the media pack, her chin up and eyes still brimming. "Is it left up to me to start?" she asked.

She looked around for the right words, and a soft, urgent voice came from the crowd, "Let it go!" Myrlie clenched her hands and raised them in the air. She looked up at the heavens and shouted, "All I want to do is say, 'Yay, Medgar! Yay!' "

"It's about time," said Darrell, standing beside her. Reena stood on the other side, hiding her eyes behind dark glasses. They closed in around their mother while she collected her composure. Her voice smoothed out, and she was pensive again.

"You all know that this has been a very long battle," she began. "It has been thirty years and sometimes I think my children and I have lived double that, with the stress, strain, the turmoil, the emotional devastation."

She thanked by name the prosecutors who had seen the case through, even Charlie Crisco, who had not often been thanked in his career. She thanked the sheriff for making her "feel safe in our native home." She answered questions about the meaning of the verdict and about the long, rough road she had traveled to learn to trust the prosecutors.

She explained why she had been slow in coming down to the press conference. "I had to jump in the air," she said, "and shed some tears and raise my face and say, 'Medgar, I've gone the last mile of the way!' "

Myrlie and her grown children spent the rest of the day giving interviews and visiting old friends at the hotel. On Sunday Myrlie got up at 6 A.M. and spent all morning with a crew from *Good Morning America*. They ended up using a few seconds of her interview on the air.

Darrell and Reena were due to fly back home that night. But Darrell had one more piece of unfinished business to deal with.

Charles Evers was at home in Fayette on Saturday morning when somebody, he thinks it was a reporter, called to tell him that Beckwith had been found guilty. He flipped on the big-screen TV and watched the press conference and the hourly reports on the national news.

He could hardly believe it. The news made him happy, then sad, and then happy again. He'd never thought there would be anything other than a hung jury. He couldn't stand to care about it again. But now — guilty! It made him proud of the whites and the blacks on that jury, the witnesses, everyone.

Charles had kept his distance from this trial for a lot of reasons. He knew he couldn't be in the same courtroom with Beckwith. He couldn't just sit there and look at the man who killed his brother smirking and bouncing around in front of him. He would have to jump him and break his neck. He knew himself, and he told people that's why he didn't go to the trial.

Besides he and Myrlie still weren't getting along. He admitted it was his fault. He was bitter, he had always pushed her away, and pushed the kids away. But now, with this verdict, maybe they could be a family again. Maybe there was something could be done to correct the problem. It was up to him to make the change in himself.

Darrell called his uncle and asked him to drive up to Jackson. Darrell had to see him. He wasn't going to hear his uncle tell him that nobody loved him, or let his uncle keep up that wall, that tough-guy act. To Darrell the outcome of the trial was a transcendence, a moment that shimmers like a rare jewel, and his father's brother had to be there to make it perfect.

Charles met them Sunday afternoon at a restaurant in Jackson. Darrell, Reena, and even Myrlie hugged him.

"Uncle Charlie," Darrell said, "you're the closest thing I've got to Daddy."

Darrell was crying, and so was Charles. Charles told them he was going to make an effort to come out to see them in Los Angeles. Get to know them and their families. And they were all invited to come be part of the homecoming this June. It was important to him now.

After lunch Myrlie and her kids left to visit Medgar's statue, but Charles didn't go with them. He thought, *No need to push things too fast.*

Ed Peters went fishing right after the press conference on Saturday afternoon.

Charlie Crisco drove home to his house by the lake. He intended to spend time with his wife and daughter, lie in the hammock, drink coffee, chew tobacco, and play golf until he was ready to start all over again. A new court term would be starting in another week.

Bobby DeLaughter went right home after the Everses left for their hotel. He told friends that he got some beer and a fistful of video westerns and he didn't get up from the couch all day and all night. He just sat there with a beer in one hand and the remote control in the other. The idea was not to think about anything.

On Sunday he went to church and then rode horses in the beautiful springlike weather. On Monday he finally started to come down, wandered around in his bathrobe all morning, and just did a lot of nothing until his mind settled down.

On Tuesday Bobby was sitting alone in his office, paying bills. He hadn't planned to come in to work at all, but he'd realized he had left all his mail on his desk and he needed to pay the phone and electric bills. He was wearing a white sports shirt and khakis. He was still not taking calls — not from Hollywood, *Good Morning America*, or anyone he didn't know their mother's name.

The phone rang. He picked up the receiver and listened, frowning. "*Newsday?*" he said. "What's that? Tell him to call the *Clarion-Ledger*."

DeLaughter intended to stay scarce as long as he could. He was planning to announce his candidacy for judge in a few weeks, and he didn't want anyone to think that he was capitalizing on the verdict. Then the phone rang again, and he heard a request that he just couldn't turn down.

On Wednesday night, at 8 P.M., Charles Evers had a surprise visitor to his weekly talk show on WMPR. "Tonight our guest is Bobby DeLaughter, the assistant district attorney of Hinds and Yazoo Counties," Evers purred in his deepest, softest public-radio voice. "Welcome to 'Let's Talk.' "

Charles poured syrup all over Bobby, introducing him as "a young man who has gone out of his way to bring justice in this state, justice that was so long overdue. It made my family feel proud of you. . . . But first I want to ask you about the trial. What made you so interested in it? Why did you work so hard at it?"

Bobby cleared his throat and repeated his now-familiar answer. He talked about the "intriguing facets" of the case and how the back-shooting assassination had chilled his blood, had really got to him.

He praised the teamwork of blacks and whites. He sounded very much like a politician now. He said the case showed "that when we all pull together as a community, we can see that justice is done in our courts, whether the case is thirty days old or thirty years old." He was very relaxed and polished.

"I understand that you are anticipating running for office," Evers said. Bobby said nothing.

"I want you to know that if you do run, there are a lot of people who believe in what you stand for," Evers continued. "I want you to know this is one old seventy-one-year-old man who will love you as long as there is breath in my body . . . for what you did for us."

A week later, Bobby DeLaughter stood on the front steps of the Hinds County Courthouse. With local television cameras rolling and a small crowd gathered, he announced his candidacy for appeals court judge. He ran unopposed in the Democratic primary.

Ed Peters decided he might run for D.A. again after all.

In the weeks after the trial Beckwith lived in his familiar cell in the hospital wing of the Hinds County Detention Center. All the guards knew him. Friends who visited him found him hobbling around on crutches. It turned out he had tripped over the trailer hitch on his car up in Batesville. He had sat through the whole trial with a small fracture in his lower leg, but he hadn't told anyone about it.

Coxwell worked on the appeal and tried to organize bail for his client. If he got Beckwith out on an appeal bond, he would probably be out for the rest of his life. But Judge Hilburn had left town for a vacation, so it was hard to get a hearing scheduled. Two months later Hilburn officially rejected Beckwith's request for a new trial. There would be no bail. Coxwell and Kitchens intended to appeal right on up to the U.S. Supreme Court, but Beckwith would stay in jail.

Coxwell's new wife was expecting a son that summer. It would be his first child. It was too soon to tell how much the Beckwith case had harmed his practice, but he suspected it hadn't helped him. Slowly his life came back to something like normal. In the beginning, he had thought that he and Bobby DeLaughter could get past this trial and come out friends. He didn't think so anymore. All he would say when asked about Bobby was, "I wish him well with his career."

Myrlie Evers spent the next month on the road, stopping in at the national NAACP convention in New York, fulfilling the speaking engagements she had put off. By the middle of March she was back home in Oregon. She had started writing her memoirs while sitting in her lonely motel room in Batesville. She wanted to record everything — how it felt, how the old memories came rushing back. She needed peace and time to write.

Myrlie wanted to see spring settle over the Cascades, sit at home with Walter, and let it finally sink in: it was done. Knowing that lifted weight off her shoulders, lightened her very bones, and she let the relief wash over her like a breeze.

She thought: *This must be how it feels to be free.*

The Klan was surprisingly placid in the days and weeks following the verdict. Richard Barrett was the only neo-Nazi to try to capitalize on the trial. He announced a "symposium" on the Beckwith case titled "Black-balling Beckwith, Whitewashing Evers." Barrett booked a room in the Old Capitol Building, now a museum, for Tuesday, February 8. He undoubtedly thought the trial would still be going on and he could attract some of the national media on their lunch break. As it turned out, only three of his own black-shirted acolytes and one old man in a business suit showed up for the seminar. A photographer came but left without taking pictures.

The only reported Klan incident, which seemed to have no connection with the case, happened a few weeks later. Three luckless young white boys burned a cross in the yard of an interracial couple in Walthall County. A friend immediately ratted them out to the FBI, and now they were facing a minimum of five years in federal prison.

Not only right-wing ravers were unhappy about the way the trial had turned out.

Since the case had been handled like a murder trial, not a political trial, there was a lingering feeling of unfulfillment among those who'd wanted it to be more. The conspiracy crowd was disappointed that the dirty laundry had not been dragged out. The man, and not the state, had been put on trial after all. The alleged complicity of the police, the culpability of the politicians, and the likelihood of at least one accomplice — these issues had been handled so lightly and fleetingly by Beckwith's defense lawyers that suspicious-minded people, and there were enough of them in Mississippi, started to wonder whether it hadn't been a deliberate cover-up.

Before long there were stories circulating that "the government" had rushed the case through the court, that "they" had prevented the real criminals from being exposed. The conspiracy crowd was muttering for blood.

They might still have their day. The Beckwith verdict had kicked open the way for new trials in the twenty-eight-year-old Vernon Dahmer case and possibly the Neshoba County murders of Goodman, Chaney, and Schwerner, which had never been tried in state court. Sam Bowers was, again, the target. Before long an African-American CBS correspondent would be chasing him through a church parking lot in Laurel, demanding to know whether he had ordered Dahmer's murder. A panicked Bowers squealed, "You're not listening," as he scrambled to escape.

So many murders had gone unresolved. Myrlie Evers herself was talking about setting up a Nuremberg-type commission to investigate old civil rights atrocities and hunt down the criminals, just as the Jews had pursued the Nazis after the war.

A few weeks after the Beckwith verdict the Mississippi legislature, which was still overwhelmingly white, voted funding to reopen the Dahmer case. "Those people who were killed back during that time are just as dead today as the day they died," said Dahmer's son, Dennis, who, like Darrell Evers, was forty. "And those individuals who did it are just as guilty today as they were the day they did it."

Along with the reopening of old civil rights cases, the Sovereignty Commission papers were on the verge of being released in some form to the public. The upheaval of memory and retribution and the exorcism of the ghosts of Mississippi were not over yet.

Whether you call the trial of Byron De La Beckwith a miracle or a travesty, it is hard to argue against the symmetry of the event. The story of Medgar Evers had come full circle. There was a balancing of the books. People who were hoping to hear the word "guilty" describe a peculiar physical sensation when the verdict was read. For a moment the components of the universe seemed to click into place, like an engine that suddenly catches and comes to life. For an instant the world took on a clarity and logic. The cops, the prosecutors, and the state itself, awash as they were in public and private sins, achieved a brief and shining moment of grace.

After the courtroom doors swung shut, the reporters and news crews caught their flights to Atlanta and New York, and another edition of the *Clarion-Ledger* was put to bed, what remained was still Mississippi, haunted ground: a place at war with its own history and destined to repeat its past, like a soul being reborn again and again until it gets it right.

Acknowledgments

FIRST OF ALL, thanks to Myrlie Evers, Bobby DeLaughter, and Charles Evers, who made this book possible.

Thanks to Bill Phillips, my editor at Little, Brown, and his colleagues Jordan Pavlin, Steve Schneider, and David Coen, who all went the distance; Kris Dahl and Gordon Kato at ICM; and David Hirshey, Mark Warren, and Will Blythe at *Esquire*.

I owe special thanks to Joe and Cynthia Speetjens, my friends and tour guides in Mississippi; Joseph Dumas, Michelle Hudson, and Clarence Hunter for their invaluable assistance; Alex and Pat Malouf for their gracious hospitality; Ed Peters, Benny Bennett, Charlie Crisco, Doc Thaggard, and the Hinds County District Attorney's staff; Henry Brinston, Merrida Coxwell, Darrell Evers, Kim McGeoy, Erle Johnston, John R. Salter, Jr., and Ben Windstein.

I offer my gratitude to the following people for their time and assistance: Dr. Margaret Walker Alexander, Reuben Anderson, Sam Baily, Thelma Beckwith, Alvin Binder, Fred Blackwell, Liz Blankenship, Dr. Albert Britton, C. C. Bryant, Sara Bullard, Betty Carter, Ben Chaney, Kenneth Dean, Morris Dees, Dave Dennis, Delmar Dennis, Jack Ditto,

John Doar, Barbara Dunn, John Emmerich, John Evans, John Fox, Elmore Greaves, Dick Gregory, Clarie Collins Harvey, Constance Slaughter Harvey, Aaron Henry, Breland Hilburn, Jerry Himelstein, Jim Ingram, Jerry Dell Jefferson, Elizabeth Evers Jordan, Vernon Jordan, Bern and Franke Keating, Ed King, Morris Kinsey, Bill Kirksey, Henry Kirksey, William Kunstler, Gordon Lackey, Ken Lawrence, Chokwe Lumumba, Governor Ray Mabus, Robert Malouf, William McIlhany, Thorn McIntyre, James Meredith, Bill Minor, Jerry Mitchell, Thomas Moore, Lane C. Murray, C. B. Needham, Jack Nelson, Mike Riley, Rena Roach, Joe Roy, Fred Sanders, Gordon Saucier, R. L. T. Smith, Jr., Dr. E. J. Stringer, Grace Sweet, Nolan Tate, Jr., Hon. Bennie Thompson, Charles Tisdale, Bill Waller, Hollis Watkins, Thompson B. Webb, Danny Welch, James Wells, William Wessel, Walter Williams, Allan Wood, Aurelia Young, the able staffs of the Mississippi Department of Archives and History, the Eudora Welty Library, the Southern Poverty Law Center, and the dozens of others who offered their help, including those who asked not to be mentioned by name.

For their support and encouragement along the way: Joseph and Josephine Vollers, F. W. "Boo" Campbell, Judy and Mert Martin, Joe and Annette Vollers, Chuck Vollers, Mary Motley Kalergis (fearless reader), Gordon Baptiste, David Petzal, and Peter Herbst. And, of course, thanks to my husband, Bill Campbell, who put up with hardship and neglect for three years and kept his sense of humor.

Thanks to all the brave men and women of Mississippi and most of all to Medgar Evers, who lives on.

Notes

CHAPTER 1: GHOSTS OF THE OLD SOUTH

I met Byron De La Beckwith in his cell in the Hinds County Detention Center on August 1, 1992. We had been corresponding since January 1991, when I had begun my research into this case as an assignment for *Esquire* ("The Haunting of the New South," *Esquire,* July 1991, 58). I persistently asked Beckwith for a formal interview. He would do this only for money; his fee was five thousand dollars. I refused to pay him and continued to refuse after I began work on this book. He did, on occasion, volunteer to answer specific questions in writing, and I have used this material at times in this book, particularly his memories of his early life in California.

Sometimes his letters were cordial, even witty (he would sign them "De La in de dungeon"); often they were vaguely ominous. For instance, he wrote me a postcard on March 1, 1991, after I first refused to pay for an interview: "Dear young woman — . . . You don't look like one but you sure are. By their fruits we do know thee." A year later, after further attempts to cash in on the book I was by then writing: "Of course, what you are doing for a living does not pay that well — nor for long. Ooops." He underlined the word "living" and drew an arrow to the phrase "nor for long," writing next to it, "Notice. No sarcasm intended here."

Beckwith's lawyers were trying to keep reporters away from him, and he was not expecting me to visit him in jail. In fact for several minutes after we were introduced, he did not seem to realize who I was, even though he had seen my picture and knew my name. Finally he turned to me in his cell and said, "Now, where did you say you were from?" I fully expected him to throw me out, but he didn't. In fact he laughed, as if it were a terrific practical joke. "Careful, Delay," one of his friends said. "She's got a photographic memory, and this is all gonna end up in her book." Beckwith announced to his friends that he didn't care if I wrote about our meeting. They nodded agreement. As far as I was concerned, that put everything on the record.

After about an hour Beckwith finally lost his temper and evicted me. I was not able to use a tape recorder or even take notes, and although I do not normally have a "photographic memory," in this case I did remember, precisely, everything that was said, and how it looked.

CHAPTER 2: DECATUR

I first interviewed Charles Evers in August 1991. I interviewed him a dozen or more times during the three years I spent researching this book. Much of the Evers family history comes from these conversations, as well as from interviews with Elizabeth Evers Jordan, Medgar and Charles's sister; C. B. Needham, a childhood friend who still lives in Decatur; and Myrlie Evers. The best printed sources are *For Us, the Living* by Myrlie Evers with William Peters (Garden City, N.Y.: Doubleday, 1967); *Evers* by Charles Evers with Grace Halsell (New York: World Publishing, 1971); and "Why I Live in Mississippi" by Medgar Evers as told to Francis H. Mitchell, *Ebony*, November 1958, 65–70. Many stories of Medgar's and Charles's childhoods were first recorded in *Evers*, including the death of Eddie Grimm and Charles's early business ventures.

CHAPTER 3: THE VETERAN

Two books cover Byron De La Beckwith's early years: *Portrait of a Racist: A Revelatory Biography of Byron De La Beckwith, Written by His Own Nephew* by Reed Massengill (New York: St. Martin's Press, 1994) and *Glory in Conflict: A Saga of Byron De La Beckwith* by R. W. Scott (Camden, Ark.: Camark Press, 1991). The latter is Beckwith's "authorized biography," a self-published paperback that he hawked from his jail cell to raise money. Some information, such as that regarding Beckwith's father's letters and Beckwith's relationship with his guardian, originated here.

The quotation on page 20 is from *Southern Belle* by Mary Craig Sinclair (New York: Crown, 1957), 11–13.

I relied on *Line of Departure: Tarawa* by Martin Russ (New York: Doubleday, 1975) for much of the information on Beckwith's combat experience in World War II.

I found other nuggets of Beckwith's family history in court records in Colusa, California, clips from the *Colusa Sun*, and the genealogical collection at the Mississippi Department of Archives and History in Jackson, which includes the Southworth and Yerger family histories.

See also "The Colonel's Grandson," *Newsweek*, July 8, 1963, 22–23.

Beckwith's musings on the "dusky races" comes from a BBC television interview conducted in the summer of 1991.

Information on Beckwith's childhood and early adulthood comes from interviews with dozens of his relatives and acquaintances in Greenwood. Many asked not to be identified as sources.

CHAPTER 4: BRAVE NEW WORLD

I first interviewed Myrlie Evers at her office in Los Angeles on February 6, 1991, while I was on assignment for *Esquire*. I had several formal, taped interviews with Evers during the course of my research for this book, including one long session at her home in Oregon on September 11, 1992, and dozens of telephone conversations. Details about Medgar and Myrlie Evers's childhoods and their life together are compiled from these interviews, as well as from her memoir, *For Us, the Living*, and various published sources.

Details of Charles Evers's military exploits come from interviews with him and appear in *Evers*. The story of the Evers brothers' attempt to vote in 1946 has been retold many times. This version comes from interviews with Charles Evers, C. B. Needham, and Medgar Evers's 1958 article in *Ebony*.

I interviewed Thomas Moore in Mound Bayou, Mississippi, on September 25, 1992. The history of Mound Bayou is in Hodding Carter's *Lower Mississippi* (New York: Farrar and Rinehart, 1942).

An excellent study of American apartheid is Neil R. McMillen's *Dark Journey: Black Mississippians in the Age of Jim Crow* (Urbana: University of Illinois Press, 1989).

CHAPTER 5: BLACK MONDAY

I interviewed E. J. Stringer by phone on June 8, 1992. The passage about Medgar Evers's relationship with his father and information about his father's death are based on interviews with Charles Evers and Myrlie Evers and on accounts in *For Us, the Living* and *Ebony*.

The most helpful books about the rise of the Citizens' Councils are *The South Strikes Back* by Hodding Carter III (New York: Doubleday, 1959) and *The Citizens' Councils: Organized Resistance to the Second Reconstruction* by

Neil R. McMillen (Urbana: University of Illinois Press, 1971). See also *My Soul Is Rested: The Story of the Civil Rights Movement in the Deep South* by Howell Raines (New York: Penguin, 1983). Quotations are taken from *Black Monday* by Tom Brady (Winona: Association of Citizens' Councils of Mississippi, 1955).

CHAPTER 6: THE ASSOCIATION

The Papers of the National Association for the Advancement of Colored People (NAACP Papers) are housed in the Library of Congress, Manuscript Division, and selections are available on microfilm. Since they are being reorganized, I have omitted box and section numbers.

I interviewed Gloster Current by telephone on March 15, 1993. Other sources for NAACP history include *An American Dilemma* by Gunnar Myrdal (New York: Harper & Brothers, 1944); *A Man Called White* by Walter White (New York: Viking, 1948; reprint, New York: Arno Press, 1969); and *Standing Fast: The Autobiography of Roy Wilkins* by Roy Wilkins with Tom Mathews (New York: Viking, 1982).

The negotiations for Medgar Evers's employment are found in the NAACP Papers in letters from Current to Wilkins (November 19, 1954) and from Ruby Hurley to Evers (November 29, 1954). Evers's report is contained in an undated draft and incorporated in "Report on Mississippi Situation," Current to Wilkins (December 13, 1954). The description of Hurley comes from Myrlie Evers and Vernon Jordan, who was once the NAACP's Georgia field secretary. The descriptions of Reverend George Lee's murder come from eyewitness accounts compiled in the NAACP papers from May 1955. The flap involving Hurley, Current, Wilkins, and Evers is documented in the branch files from this month.

CHAPTER 7: THE STIRRING

The murder of Emmett Till is one of the most written about lynchings in the South. The trial testimony was covered by major newspapers, including the *New York Times*. The best sources are *A Death in the Delta: The Story of Emmett Till* by Stephen J. Whitfield (New York: Free Press, 1988) and "Approved Killing in Mississippi" by William Bradford Huie, *Look*, January 24, 1956. Charles Evers's and Myrlie Evers's recollections are included in this chapter.

The shooting of Gus Courts is documented in the NAACP Papers from 1955 and in *Standing Fast*.

The NAACP membership statistics are in the NAACP Papers in a letter from Current to Evers (September 26, 1956). The account of Medgar Evers's insurrection at the NAACP convention appears in *Thurgood Marshall: Warrior at the Bar, Rebel on the Bench* by Michael D. Davis and Hunter R. Clark (New York: Citadel Press, 1994), 201–202.

CHAPTER 8: THE SPY AGENCY

As of this writing, the Sovereignty Commission's secret files are locked in the basement of the Mississippi Department of Archives and History, awaiting a final disposition of the long court case to release them to the public (see Chapter 22). Since the suit was first brought in 1977, bits and pieces of the files have been leaked to the media. In 1989 a cache of Sovereignty Commission file copies that were included in the papers of the late Governor Paul Johnson were ruled unrestricted by a Mississippi judge and are available at the University of Southern Mississippi, Hattiesburg. Later that year a few thousand additional pages wound up in the hands of the *Clarion-Ledger*. About a year after I began working on this book, I was able to get my own set of "secret" files. The information in this chapter is drawn directly from the files and was checked against primary sources as often as possible. For instance, I interviewed Elmore Greaves in Jackson on November 18, 1992, and he confirmed his involvement in the scheme to arrest Evers and Wilkins.

Former Sovereignty Commission director Erle Johnston wrote a book on the subject: *Mississippi's Defiant Years: 1953–1973* (Forest, Miss.: Lake Harbor, 1990).

John Dittmer refers to the Sovereignty Commission papers in his invaluable study *Local People: The Struggle for Civil Rights in Mississippi* (Urbana: University of Illinois Press, 1994).

The details of Beckwith's divorces from his first wife are documented in justice court records in LeFlore County (*Mary Louise Williams Beckwith v Byron De La Beckwith*, nos. 12,795, 12,882 [1960], 13,565 [1962]). Reed Massengill's *Portrait of a Racist* probes this relationship at length and is an important source of Beckwith history and arcana, including the psychiatrist's analysis.

CHAPTER 9: THE FREEDOM RIDERS

The account of Medgar Evers's assault outside the Hinds County Courthouse comes from documents in his FBI file obtained through the Freedom of Information Act. This incident is recounted in file no. 44-1250, the result of a limited investigation requested by John Doar on March 29, 1961. G. W. "Red" Hydrick's arrest is covered in the *Jackson State-Times*, March 30, 1961. Burke Marshall's statement was quoted in the *Pittsburgh Courier*, April 8, 1961. I interviewed Doar at his law offices in New York on April 21, 1992.

The story about James Eastland's deal for Harold Cox is often repeated. This version comes from Arthur M. Schlesinger's *Robert Kennedy and His Times* (New York: Houghton Mifflin, 1978), as does Kennedy's comment on civil rights.

Evers's opposition to the Freedom Riders in Mississippi and Wilkins's statement to James Farmer are from *Freedom Bound, A History of America's Civil Right's Movement* by Robert Weisbrodt (New York: W. W. Norton, 1990), 55–56. Other information comes from interviews with Alvin Binder in Jackson, 1992 and 1993, and Vernon Jordan in Washington, D.C., October 1992 and May 1993.

CHAPTER 10: OLE MISS

The Ole Miss riots are well documented, and I used multiple sources and eyewitness accounts for this chapter. James Meredith tells his story in *Three Years in Mississippi* (Bloomington: University of Indiana Press, 1966). I interviewed Meredith in Jackson on January 15, 1992. Beckwith's attempt to participate is recounted in *Glory in Conflict*.

CHAPTER 11: THE JACKSON MOVEMENT

I am indebted to John R. Salter, Jr., for much of the information in this chapter. I interviewed him by telephone several times and referred often to his book *Jackson, Mississippi: An American Chronicle of Struggle and Schism* (Hicksville, N.Y.: Exposition Press, 1979).

I interviewed Dick Gregory by telephone on August 18, 1993, and referred to his memoir, *Nigger* (with Robert Lipsyte, 1964; reprint, New York: Washington Square Press, 1986), to help recreate some scenes. Some details of the firebombing of the Evers house and other incidents come from *For Us, the Living*. I also interviewed Ed King, Dave Dennis, Gloster Current, Myrlie Evers, R. L. T. Smith, Jr., Sam Baily, and Aaron Henry.

CHAPTER 12: THE LAST WARNING

Salter and other participants contributed to this account. Martin Luther King, Jr.'s taped conversation regarding Wilkins comes from Taylor Branch's *Parting the Waters: America in the King Years 1954–63* (New York: Touchstone, 1989), 816. The book also discusses Wilkins's long feud with King. The words with which Medgar Evers told Dick Gregory that his son was dead come from *Nigger*, 182.

The telegram from Charles Diggs to the White House and the response from Lee White can be found in the microfilm collection of documents titled *Civil Rights During the Kennedy Administration, 1961–1963* from the Kennedy Library.

Other sources include Dave Dennis, W. C. Shoemaker, Henry Kirksey, Gene Young, Charles Evers, Henry Lamb, Clarie Collins Harvey, and Aurelia Young, who kindly shared her diary from this time with me.

CHAPTER 13: THE HOUR OF LEAD

The details of Medgar Evers's murder come from many sources, including witness descriptions, investigators, police records, court documents, and interviews with Myrlie Evers, Darrell Evers, James Wells, Aurelia Young, Dr. Albert Britton, Gloster Current, and Charles Evers. The scene in which he learns of Medgar's murder was recounted in *Evers* and in various interviews. Part of the text of Myrlie Evers's speech is in *For Us, the Living,* 310, and in the *New York Times,* June 13, 1963.

CHAPTER 14: FUNERAL

Again I have relied as often as possible on first-person accounts from Myrlie Evers, John Doar, Dave Dennis, John Salter, William Kunstler, Vernon Jordan, and newspaper reports. Salter's book, *Jackson, Mississippi,* contains details of the police confrontation after the funeral. Charles Evers recalled the funeral in *Evers,* 111, and in interviews.

CHAPTER 15: A PAWN IN THE GAME

I interviewed Thorn McIntyre in Montgomery, Alabama, on February 13, 1992. Other details come from police and court records. I interviewed Bill Waller in Jackson on June 6 and 16, 1992, and John Fox on December 16, 1991. Myrlie Evers has often described the depression she suffered after her husband's murder. The visits to the psychiatrist are mentioned in the NAACP Papers, as are other events described in this chapter.

CHAPTERS 16 AND 17: TRIAL BY AMBUSH AND THE VARMINT HUNTER

These chapters were reconstructed from the authenticated transcript of the first trial, newspaper accounts, and interviews with Bill Waller, John Fox, and Myrlie Evers. "The Trial of Delay Beckwith" by Harold Martin, *The Sat-*

urday Evening Post, March 14, 1964, 77–82, is the best magazine article on the first trial. See also "Notes on the Beckwith Trial," by Jeannine Herron, *The Nation,* February 24, 1964, 179–181.

CHAPTER 18: THE SECOND TRIAL

It appears that no transcript was made of the second Beckwith trial, and the court reporter's notes have not been found. I was able to reconstruct testimony from newspaper articles at the time, including the *New York Times* and, most helpful of all, the *Greenwood Commonwealth.*

During my encounter with Beckwith in his cell in 1992, he talked about the taxi drivers' testimony and how one of the cabbies "decided not to lie for Bill Waller after a group of good white men beat him with a stick." He maintained he would never have done such a foolish thing as ask a cabdriver for directions to Medgar Evers's house.

I have interviewed Gordon Lackey several times, including one lengthy, taped interview in Greenwood on January 31, 1991. He denied being a Klan member in that interview. He said he "never felt it was productive." In 1994 I asked him again whether he was a member of the White Knights and if he had recruited Beckwith into that group. He denied it, but he told me that anyone who told you he was a White Knight couldn't be one. It was a secret organization. Or so he'd heard.

CHAPTER 19: THE LONG SUMMER

Myrlie Evers's adjustment to life in California is recorded in an article titled "Why I Left Mississippi," *Ebony,* March 1965, 25–28. Other details of the move can be found in the NAACP Papers. Charles Evers often described how Medgar's memory steered him away from violence. One instance can be found in *Evers,* 114.

I interviewed Dave Dennis in Jackson on March 24, 1993, and by telephone. Dennis also discussed Freedom Summer tactics in *My Soul Is Rested,* 273–278.

I spoke to Delmar Dennis several times by telephone and interviewed him in Sevierville, Tennessee, on January 10, 1992. Other background can be found in *Klandestine* by William H. McIlhany II (New Rochelle, N.Y.: Arlington House, 1975).

The murders of the three civil rights workers are well documented. One of the best books on the subject is *We Are Not Afraid* by Seth Cagin and Philip Dray (New York: Macmillan, 1988; New York, Bantam, 1991).

The "Dear Wonderful Friends" letter is in the Paul Johnson Papers at the University of Southern Mississippi, in a file marked "Klan."

I owe the description of Delay and Willie Beckwith fighting in their trailer to *Portrait of a Racist,* 225–226, as well as witnesses in Greenwood.

The scene of Charles Evers at the Philadelphia courthouse is found in *We Are Not Afraid,* 379–380, and reconstructed from newspaper accounts.

The text of Dave Dennis's eulogy appears in *Eyes on the Prize: America's Civil Rights Year 1954–1965* by Juan Williams (New York: Penguin, 1988), 239–240.

Van Riper's decision not to "blow the case" comes from his testimony at Beckwith's third trial, February 1, 1994.

CHAPTER 20: WHITE KNIGHTS

Beckwith's testimony is found in the report of the House Committee on Un-American Activities, *Activities of Ku Klux Klan Organizations in the United States,* 89th Congress, January 12, 1966, 2698. Rules and rituals of the White Knights are described in *The Present-Day Ku Klux Klan Movement,* 90th Congress, December 11, 1967.

Fred Sanders told me about his encounter with Beckwith in 1967. Beckwith's campaign interview is in *The Southern Review,* July 15, 1967, 5. Delmar Dennis recalled meeting Beckwith in our interview in January 1992. Voter statistics come from Frank R. Parker, *Black Votes Count: Political Empowerment in Mississippi after 1965* (Chapel Hill: University of North Carolina Press, 1990), 32.

The outcome of the Neshoba County case is in *We Are Not Afraid* and in *Attack on Terror: The FBI Against the Ku Klux Klan in Mississippi* by Don Whitehead (New York: Funk and Wagnall's, 1970).

The rise of Swiftism is documented in *Blood in the Face* by James Ridgeway (New York: Thunder's Mouth Press, 1990) and *Hate Groups in America, A Record of Bigotry and Violence,* a publication of the Anti-Defamation League of B'nai B'rith (New York, 1988).

I owe details of Beckwith's bombing arrest to the New Orleans Police Department report and the sharp memories of Ben Windstein and John Evans, the arresting officers. Court records and trial transcripts from Beckwith's state and federal trials are on file with the Louisiana Supreme Court appeal under *State of Louisiana v Byron De La Beckwith,* no. 58,586, February 28, 1977.

Al Binder, who died in 1993, was an invaluable source who sat for three interviews (August 23 and October 14, 1991; January 13, 1993) and copied many documents from his files. The ADL office in New Orleans kept meticulous clipping files on the case, for which I am grateful. Some information about the FBI's relationship with Mississippi's Jewish community comes from Jack Nelson's *Terror in the Night: The Klan's Campaign Against the Jews*

(New York: Simon & Schuster, 1993). Other sources who prefer not to be named also contributed to this account.

Beckwith's life at the old Melton place is described in several sources but most vividly in *Glory in Conflict.* The incident with the photographer and writer appears in "My Friend the Nazi" by John R. Miller, *Tropic Magazine* (*The Miami Herald*), June 10, 1990, 12–13.

CHAPTER 21: HOMECOMING

I interviewed both Lane C. Murray and Charles Evers about their meeting in Natchez and their unusual friendship. Sources for Evers's political career include Jason Berry, *Amazing Grace: With Charles Evers in Mississippi* (New York: Saturday Review Press, 1973), which (64–71) is a source for the scene in which Evers returns to Decatur, and Erle Johnston, *Politics: Mississippi Style* (Forest, Miss.: Lake Harbor, 1993), where Owen Brooks's open letter is quoted on page 286. See also "We Can't Discuss White People Anymore . . ." by Walter Rubager, *New York Times Magazine,* August 4, 1968. Evers's financial problems have been covered in the *Clarion-Ledger* and are outlined in documents filed in U.S. Bankruptcy Court, Southern District of Mississippi, case no. 90-01503.

CHAPTER 22: MISSISSIPPI TURNING

Statistics are drawn from *Black Elected Officials, Local People,* and various other sources. I interviewed Margaret Walker Alexander on January 26, 1991. Her speech is reprinted in *Mississippi Writers: Reflections of Childhood and Youth,* vol. 2, ed. Dorothy Abbott (Jackson: University Press of Mississippi, 1986), 608.

The remainder of the chapter comes from interviews with the subjects mentioned, articles in the *Clarion-Ledger,* and many days spent sitting around the district attorney's office in Jackson over many months. Most of the scenes and dialogue in this and the following chapters were directly observed. Other incidents and conversations were described to me by people who were there.

CHAPTER 23: THE CASE

I interviewed Bobby DeLaughter on January 24, January 28, and August 26, 1991, and February 22, 1994. I was able to re-create the investigation with his help and the help of Ed Peters, Charlie Crisco, Doc Thaggard, and Benny Bennett. Al Binder and Bill Kirksey offered their insights into the Beckwith case and observations about their friend and colleague DeLaughter.

CHAPTER 24: THE STATUE

I rode with Charles Evers on the campaign trail on October 1, 1991, and was with him in Fayette on Election Day, November 5, 1991. It was there that I interviewed Elizabeth Evers Jordan, who came to help with the campaign.

I spoke to Merrida Coxwell several times before and after the trial. Kirk Fordice's career as governor is well documented in the *Clarion-Ledger*. Kim McGeoy's meeting with Judge Breland Hilburn was in the presence of a court reporter, who transcribed the dialogue. The affidavits supporting bail for Beckwith are on file in the Hinds County Circuit Court under *State of Mississippi v Byron De La Beckwith*, no. 90-3-3495, as are various hearing transcripts. I first interviewed Darrell Evers in Jackson on June 29, 1992, and have spoken to him many times since by phone.

CHAPTER 25: HURRICANE SEASON

The opening quote from Beckwith comes from a letter to me dated May 11, 1992. The accounts of Beckwith's court appearances are from court documents, newspaper records, and my notes. I was present for every one of his appearances in Mississippi except his arraignment. The legal arguments summarized in this chapter are found in briefs filed with the Supreme Court of the State of Mississippi, *Byron De La Beckwith v State of Mississippi*, no. 91-KA-1207.

Again dialogue recorded in this chapter was either witnessed by me or reconstructed by someone who was there. When I describe what people were feeling or thinking, it is because I have asked them what was going through their minds.

For Bob Moses and the Algebra Project see Alexis Jetter, "Mississippi Learning," *New York Times Magazine*, February 21, 1993, 28.

The encounter between the Beckwiths and the young reporter was described in Beverly Pettigrew Kraft, "Beckwith's Son Wins Case Against Reporter," *Clarion-Ledger*, February 17, 1993. Myrlie Evers described her thoughts during the anniversary ceremonies in an interview in Jackson, June 12, 1993.

CHAPTER 26: BATESVILLE

Mike Riley of *Time* magazine was kind enough to share a transcript of his telephone interview with Beckwith from January 14, 1994. A good background on Batesville is found in Jerry Mitchell, "And a River Runs through Panola's Racial, Economic Divide," *Clarion-Ledger*, January 17, 1994.

CHAPTERS 27 AND 28: THE TESTIMONY OF GHOSTS AND THE
LAST MILE OF THE WAY

I interviewed Ed Peters in Jackson on February 10, 1994. Peters, along with
Bobby DeLaughter, Cynthia Speetjens, John Davidson, Henry Brinston, Myrlie Evers, Darrell Evers, Benny Bennett, Charlie Crisco, Charles Evers, Merrida Coxwell, and others helped reconstruct the events surrounding the trial.

A transcript of Jim Kitchens's conversation with Martha Jean O'Brien was
entered into the evidence file in *Mississippi v Beckwith.*

I spoke to Gordon Lackey by phone on June 12, 1994, and asked him
again about his whereabouts on the night of June 11–12, 1963. He said that
he had been drinking with National Guard buddies in honky-tonks near
Camp Shelby, and that he never went to Jackson that night. He told me that
he had once owned a blue International Harvester pickup, but it was a 1964
model. He said he had nothing to do with the murder of Medgar Evers and
he continues to believe that Byron De La Beckwith is an innocent man.

Beckwith was not allowed out on bail after his conviction, and remained
in the Hinds County Detention Center while his lawyers prepared his appeal.
He spent his days reading the Bible, exercising on the mini trampoline that
he was allowed to keep in his cell, and, as always, writing letters. One of his
most frequent pen pals was Harry Rosenthal, the lawyer who had put up his
bond during the trial. Despite evidence to the contrary, Beckwith had decided that Rosenthal was actually a Christian, and he addressed him in correspondence as "My Compatriot benefactor par excellence." Rosenthal, who
says that he helped Beckwith out because he felt Beckwith's rights had been
denied, told me that he felt "rewarded" that Beckwith trusted him. "Beckwith
said 'I'll never curse a Jew again,' " said Rosenthal.

The lawyer has allowed some of his correspondence from Beckwith to be
made public. In these letters Beckwith says he was searching for an out-of
state, big-name lawyer to take up his case. He complained bitterly about
Coxwell and Kitchens, "known liberals" whom he said were "sitting on their
asses" while he rotted in jail. "Harry, they think I will live forever and hell yes
. . . I will," he wrote. "Byron De La Beckwith Ain't Done Yet."

Index